THE
NEW YORKER

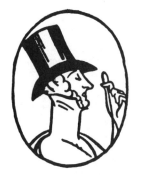

ALBUM

OF DRAWINGS

1925~1975

PENGUIN BOOKS

Penguin Books Ltd, Harmondsworth,
Middlesex, England
Penguin Books, 40 West 23rd Street,
New York, New York 10010, U.S.A.
Penguin Books Australia Ltd, Ringwood,
Victoria, Australia
Penguin Books Canada Limited, 2801 John Street,
Markham, Ontario, Canada L3R 1B4
Penguin Books (N.Z.) Ltd, 182–190 Wairau Road,
Auckland 10, New Zealand

First published in the United States of America by
The Viking Press 1975
First published in Canada by
The Macmillan Company of Canada Limited 1975
First published in Great Britain by André Deutsch Ltd 1976
Published in Penguin Books 1978
Reprinted 1978, 1979, 1981, 1982, 1985

LIBRARY OF CONGRESS CATALOGING IN PUBLICATION DATA
Main entry under title:
The New Yorker album of drawings, 1925–1975.
Cartoons originally published in the New Yorker.
1. American wit and humor, Pictorial.
1. New Yorker (New York, 1925–   )
NC1428.N453 1978   741.5′973   78-9669
ISBN 0 14 00.4968 1

Printed in the United States of America by
Murray Printing Company, Westford, Massachusetts

Design and layout by Carmine Peppe, of *The New Yorker* staff

This book is dedicated to James M. Geraghty—friend and guiding spirit of comic artists, Art Editor of *The New Yorker* from 1939 through 1972.

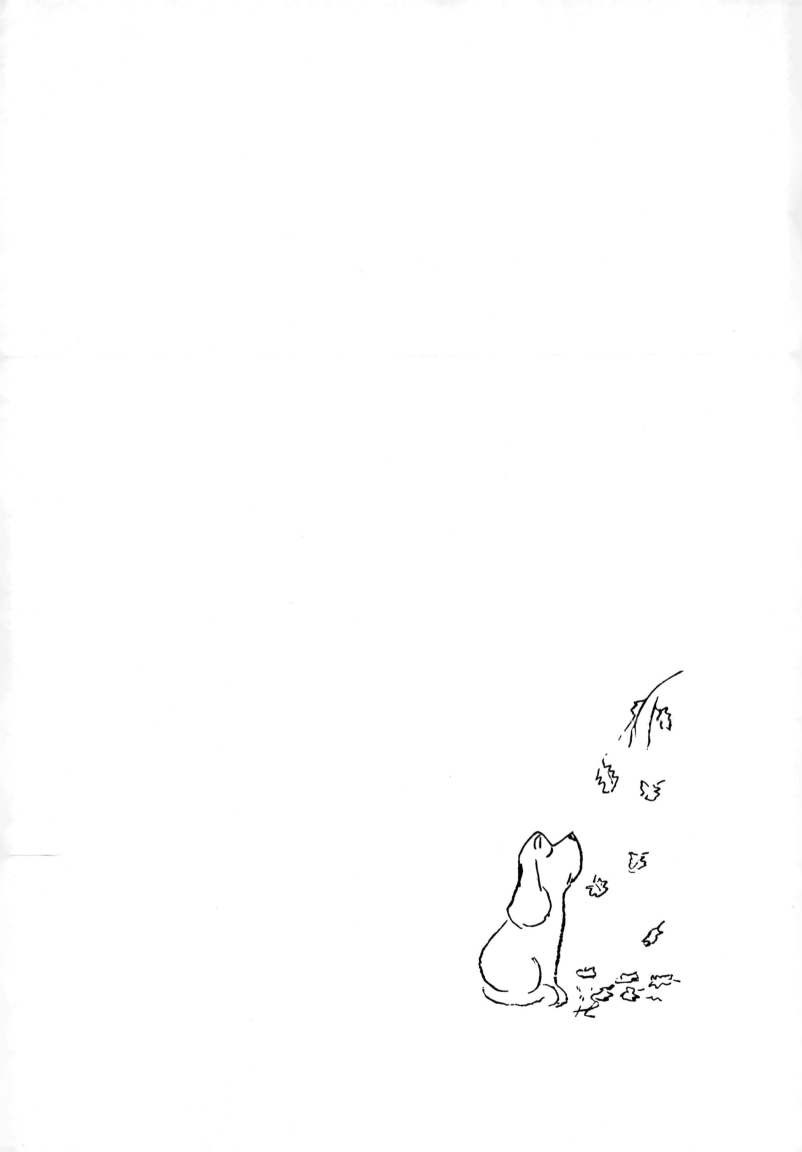

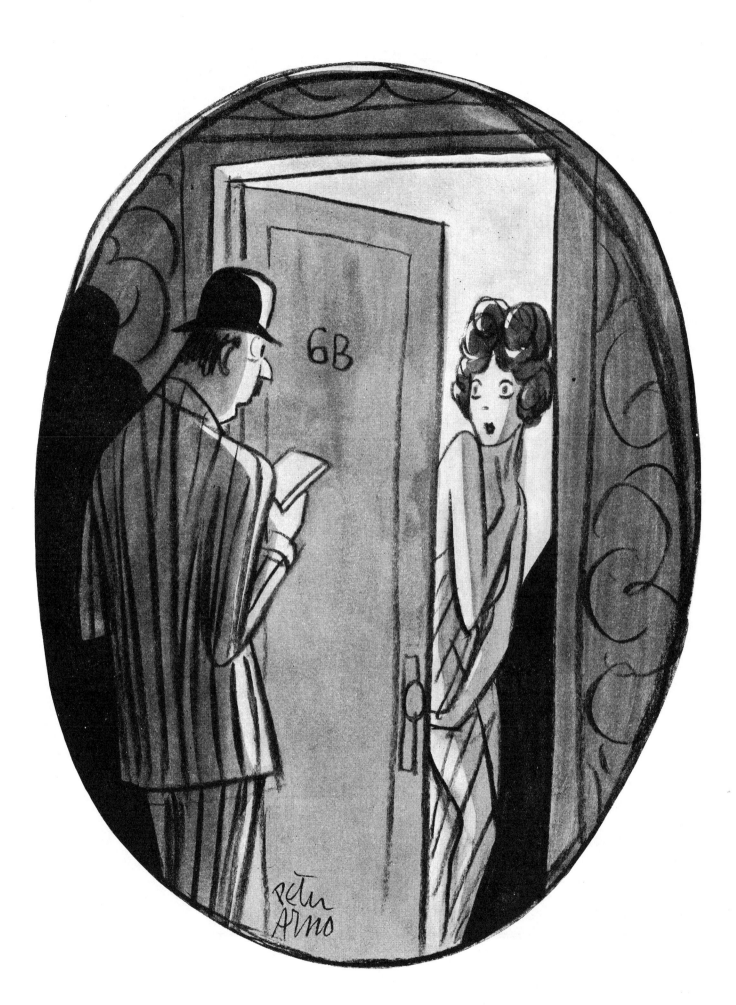

*"I'm checking up for the company, Madam. Have you any
of our Fuller Brush men?"*

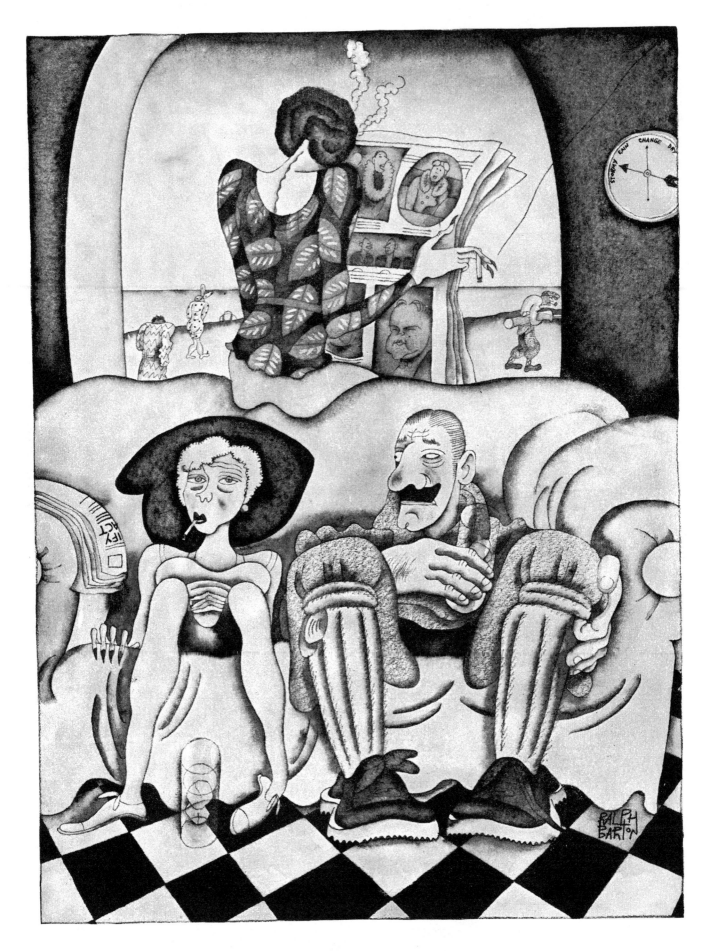

THE 1930'S

Weekend Guests—Sunday Morning after Saturday Night

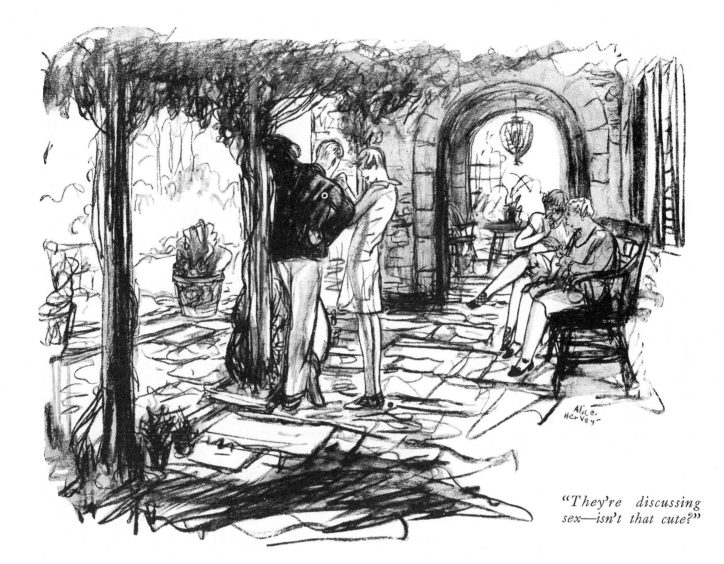

"They're discussing sex—isn't that cute?"

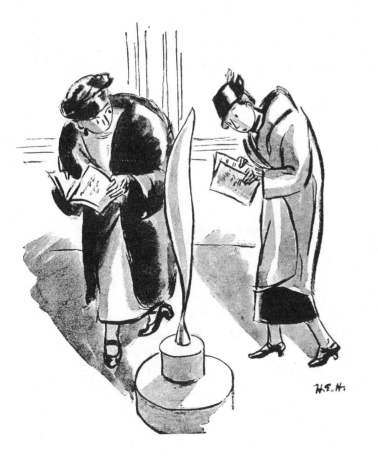

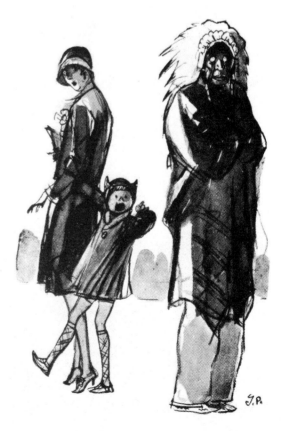

"Quick, mama—look! President Coolidge!"

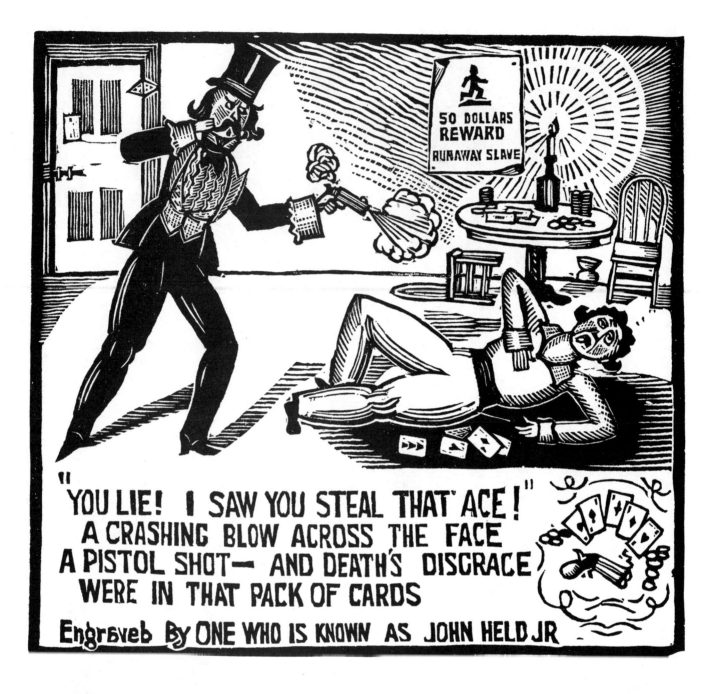

The Rise and Fall of Man

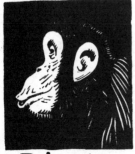 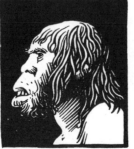 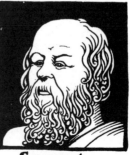 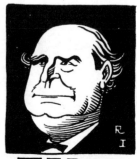

Primate   Neanderthal Man   Socrates   W. J. Bryan

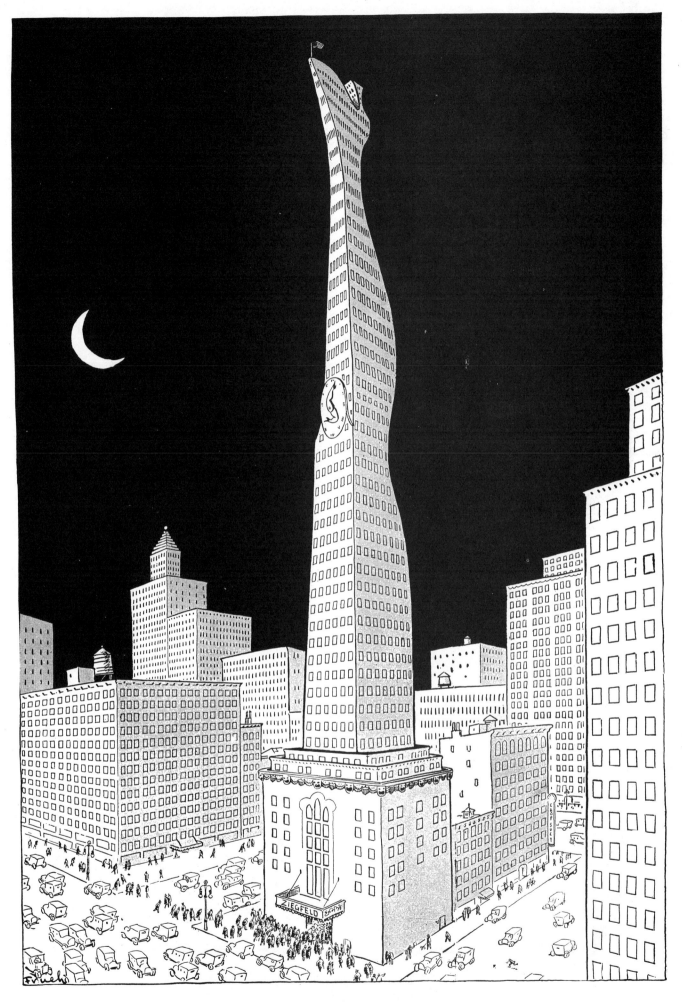

SUGGESTED DESIGN

Chicagoans to Build Theatre for Ziegfeld—Signs Contract for 44-story Building—To Establish Mid-West Centre for Glorification of the American Girl—NEWSPAPER HEADLINE

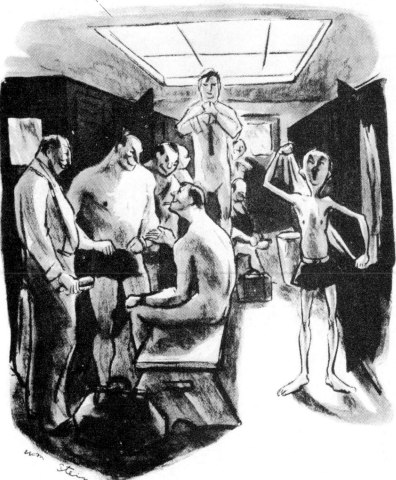

"Oh, Mademoiselle from Armenteers."

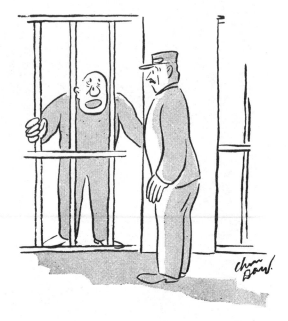

"Hey, what about dames?"

"His father wants him to be a lawyer, but I want him to go into a bank. It's always so nice and cool in a bank."

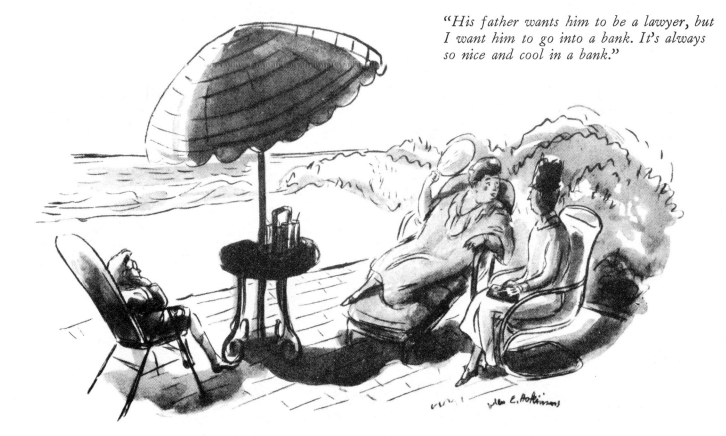

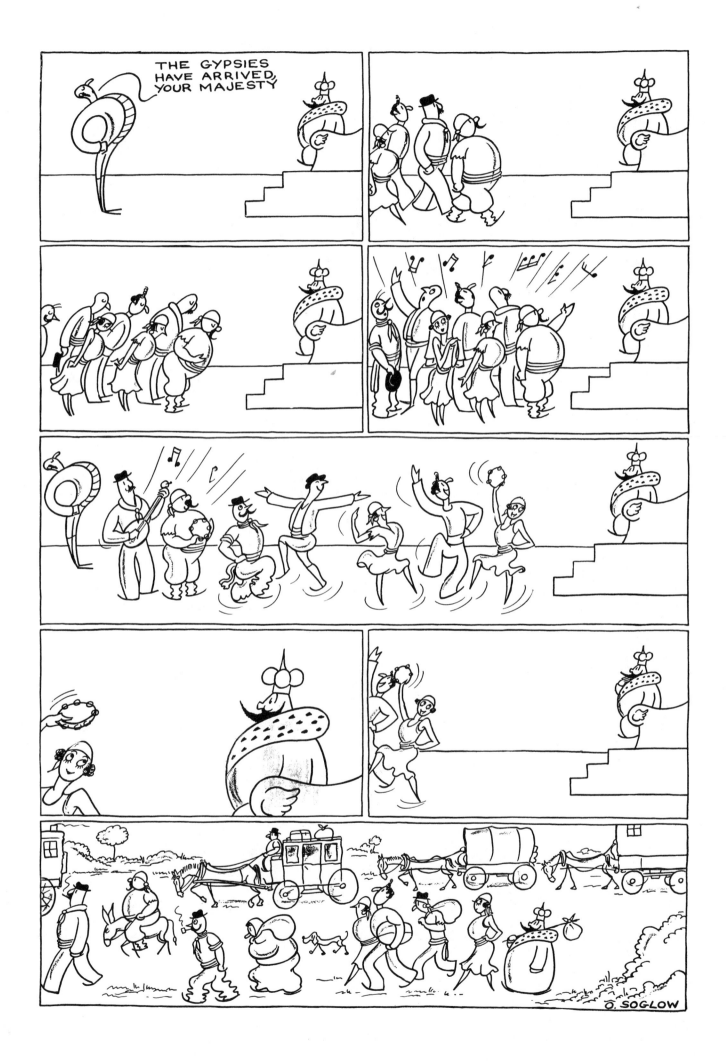

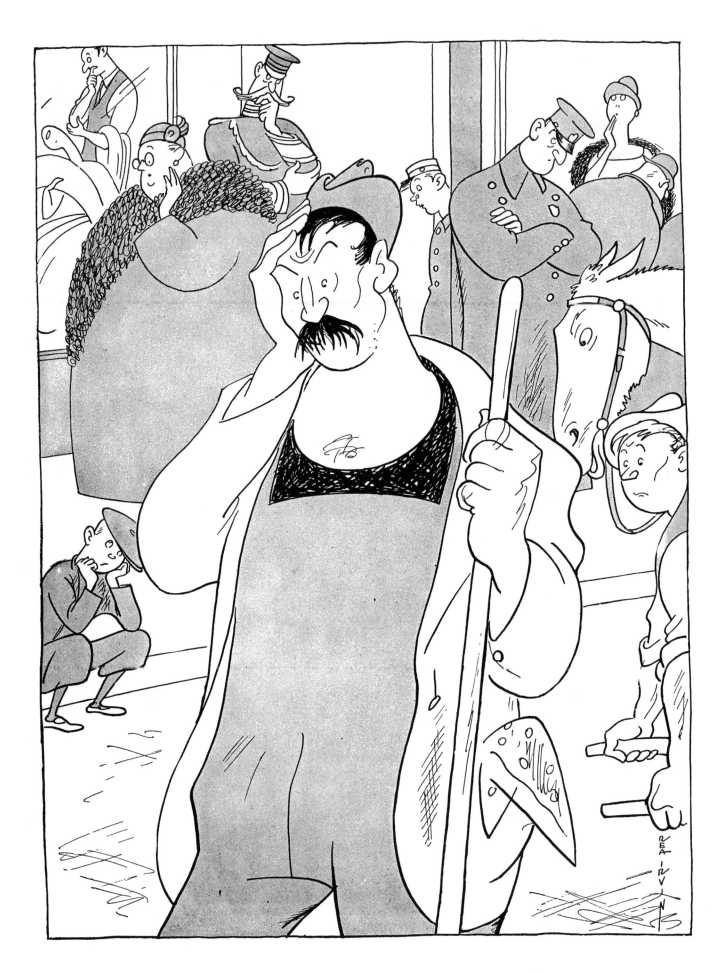

"*People slowly accustomed themselves to the idea that the physical states of space itself were the final physical reality.*"

—PROFESSOR ALBERT EINSTEIN

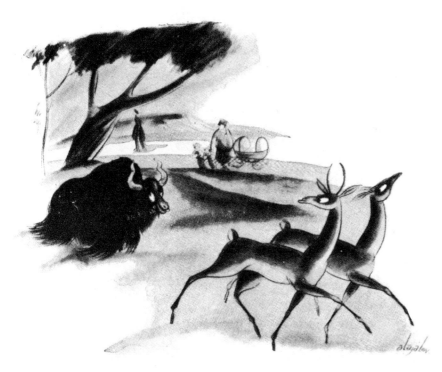

"Good Lord! Here comes that impossible yak again!"

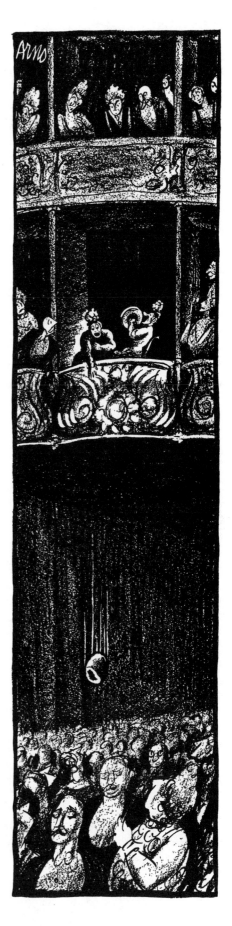

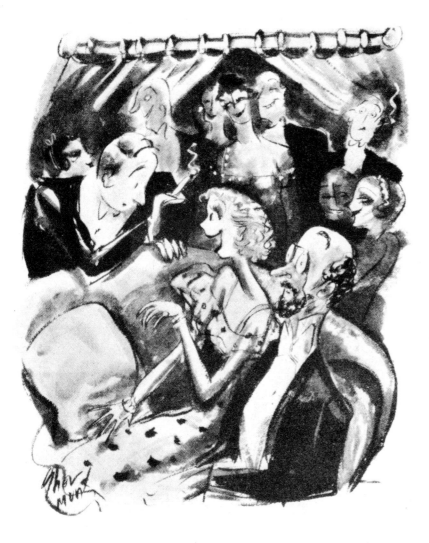

"Professor Furbush has been telling me about the N'gambi fertility rites—and guess what they turn out to be!"

"Whoops! There goes me muff!"

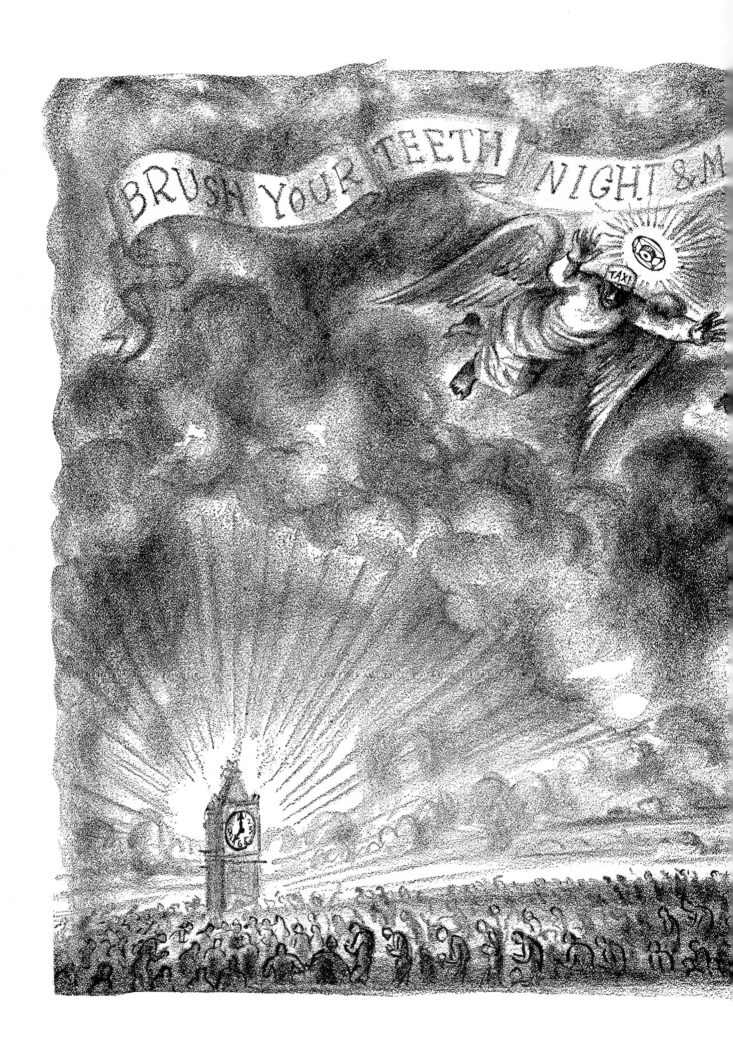

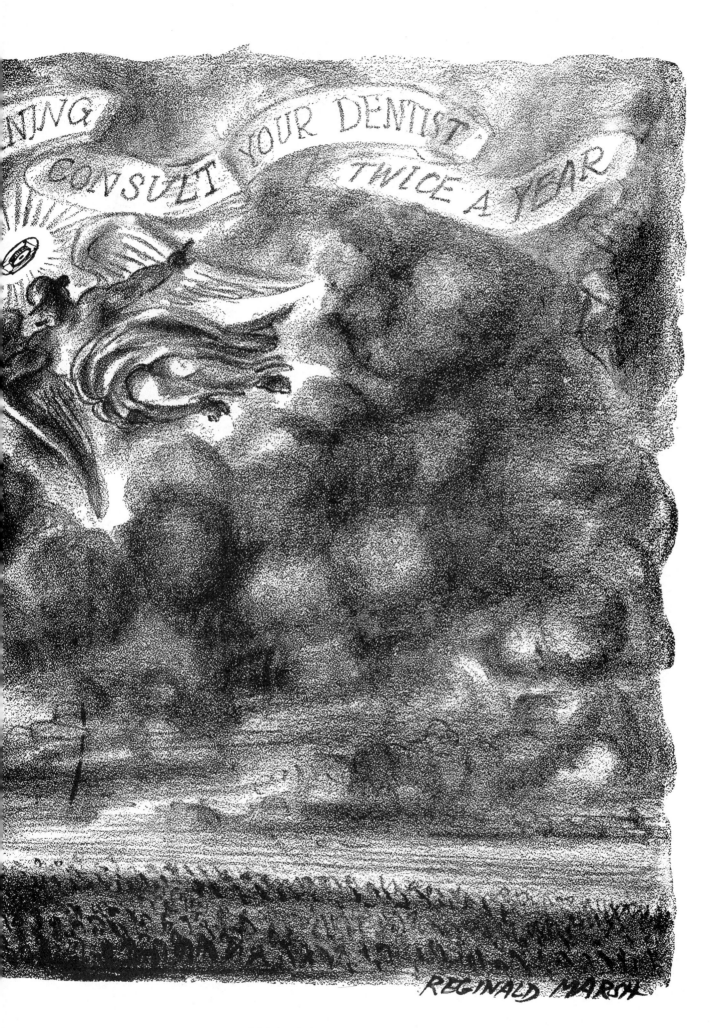

THE ANGELUS

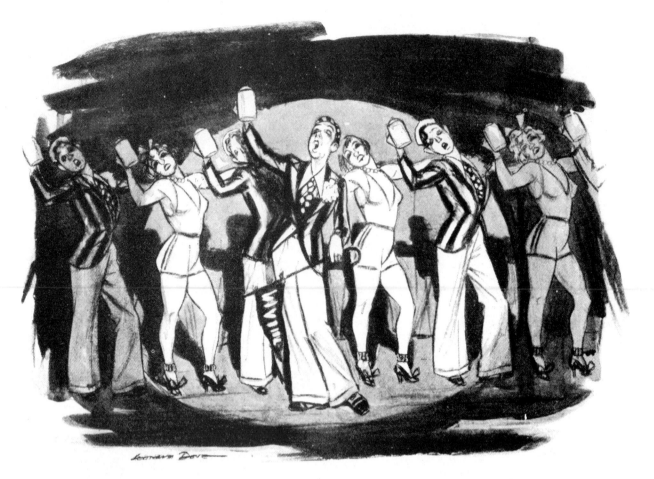

"To the Gods—to the Fates—to the Rulers of Men and their Destinies . . ."

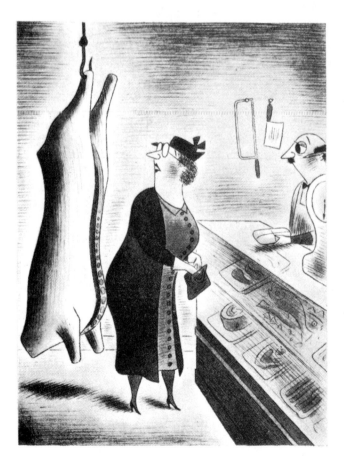

"I _beg_ your pardon."

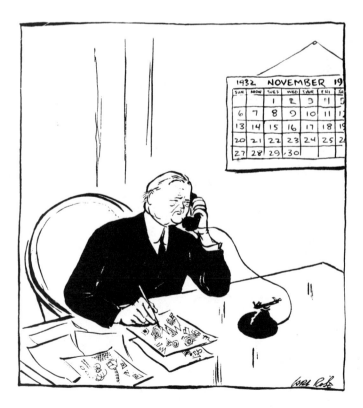

"Hello, Governor Roosevelt. You haven't got a good idea for a Thanksgiving proclamation, have you?"

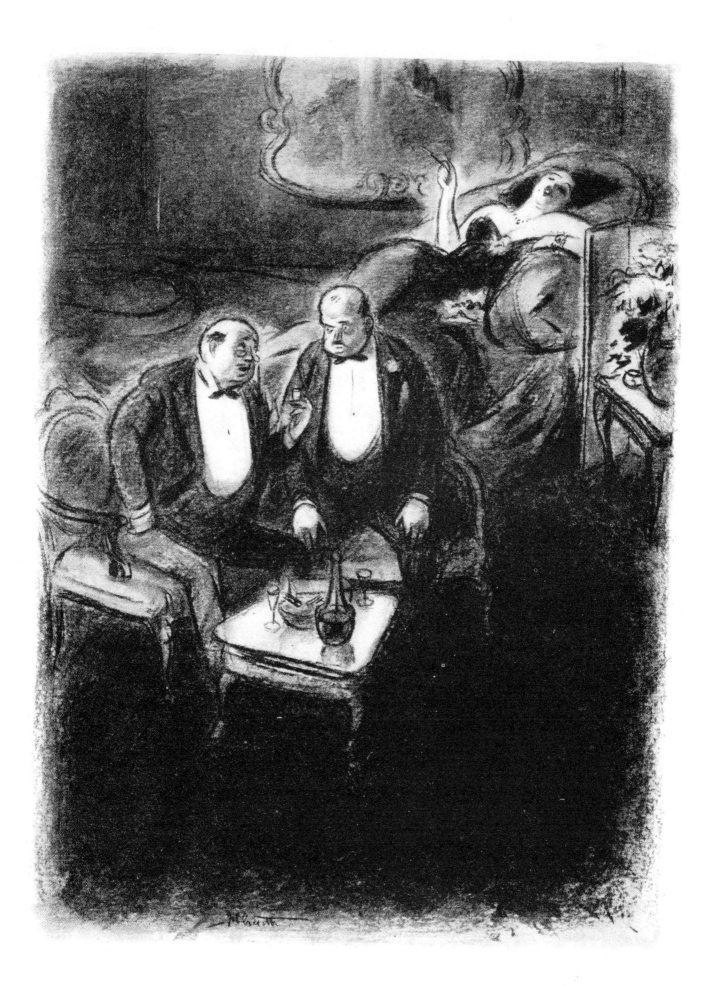

"*I never told her about the Depression. She would have worried.*"

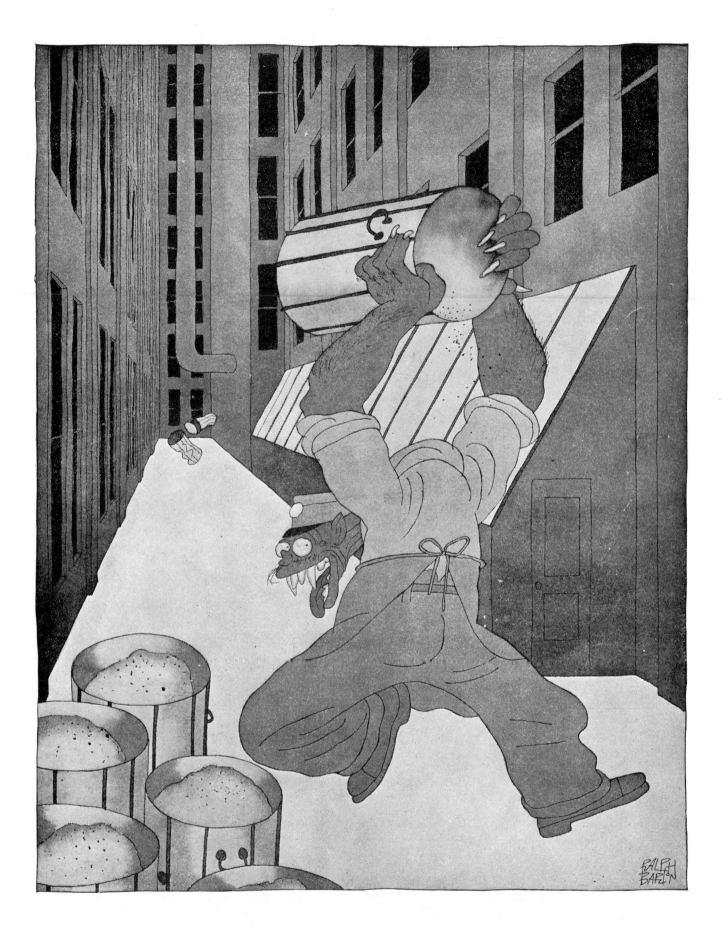

THE SORT OF THING THAT BRINGS JOY TO THE ASHMAN'S BLACK HEART

*A Whole, Nice, New, Big, Twenty-story, Co-operative Apartment House
to Wake up at Six in the Morning*

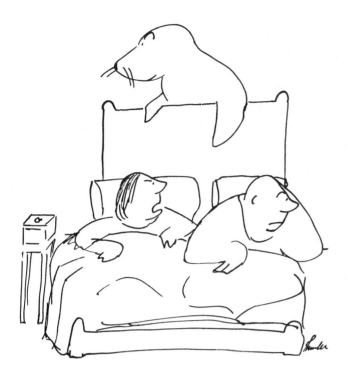

"All right, have it your way—you heard a seal bark!"

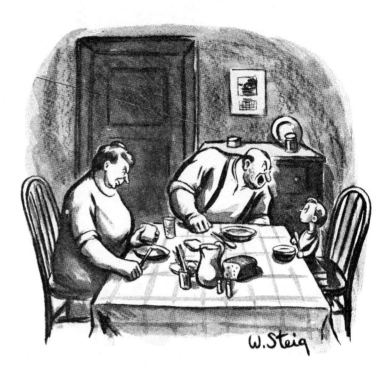

"What's wrong wit' oatmeal, if I ain't bein' too inquisitive?"

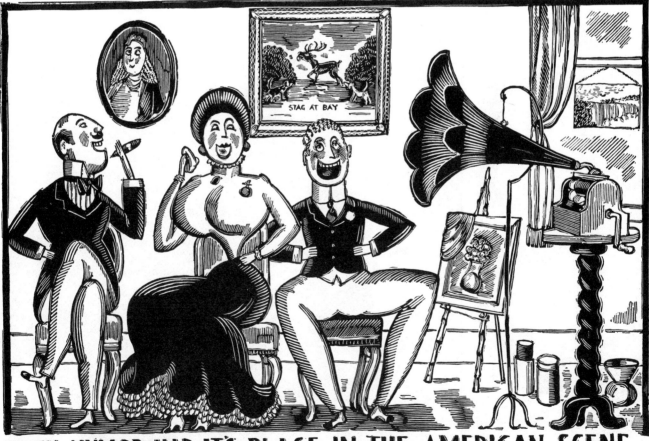

WHEN HUMOR HAD IT'S PLACE IN THE AMERICAN SCENE
Listening to "COHEN ON THE TELEPHONE"
ENG BY JOHN HELD JR THE GHOUL WHO DIGS IN THE GRAVES OF THE PAST

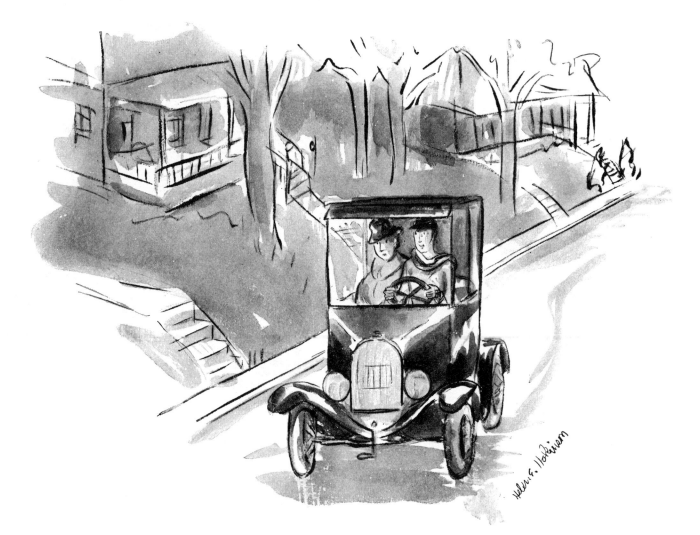

"I love driving. It gives you such a sense of power."

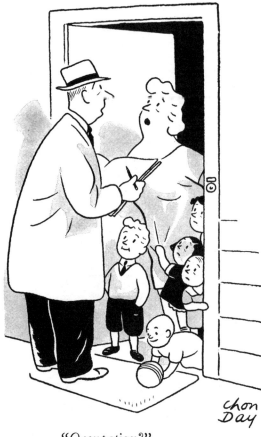

"Occupation?"
"Woman."

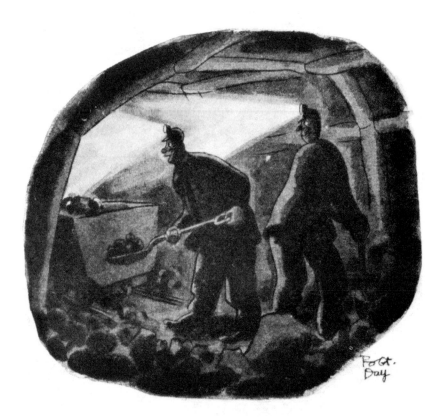

"For gosh sakes, here comes Mrs. Roosevelt!"

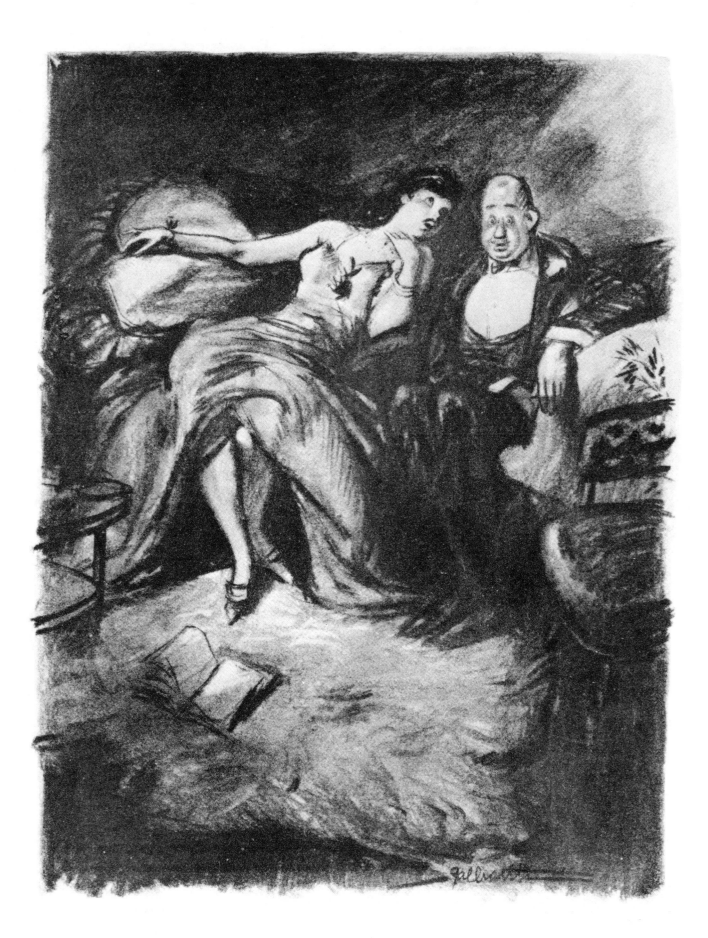

"Little things mean a lot to a girl, Mr. Goldsmith—like your coming to see me this way when you're cold sober."

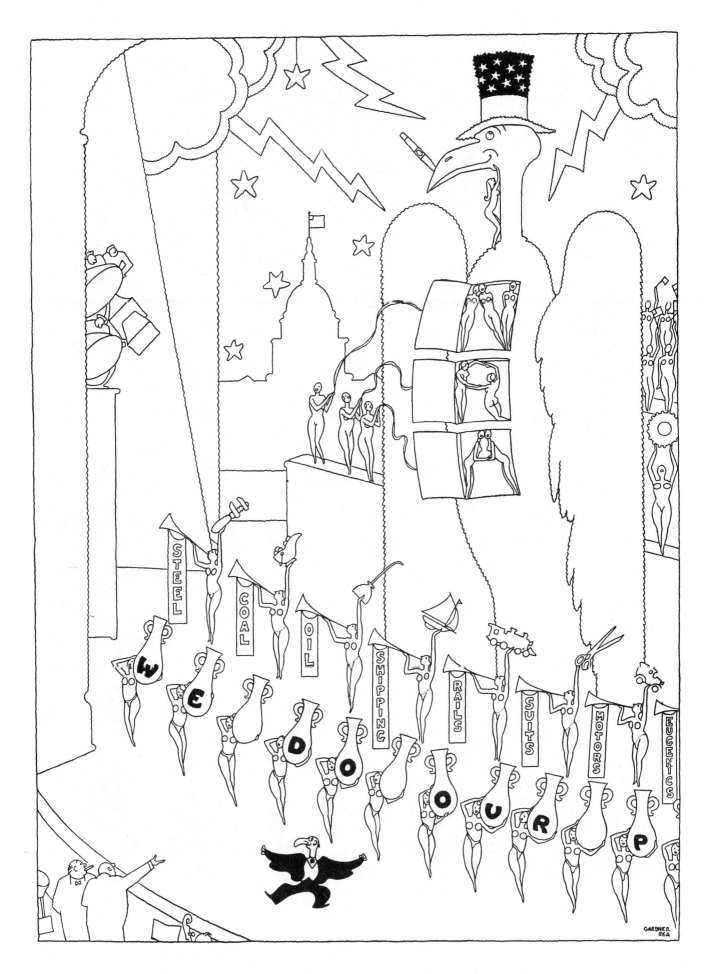

"There, Morris! If that don't bring prosperity, nothing will."

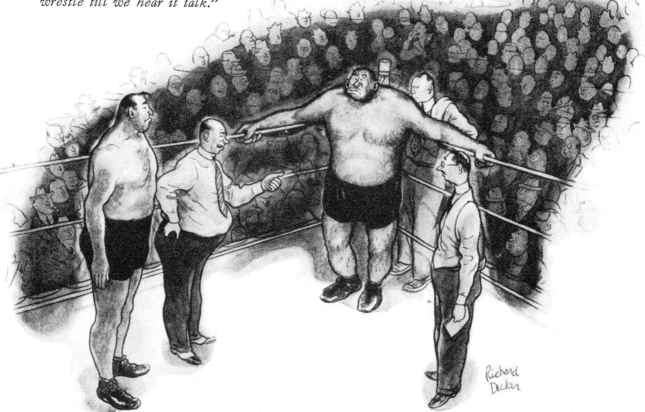

"My man don't
wrestle till we hear it talk."

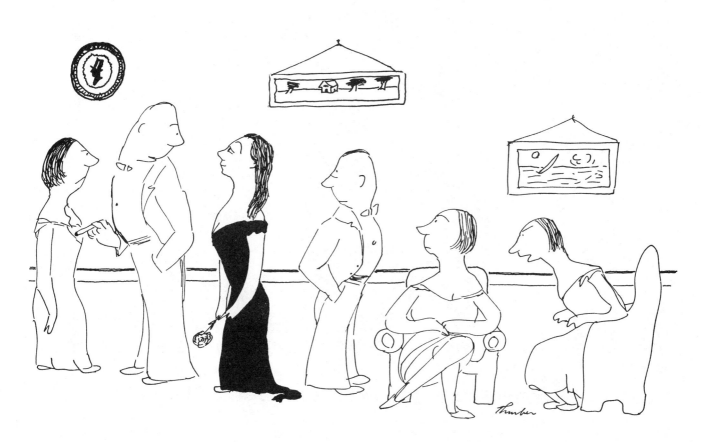

"She's been this way ever since she saw 'Camille.'"

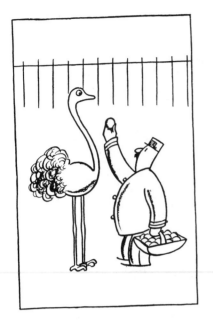 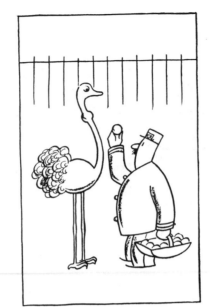 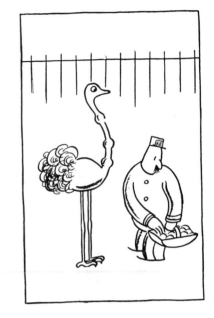

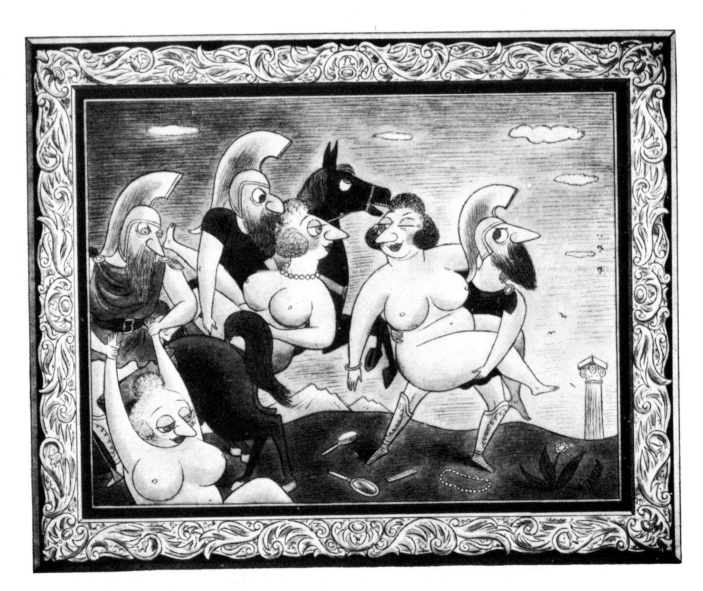

OUR MODERN GALLERY OF ANCIENT FAVORITES

Rape of the Sabines

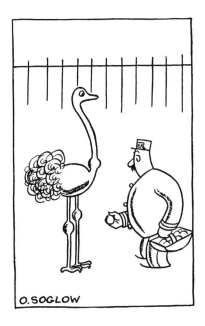

O. SOGLOW

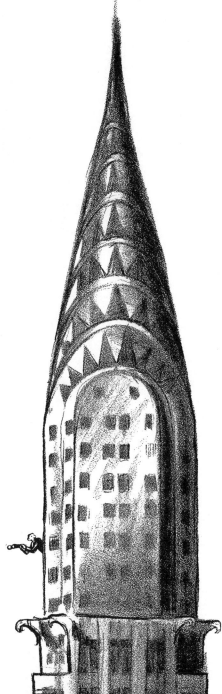

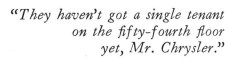

"They haven't got a single tenant on the fifty-fourth floor yet, Mr. Chrysler."

CARL ROSE

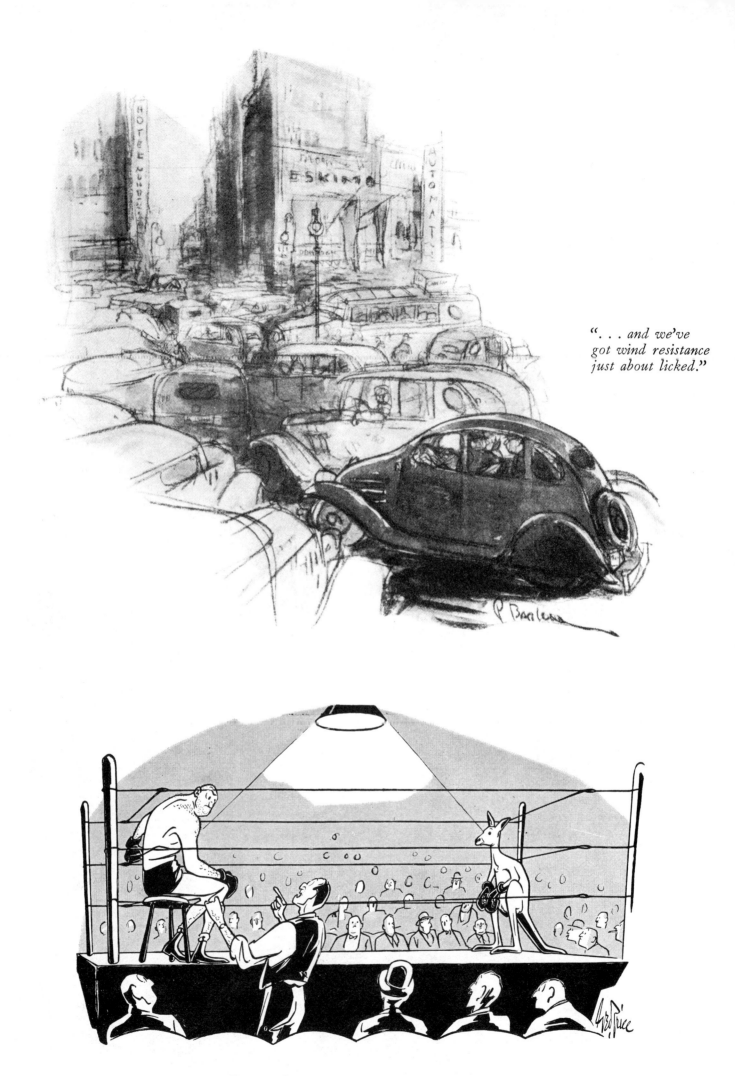

"... and we've got wind resistance just about licked."

"Remember now, you got the brains."

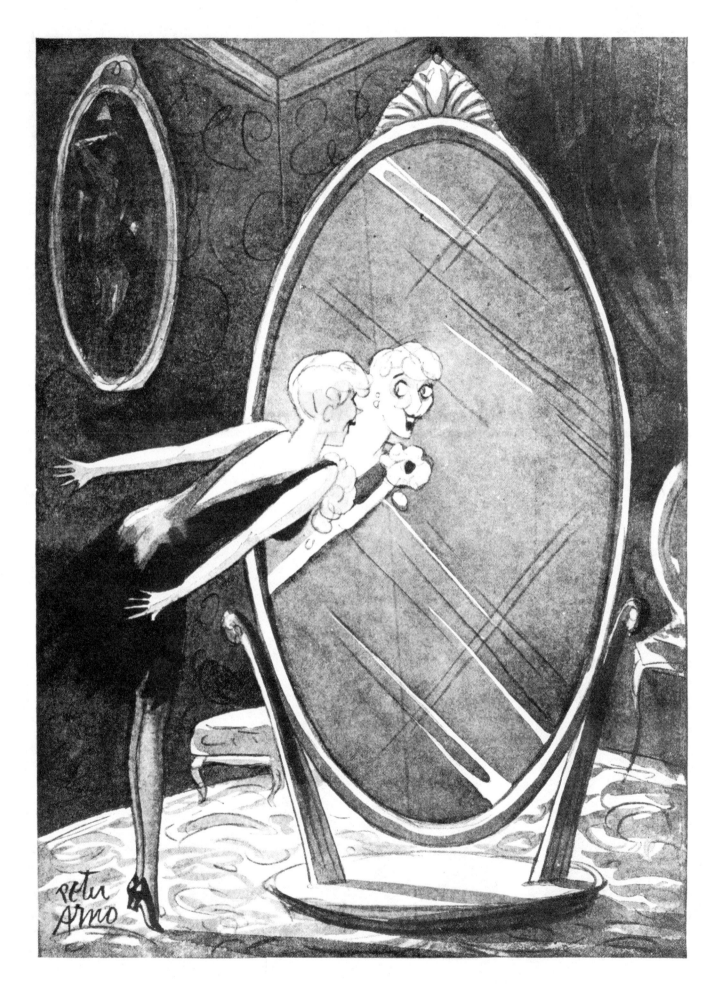

"Boo! You pretty creature!"

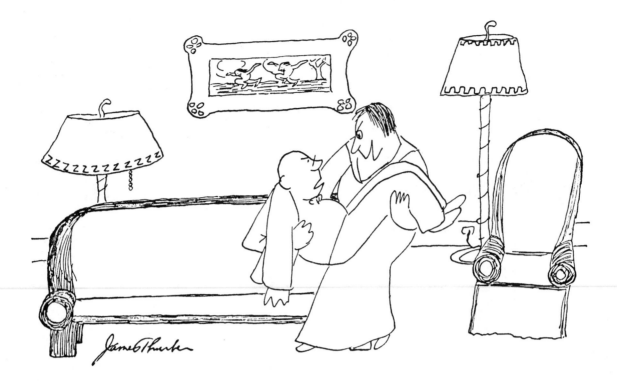

"You're going a bit far, Miss Blanchard."

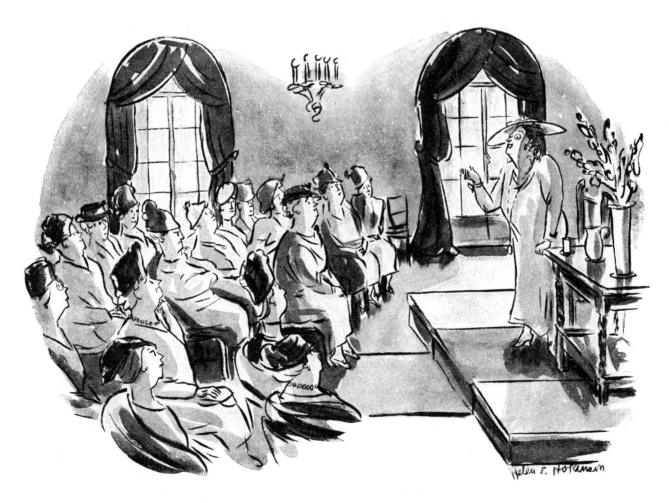

"Of course, we must draw some sort of distinction between wishing to overthrow the government and not liking the present administration."

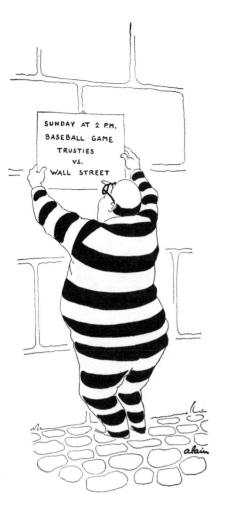

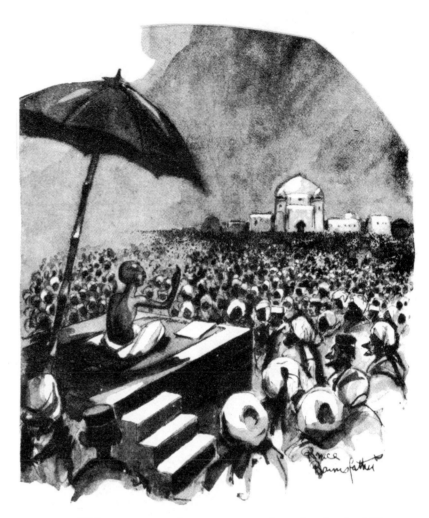

"Now can you hear me—you boys in the back?"

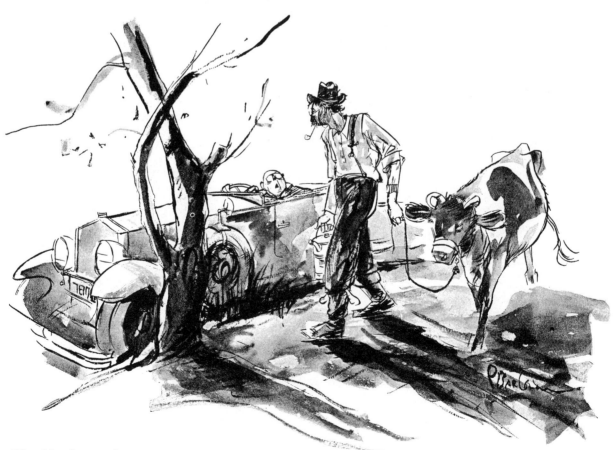

"Is this the road
to Cold Spring Harbor? Answer yes or no!"

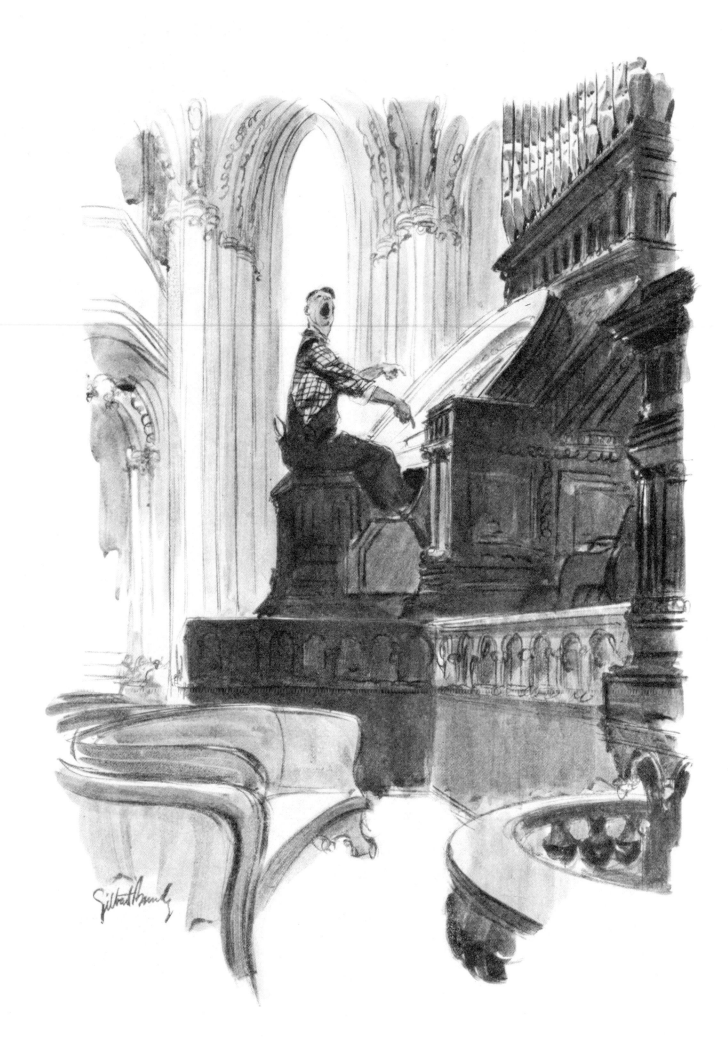

"I love coffee, I love tea. I love the girls, an' the girls love me."

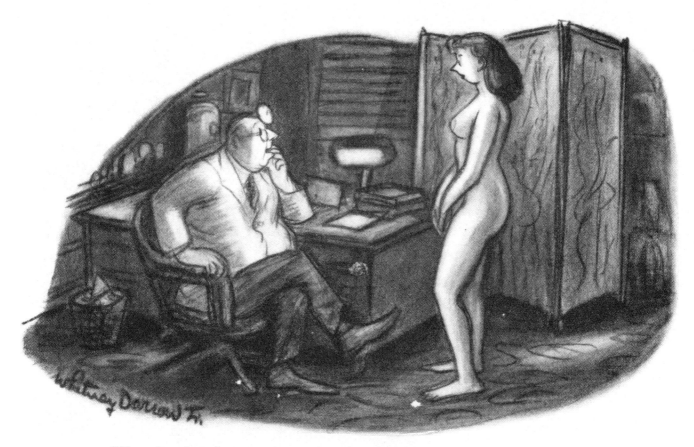

"Now just how long has this tonsil been bothering you, Miss Lorrimer?"

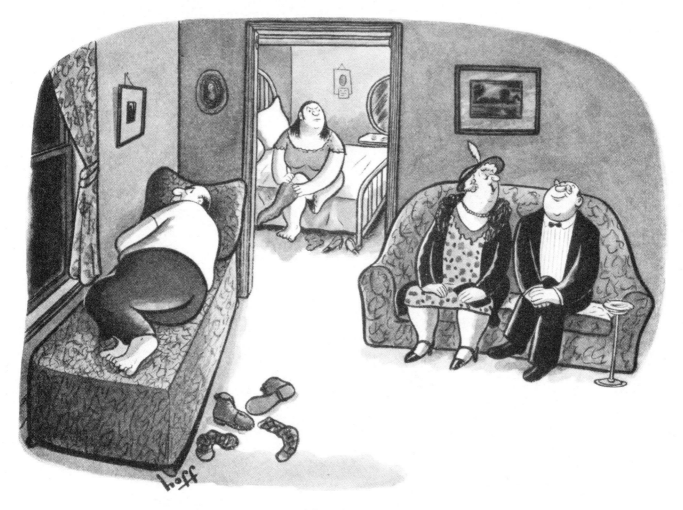

"Maybe they'd like us to say 'good night' already."

"Now, there's been a lot of loose talk going around lately about splitting the atom."

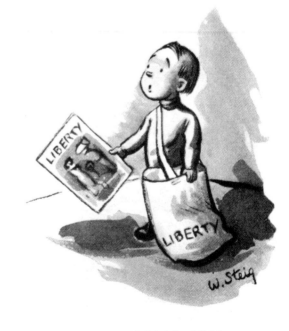

SMALL FRY

"Libiddy?"

"I used to bet my husband I'd die before he did—and I lost!"

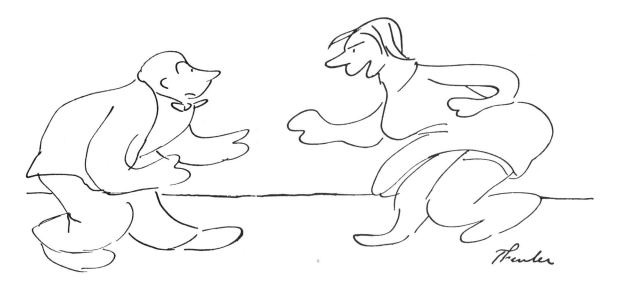

"Best two falls out of three, Mr. Montague? O.K.?"

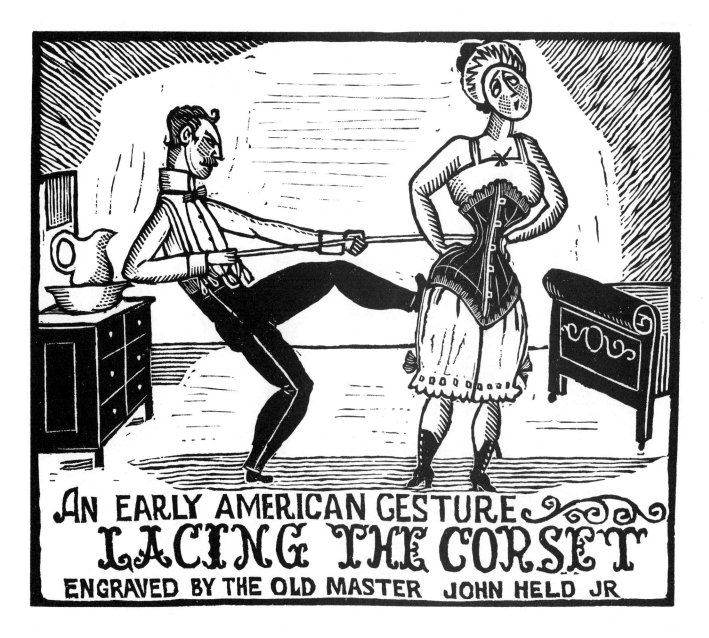

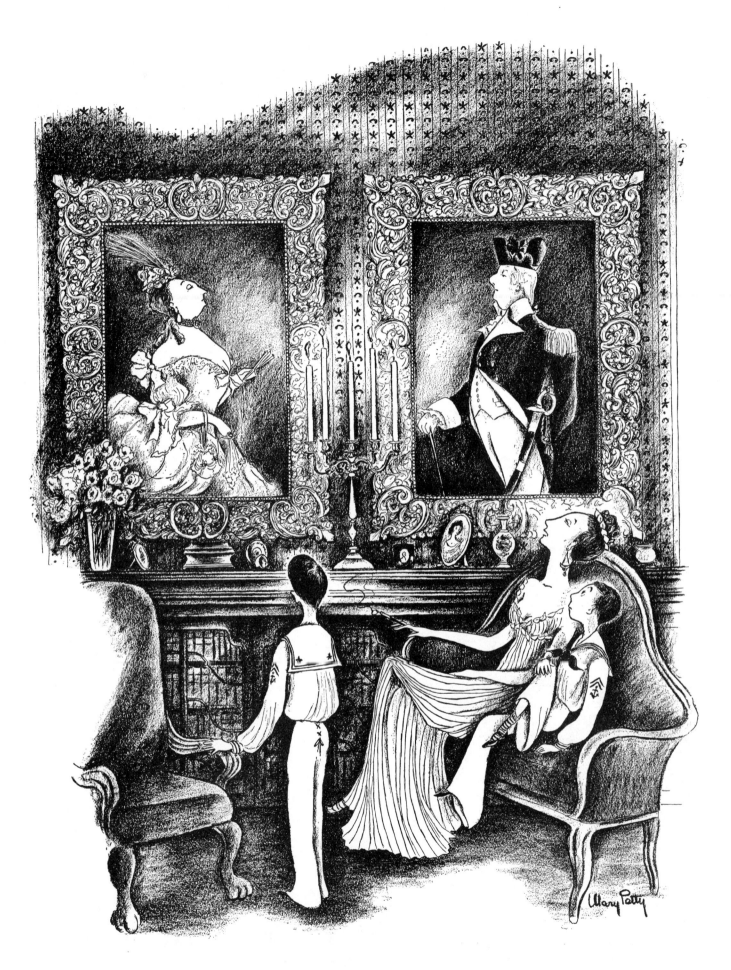

*"The Indians had him completely at bay. He saved his last shot for
your Great-Great-Great Aunt Fanny."*

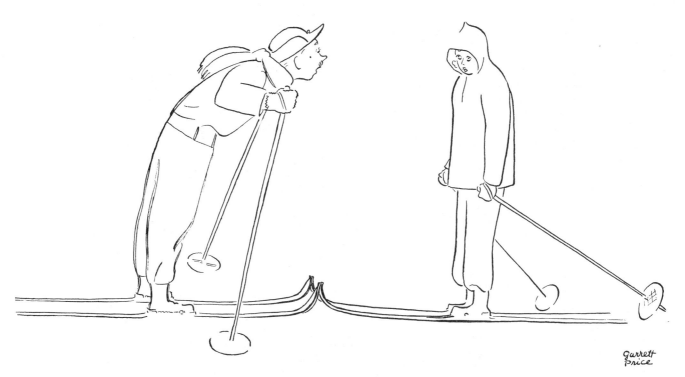

"Tira, I love you."

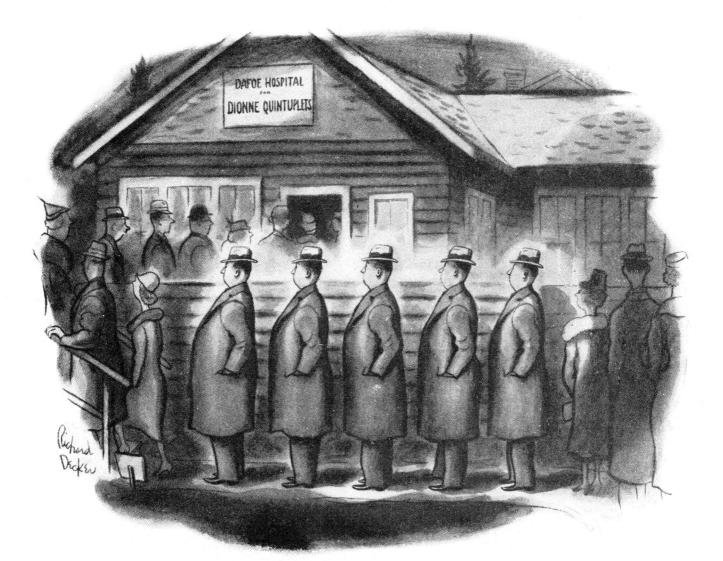

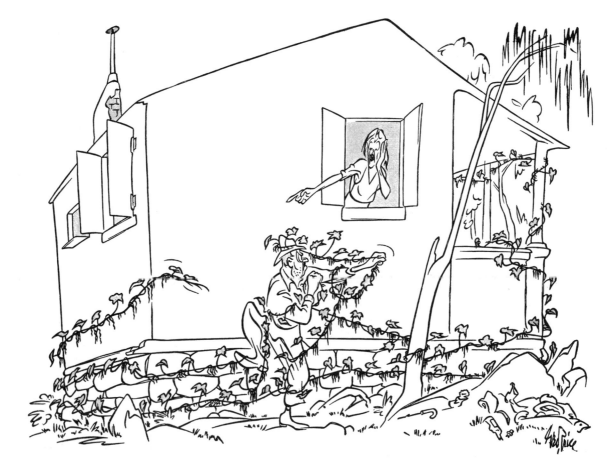

"Watch out, Fred! Here it comes again!"

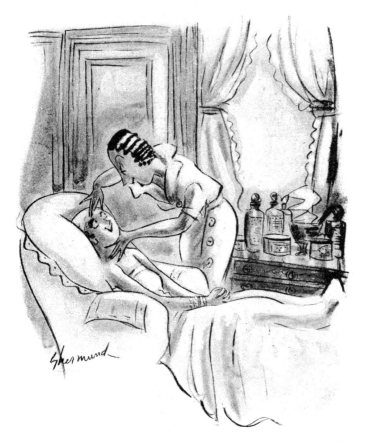

"You're one of the lucky few who
have a normal skin."

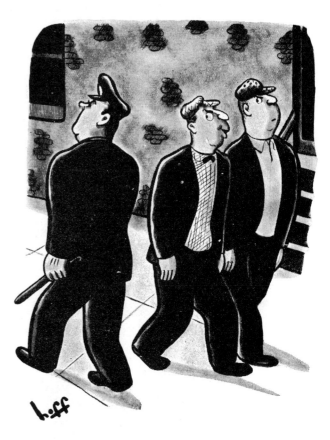

"And Mrs. Wilkins' baby—how is _she_?"

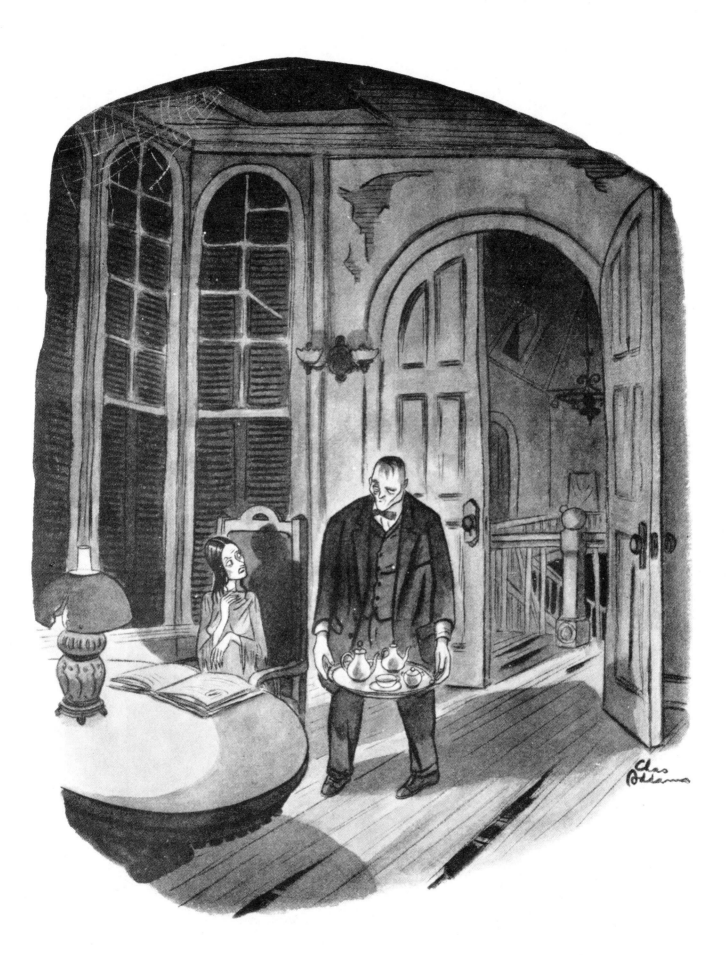

"Oh, it's you! For a moment you gave me quite a start."

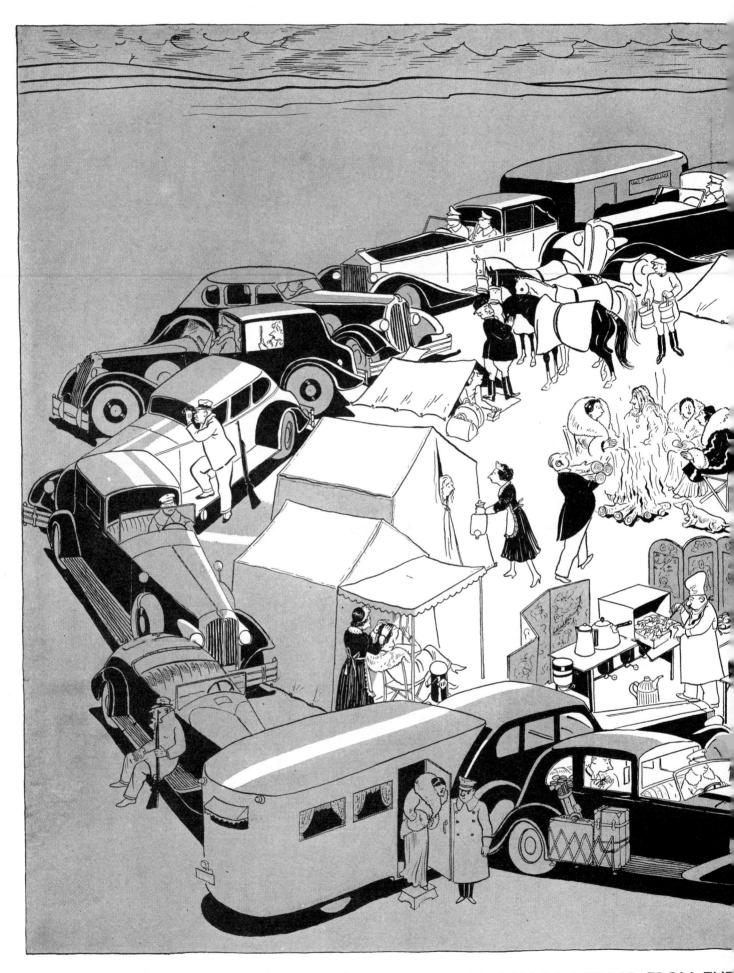

A CARAVAN OF CALIFORNIA MILLIONAIRES, FLEEING EASTWARD FROM THE

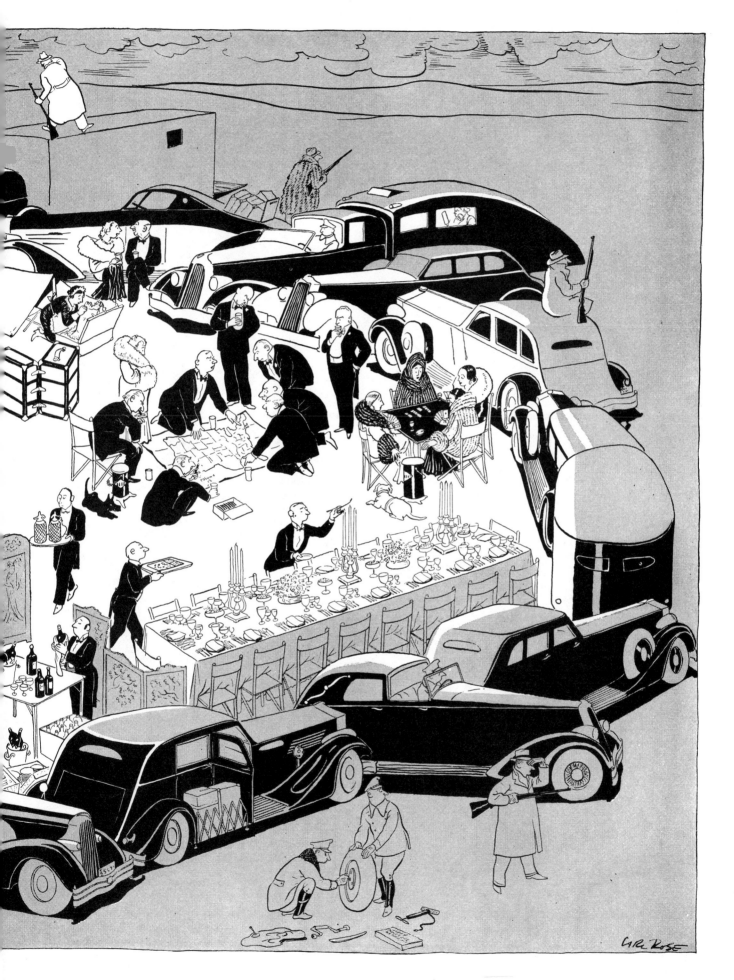

...ATE INCOME TAX, ENCAMPS FOR THE NIGHT IN HOSTILE WISCONSIN TERRITORY

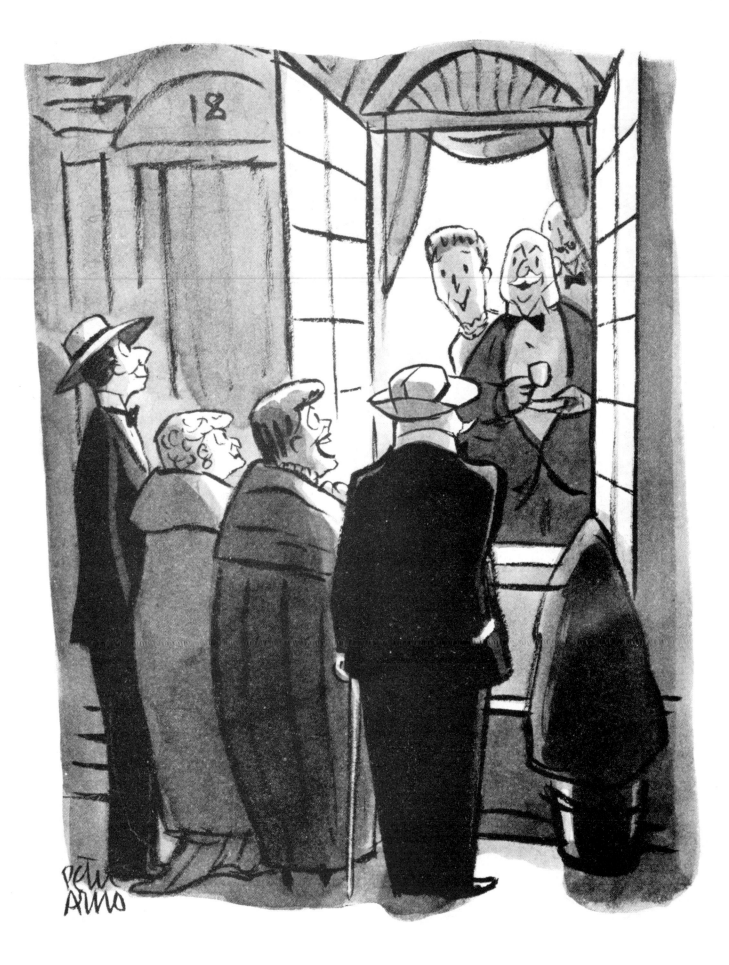

"*Come along. We're going to the Trans-Lux to hiss Roosevelt.*"

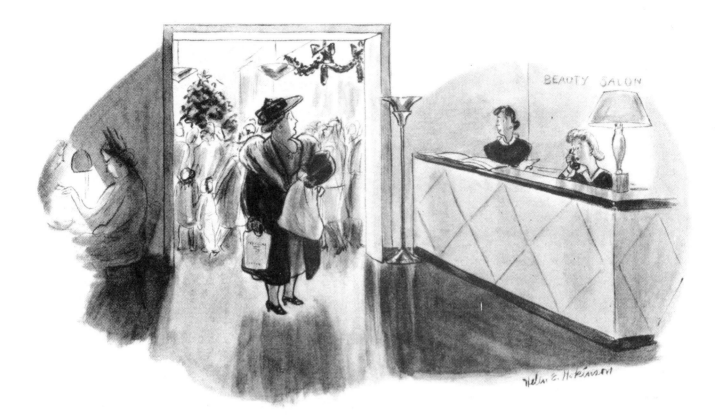

"Have you a treatment that includes lying down?"

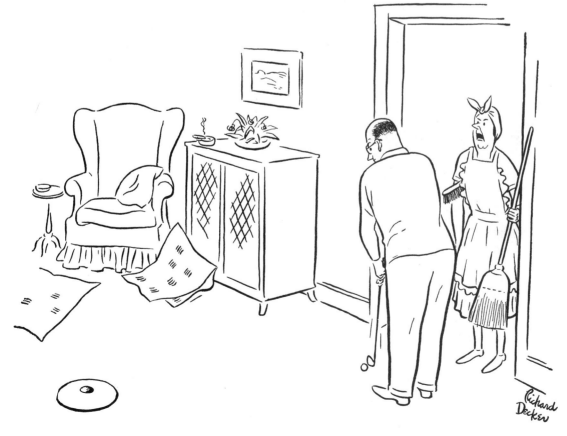

"Mind if I play through?"

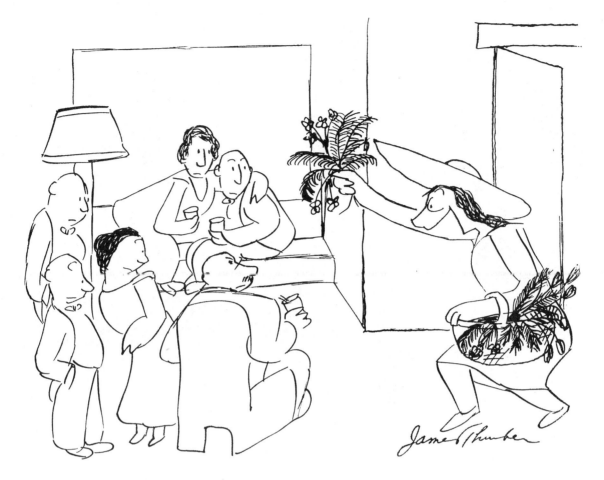

"I come from haunts of coot and hern!"

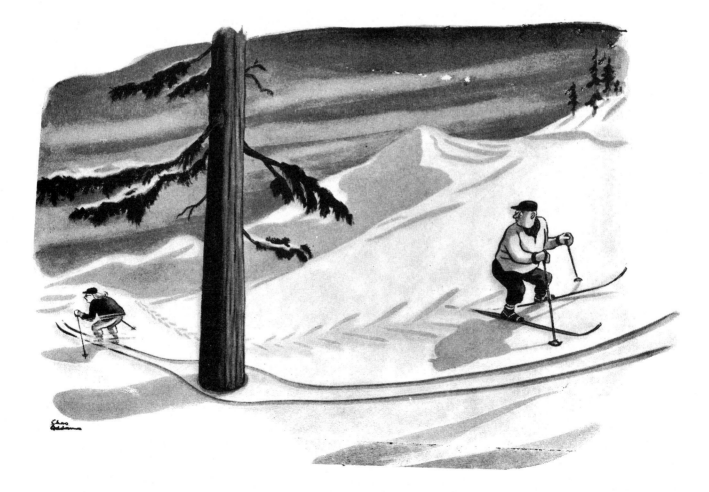

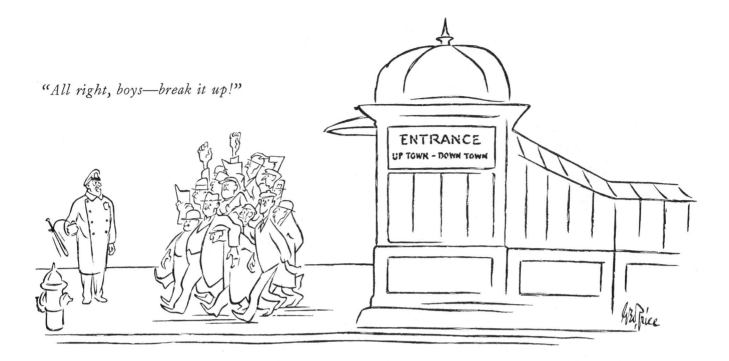

"All right, boys—break it up!"

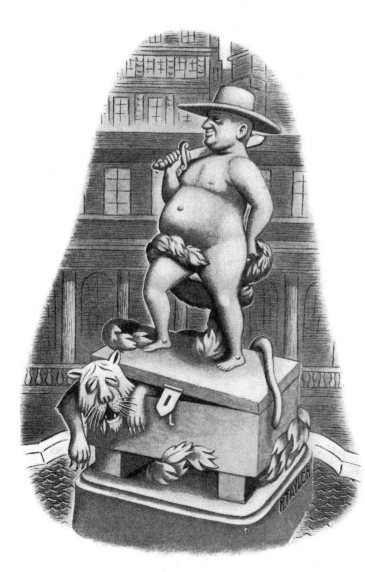

A REVISED STATUARY
FOR THE CITY OF TOMORROW

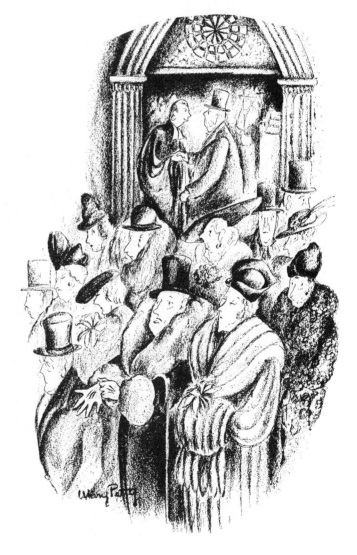

*"Everything considered, he preaches a
remarkably good sermon. It's so hard
to avoid offending people like us."*

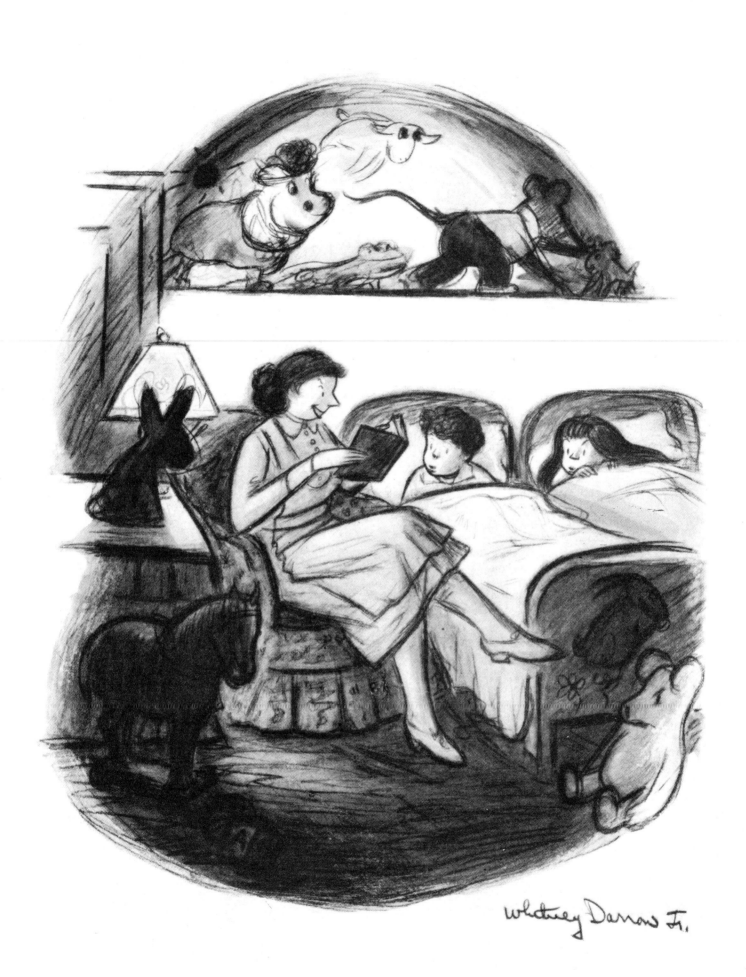

*"Coked to the gills, Beardon lunged toward the supine figure
on the red plush couch."*

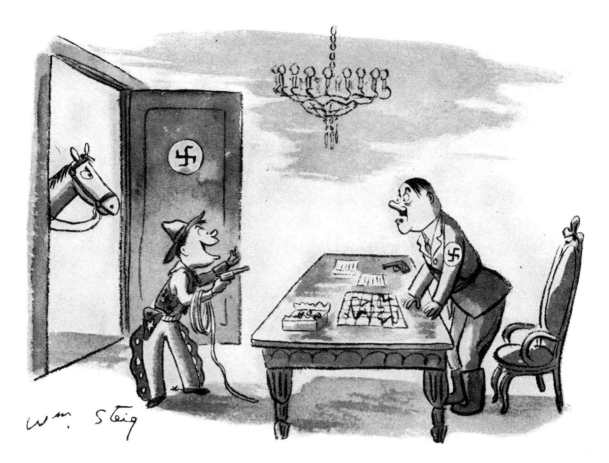

DREAMS OF GLORY

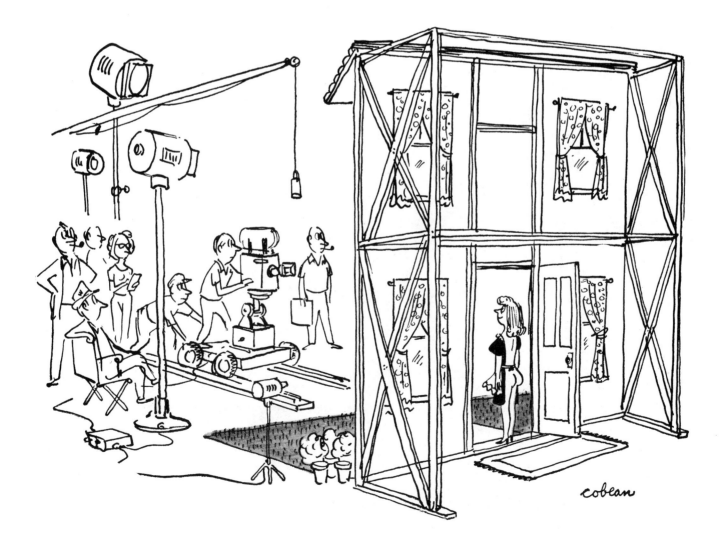

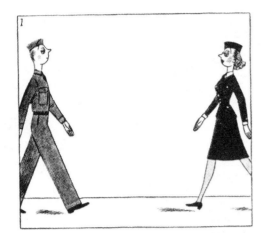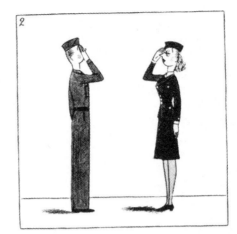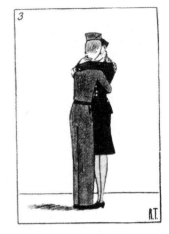

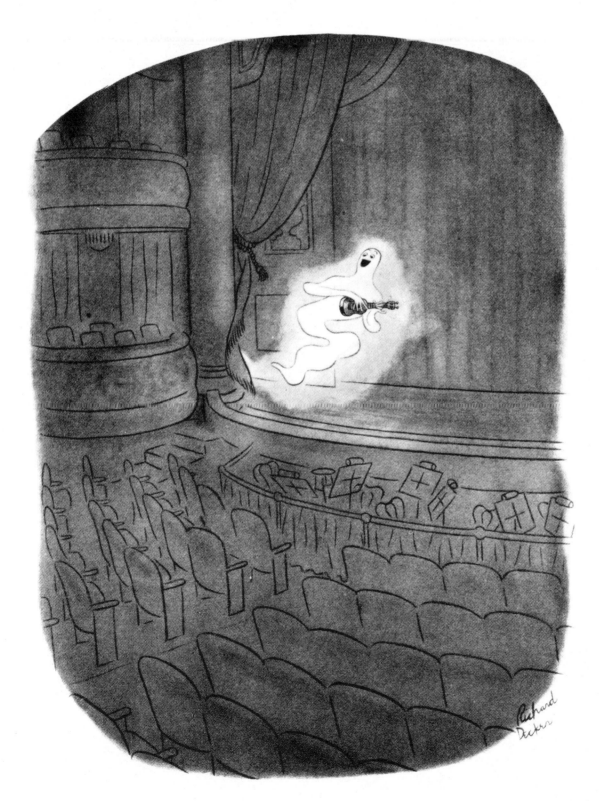

"Yes! we have
no bananas—
we have
no bananas
today."

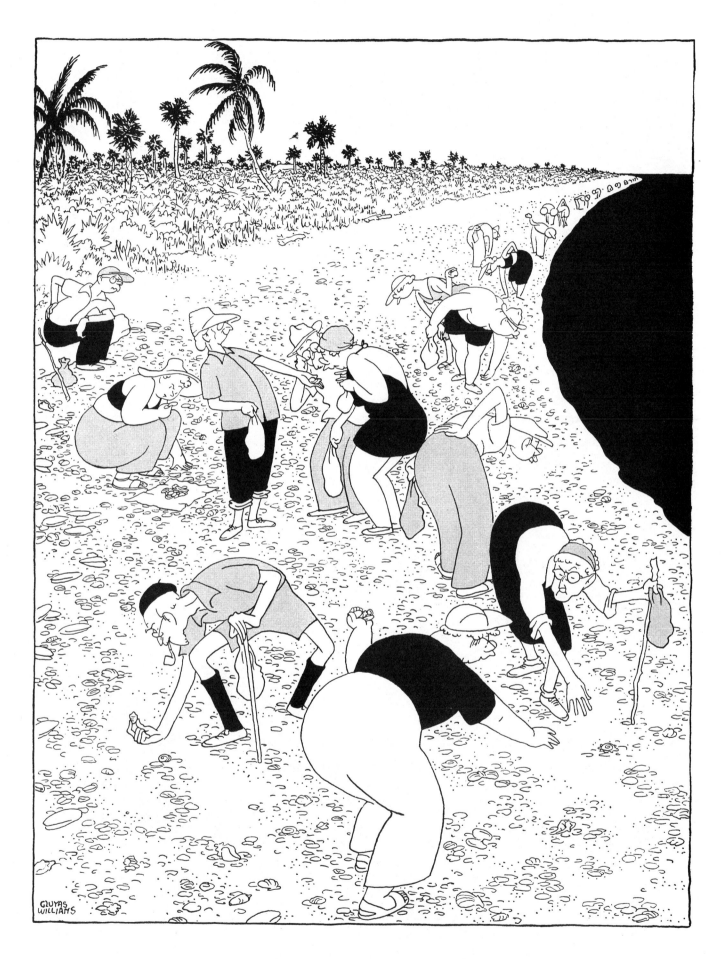

AMERICA'S PLAYGROUNDS

Shelling on Sanibel Island

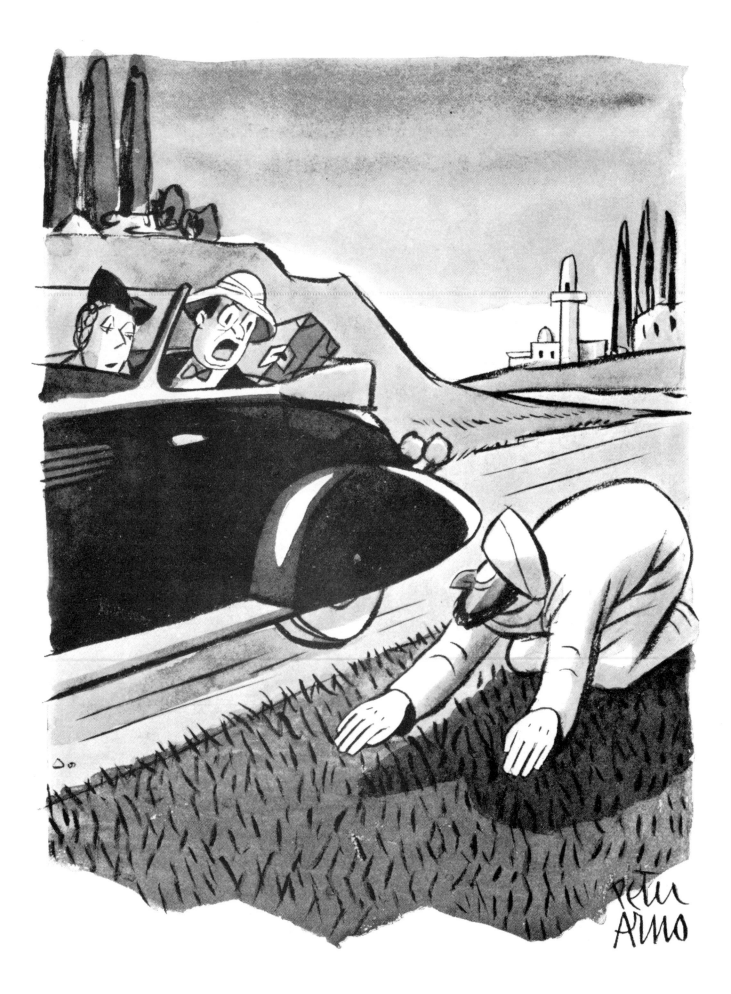

"Hey, Jack, which way to Mecca?"

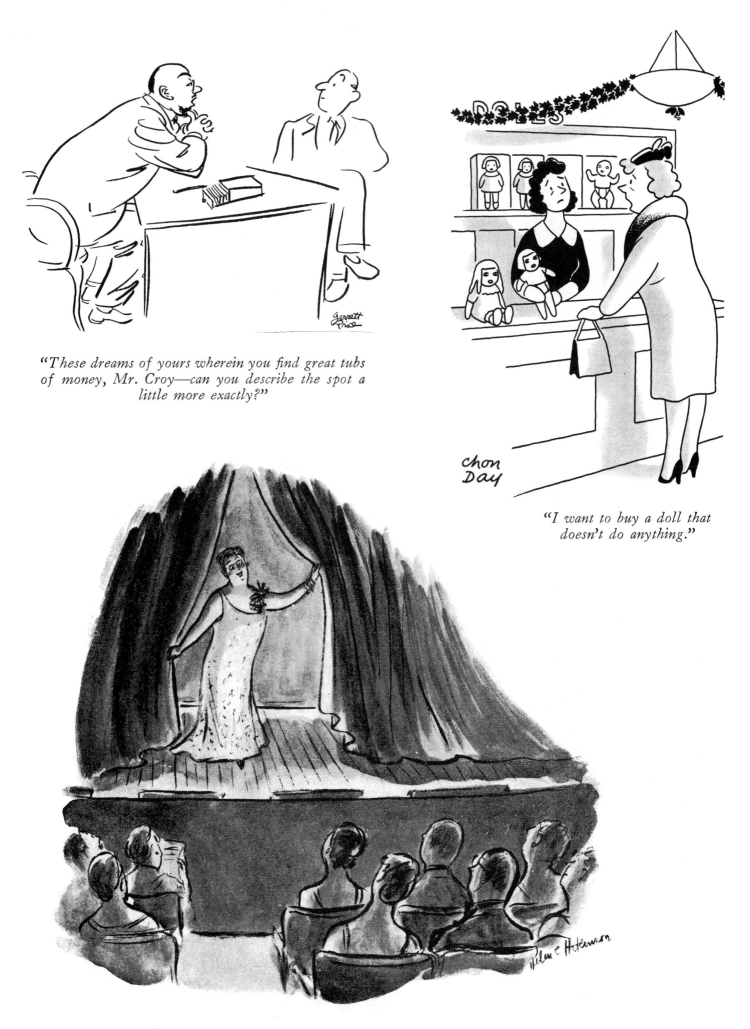

"These dreams of yours wherein you find great tubs of money, Mr. Croy—can you describe the spot a little more exactly?"

"I want to buy a doll that doesn't do anything."

"Enough of Prologue! Now let's have the play. 'The Pageant of Distinguished Bergen County Women' is under way."

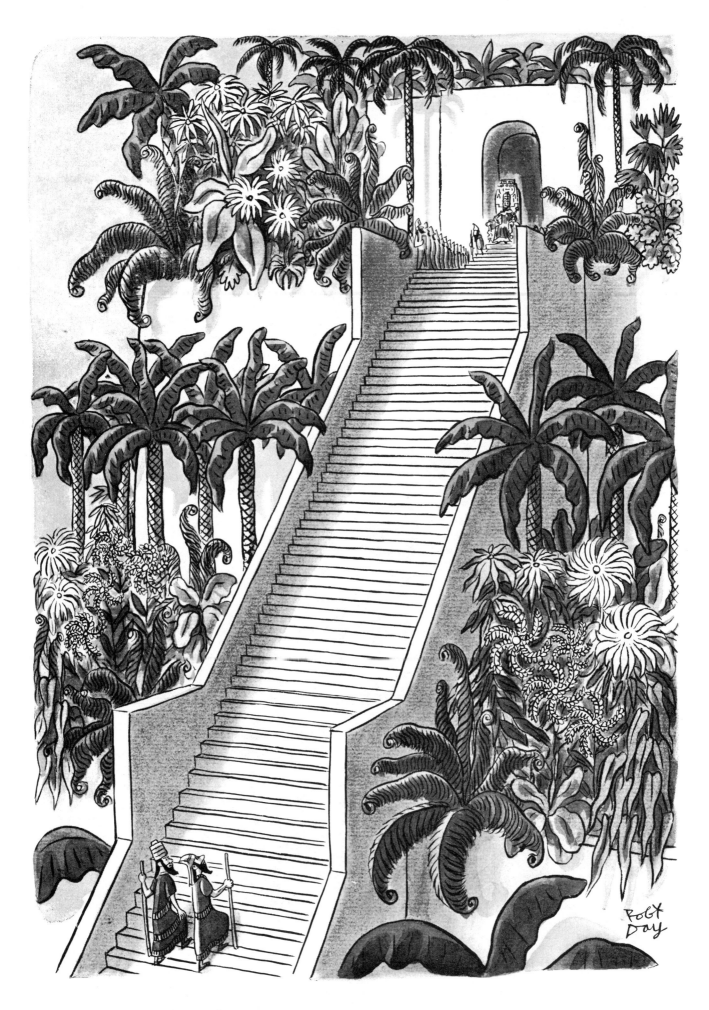

"Don't forget to compliment him on his green thumb."

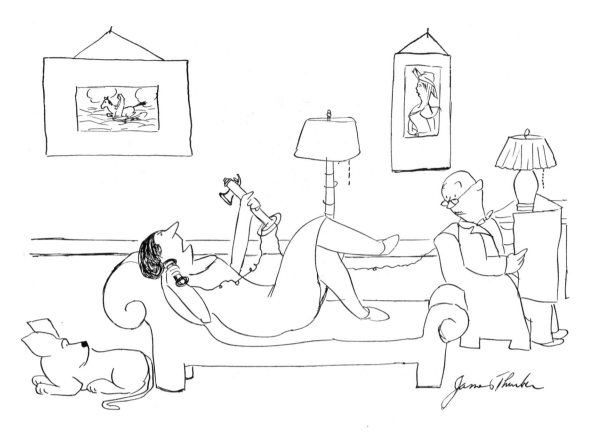

"Well, if I called the wrong number, why did you answer the phone?"

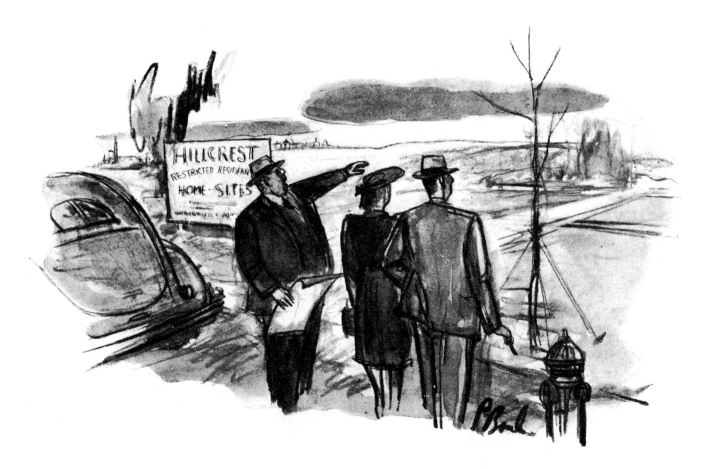

*"There's a fascinating legend about an Indian maiden in connection
with Plots 14, 15, and most of 15A."*

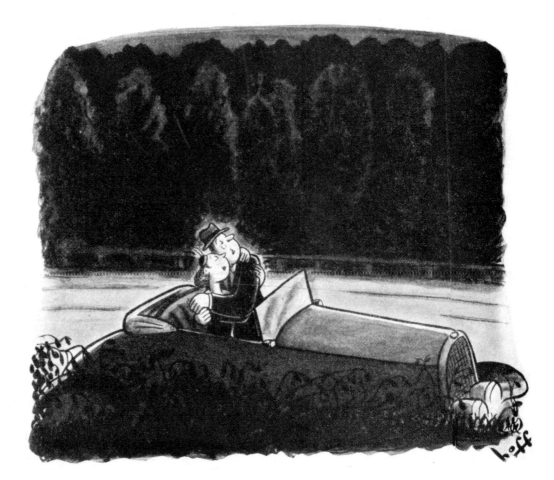

*"I just can't believe it.
A half-hour ago
I whistle at you
and now
you're in my arms."*

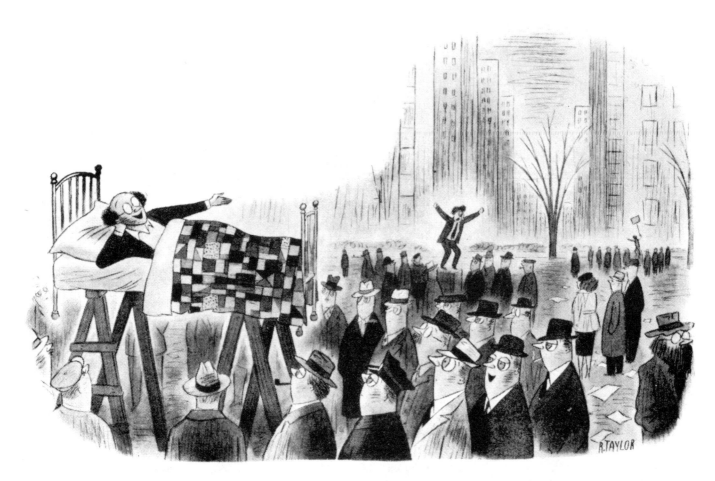

"He advocates a doctrine of peaceful resignation."

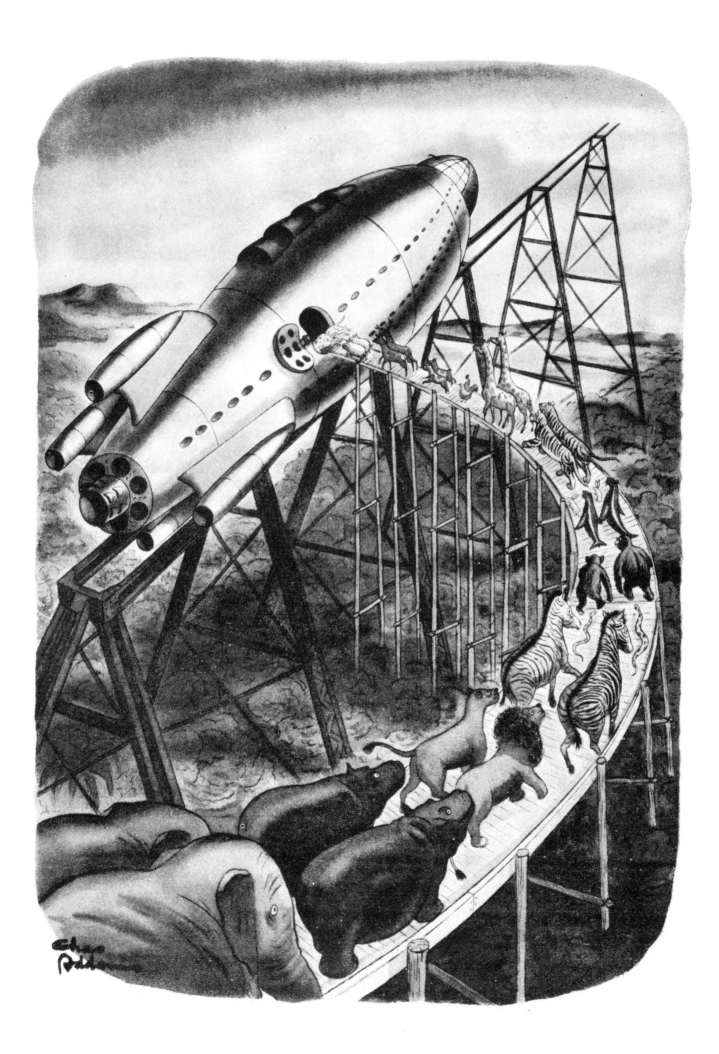

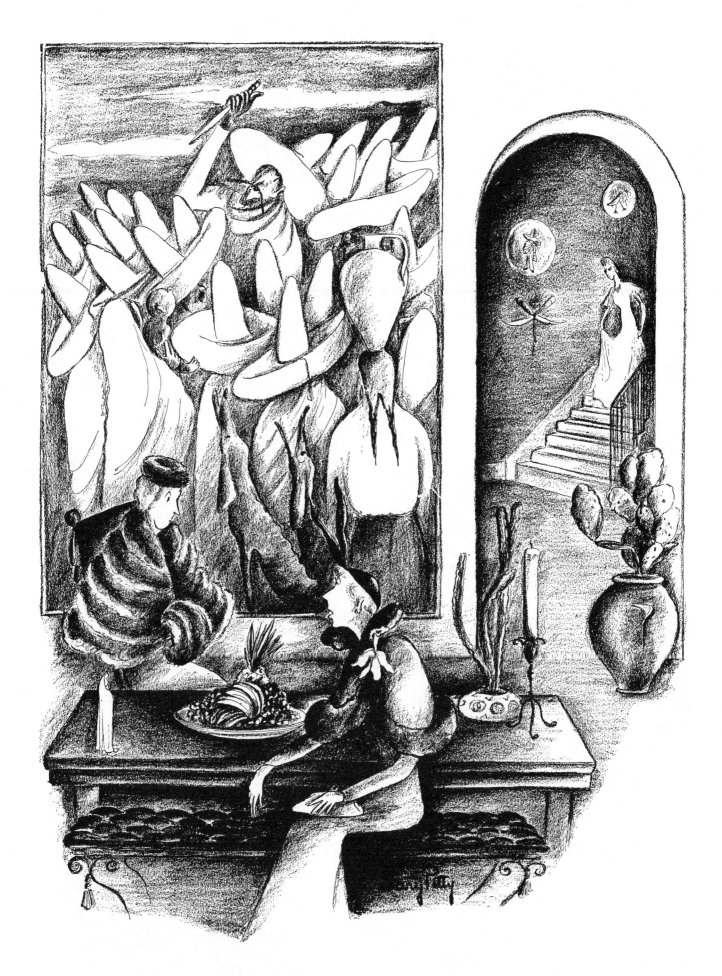

"You'd think she'd rather <u>forget</u> Mexico. She got ringworm there."

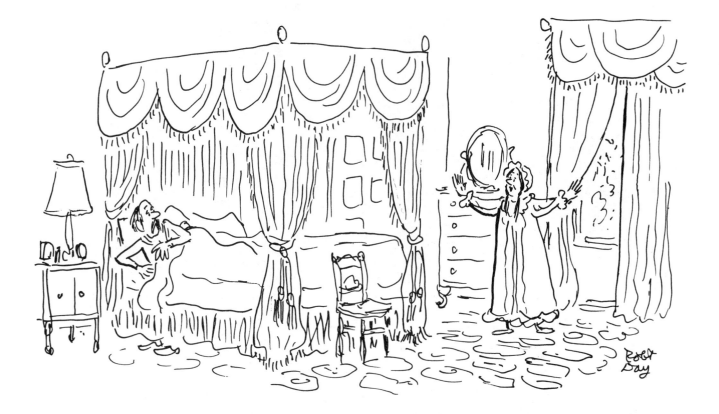

"*Get up, Richard, quick! Bedlam has broken loose in the garden! The forsythia, dogwood, andromeda, daffodils, and Mongolian azaleas are all in full bloom and going wild trying to prove that each is more beautiful than the other!*"

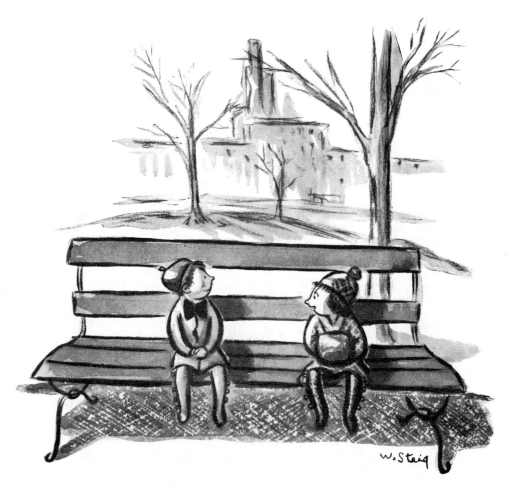

"*Well, stupid, don't just sit there.*"

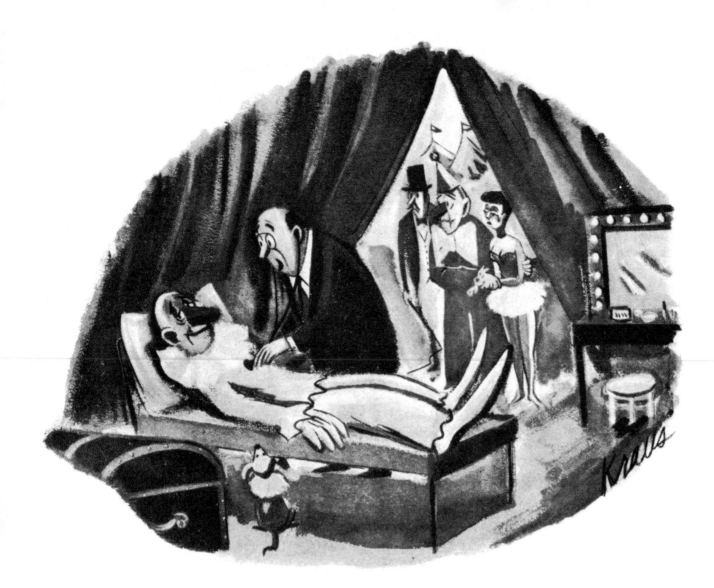

"*Good heavens, man, your heart is breaking!*"

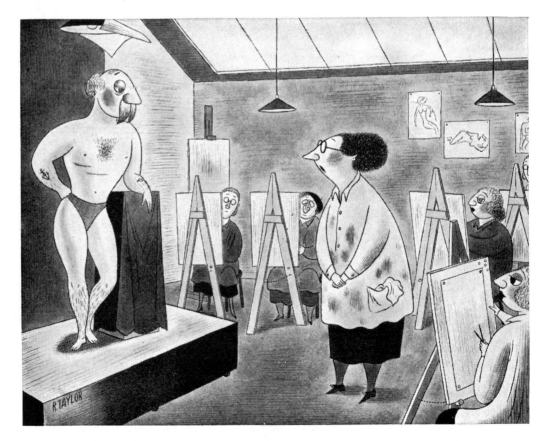

"*Couldn't we have a pose with a little more character in it, Mr. Humbolt?*"

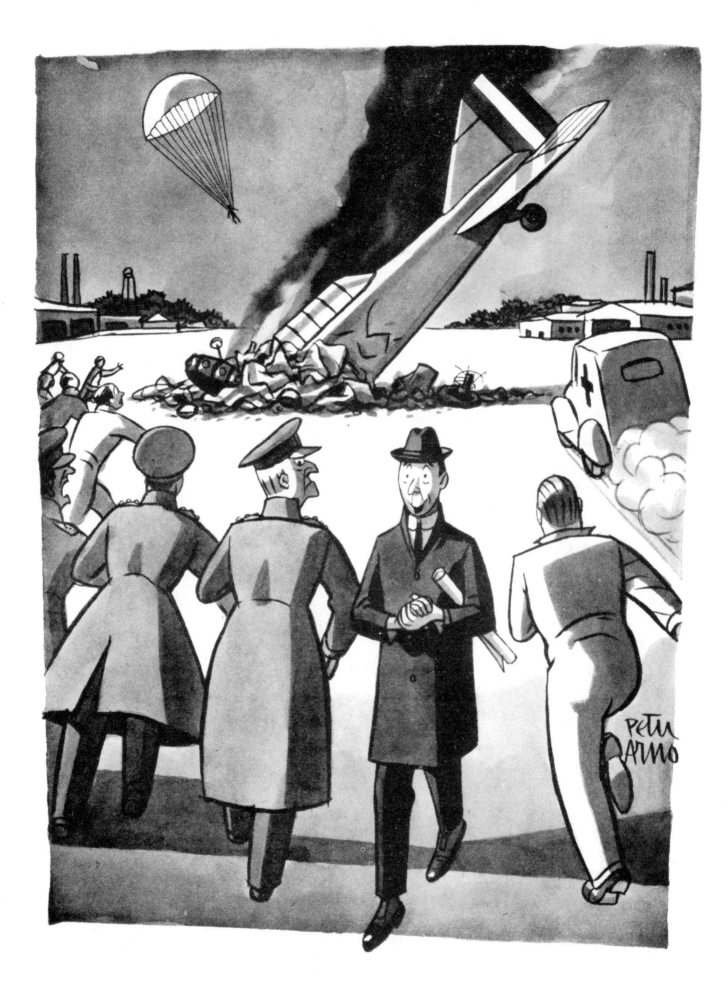

"Well, back to the old drawing board."

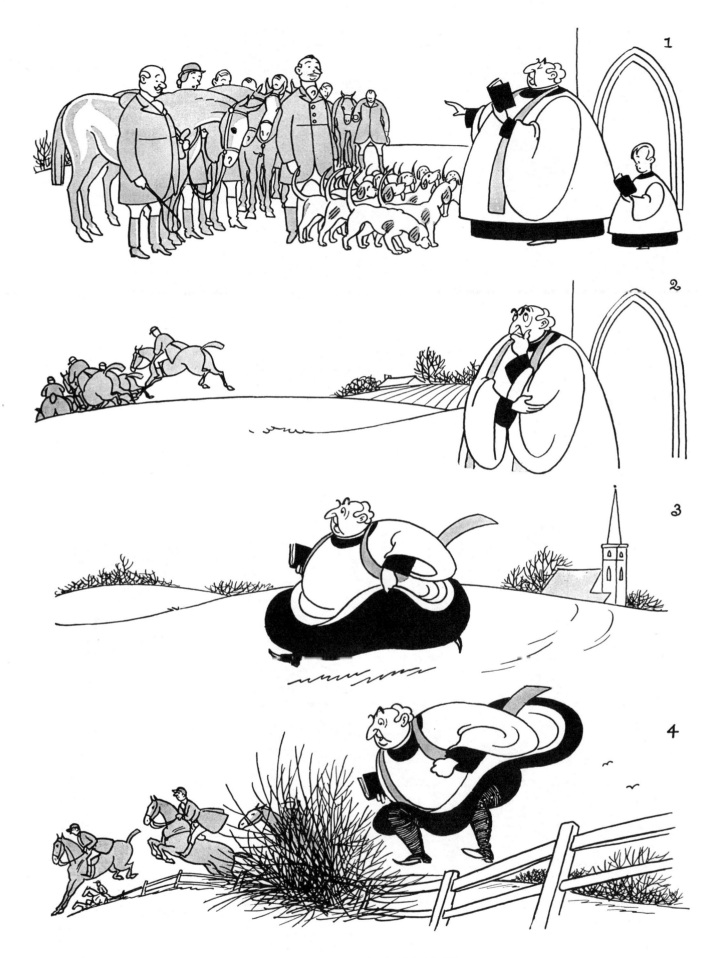

THE VICAR'S REMORSE

Having blessed the foxhounds in accordance with tradition, he feels the prick of conscience

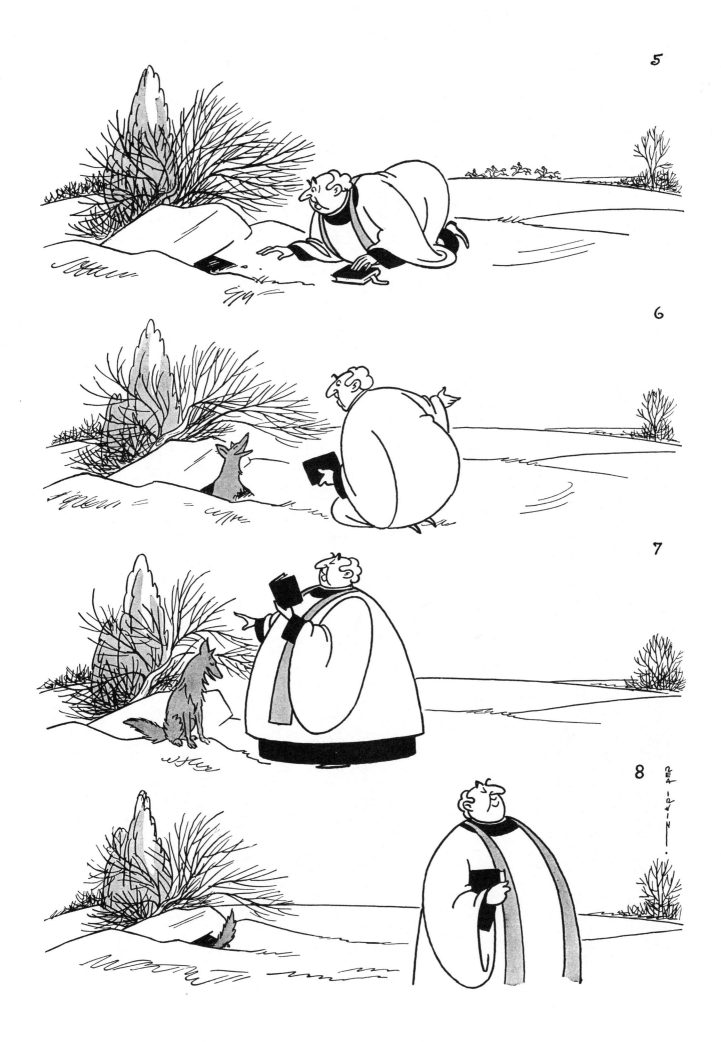

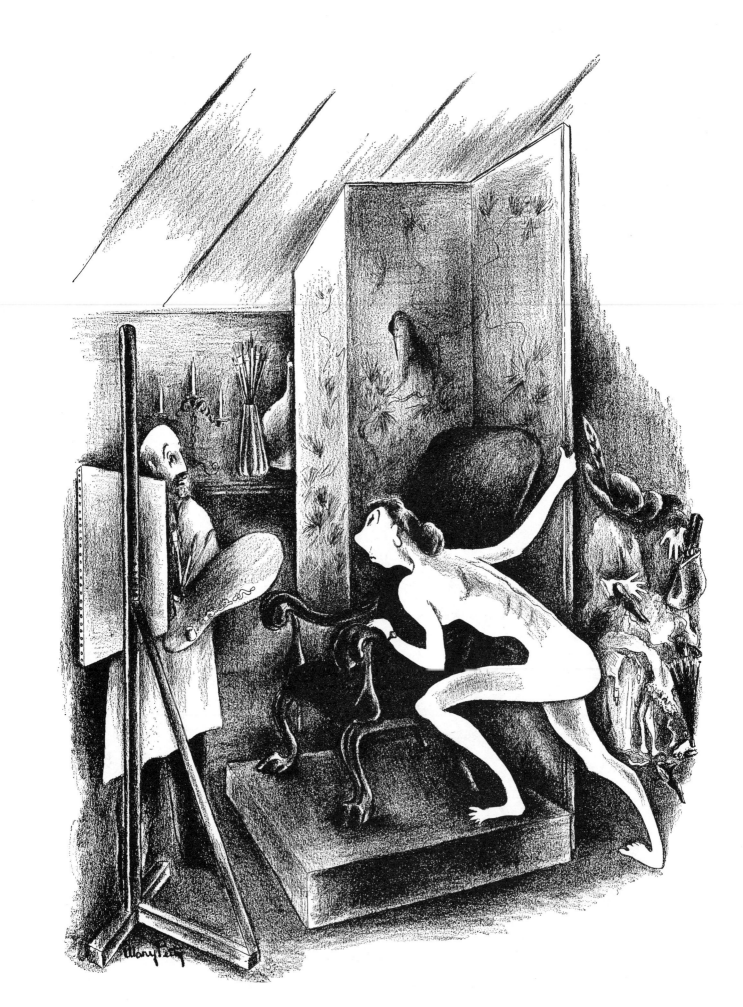

"Dear no, Miss Mayberry—just the head."

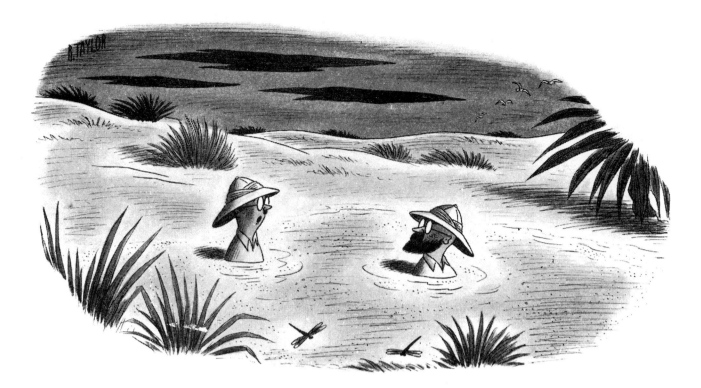

"Quicksand or not, Barclay, I've half a mind to struggle."

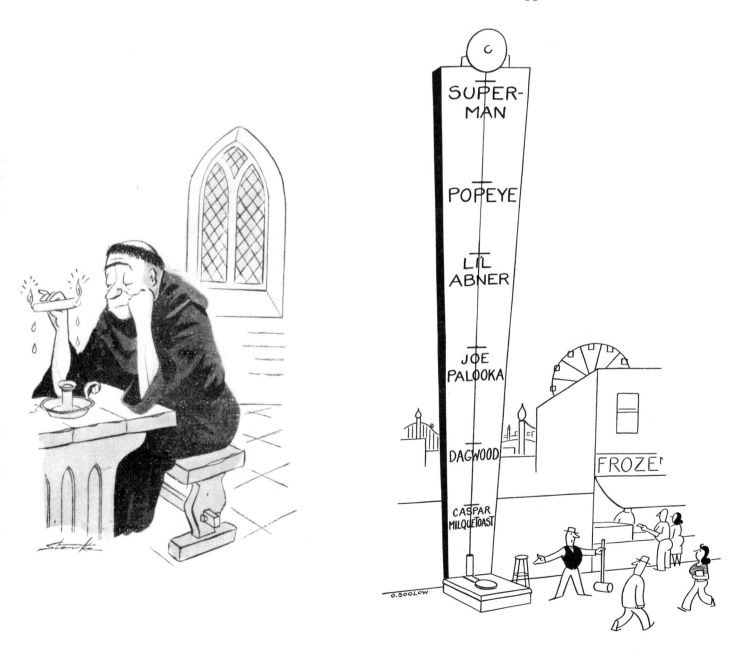

OUR NEW NATURAL HISTORY
A GROUP OF MISCELLANEOUS CREATURES

The Tantamount

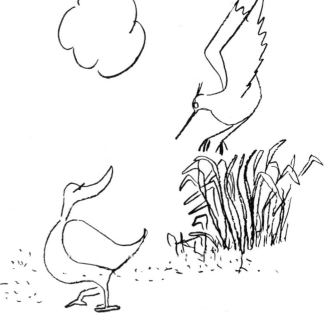

A pair of Martinets

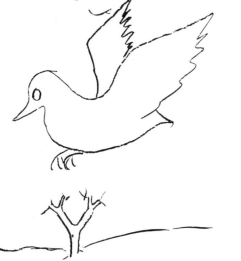

The Common Carrier

A female Shriek (right) rising out of the Verbiage to attack a female Swoon

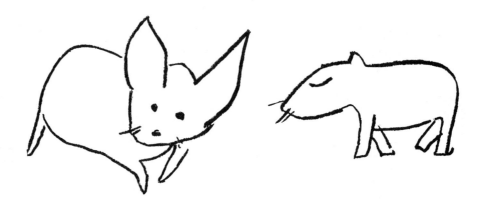

The Bodkin (left) and the Chintz

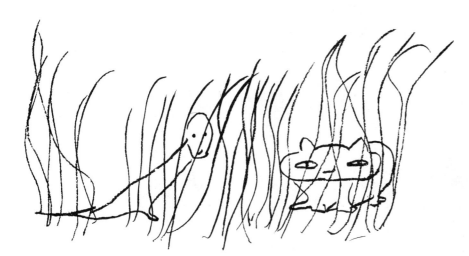

A Scone (left) and a Crumpet, peering out of the Tiffin

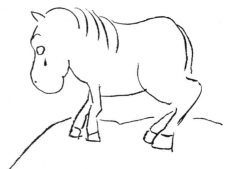

The Hopeless Quandary

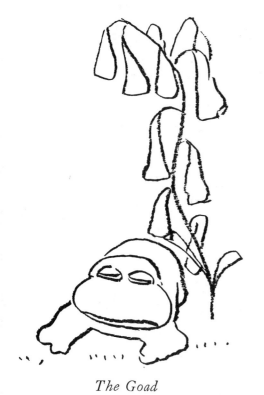

The Goad

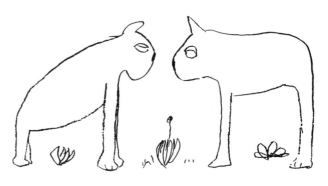

A Trochee (left) encountering a Spondee

THREE FRESH~WATER CREATURES

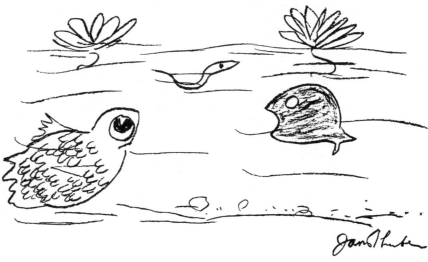

The Qualm   *The Glib*   *The Moot*

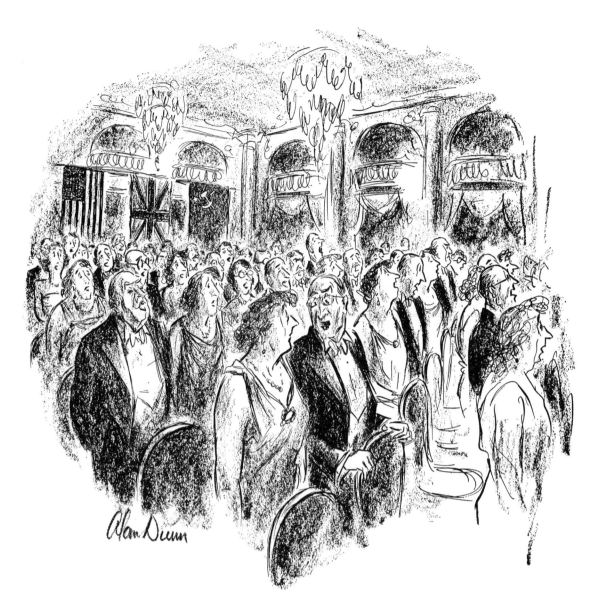

"It's the 'Internationale.' If you don't know the words, just mumble."

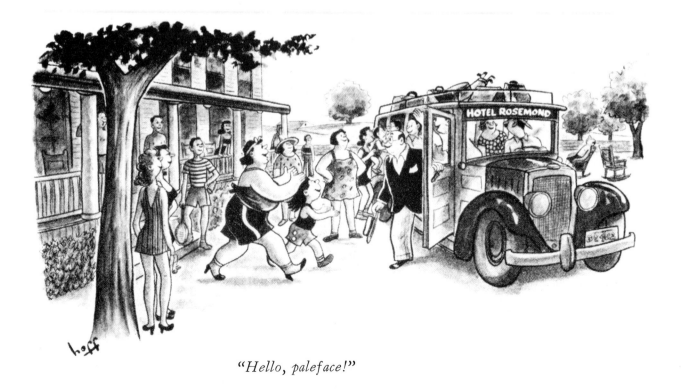

"Hello, paleface!"

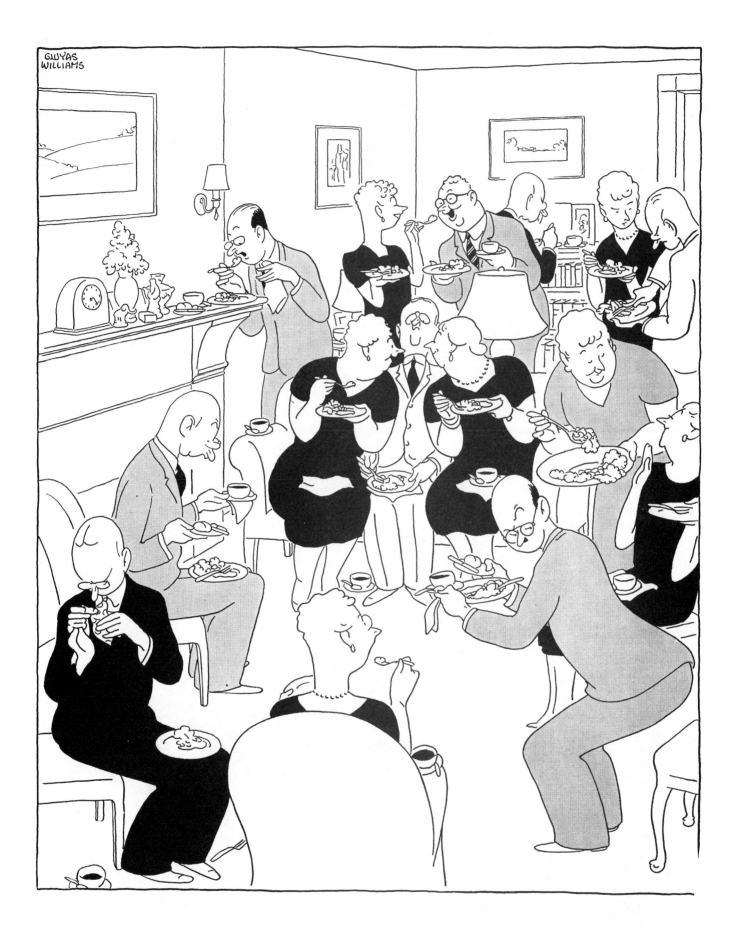

THE INNER MAN

Buffet Supper

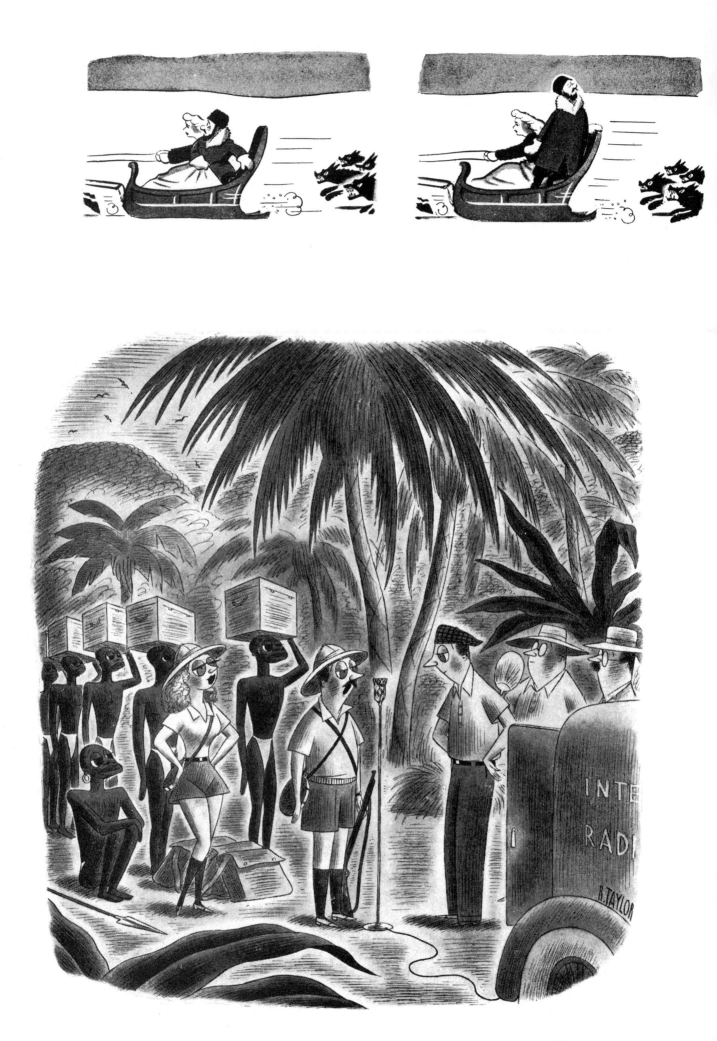

"... and now I'm off, taking with me only the bare necessities of life."

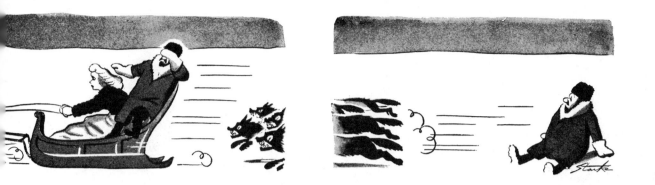

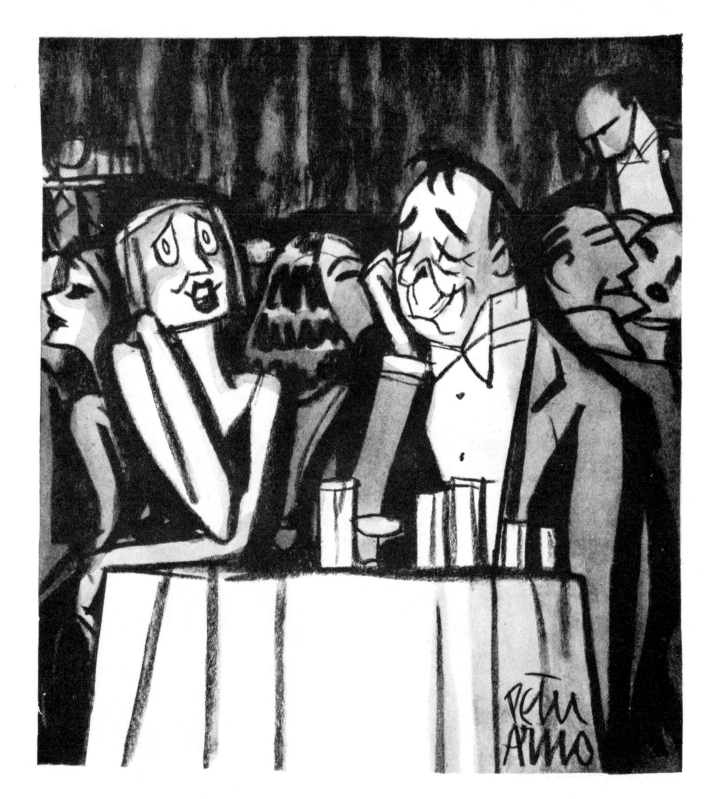

"*You're a mystic, Mr. Ryan. <u>All</u> Irishmen are mystics.*"

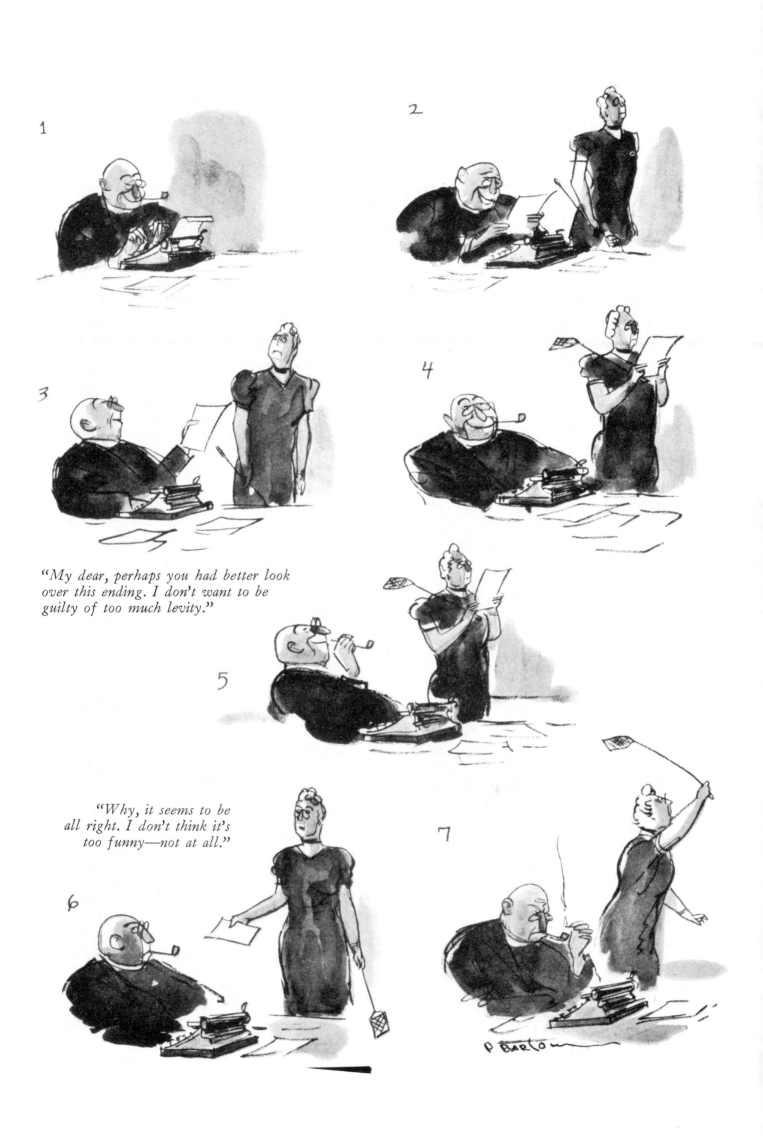

"My dear, perhaps you had better look over this ending. I don't want to be guilty of too much levity."

"Why, it seems to be all right. I don't think it's too funny—not at all."

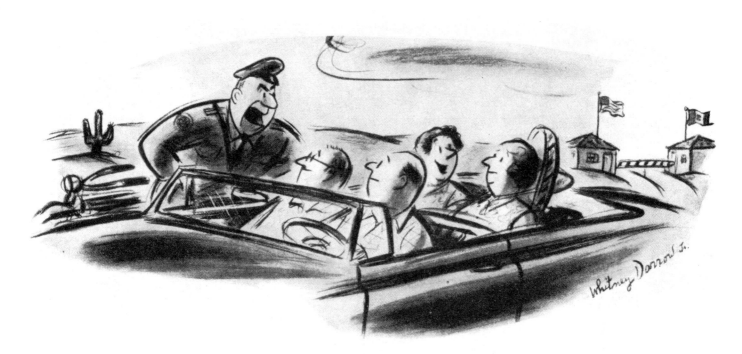

"It certainly sounds good to hear English spoken again."

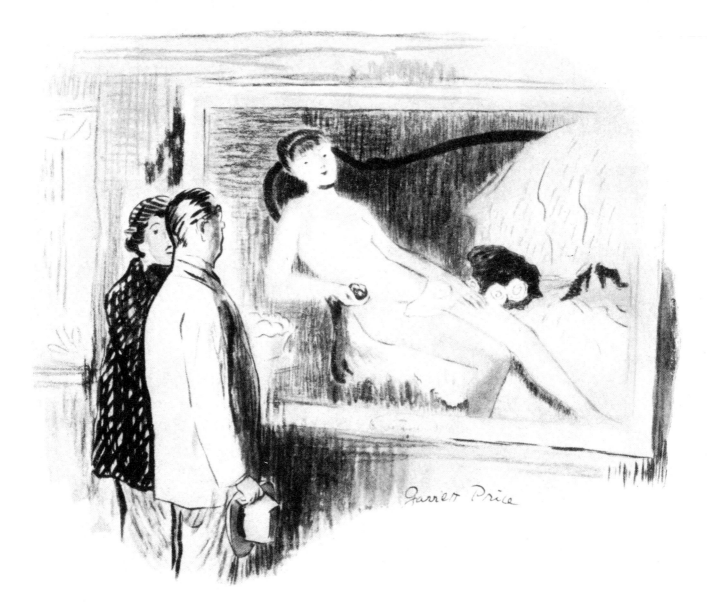

"Mama had a sofa just like that when we lived on South Elm Street."

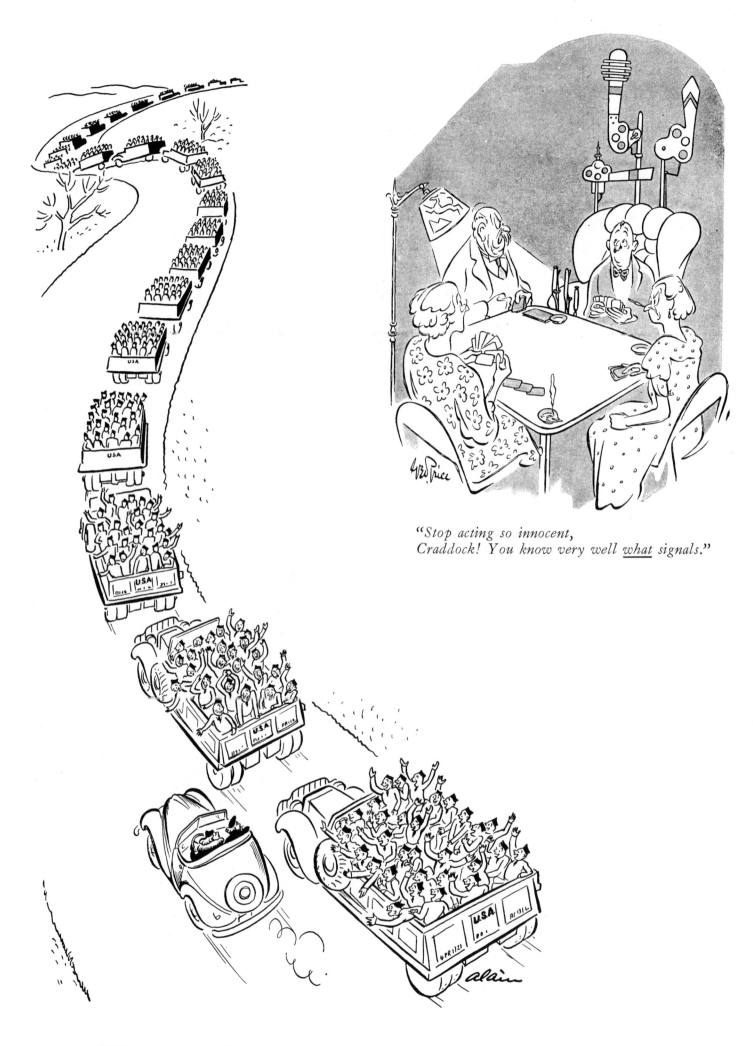

"Stop acting so innocent,
Craddock! You know very well _what_ signals."

"The best thing to do is just pay no attention."

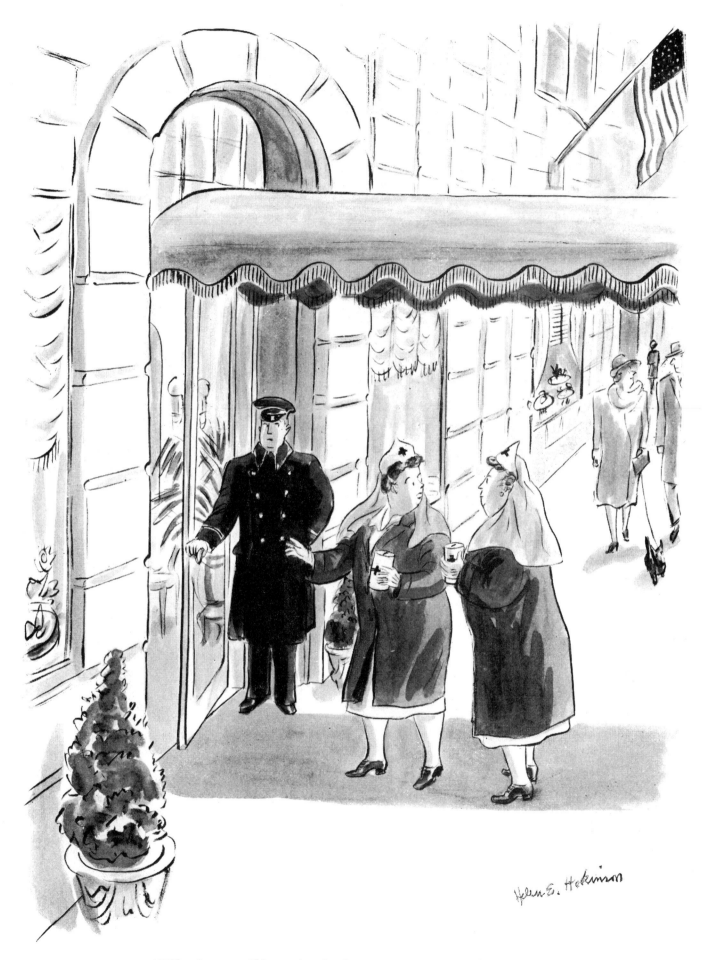

"*They're terribly strict in here. You can set the can on the table, but you can't shake it.*"

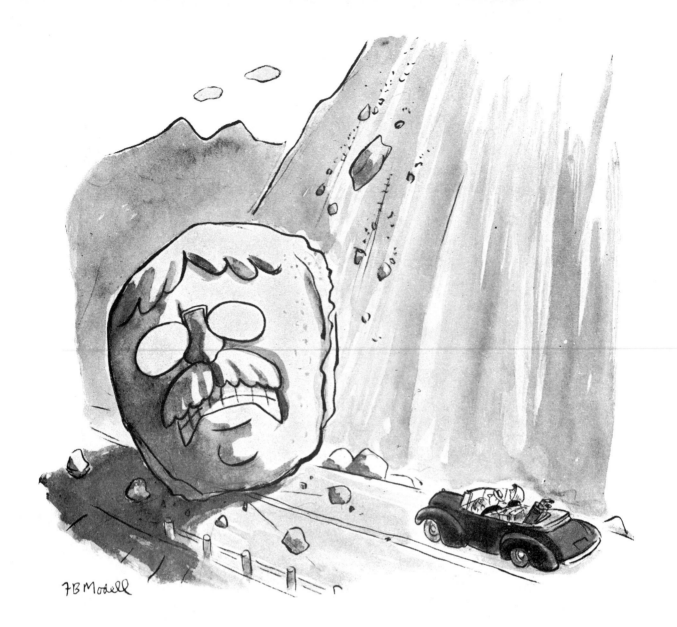

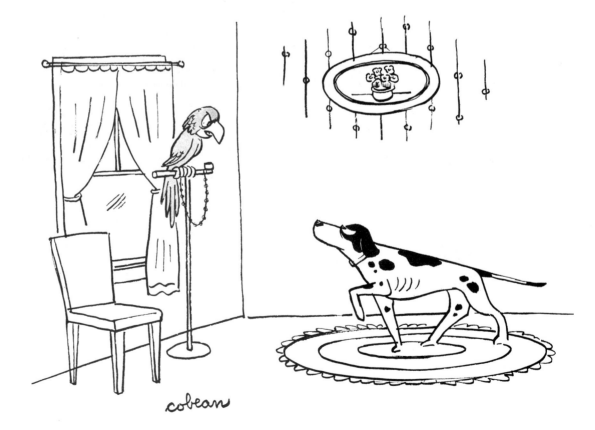

"Aw, nuts! Why don't you grow up?"

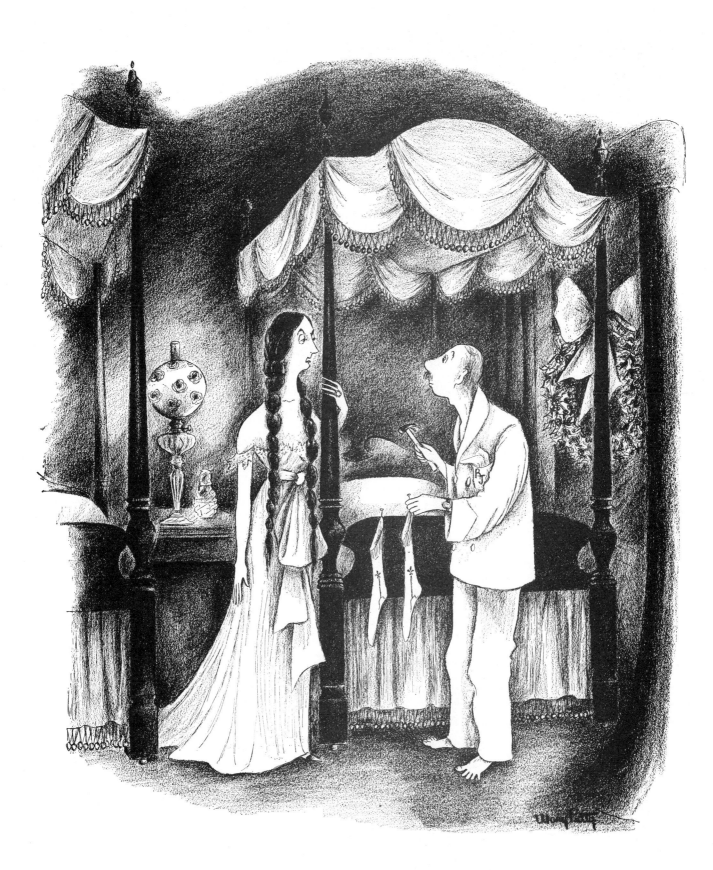

"It's time you faced facts, Rodney."

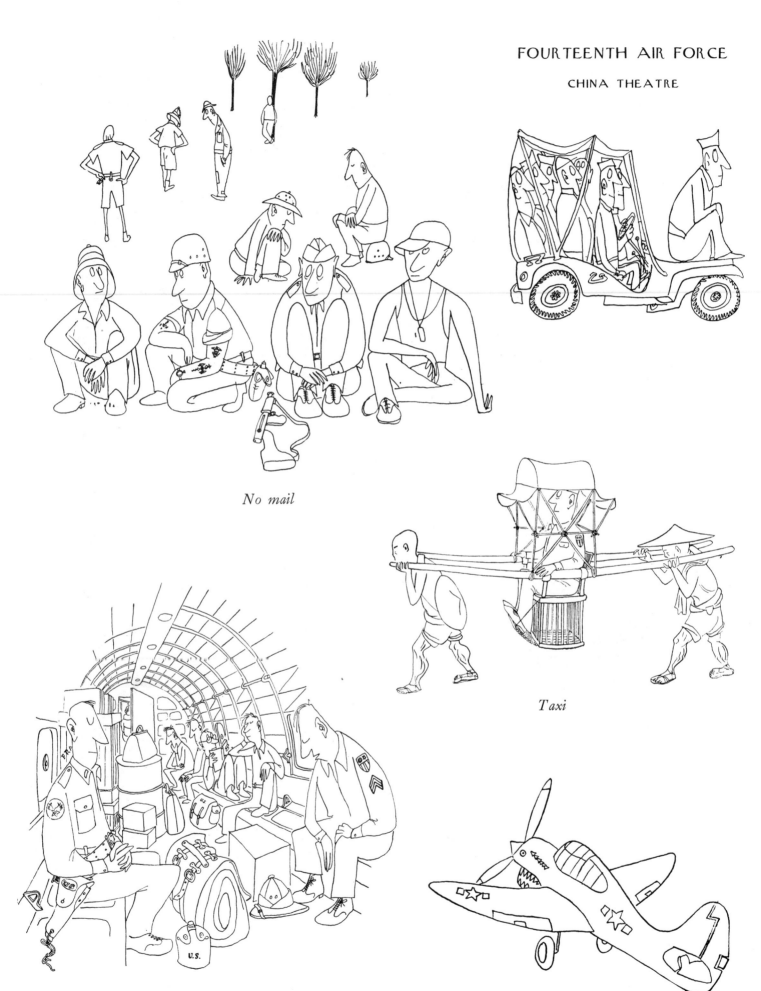

No mail

Taxi

Flying in

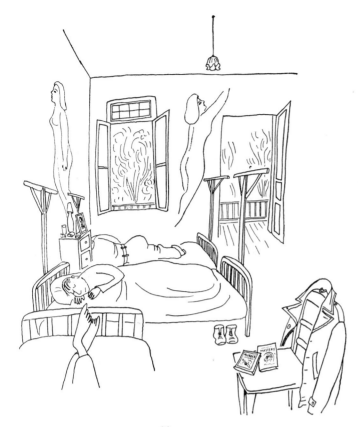

Siesta

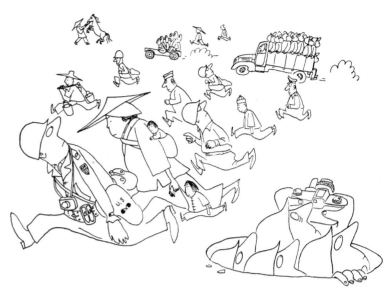

Air raid

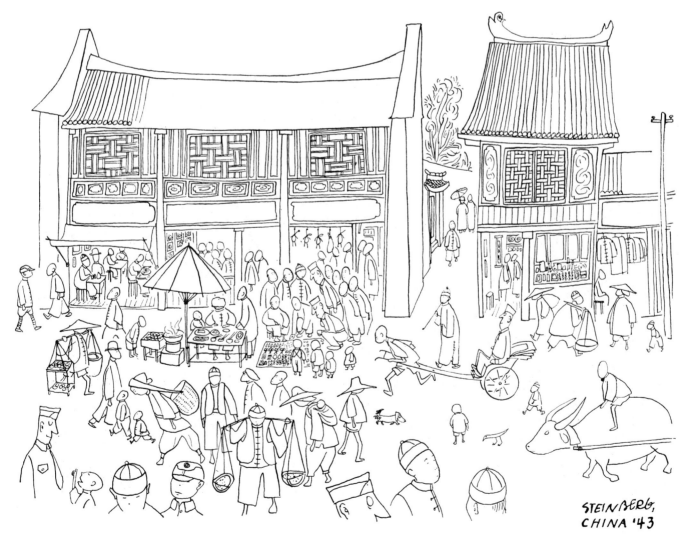

STEINBERG, CHINA '43

Main Street

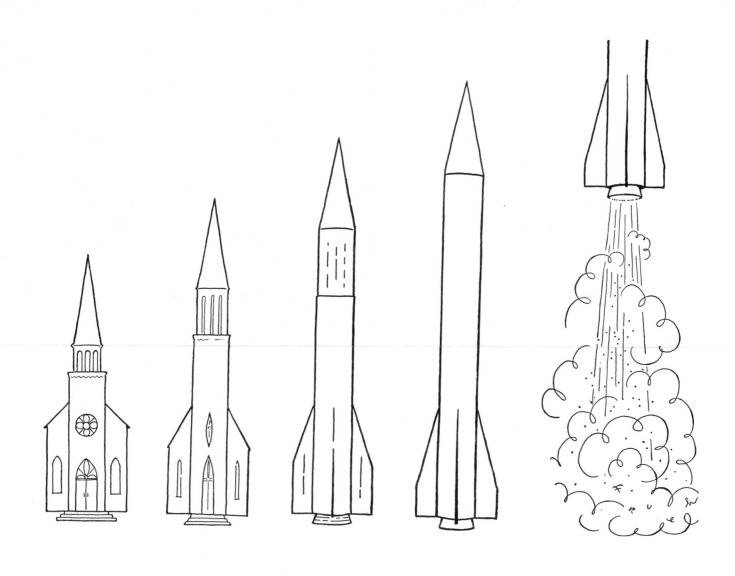

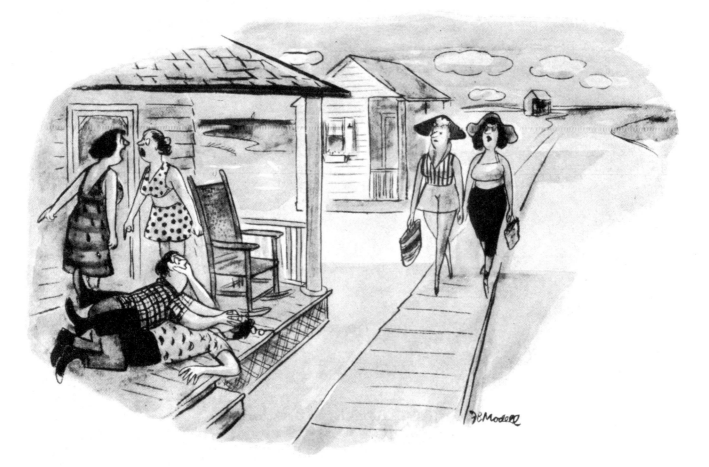

"I've always said two couples sharing a cottage is no good."

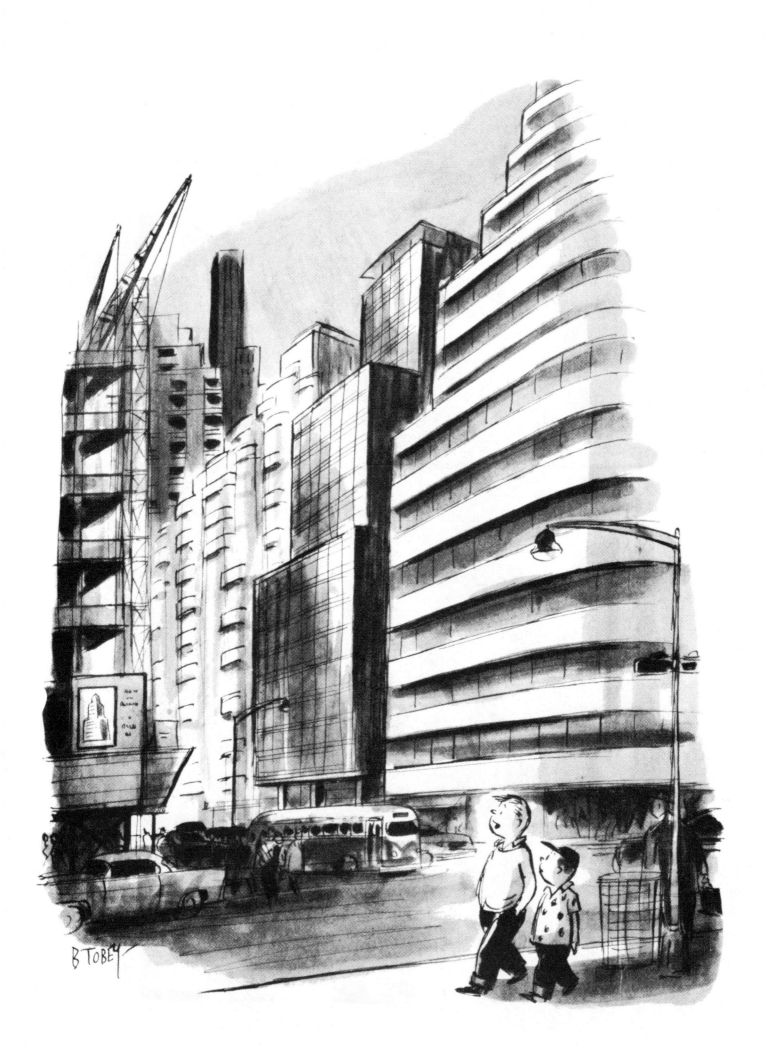

"This neighborhood sure has changed since I was a kid."

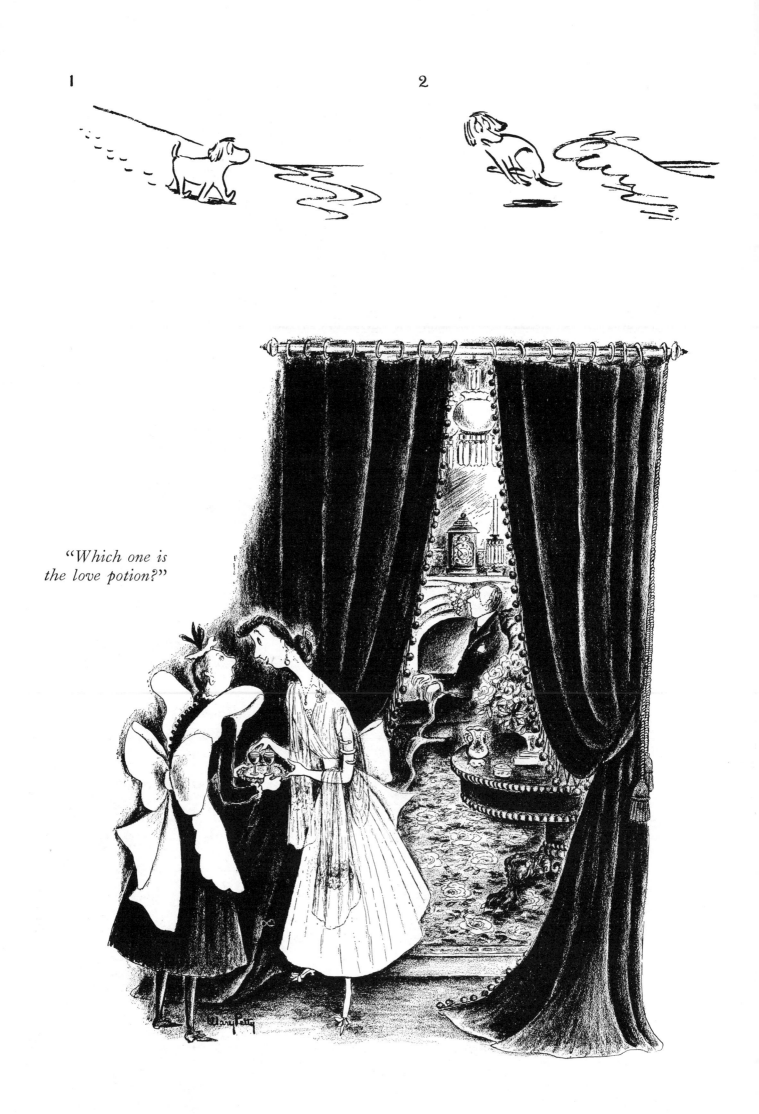

*"Which one is
the love potion?"*

3

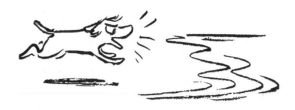

4

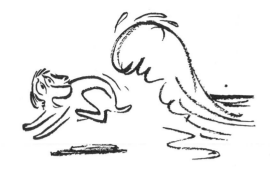

5

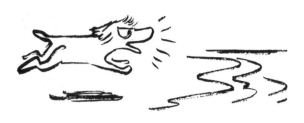

6

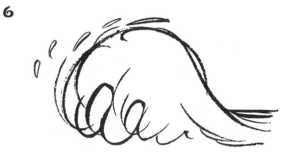

7

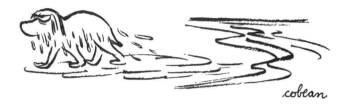

cobean

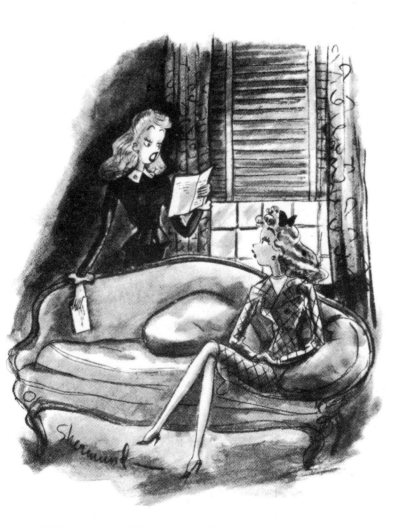

"Can they really make a Yale man a private?"

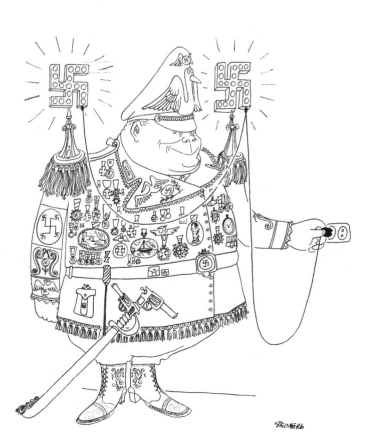

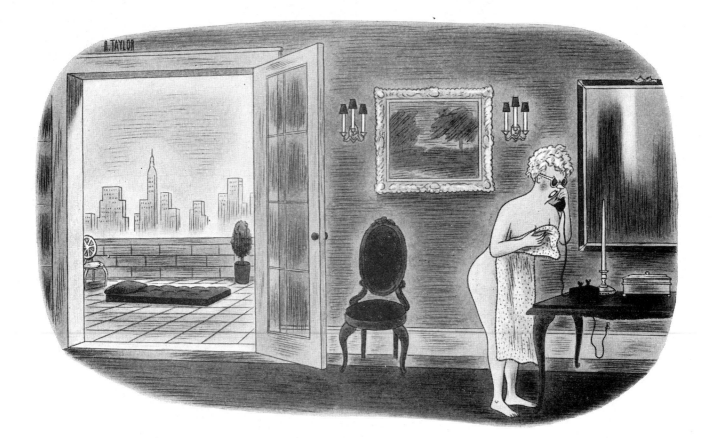

"*I want to report a helicopter.*"

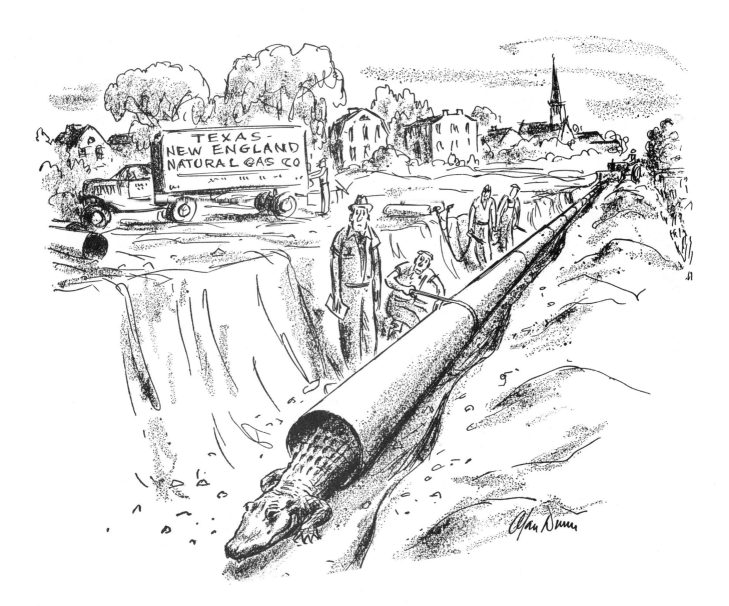

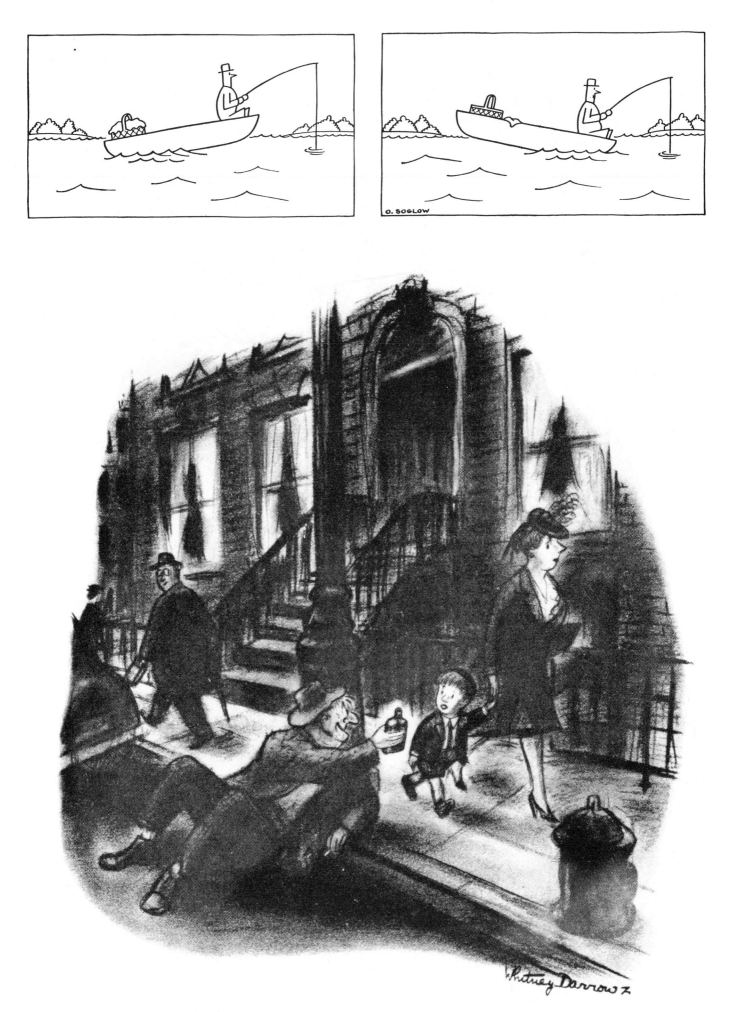

"No thank you. I don't drink."

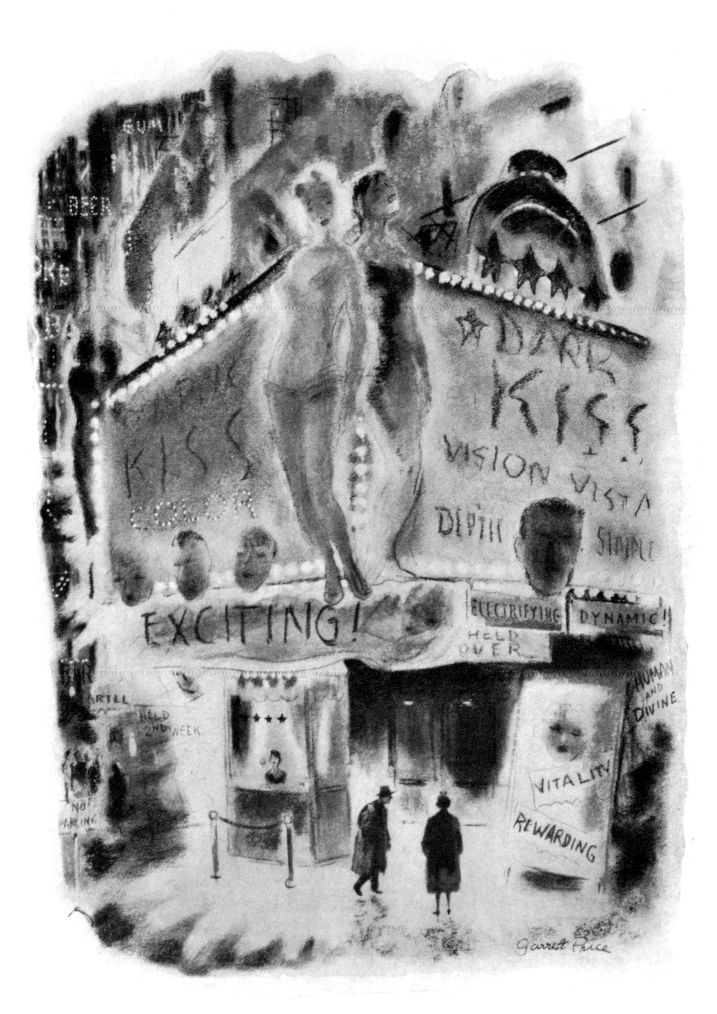

"She says it drags."

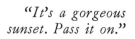

"It's a gorgeous
sunset. Pass it on."

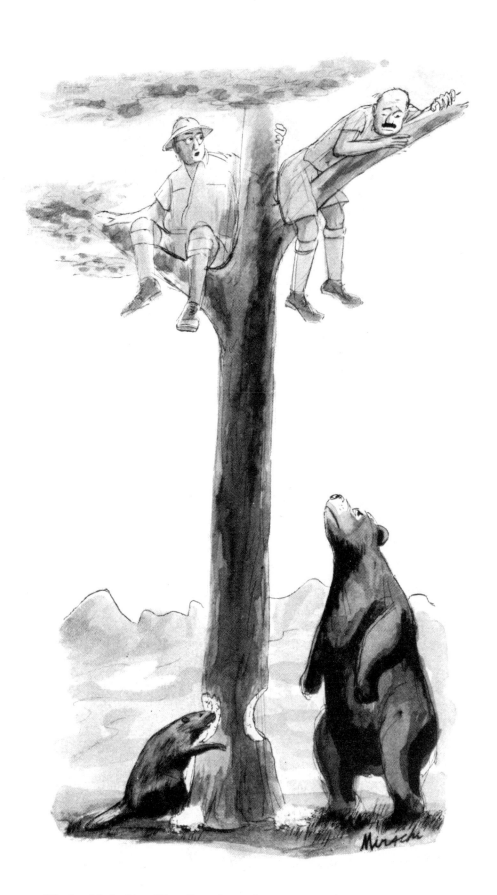

"I do think, Dr. Wurdle, that what we are witnessing here is an
example of what might well be called ecological coördination."

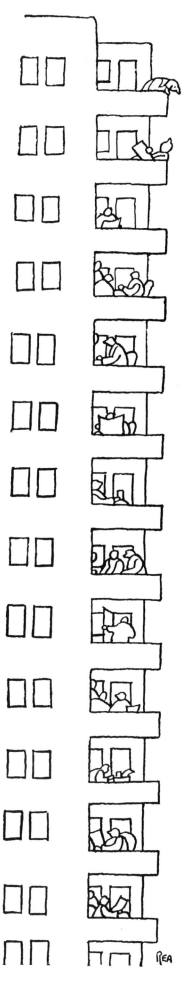

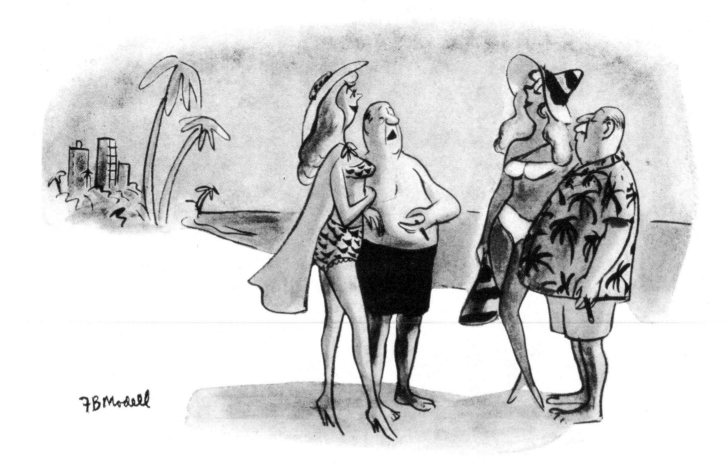

"And this is _my_ secretary—Miss Foster."

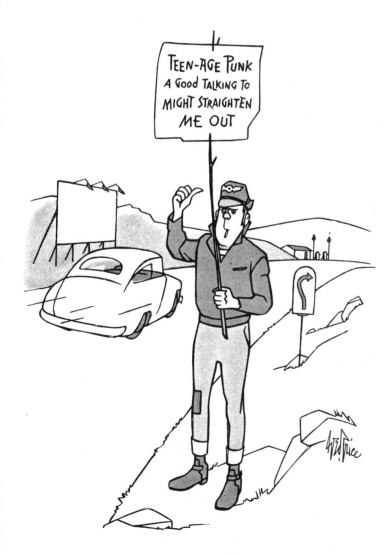

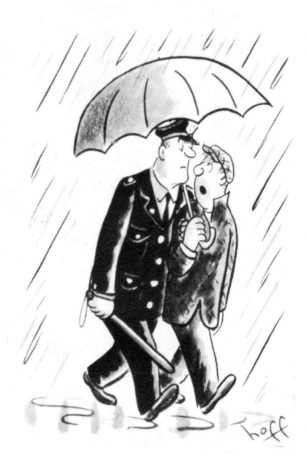

"You sure you're not picking me up on
account I got an umbrella?"

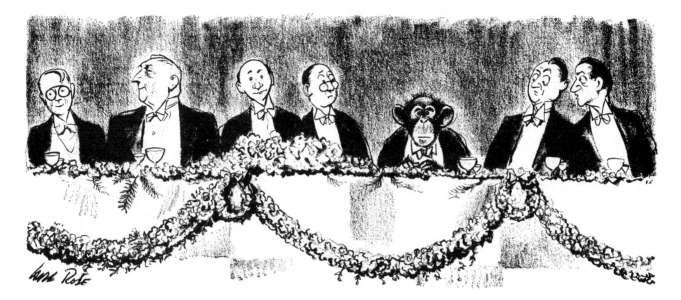

"I'm not sure,
but I think he's from the Yale Psychological School."

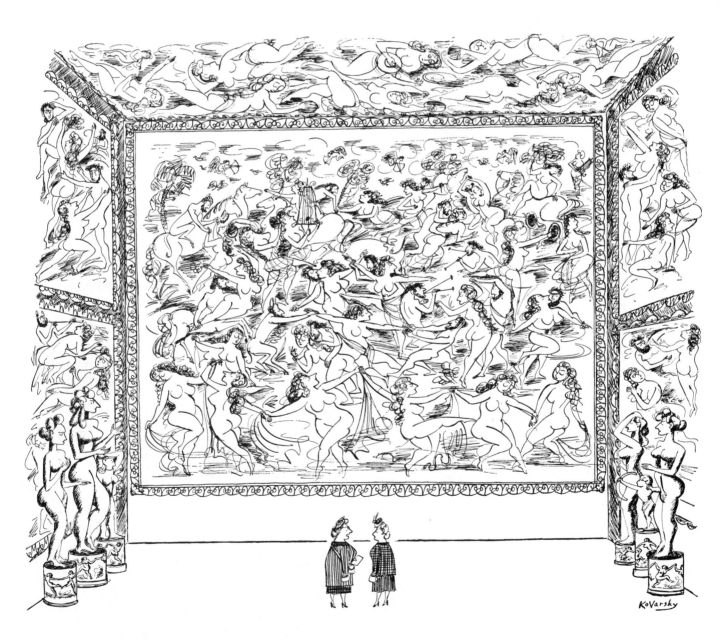

"Well, it's no wonder those Borgias and Medicis were always poisoning each other."

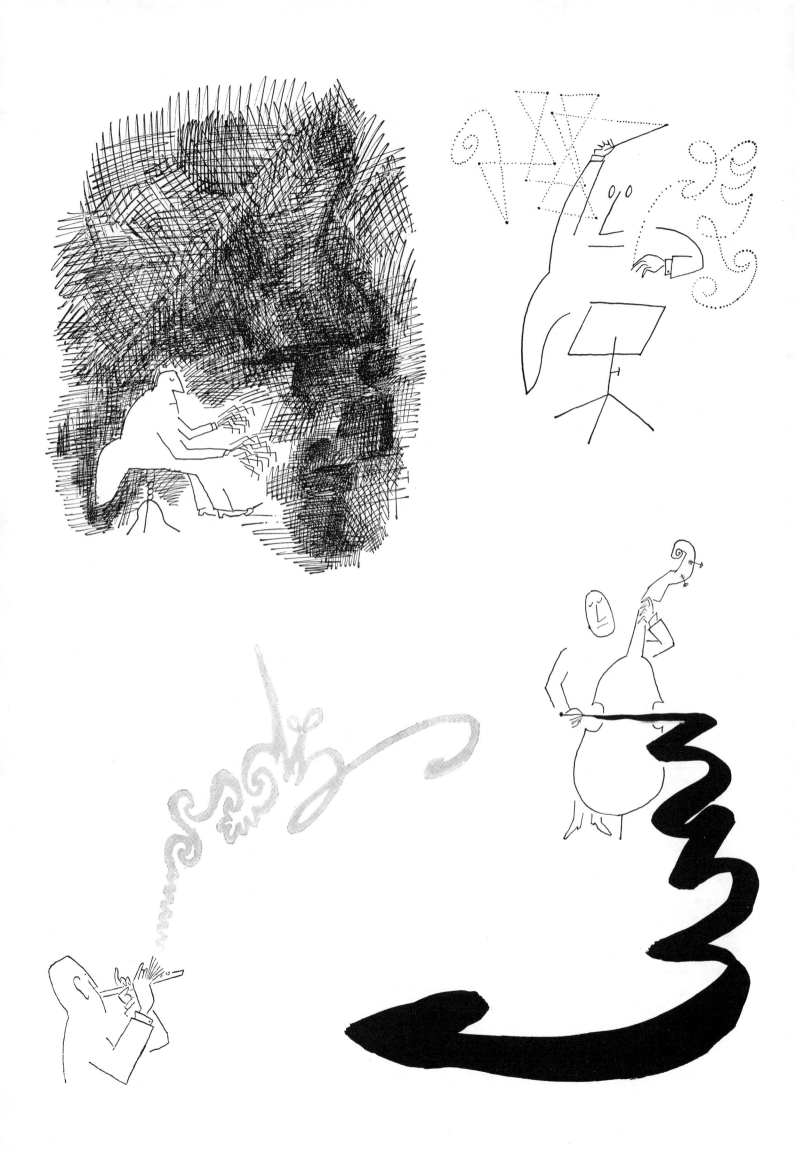

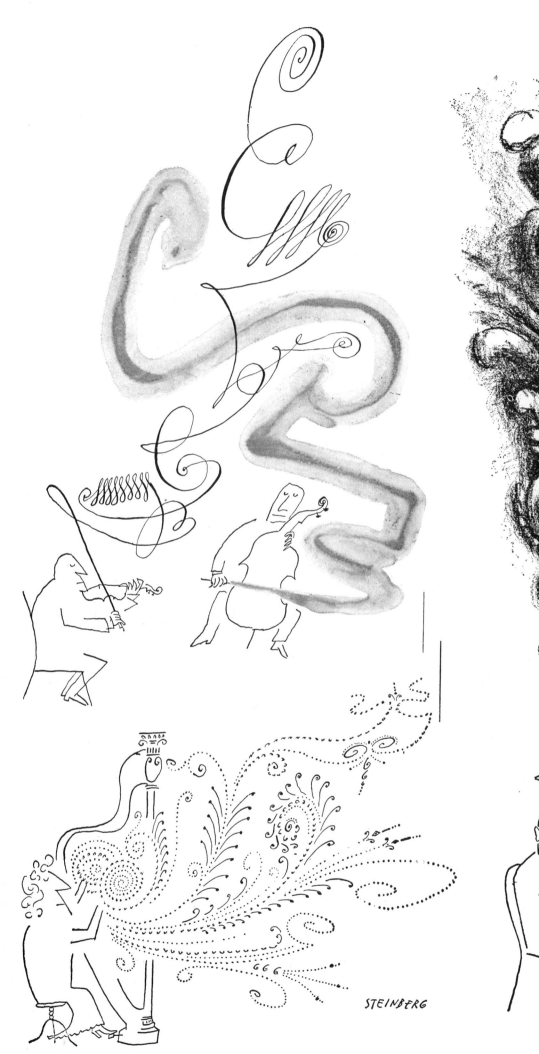
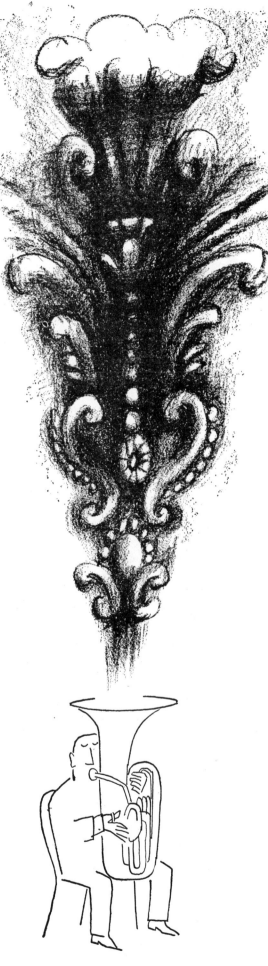

STEINBERG

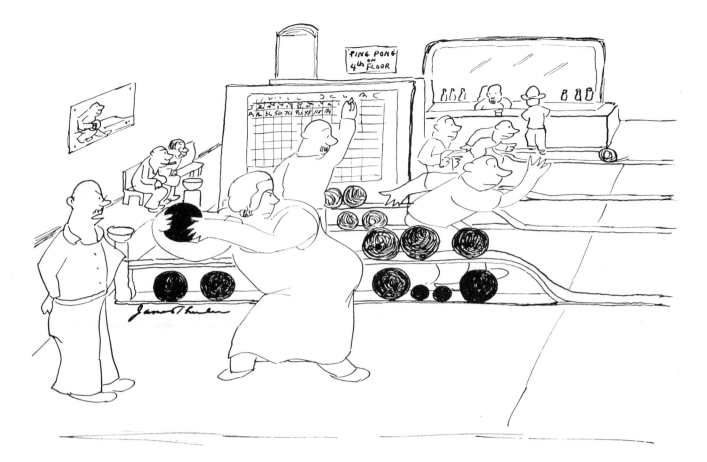

"All right, all right, try it that way! Go ahead and try it that way!"

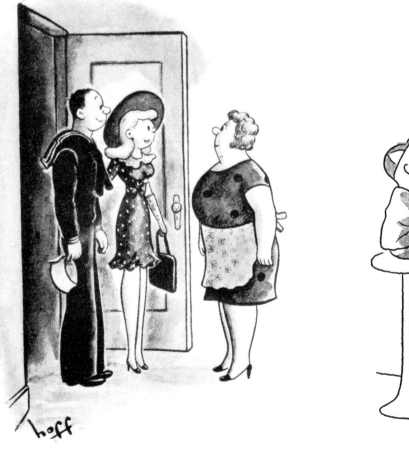

*"Mother, I'd like you to meet a member
of the armed forces."*

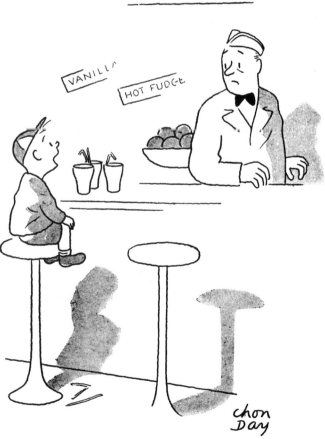

"And now I want to thank you very much."

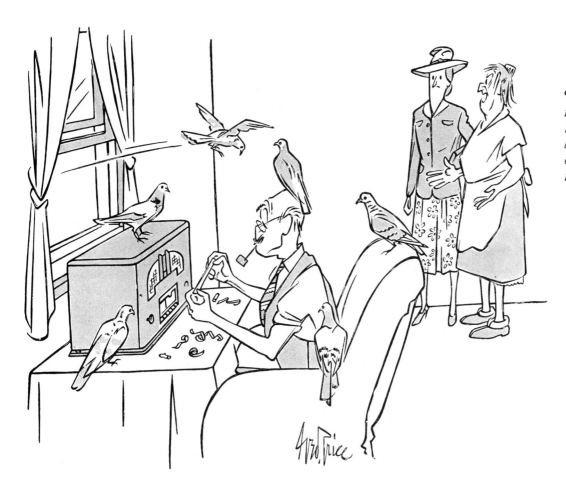

"*It's the Times' bulletins every hour on the hour, the Daily News' bulletins every hour on the half-hour, and those damn carrier pigeons in between.*"

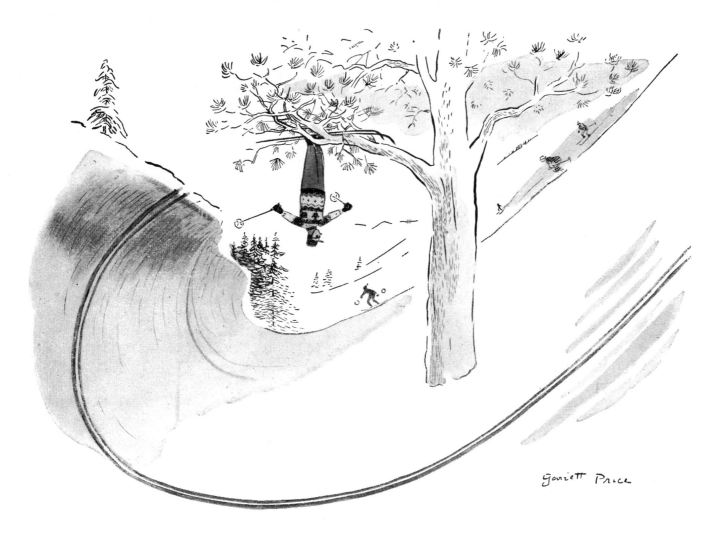

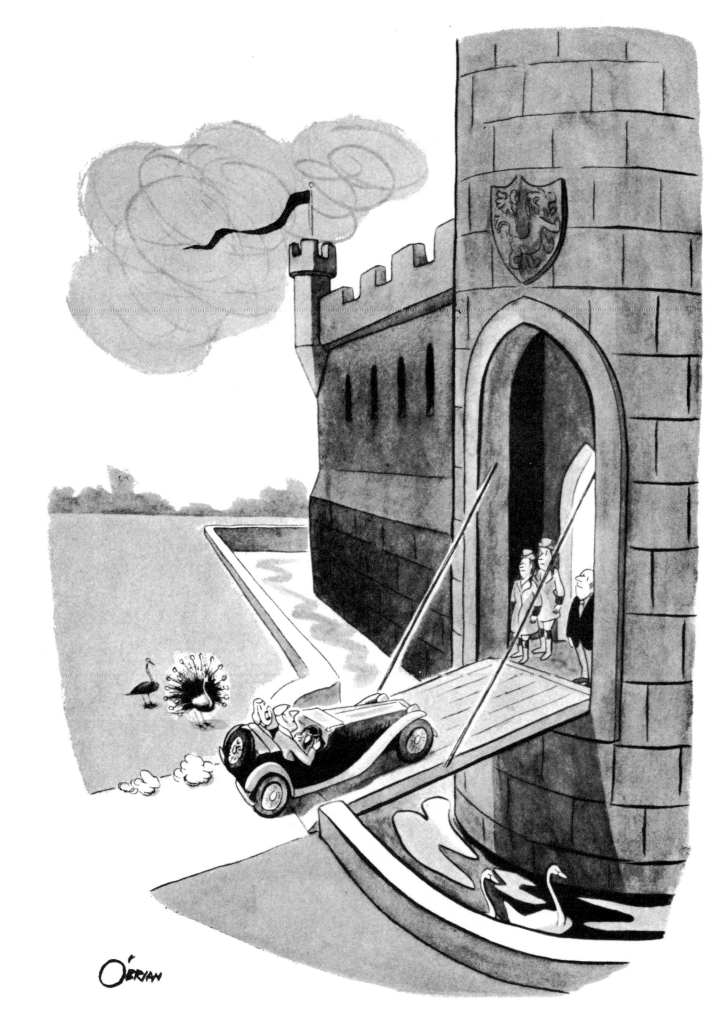

"Good heavens! I thought Duke was your nickname!"

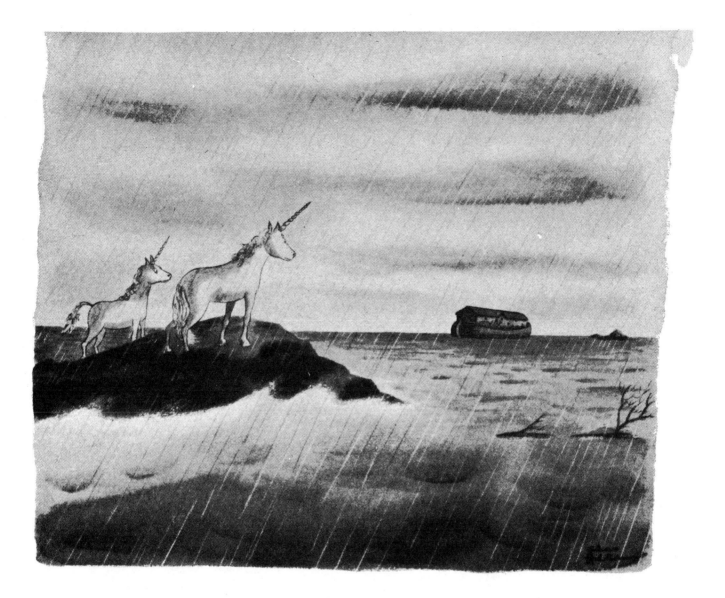

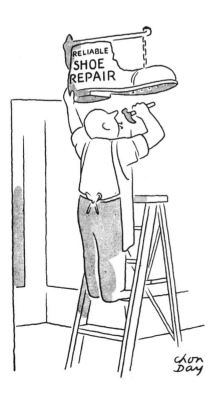

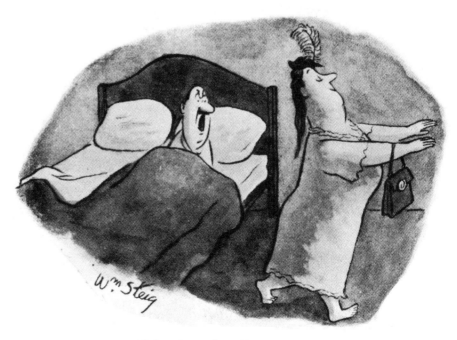

"*Macy's is closed!*"

THE DAY THE TRAINS STOPPED

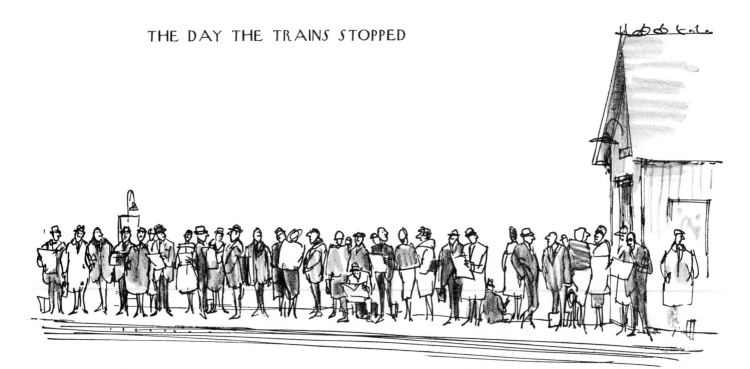

On the branch line, forty-seven people gathered between 7:47 and 10:39. When the fifth scheduled train failed to appear, Fred Fitzdyke, a commuter since 1945, said, "When I started using this line, they ran it like clockwork."

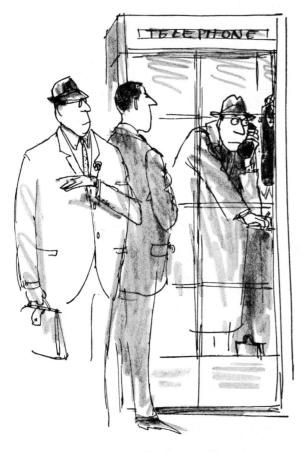

George Ward telephoned his assistant, Donald Chapman, at the office, and told him he didn't know when he would be able to get to the shop. "You'll have to carry the ball," he said to Chapman, who told him to go home and take it easy.

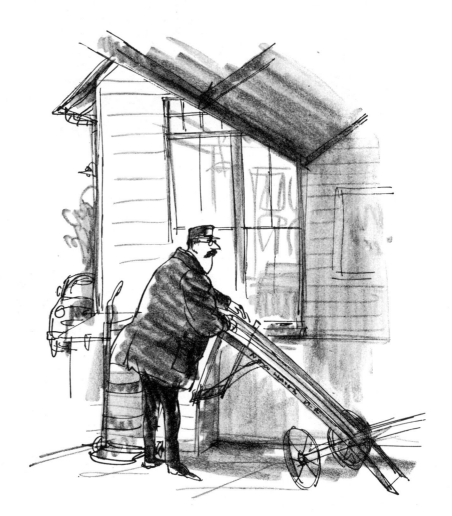

Baggagemaster Fred Folsom answered all questions by saying nobody told him anything, he didn't know anything, and he didn't know anybody who did know anything.

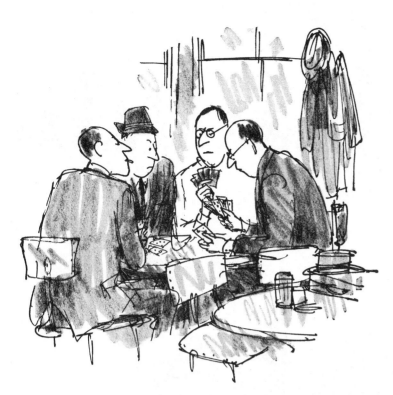

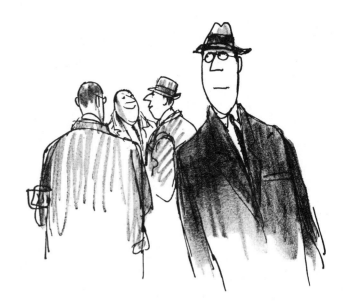

Ralph Miller, Ronald Smith, Gene Clifford, and Henry Thompson adjourned to the station luncheonette, where they played bridge until four o'clock in the afternoon.

Arthur Fenster was close to, but not actually a part of, a conversation between John Amster, Dick Burnside, Jr., and Tom Stanley, all golfers and members of the Chipowee Country Club. They were discussing their game. Fenster hoped they might start talking about the delay, so he could say something casual, like "You'd think they could make some sort of announcement. It wouldn't cost them anything."

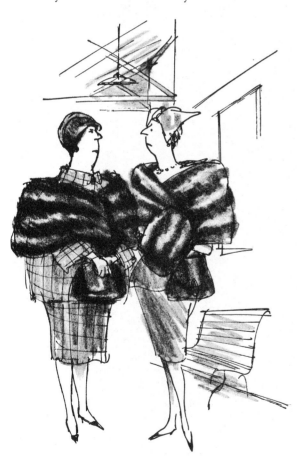

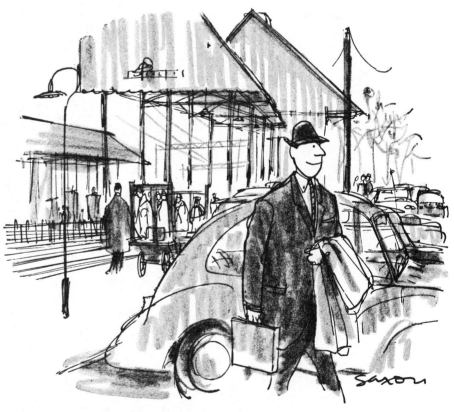

Mrs. Lewis Fisher, member of the Republican Town Committee, said to her neighbor, Mrs. Lloyd Lefcourt, "There's more to this than meets the eye." Mrs. Lefcourt, who had matinée tickets to "The Sound of Music," said, "Be that as it may, discourtesy is certainly the order of the day."

At twelve o'clock noon, it became clear to Willis Palmer that the trains were not going to arrive. That, in fact, there never again would be an 8:47 to Grand Central. He thought of his family, in the neat board-and-batten split-level on the hill—of Francine, his wife; and Bill and Debby, his two young children. He knew he would have to give up his job in New York and try to find something in the country. Something close to home. Palmer folded his "Herald Tribune" neatly, dropped it in a litter basket, and walked slowly toward his Plymouth station wagon.

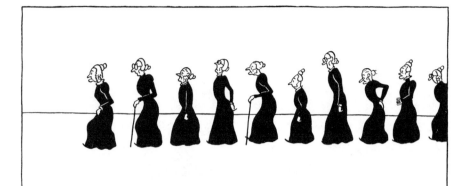

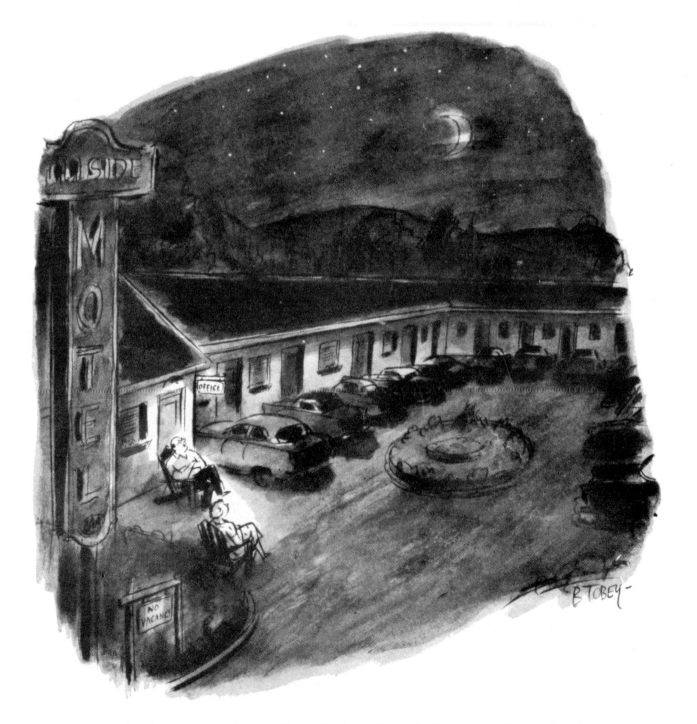

"*This is the hour I love best, when they're all tucked away and sound asleep and I'm kind of like a shepherd watching over them all.*"

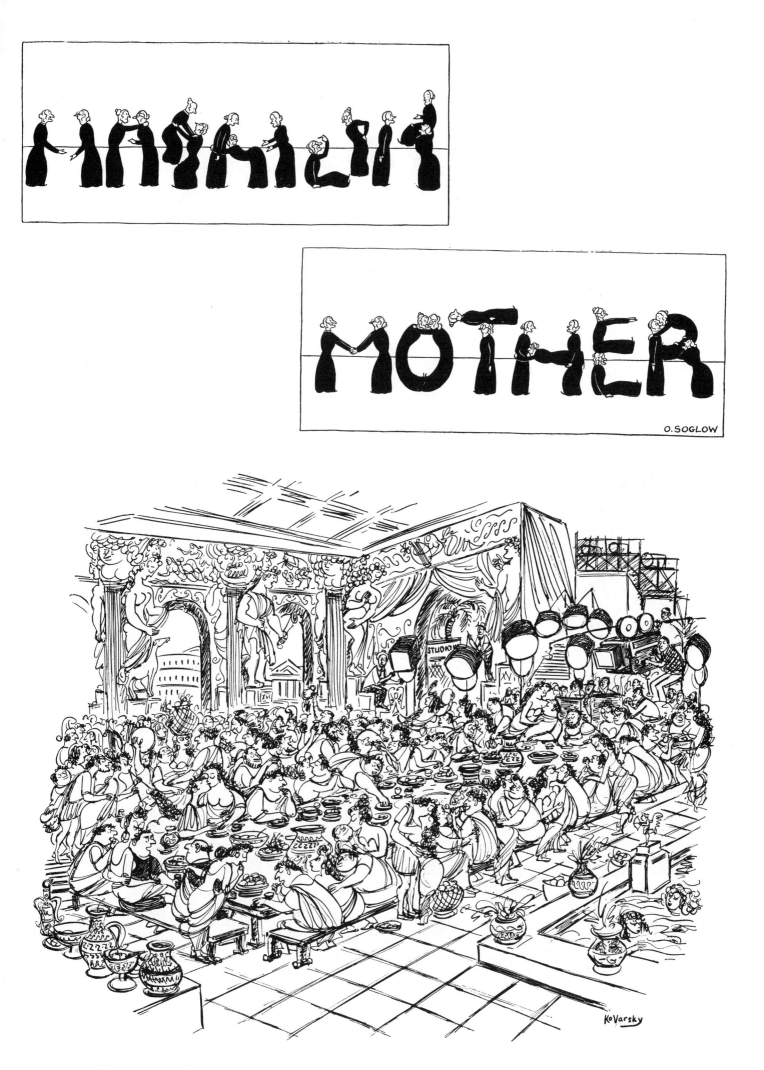

O. SOGLOW

"*I hope they have to do a retake. This cherry cobbler is delicious.*"

KoVarsky

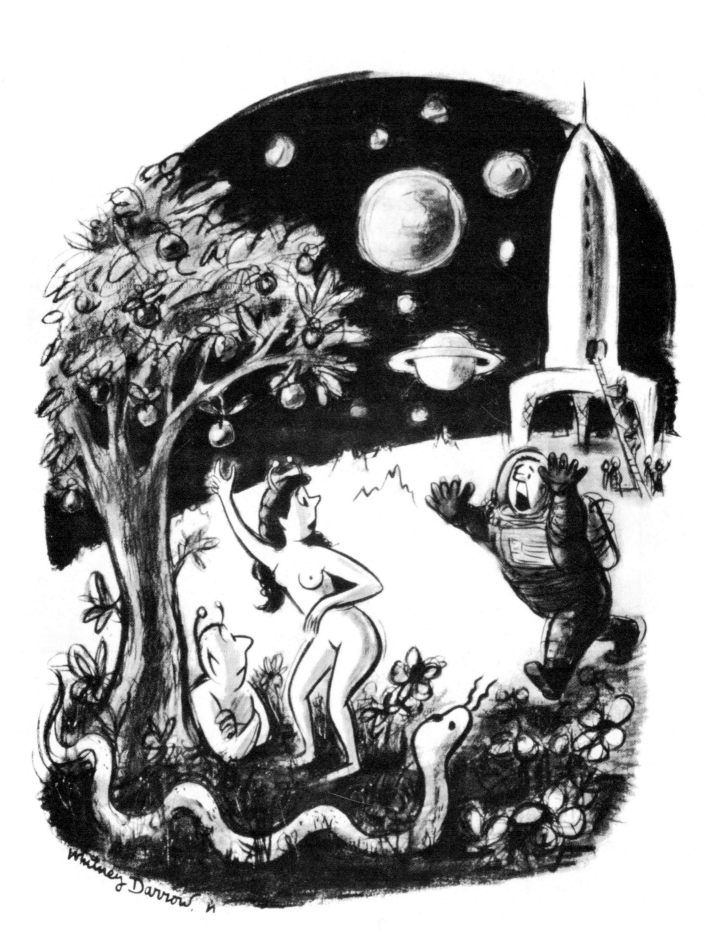

"Miss! Oh, Miss! For God's sake, stop!"

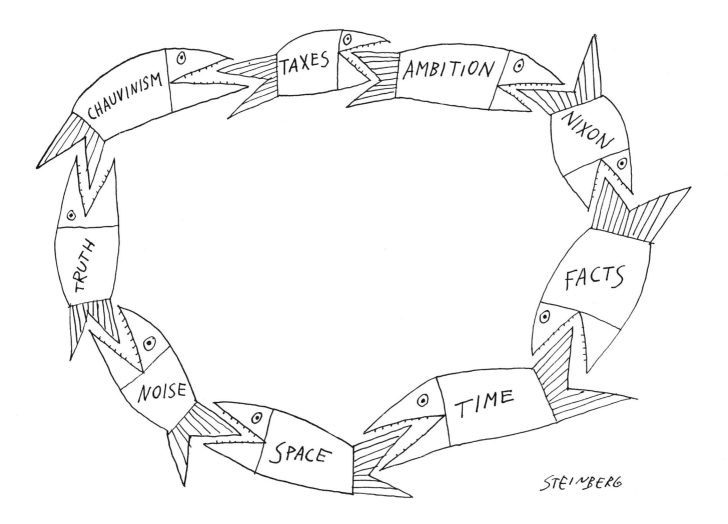

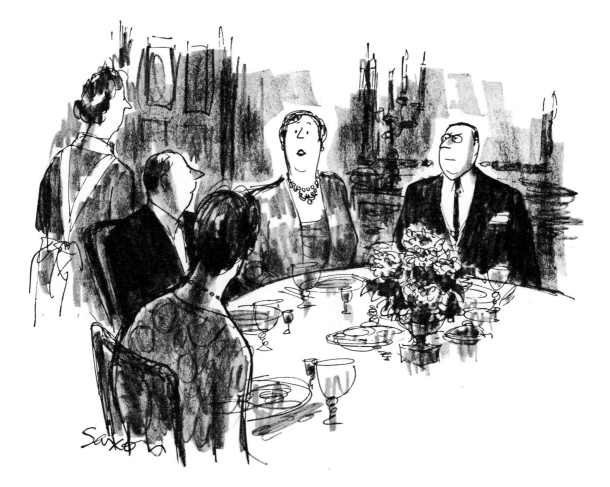

*"All I know is that they haven't had any
wild parties in Cos Cob in the six years we've lived here."*

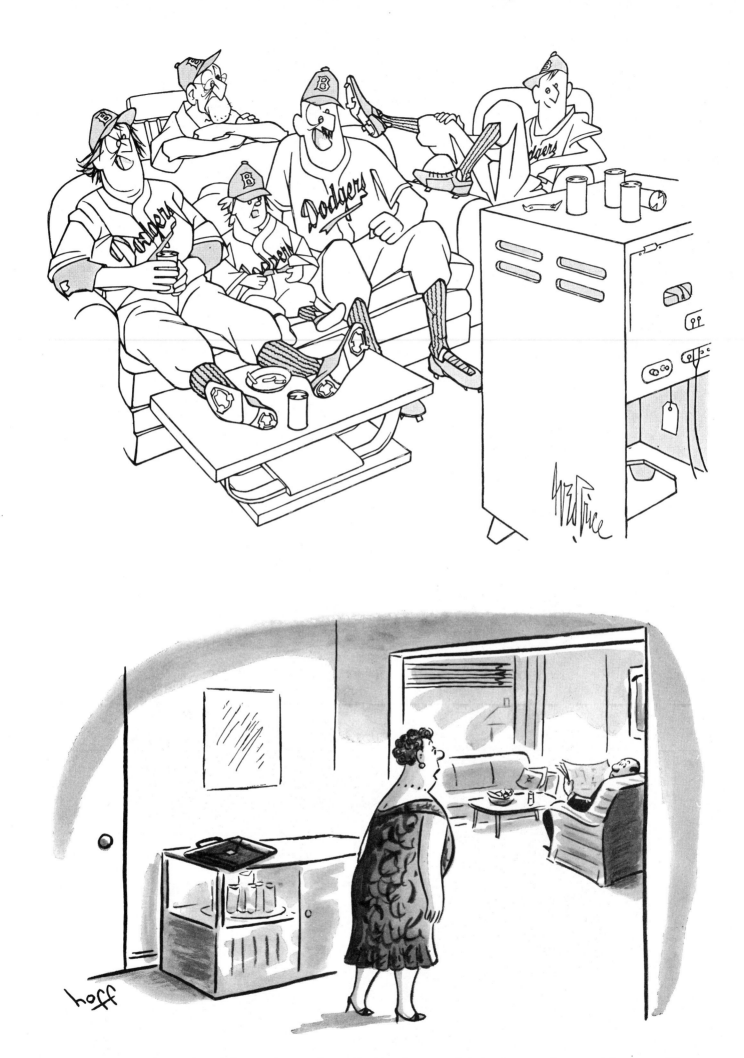

"Oh, *there* you are! Goodness, for a minute I thought your briefcase came home without you!"

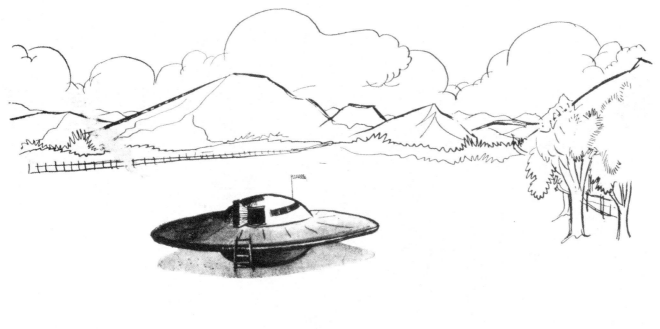

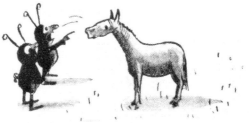

"Kindly take us to your President!"

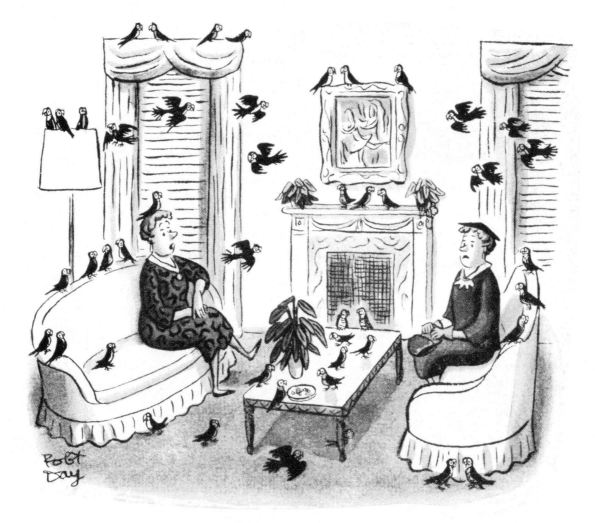

"I wish he would forget an anniversary occasionally."

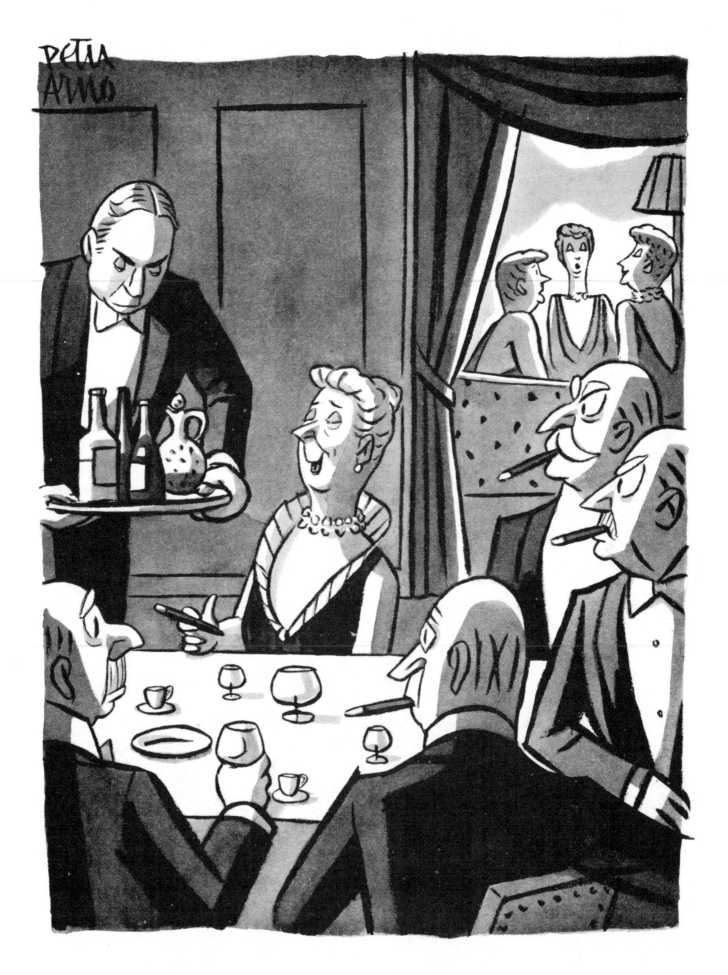

"*Thanks, no. I've had <u>more</u> than enough.*"

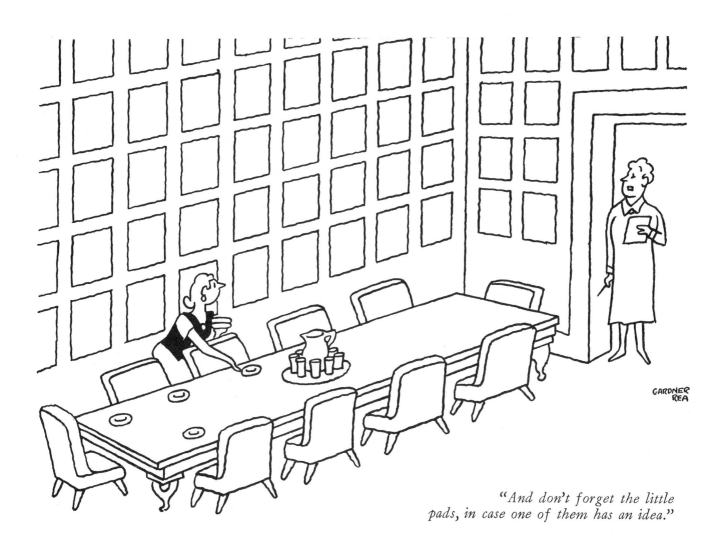

"*And don't forget the little pads, in case one of them has an idea.*"

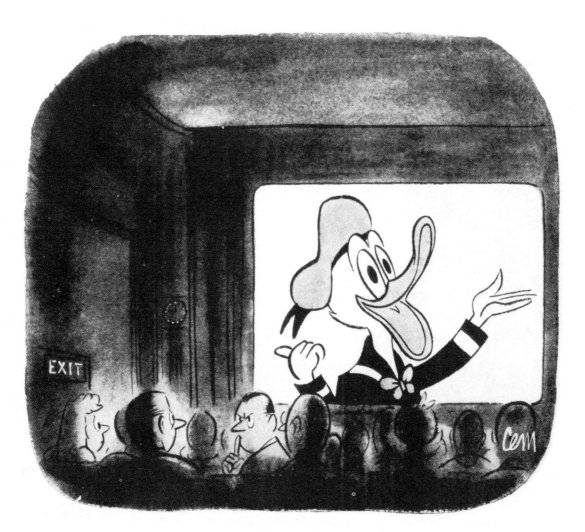

A LA RECHERCHE DU
TEMPS PERDU

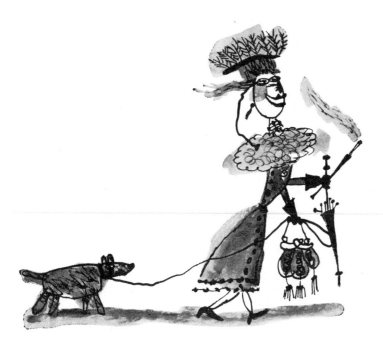

Everyone said Mrs. Mantle was crazy.

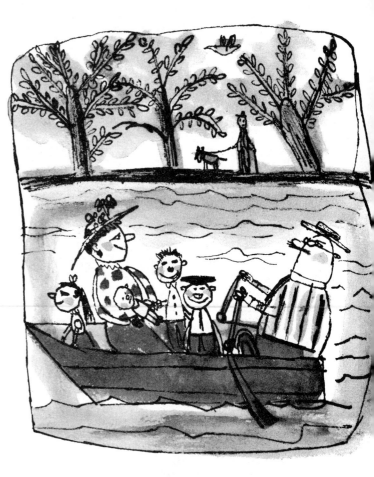

Papa was an expert rower.

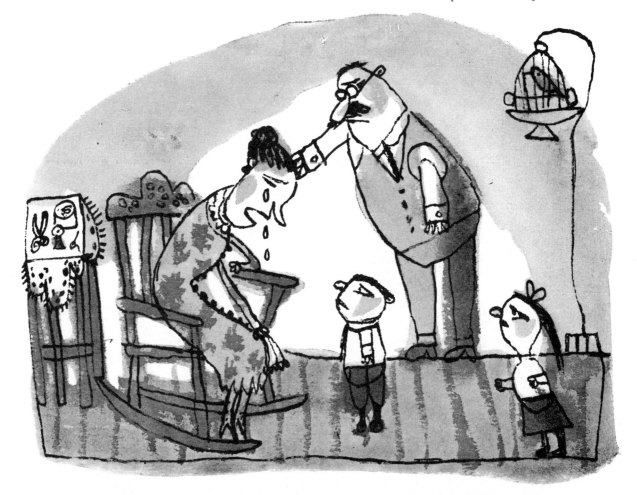

Sometimes Mama cried for days.

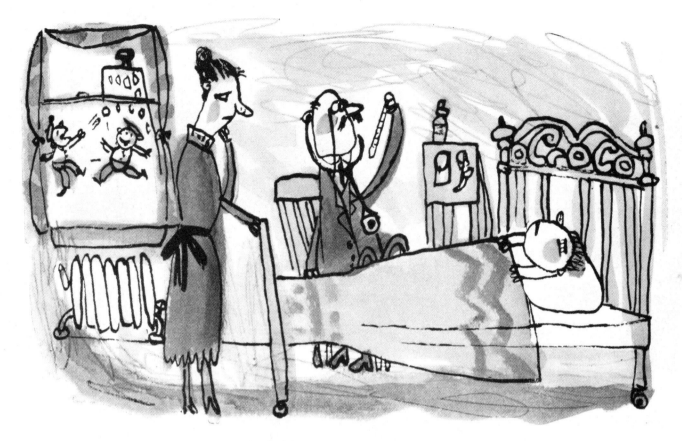

Daniel had the Spanish influenza.

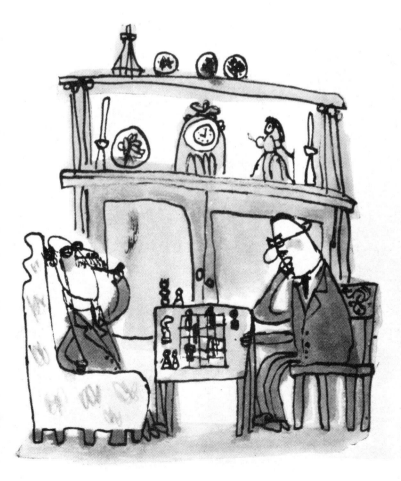

Papa said that Mr. Hoffman was a genius.

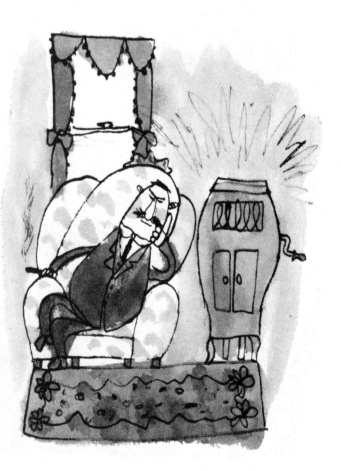

Caruso was Papa's favorite singer.

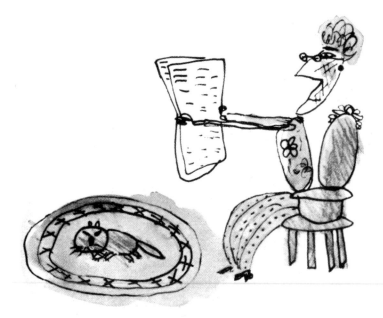

Grandma was farsighted.

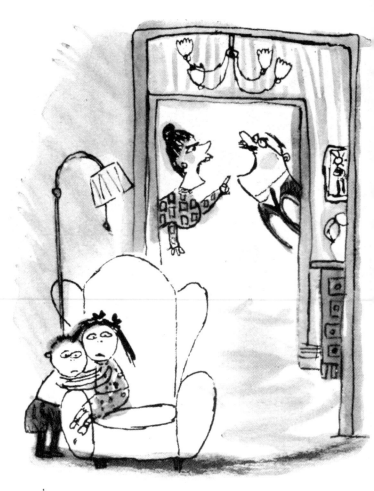

Mama and Papa never quarrelled
in front of the children.

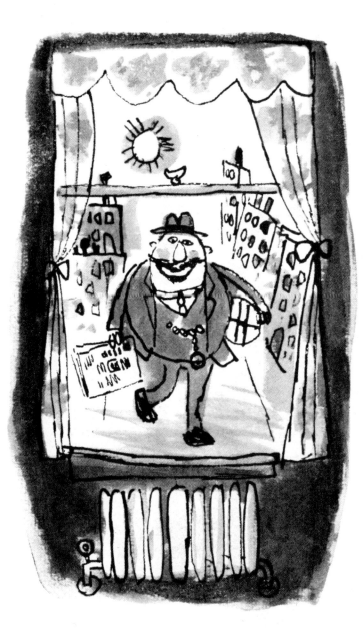

Papa came home from work at seven o'clock.

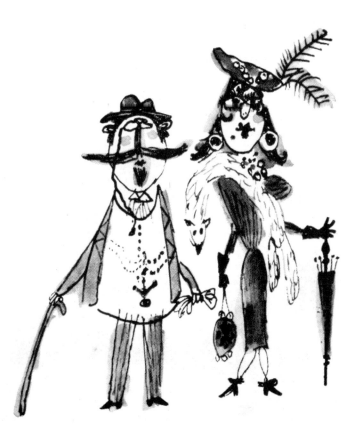

Some European friends came to visit.

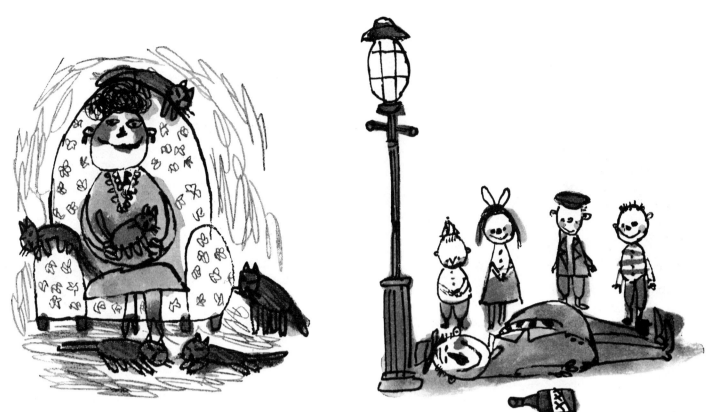

Mrs. Dixon loved cats.

Mama was very sorry for poor Mrs. Harris.

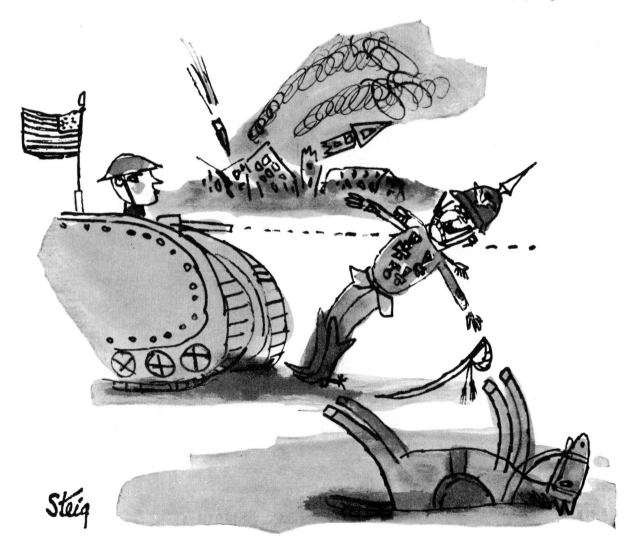

Steig

We won the war.

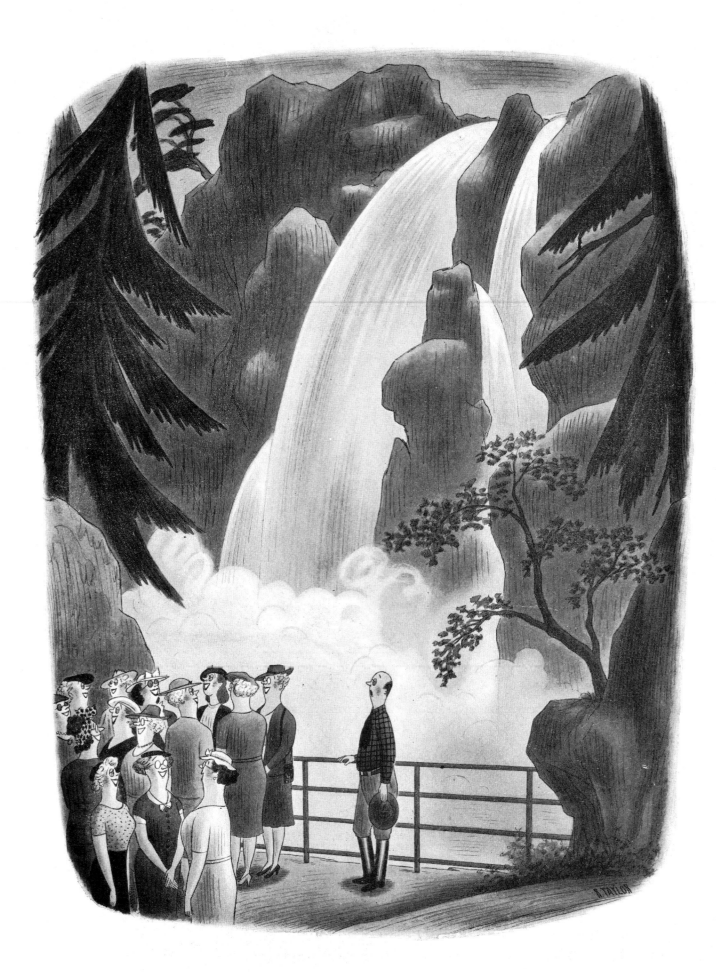

*"Now if we can all be silent for a few moments, we will
hear the thunder of the waters."*

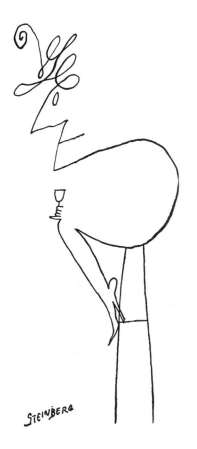

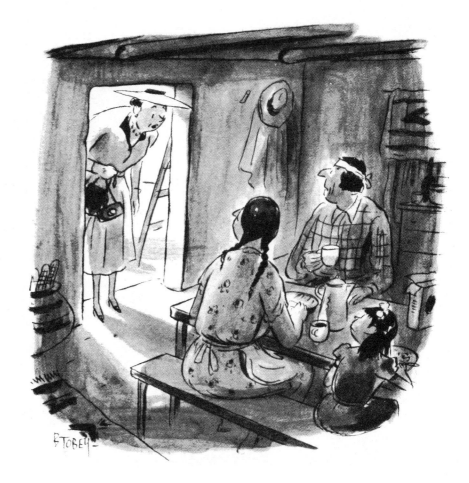

"Oh, I _beg_ your pardon! I thought you were extinct."

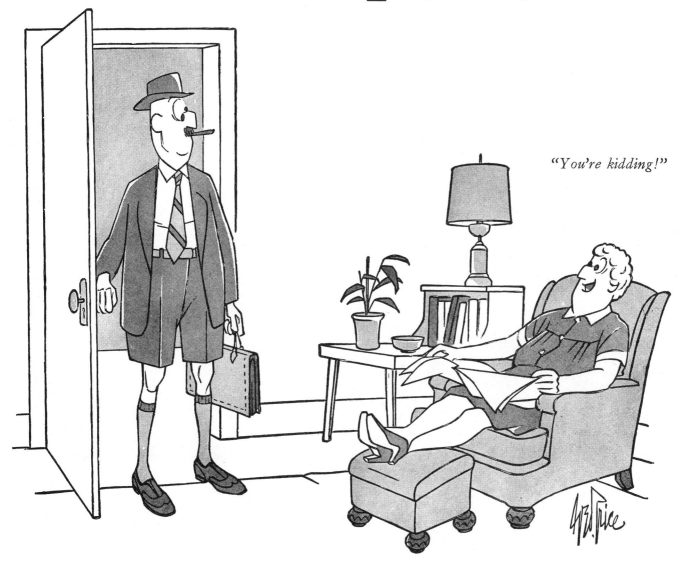

"You're kidding!"

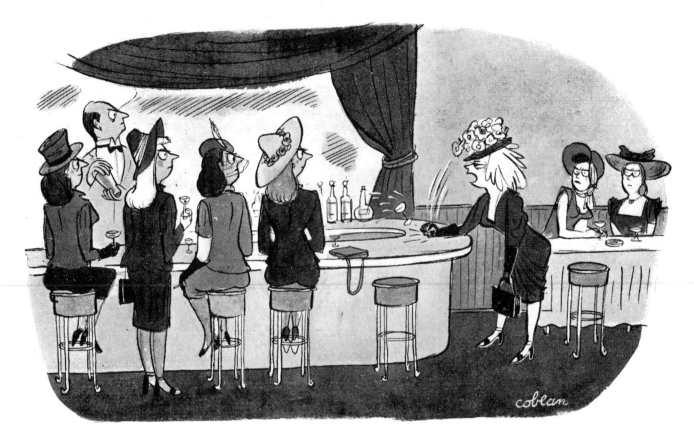

"I can lick any woman in the house!"

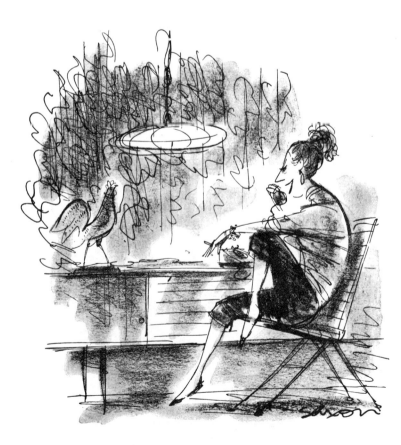

"But you must come! We're only _having_ people
who hate New Year's Eve parties!"

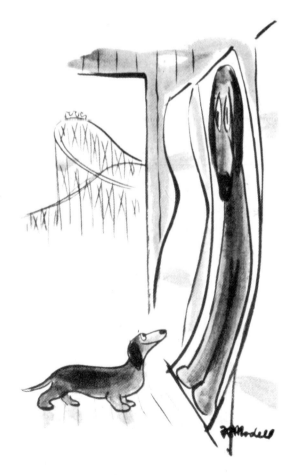

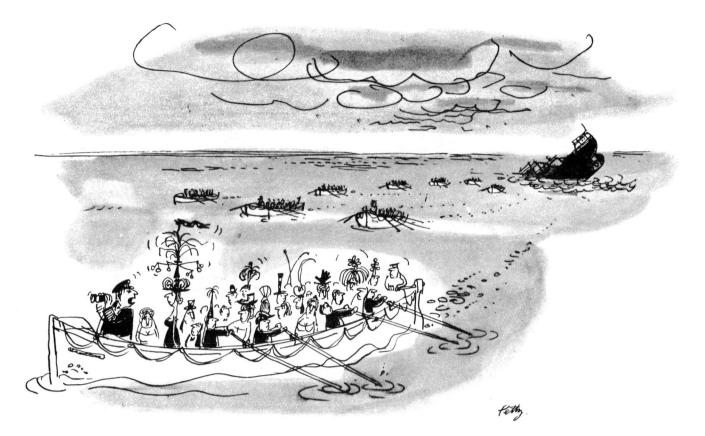

"Be patient, Madam. The judging of the funny hats will resume as soon as we get ashore."

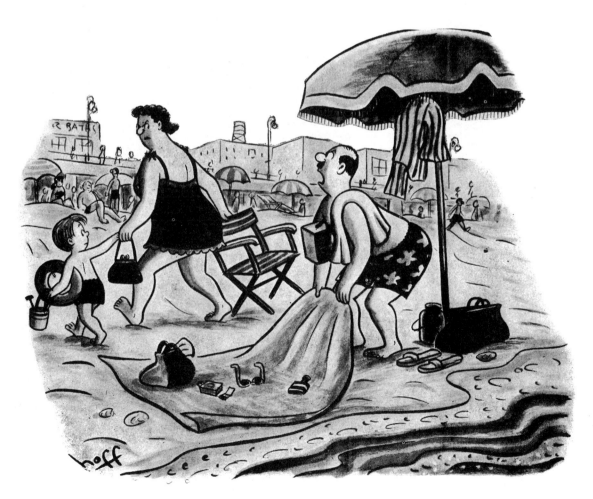

*"So we have to move! Am I
supposed to be in charge of the tides or something?"*

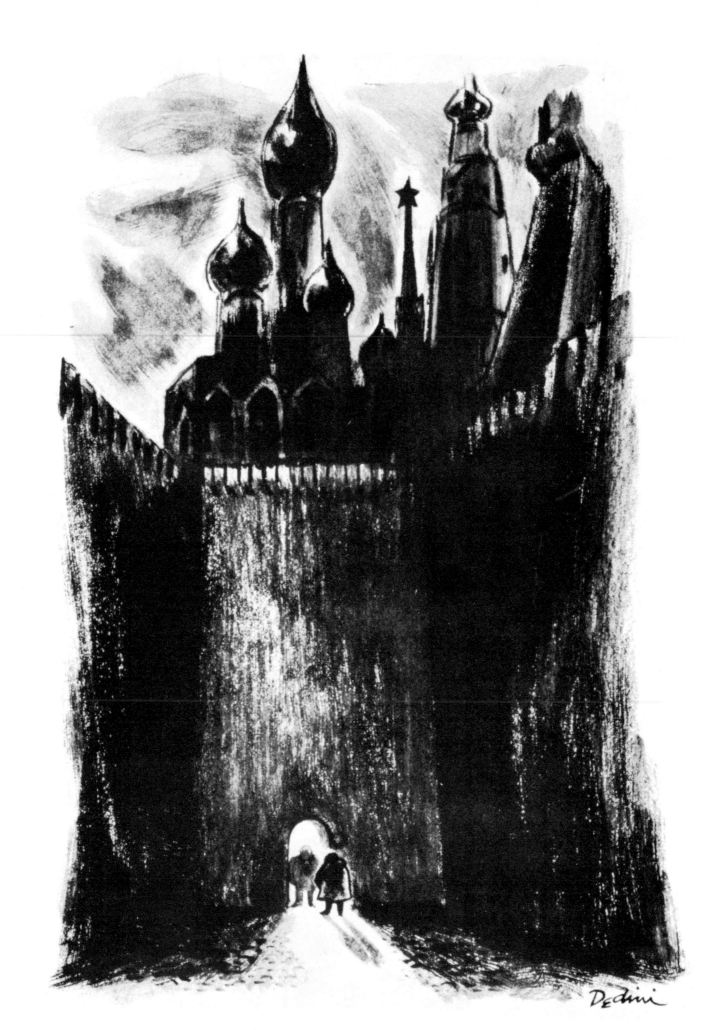

"Will you please stop bothering us, Comrade? You'll read it in 'Izvestia' when we surpass America."

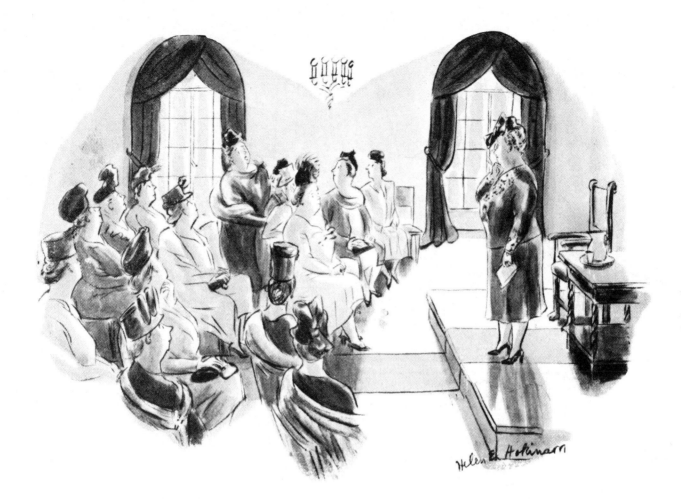

"I just want to say that I'm perfectly willing to serve as treasurer, provided every penny doesn't have to come out exactly even."

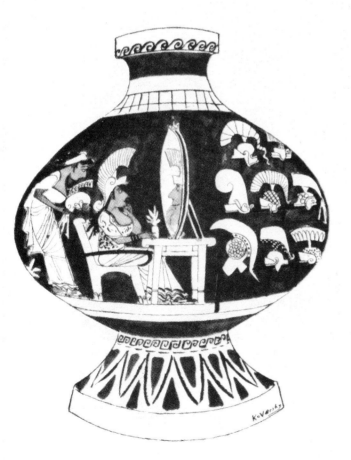

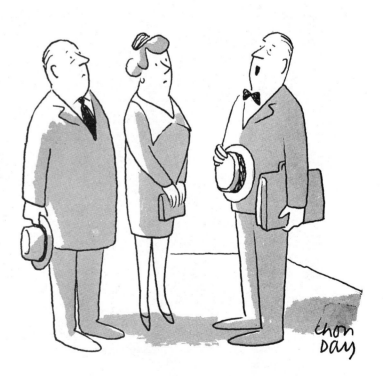

"Yes, the walls _are_ paper-thin. But you'll find your neighbor possesses a rapierlike wit, full of amusing double-entendres and profusely studded with literary allusions."

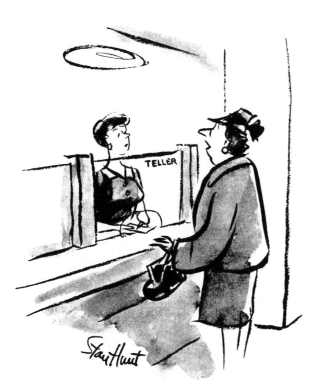

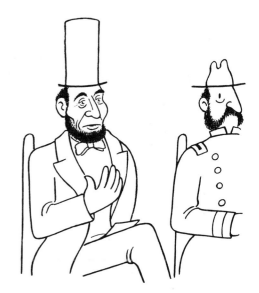

"Do your cameras photograph people who
are not holding you up?"

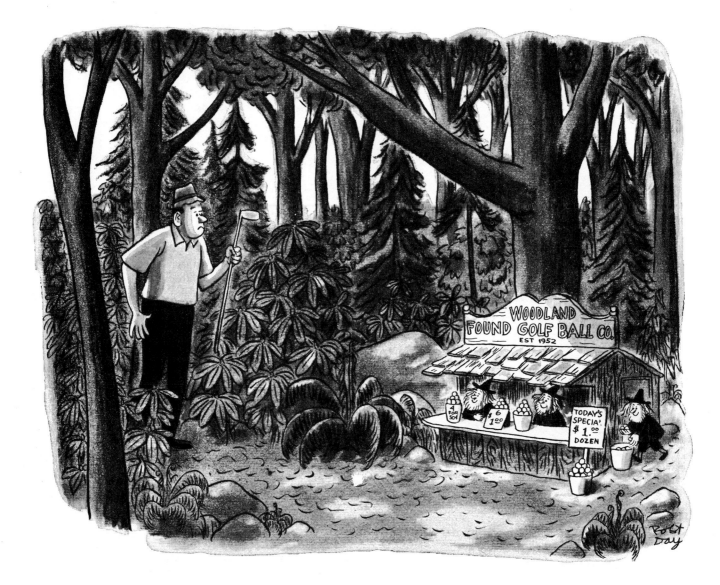

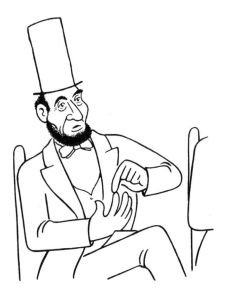
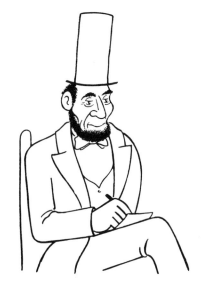
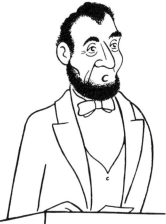

FOUR SCORE AND
SEVEN YEARS AGO---

O. SOGLOW

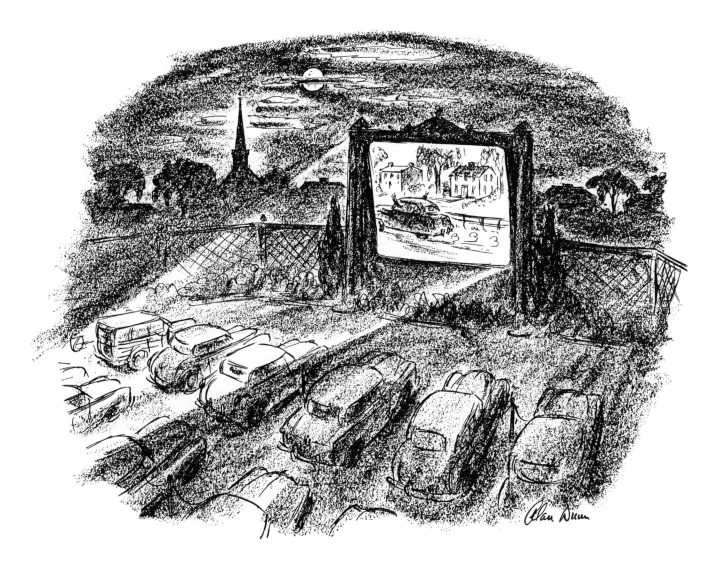

"And so we say goodbye to beautiful New England."

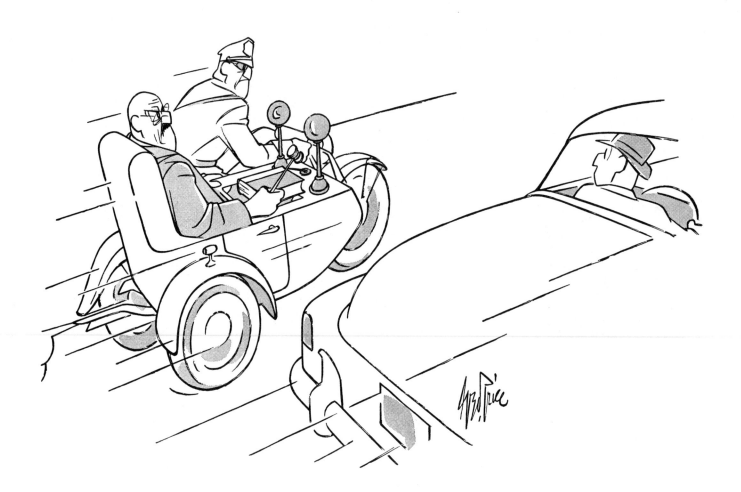

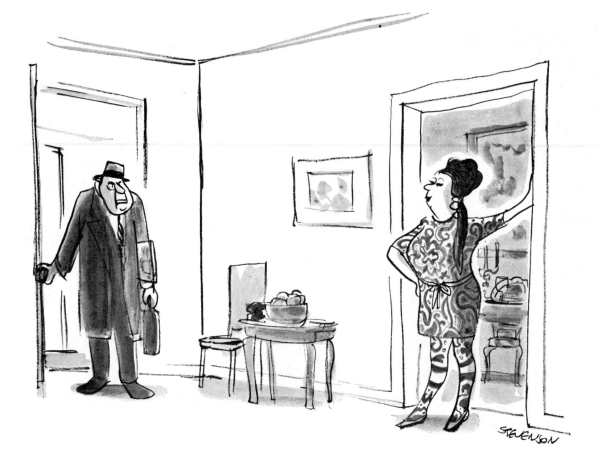

"Bertha, will you do me a favor and stop
reading those damn 'How to Save Your Marriage' articles?"

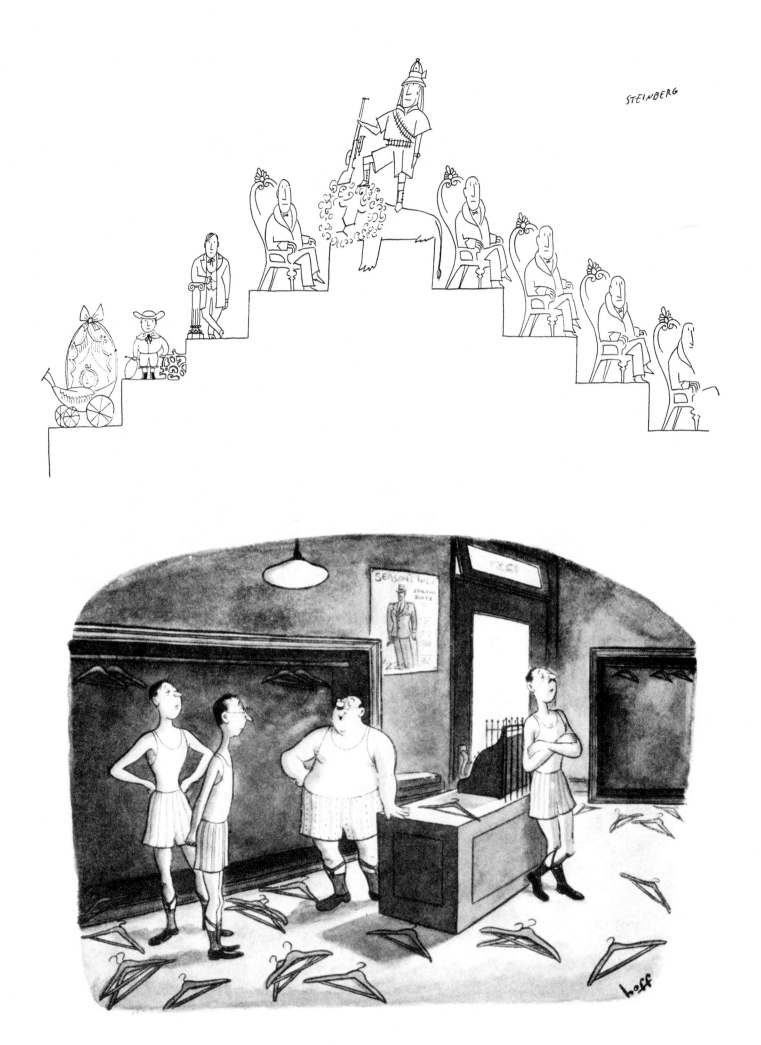

"*Most successful suit sale we ever had, I should say.*"

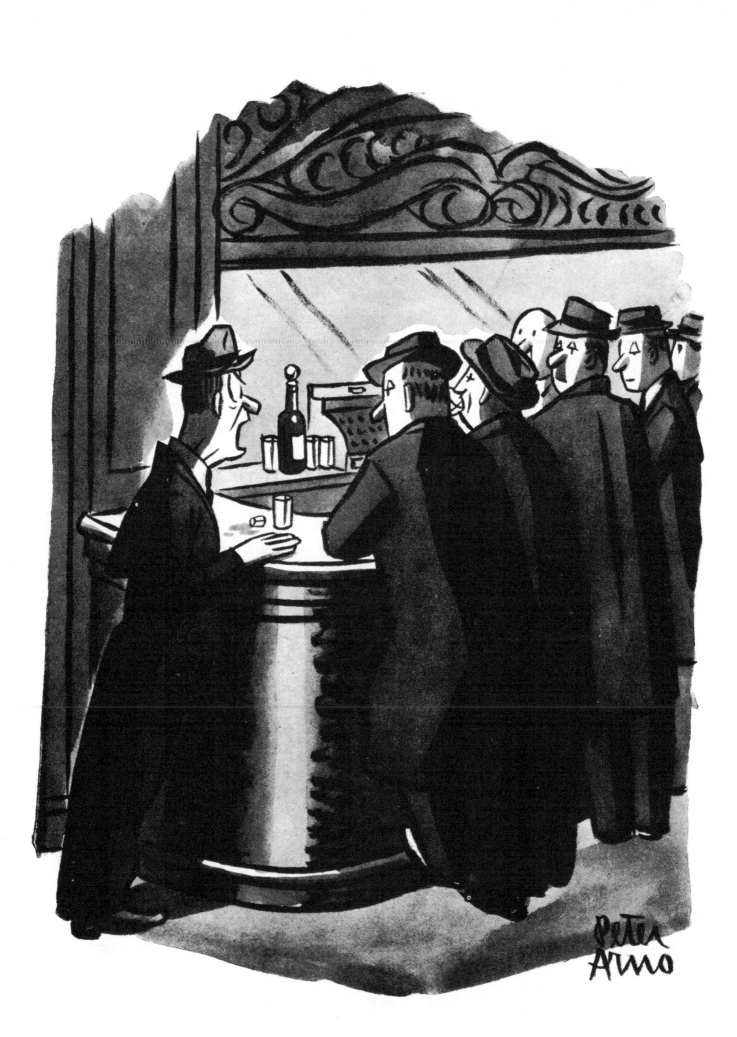

"I hate __everybody__, regardless of race, creed, or place of national origin!"

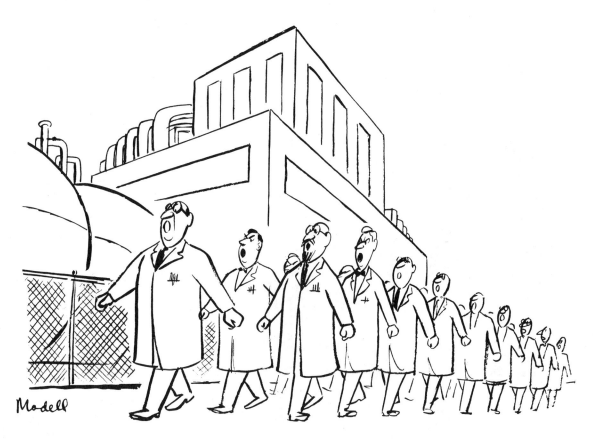

"*From the cyclotron of Berkeley to the labs of M.I.T.,*
We're the lads that you can trust to keep our country strong and free."

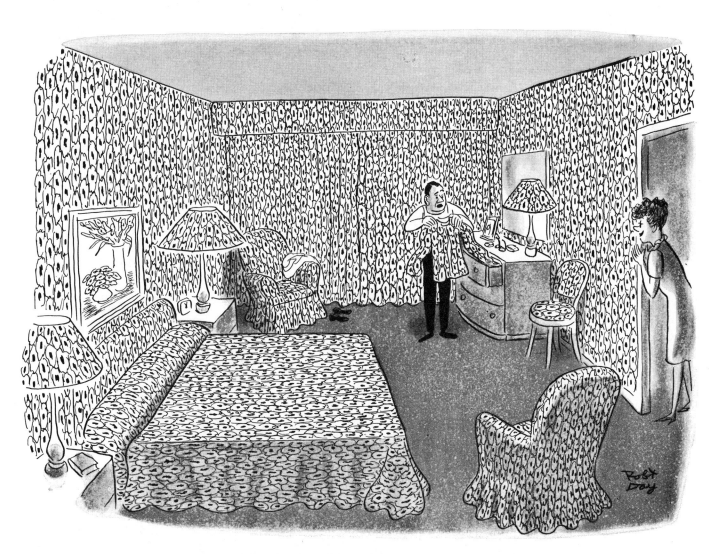

"*Good grief, Marge! Not my pajamas, too!*"

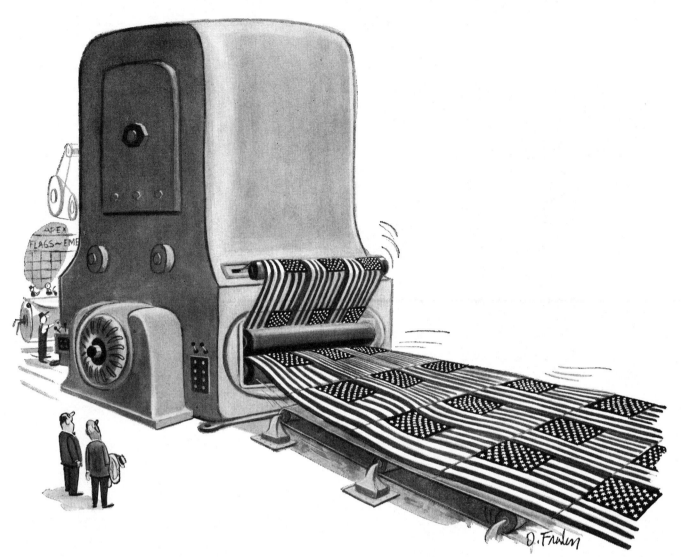

"*Now, this is our new Betsy Ross Multi-Weave unit.*"

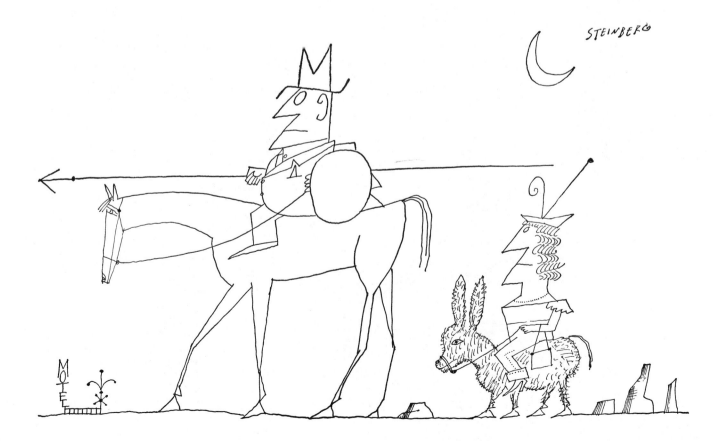

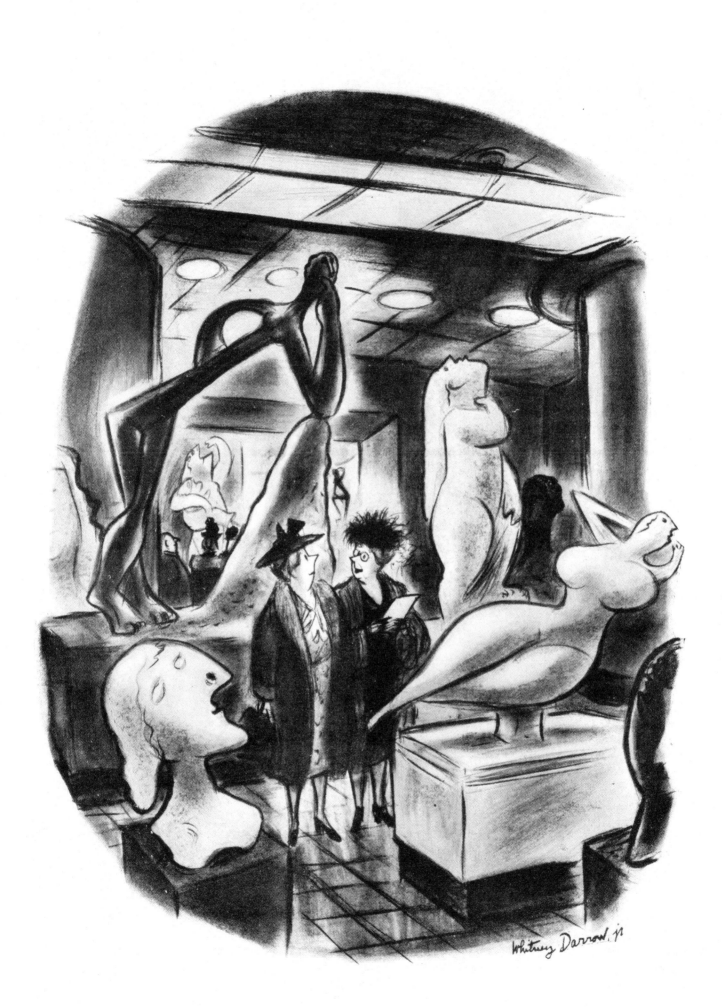

"Why doesn't he pick on his own sex for a change?"

THE COUNTRY LIFE

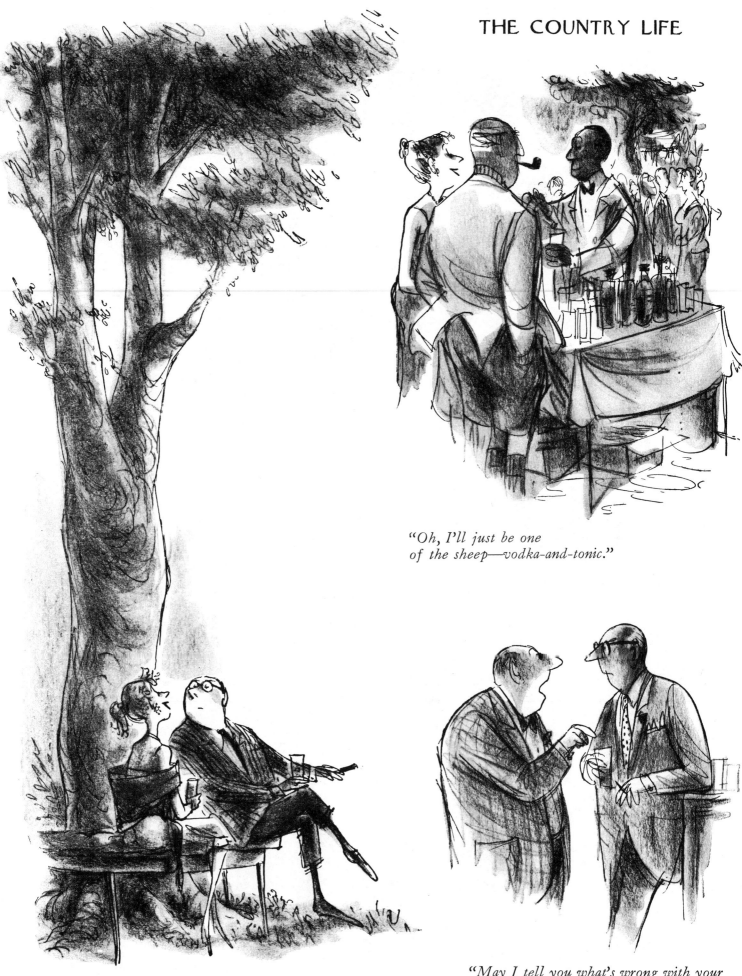

*"Oh, I'll just be one
of the sheep—vodka-and-tonic."*

*"Then if the stock splits, is my stock
automatically worth more?"*

*"May I tell you what's wrong with your
lawn? You are babying the roots. They're
not digging down."*

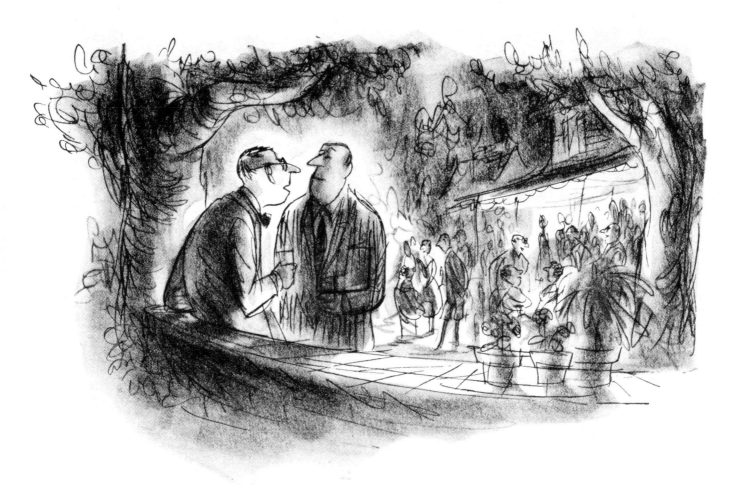

"*Do you consider all these people your friends?*"

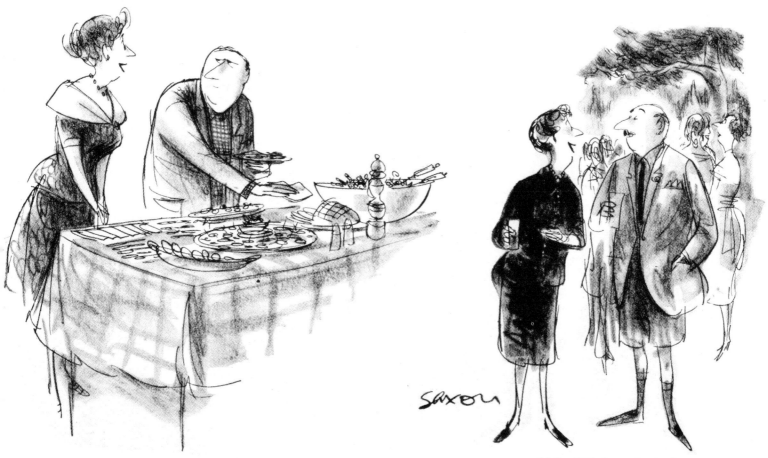

"*I'm sure you'll forgive Stewart. He has this nervous way of insulting people.*"

"*Mr. Winkett, I think your wife is just darling!*"

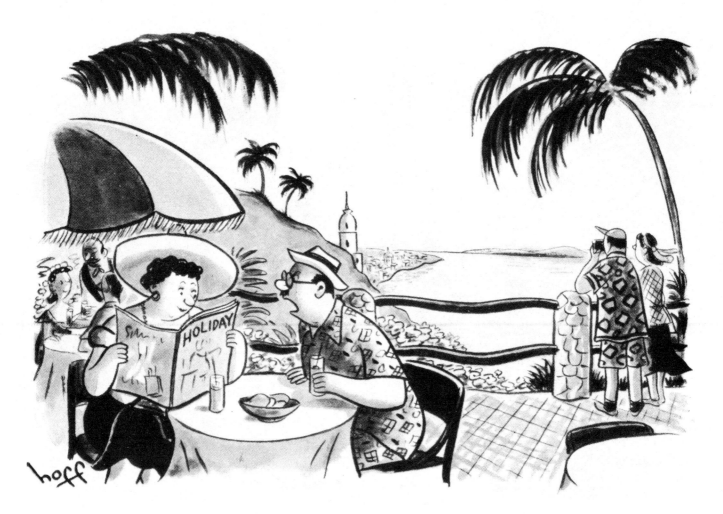

"Damn it, Alice, can't you leave well enough alone!"

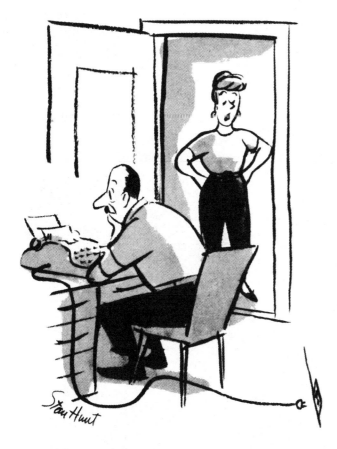

"No wonder you can't write. You're
not plugged in!"

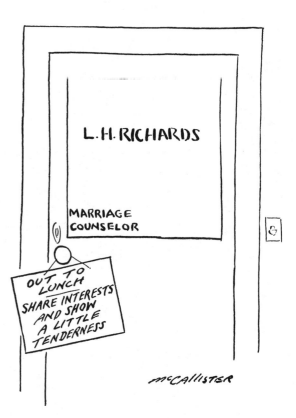

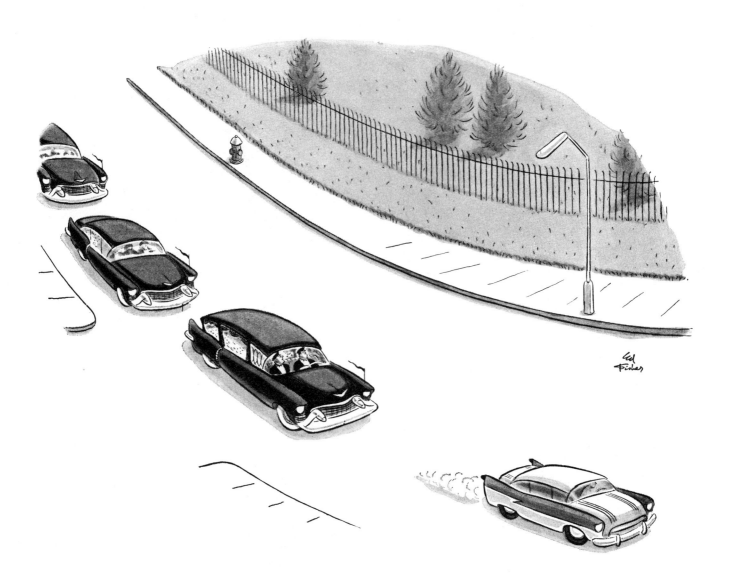

"See if you can pass that car. He would have wanted it that way."

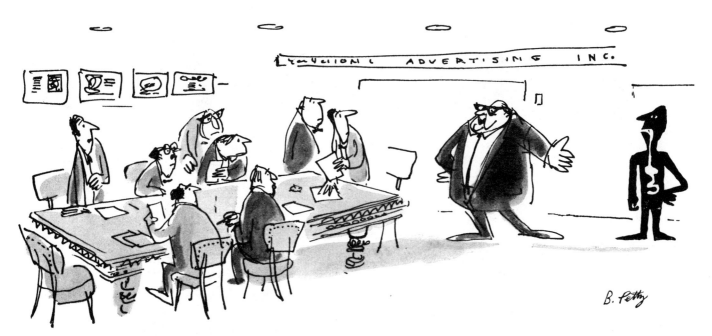

"And Mr. Fugazy here will be helping us on the aspirin account."

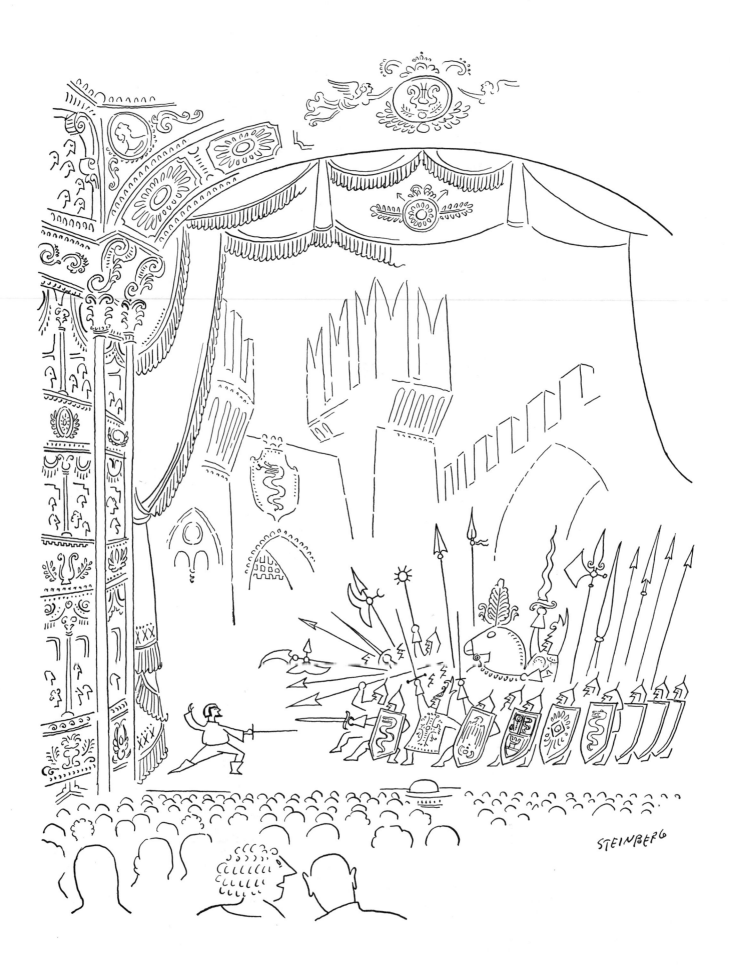

"*His wife poisons him in the third act.*"

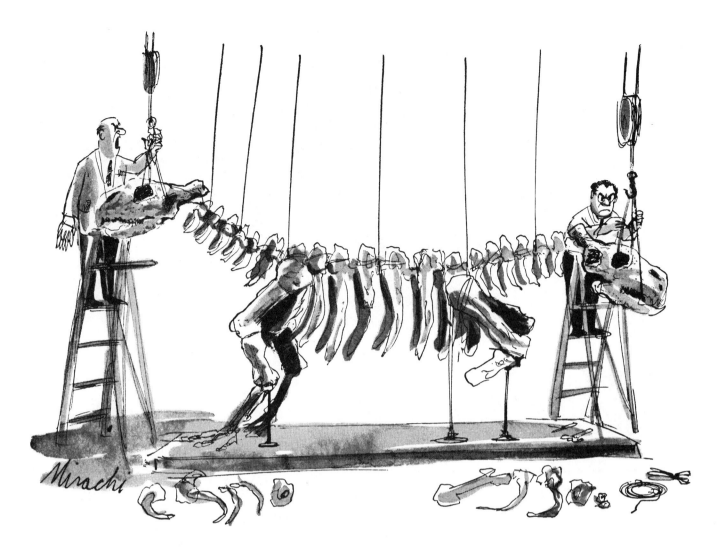

"Yeah? Well, I've forgotten more about paleontology than you'll ever know."

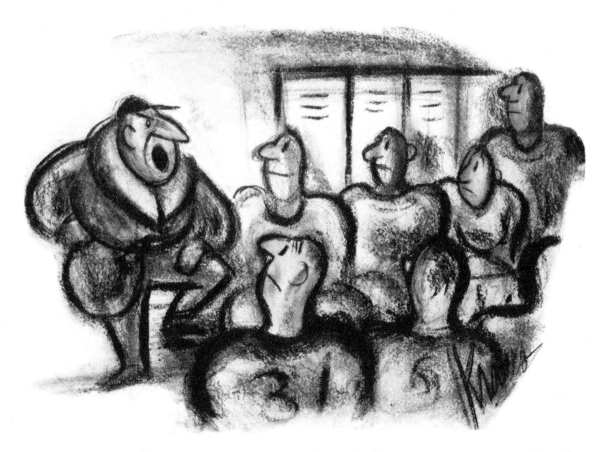

"Now, what I'd like to see in the second half is a little more unnecessary roughness."

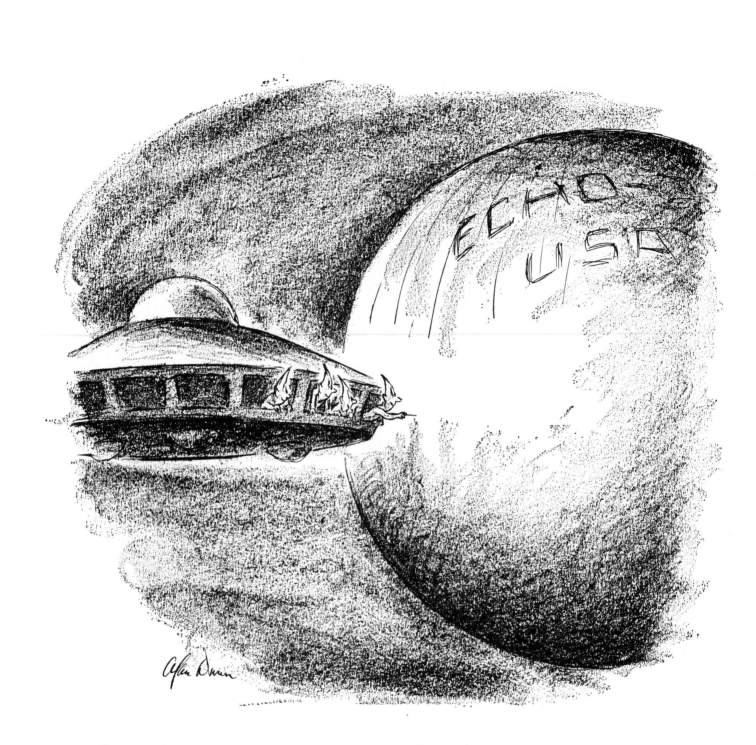

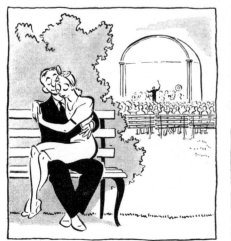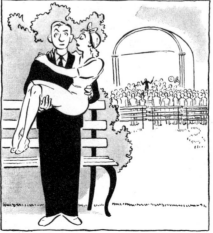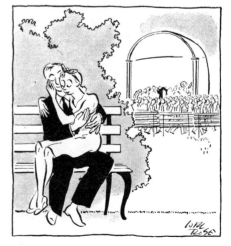

NATIONAL ANTHEM

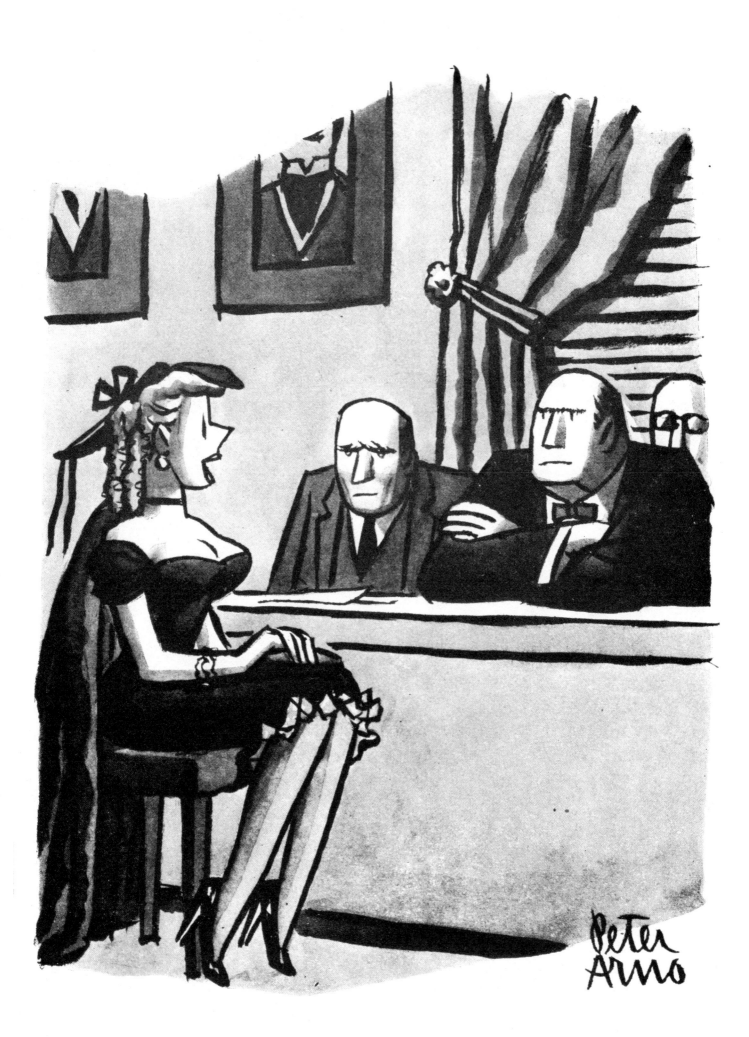

"*I really don't know if he was a Communist. We never discussed politics.*"

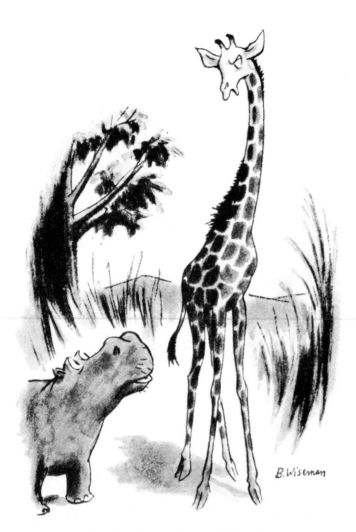

"Speak up! Speak up! How do you expect me to hear you?"

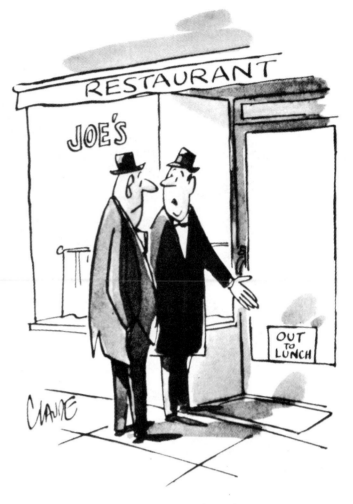

"See what I mean? Nobody gives a damn anymore!"

"Either cheer up or take off the hat."

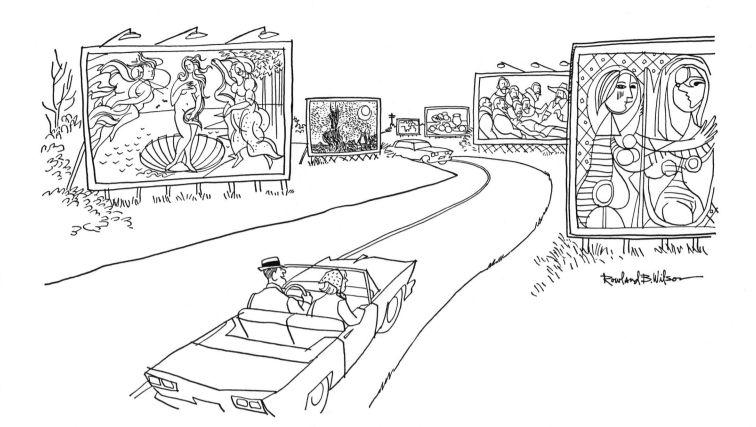

"Now, *this* *is* Highway Beautification!"

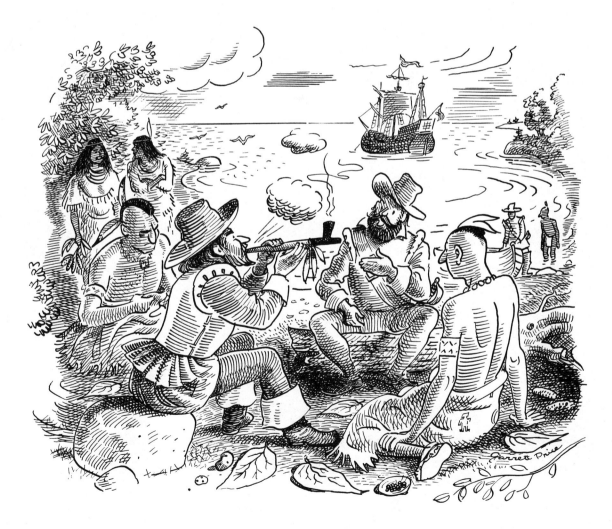

"Don't worry. If it turns out tobacco is harmful, we can always quit."

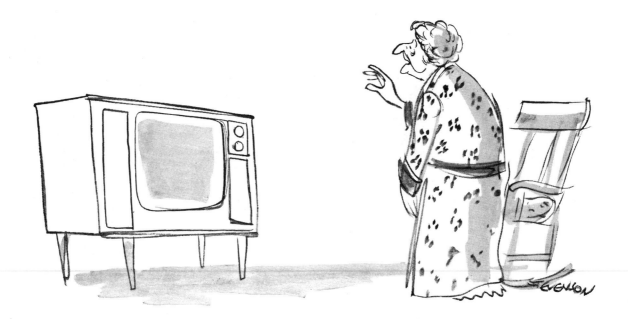

"Night-night. See you in the morning."

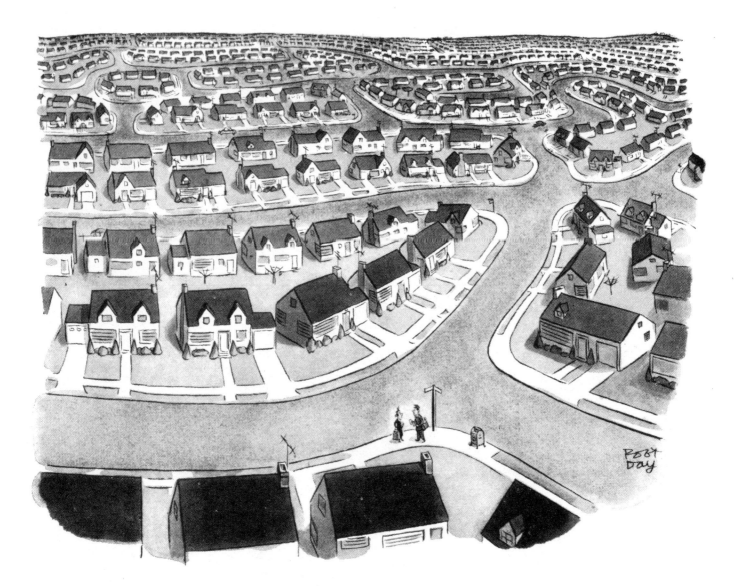

"I'm Mrs. Edward M. Barnes. Where do I live?"

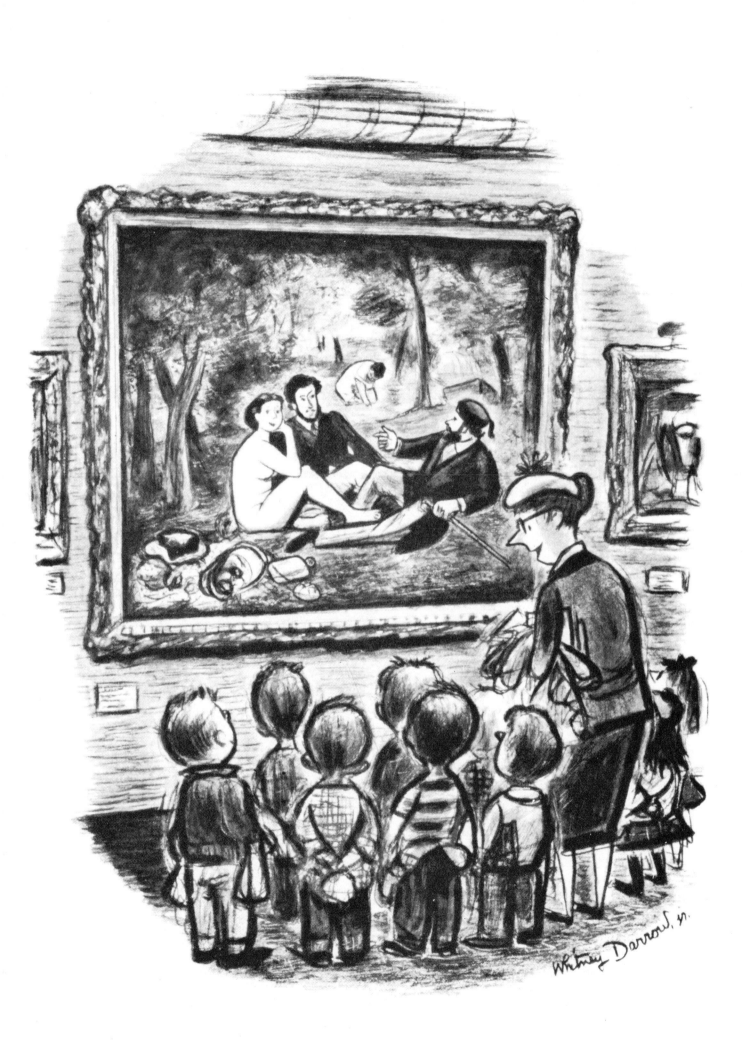

"Well, it was sort of like a cook-out."

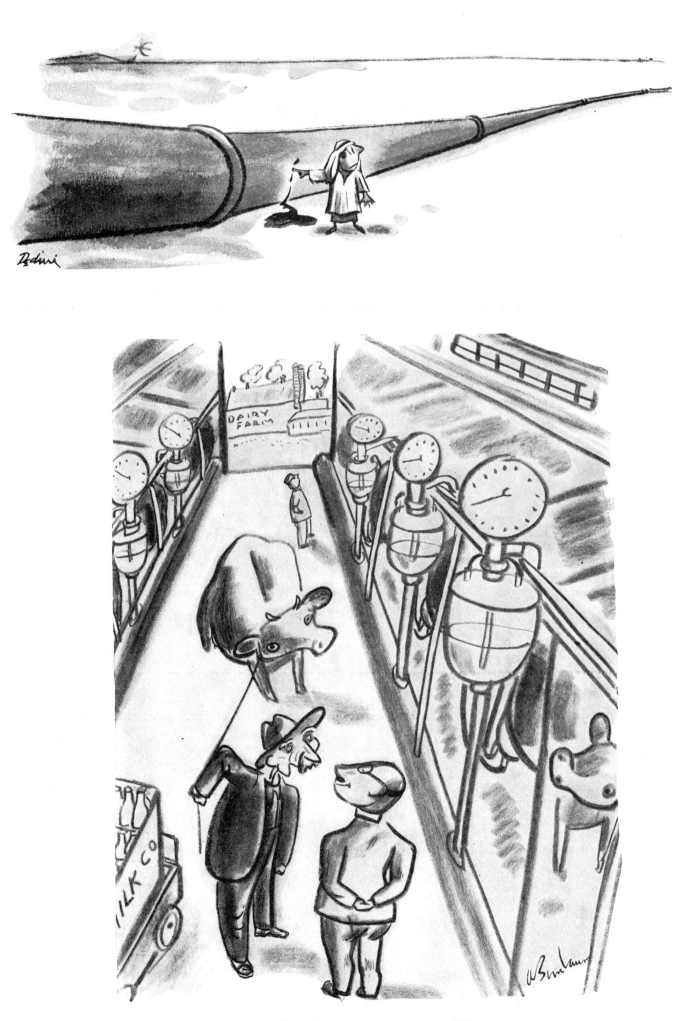

"Mind if I show my cow around?"

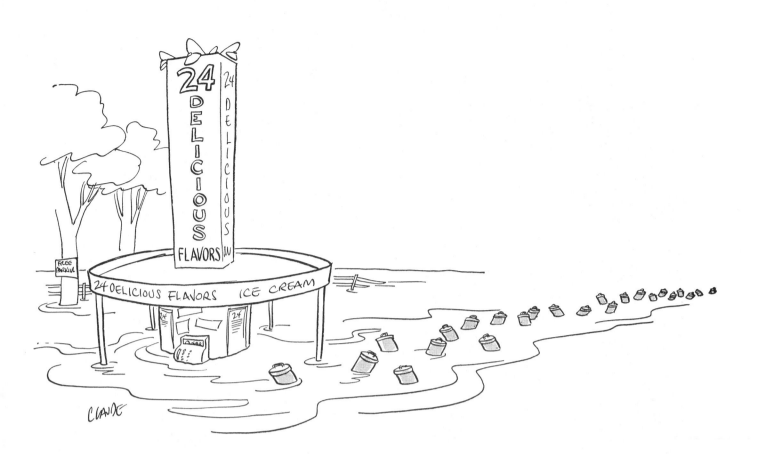

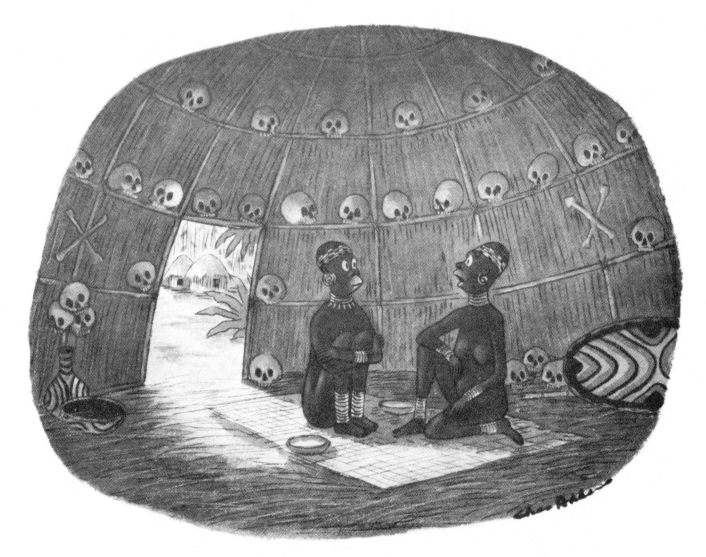

"One thing I'll say for him—he's always been a good provider."

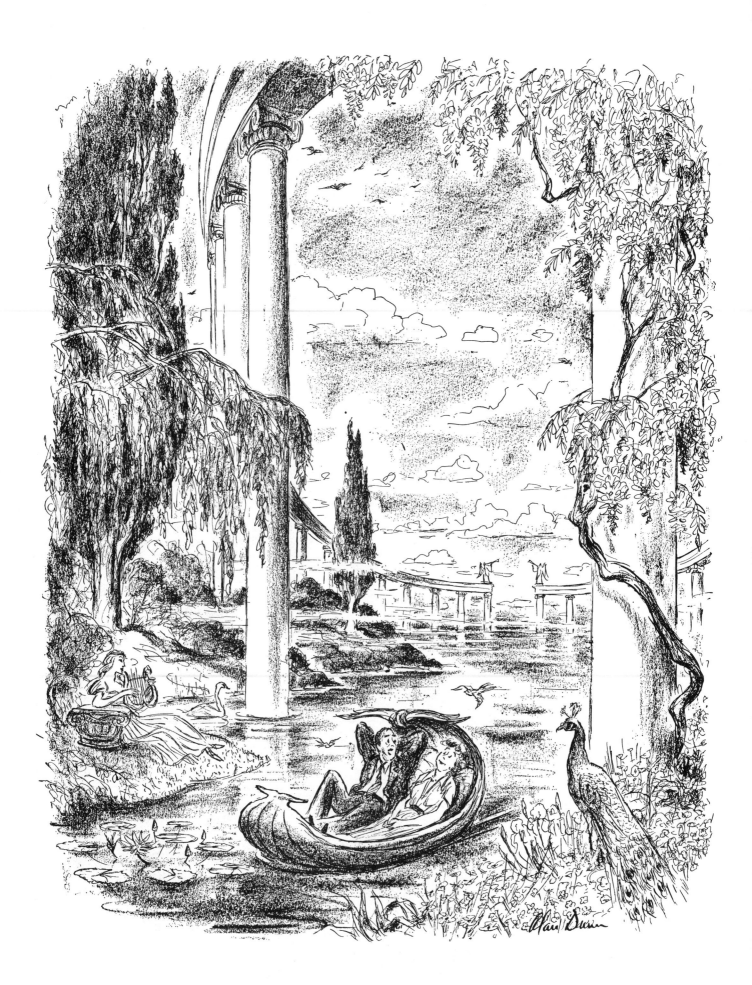

"What was the name of that tranquillizer we took?"

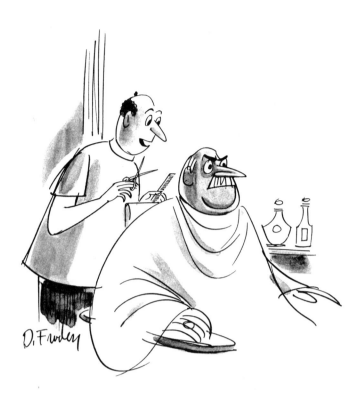

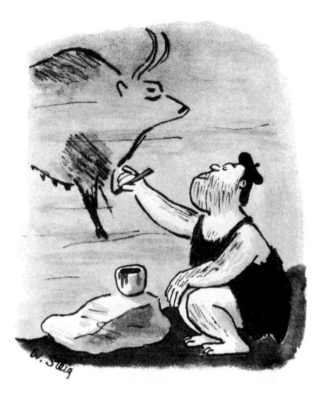

"The thing is, sir, are you referring to your status quo or my status quo?"

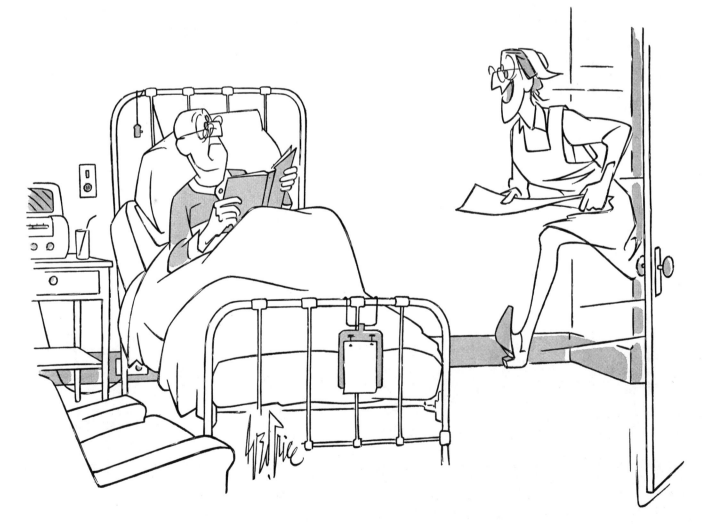

"Good news, Mr. Murdock! You can go home as soon as you fork over $593.50."

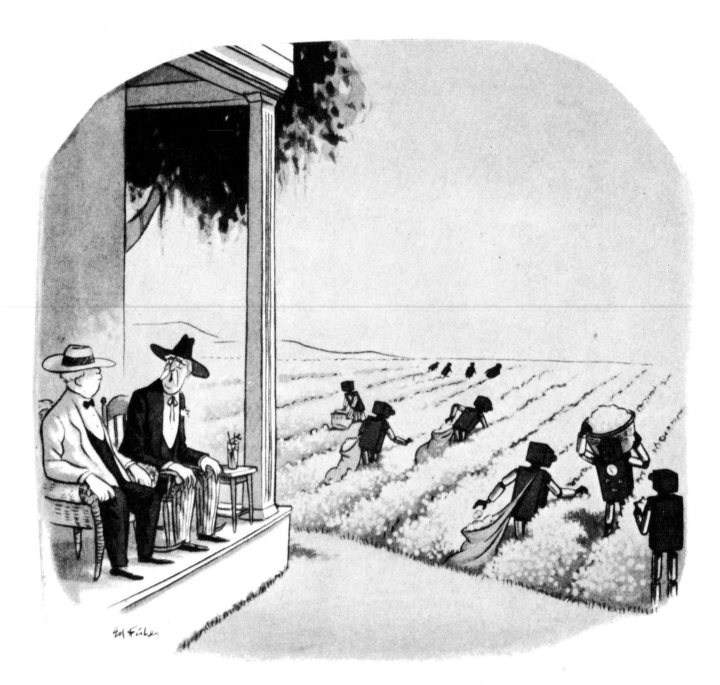

"*Know what Ah miss? Ah miss that soft, sweet singing. That's what Ah miss.*"

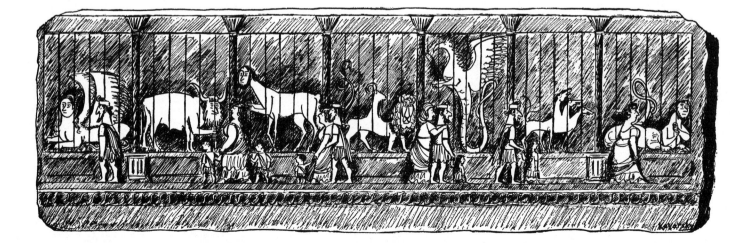

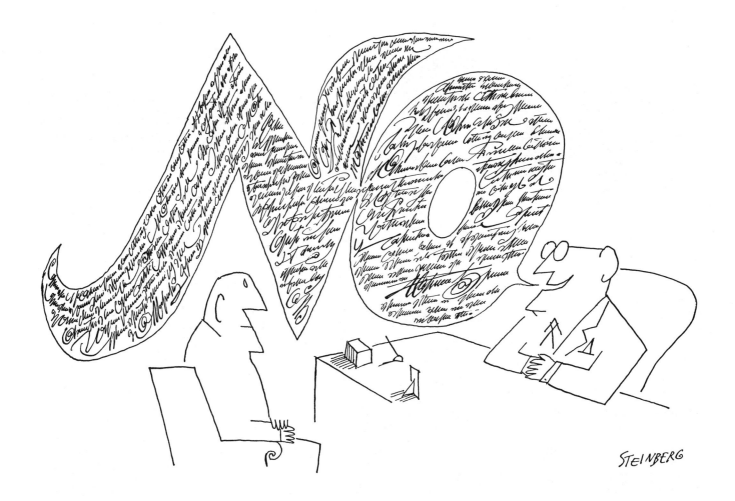

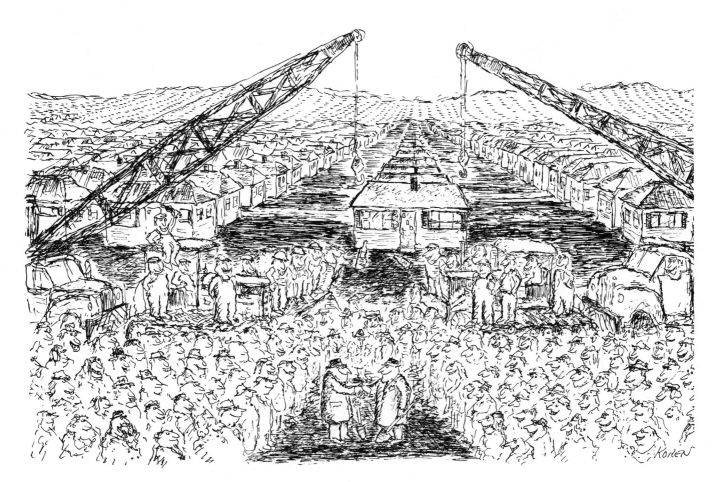

"At last! One nation, indivisible."

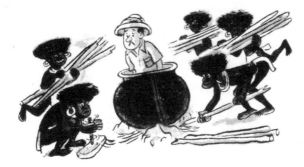 1

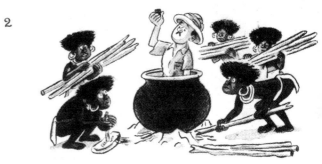 2

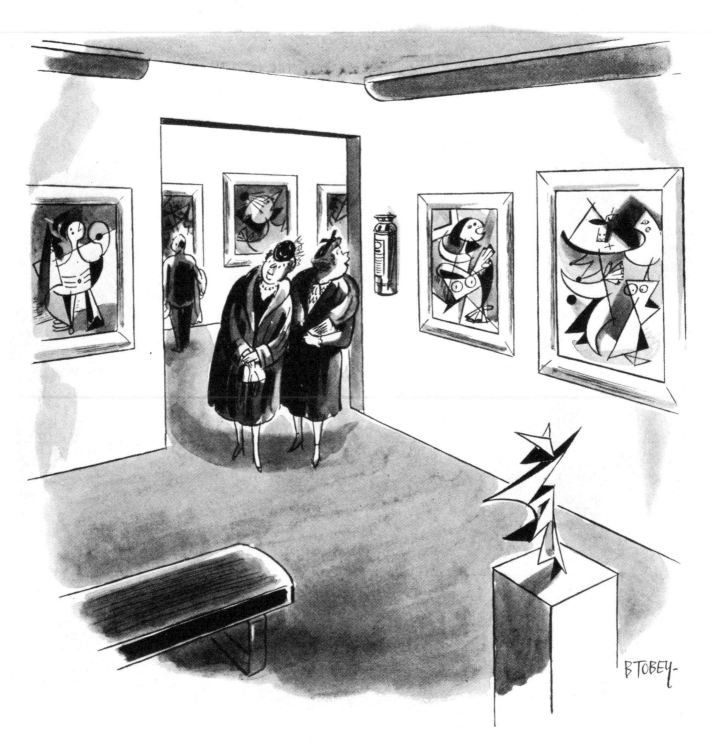

"We've already done this room. I remember that fire extinguisher."

3

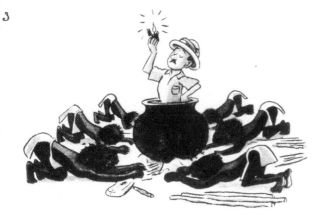

4

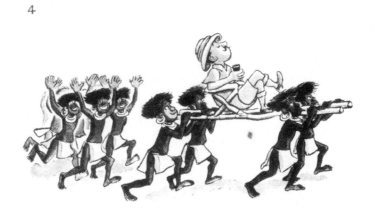

5

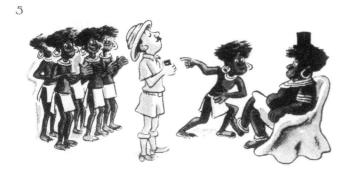

6

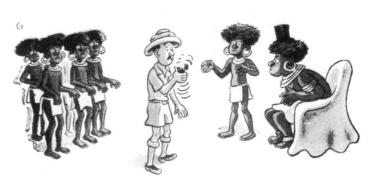

7

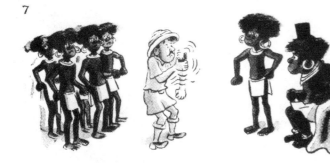

8

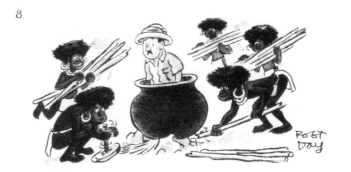

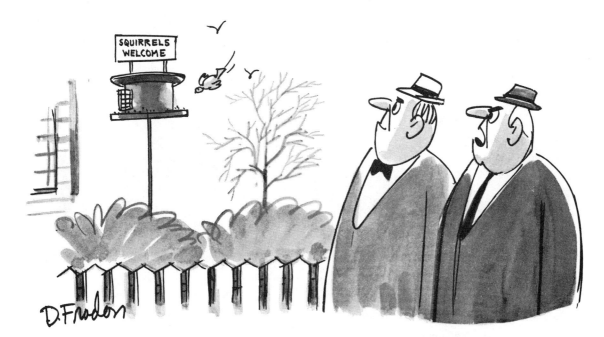

"Liberals!"

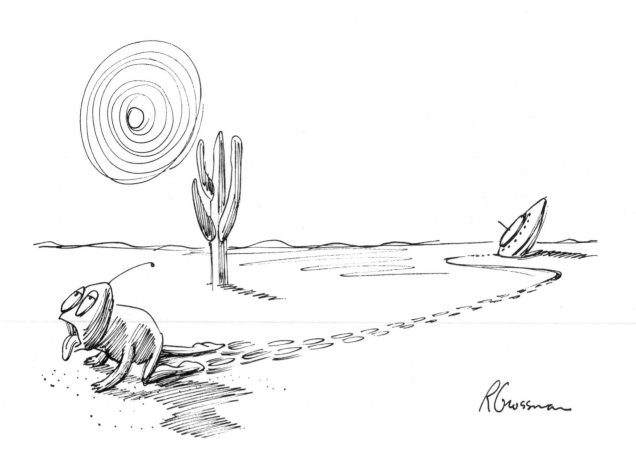

"Ammonia! Ammonia!"

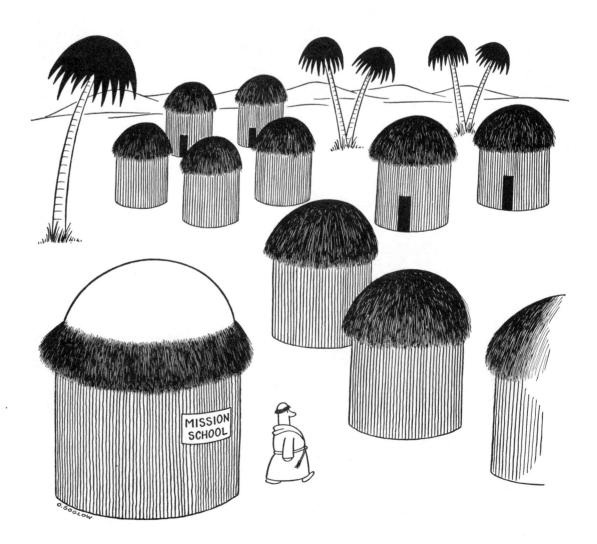

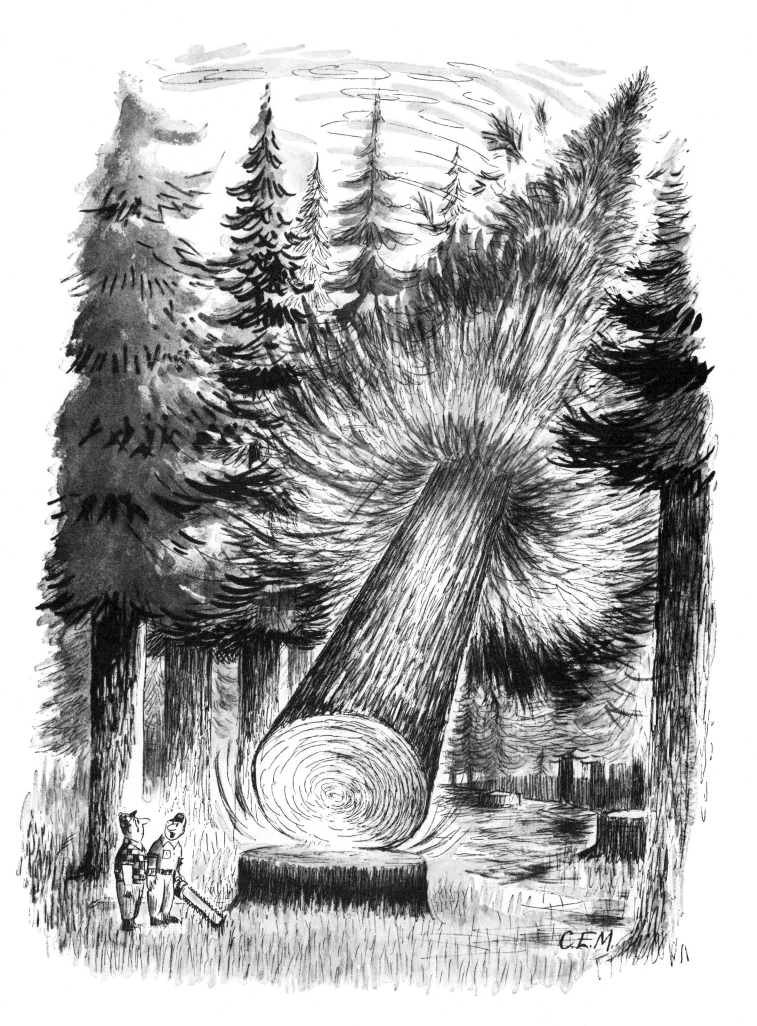

"Why, Archie, you're crying!"

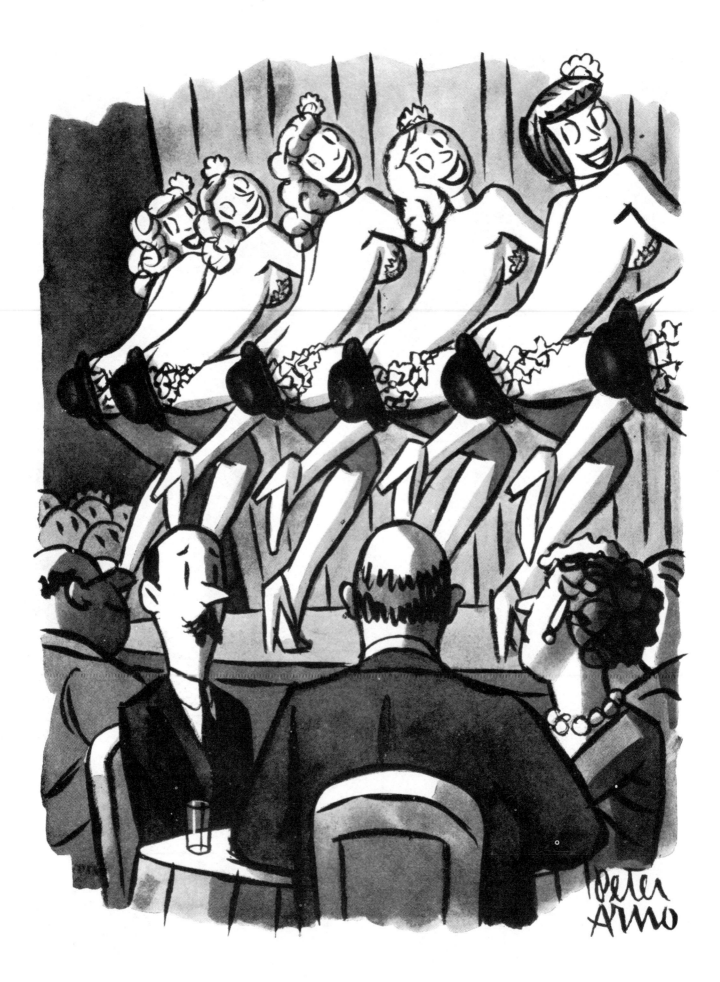

"*It isn't often one sees a bowler these days.*"

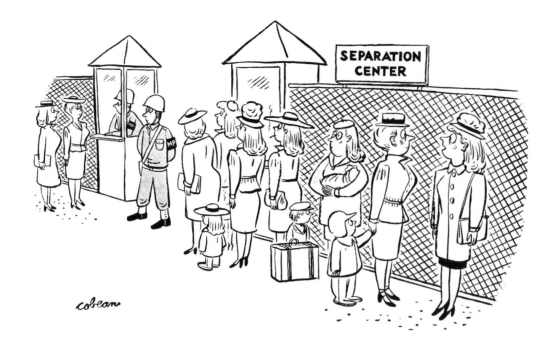
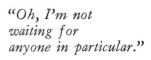

"*Oh, I'm not waiting for anyone in particular.*"

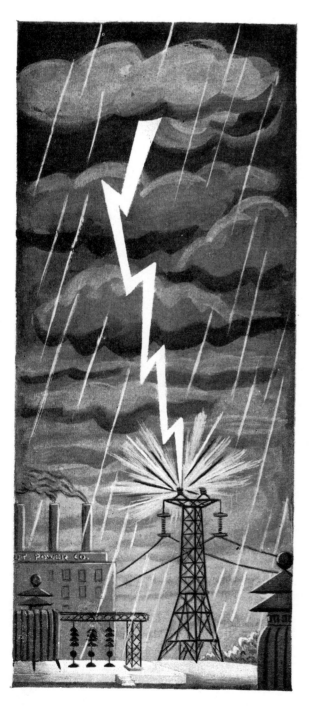
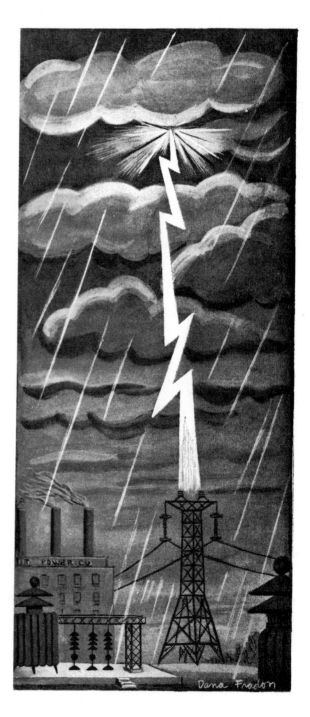

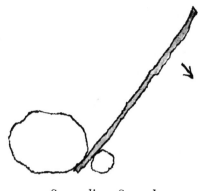

Seconding Speech

POLITICAL CONVENTION

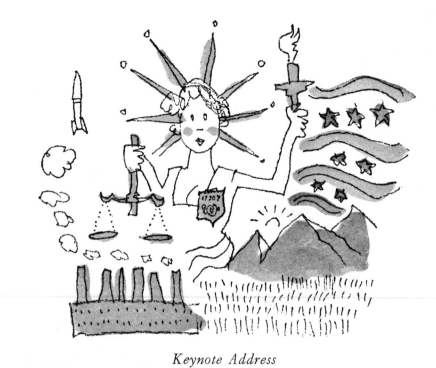

Keynote Address

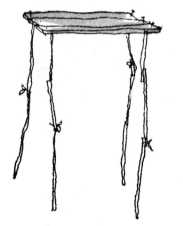

Platform

Split Delegation

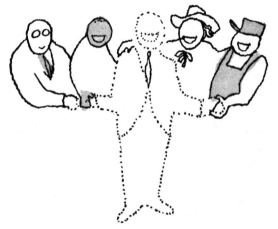

Coalition Candidate

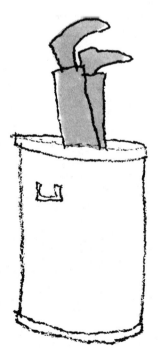

Early Drive Fails

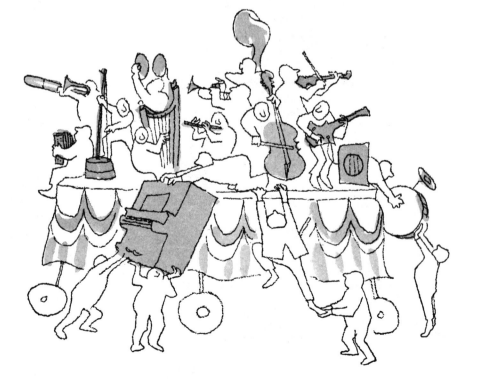

Bandwagon

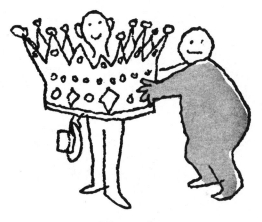

Kingmaker

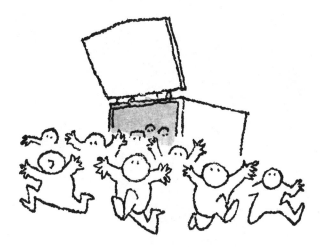

Releasing Delegates

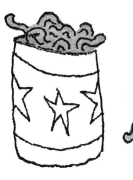

Caucus

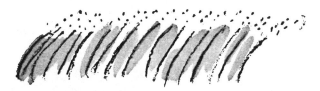

Farm Bloc

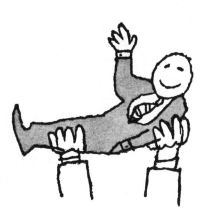

Favorite Son

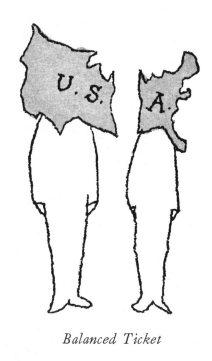

Balanced Ticket

STEVENSON

Steamroller

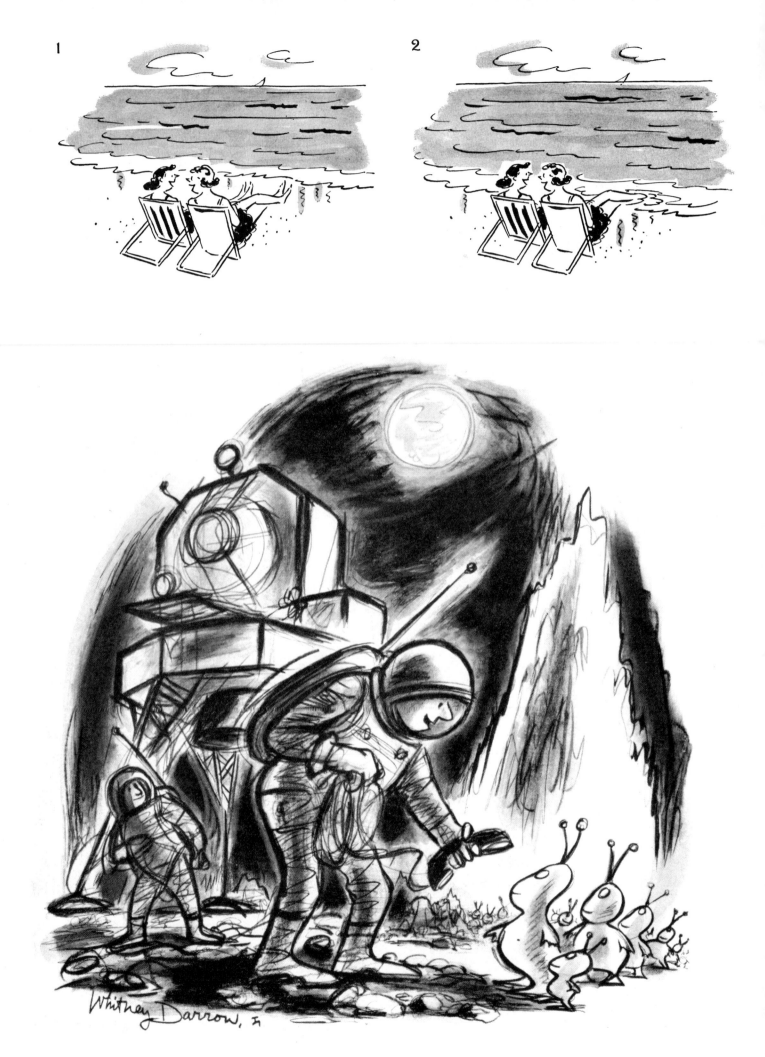

"President Johnson wants to say 'Howdy.'"

3

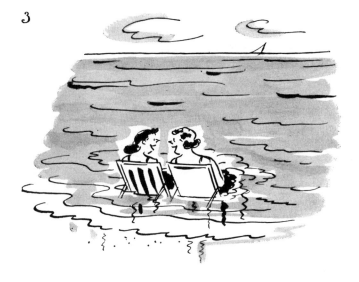

4

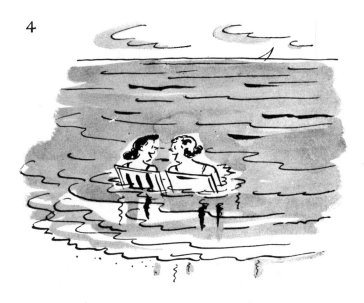

5

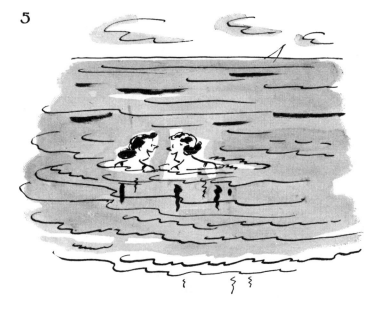

6

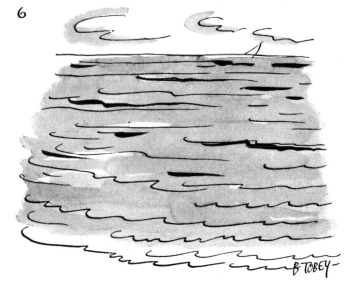

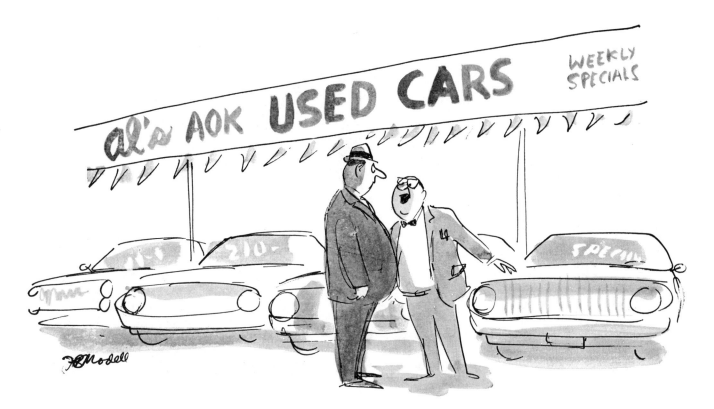

"*I happen to know Ralph Nader's mother drives this model.*"

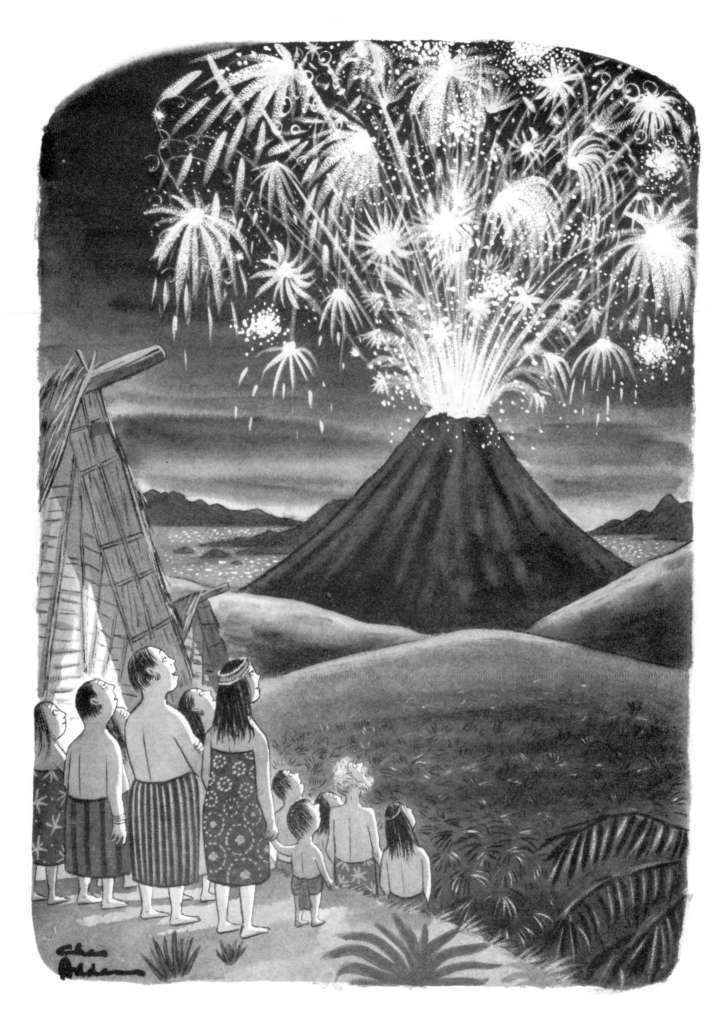

"Whatever the gods are, they aren't angry."

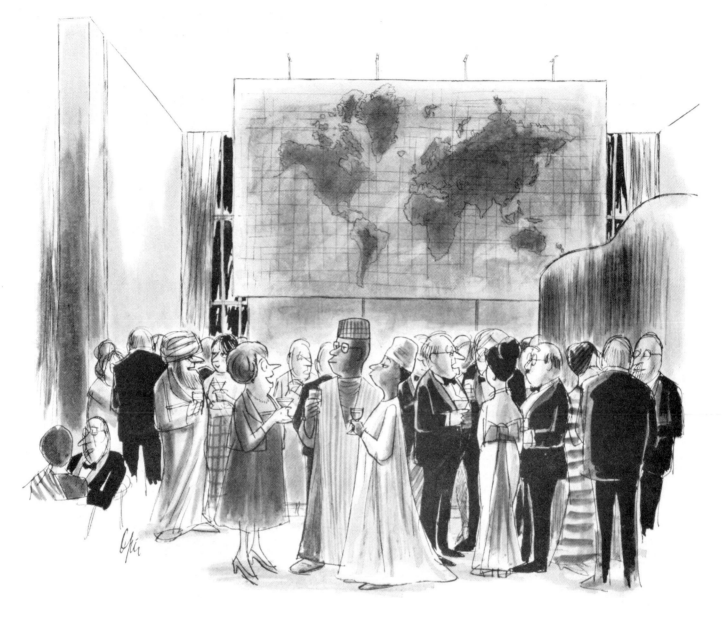

"Whereabouts in Africa are you folks from?"

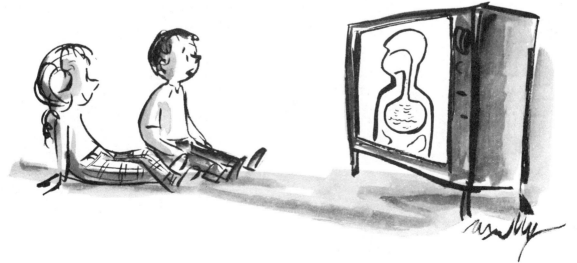

"I think that's what is wrong with me."

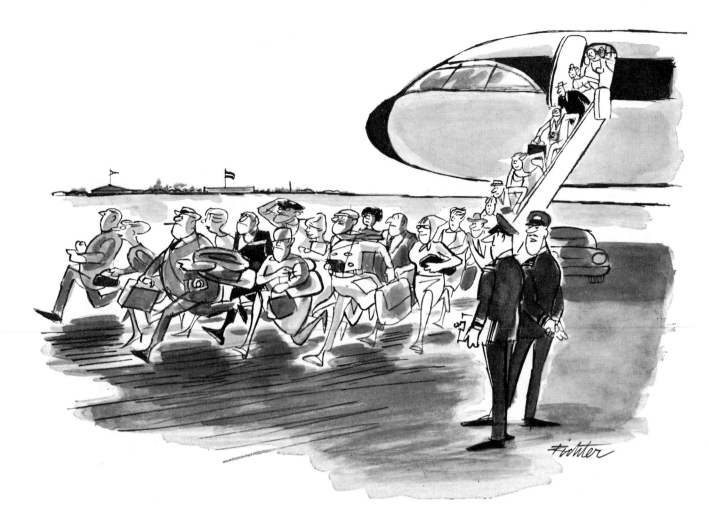

"Seventeen major European cities in twenty-one days."

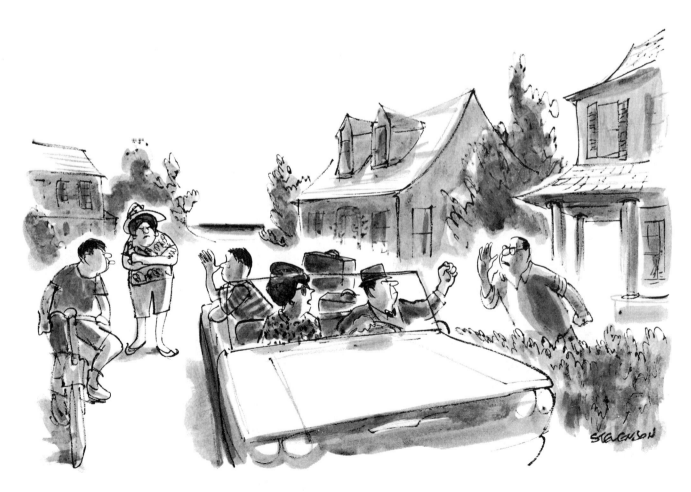

"By and large, I think last summer was more gemütlich than _this_ summer."

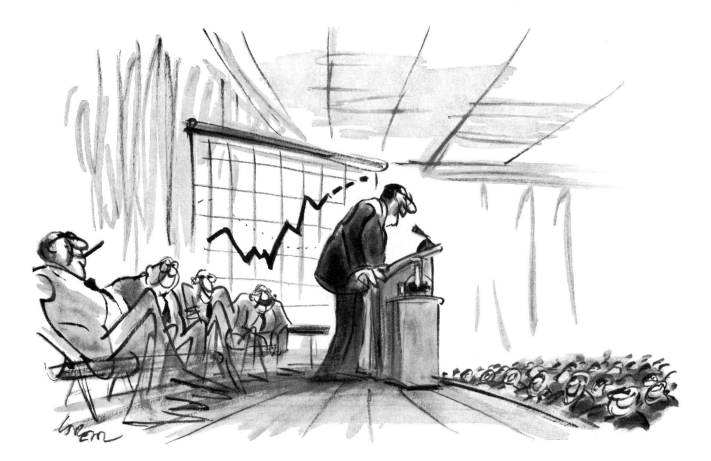

"*And though in 1969, as in previous years, your company had to contend with spiralling labor costs, exorbitant interest rates, and unconscionable government interference, management was able once more, through a combination of deceptive marketing practices, false advertising, and price fixing, to show a profit which, in all modesty, can only be called excessive.*"

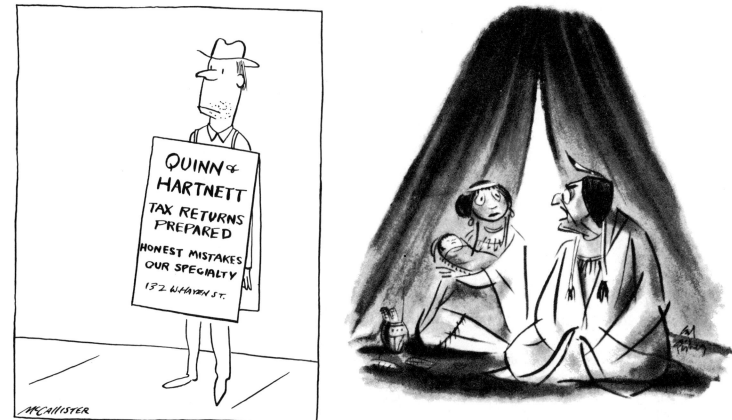

"*I'm sick and tired of living in a papoose-oriented tepee!*"

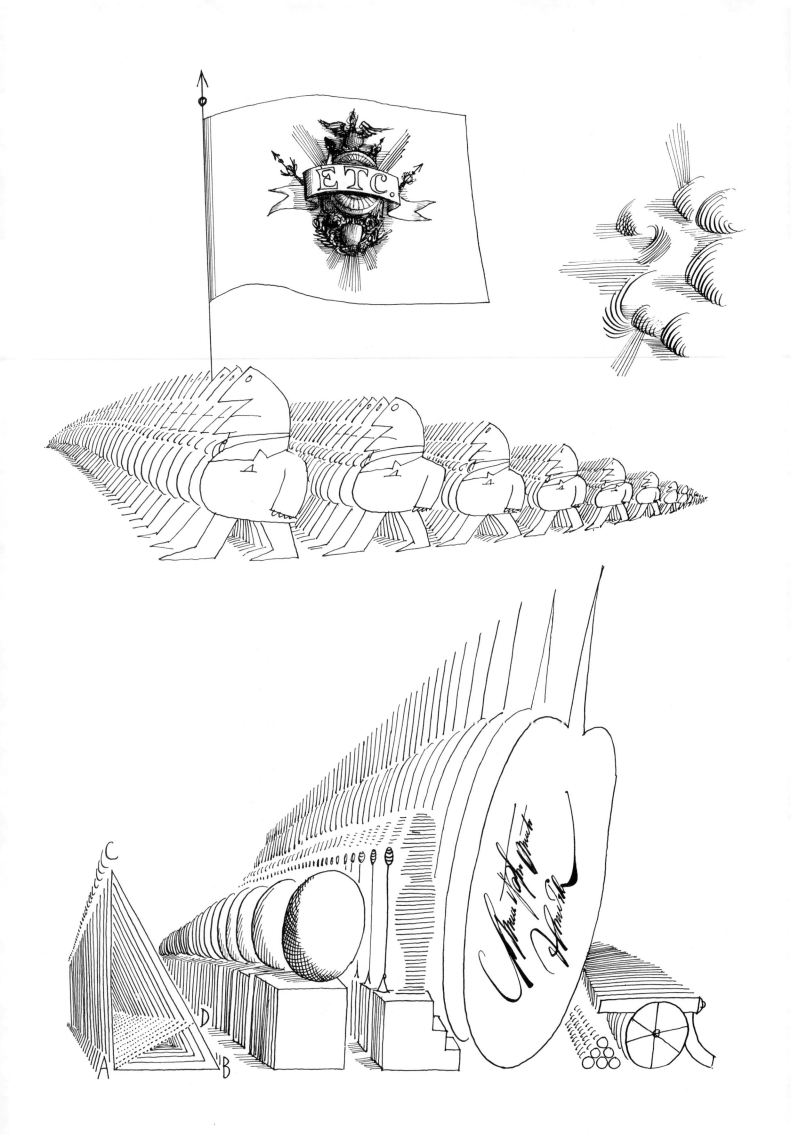

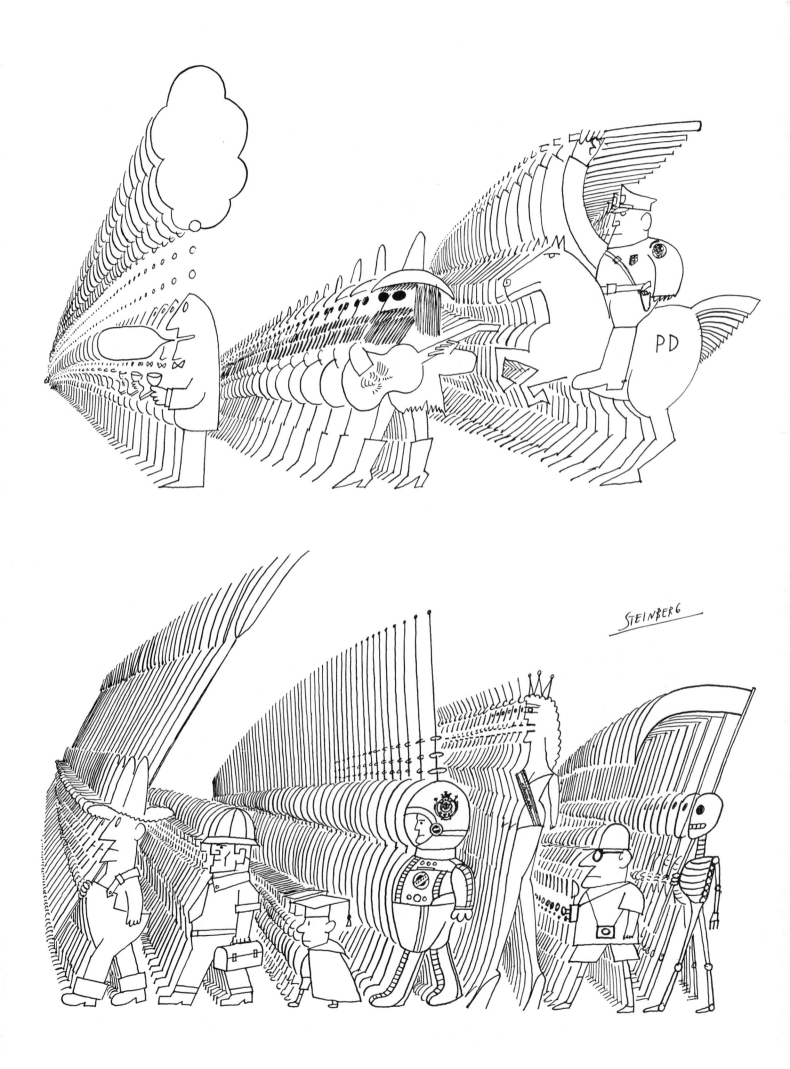

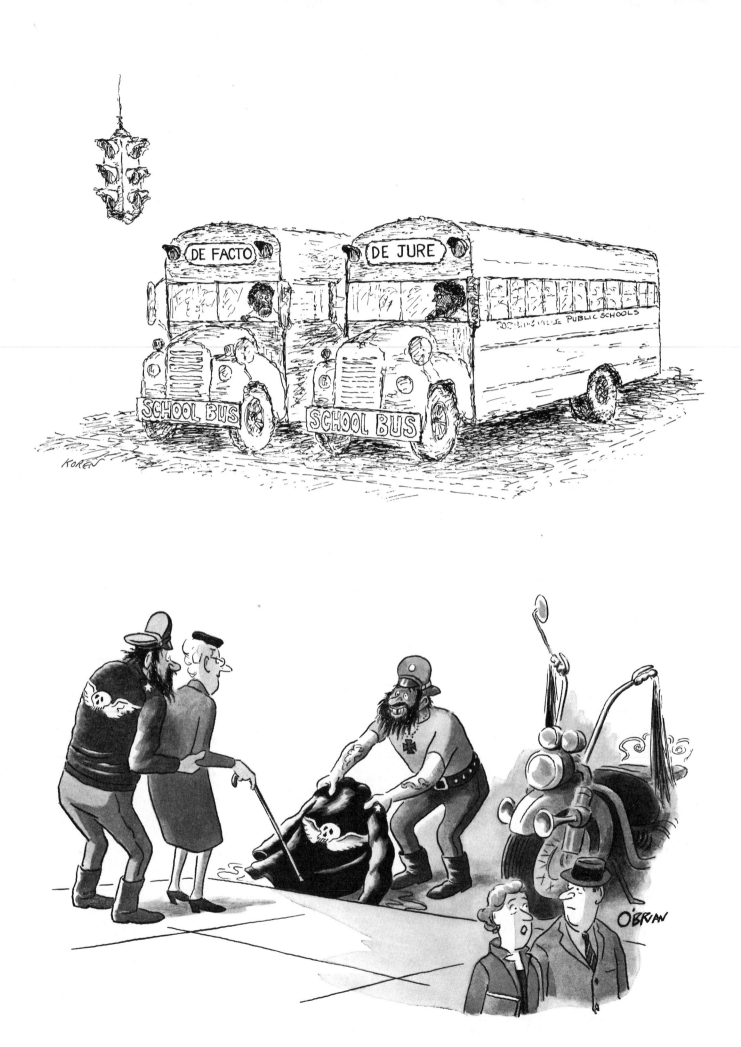

"Well, they can't be all bad."

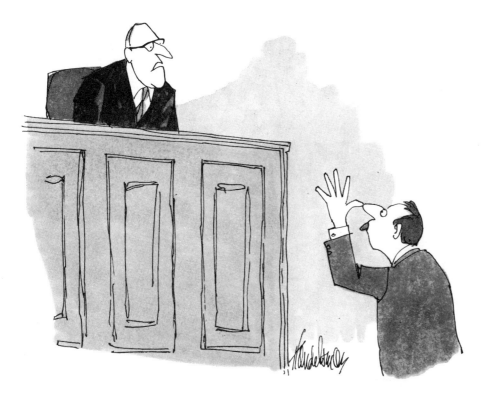

"*Mister, you're __really__ asking for justice!*"

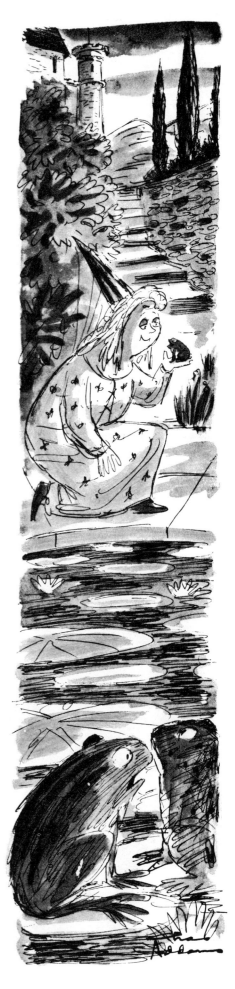

"*Personally, I can't imagine what he sees in her.*"

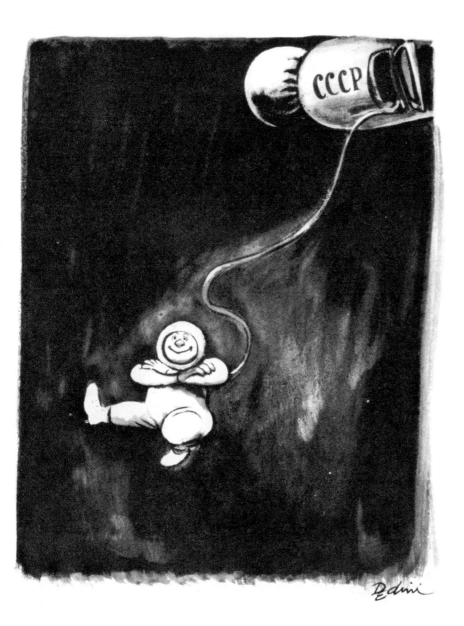

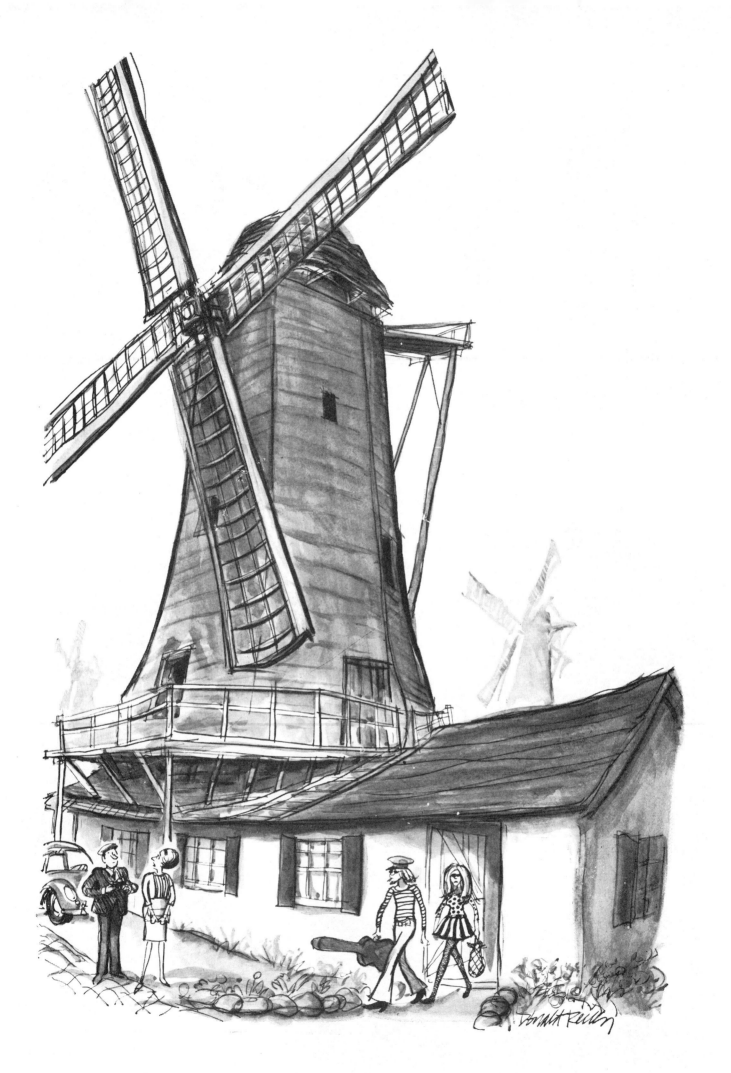

"Oh dear! I <u>was</u> hoping for something more in the way of wooden shoes."

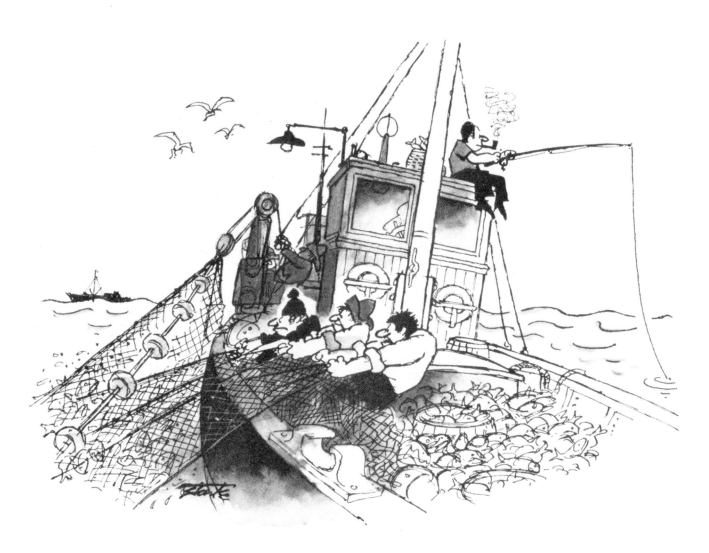

"I think it makes us all look damn silly the way Ferguson spends his off-duty time."

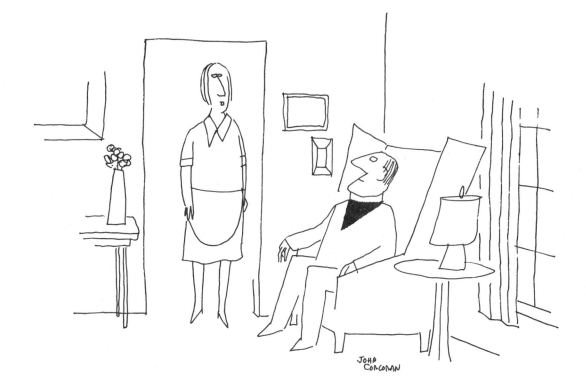

"What we are about to receive will be another ten minutes."

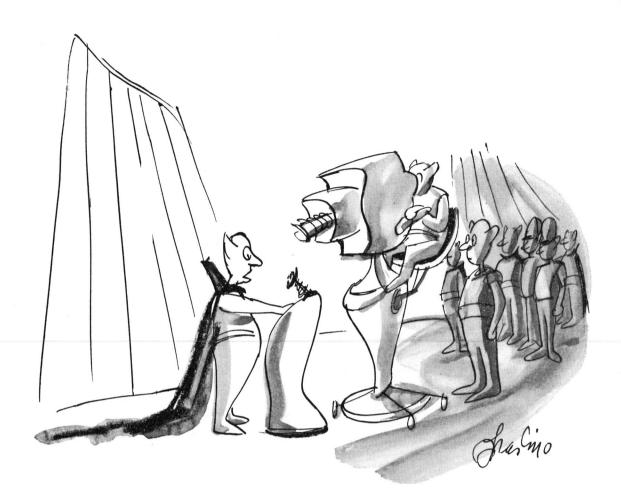

"My fellow Martians, it is with a heavy heart that I speak to you tonight. The planet Earth, with unprovoked belligerence, has landed troops on her moon."

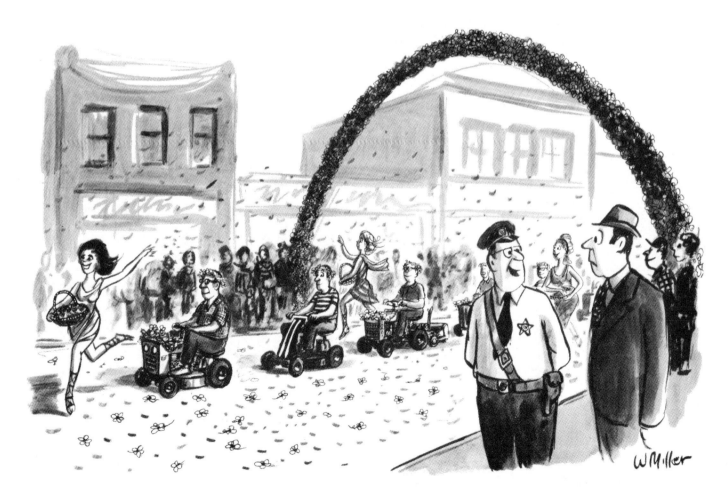

"It's one of our local customs—the annual blessing of the lawnmowers."

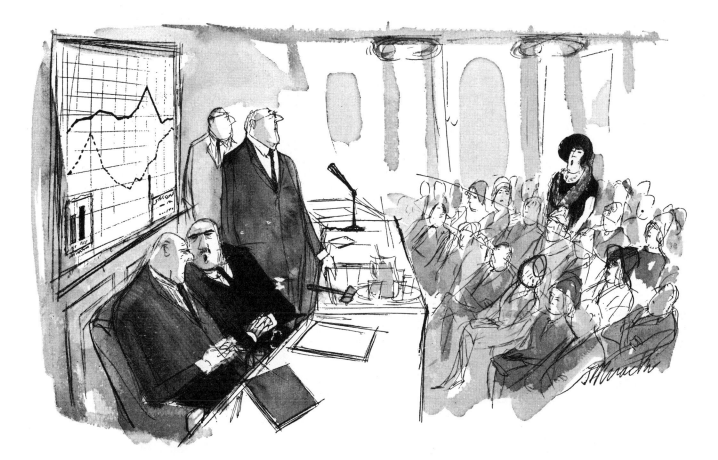

"This is the part of capitalism I hate."

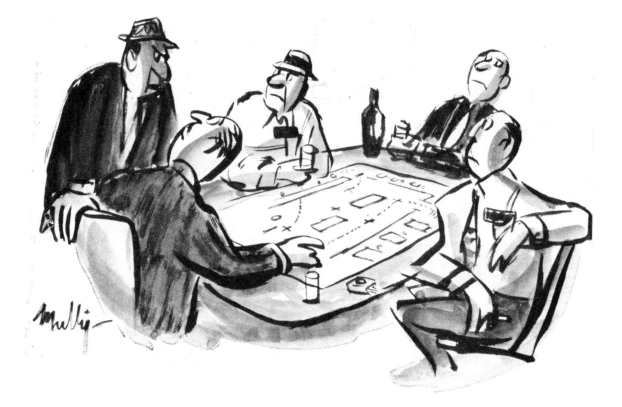

"I got news for you guys. We own that bank."

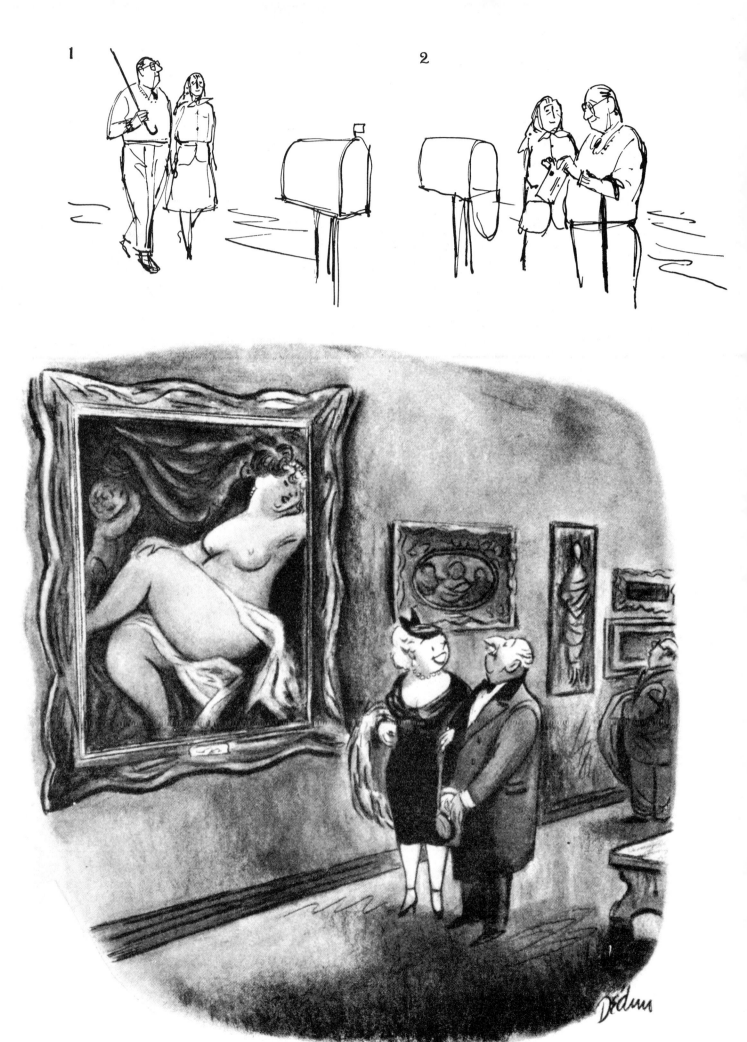

"Why, Ted, you say the sweetest things."

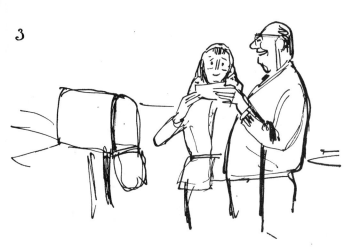

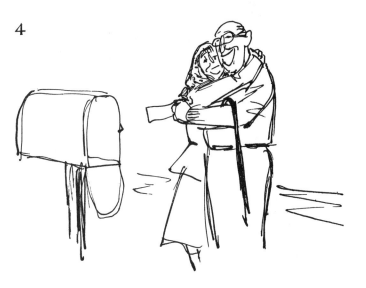

"Our first Social Security check!"

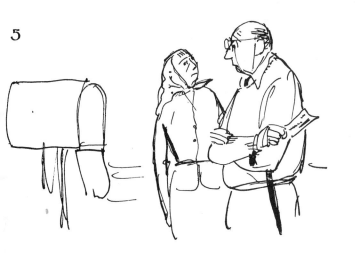

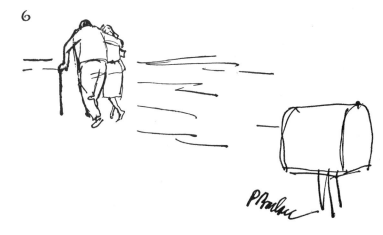

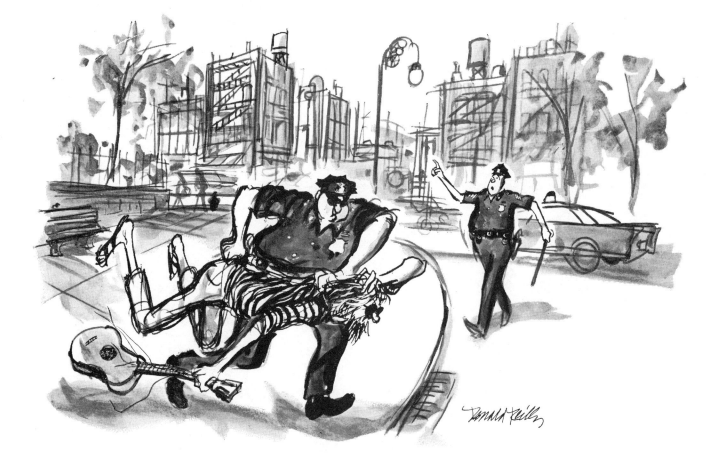

"No, no, Sweeney! _Identify_! _Empathize_!"

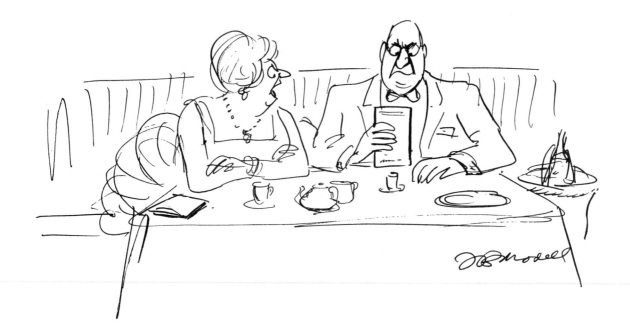

"Oh, for pity's sake! Put it on your American Express card and blow your top when you get the bill."

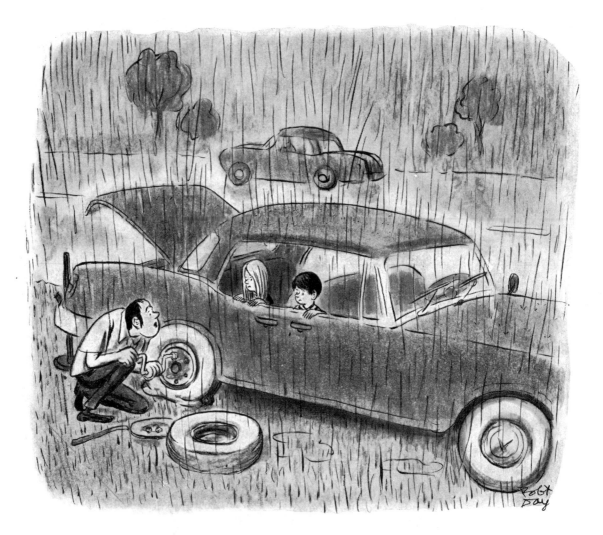

"Don't you understand? This is <u>life</u>, this is what is happening. We <u>can't</u> switch to another channel."

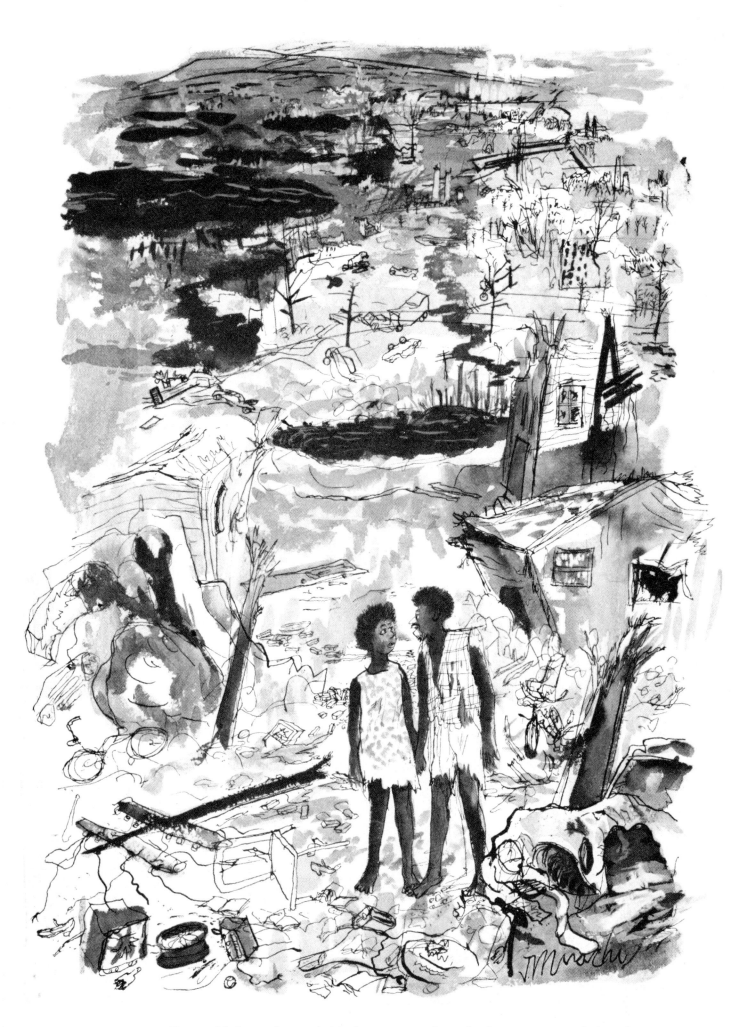

"Senator Russell would have been tickled to know that the last two remaining human beings not only are Americans but come from Georgia."

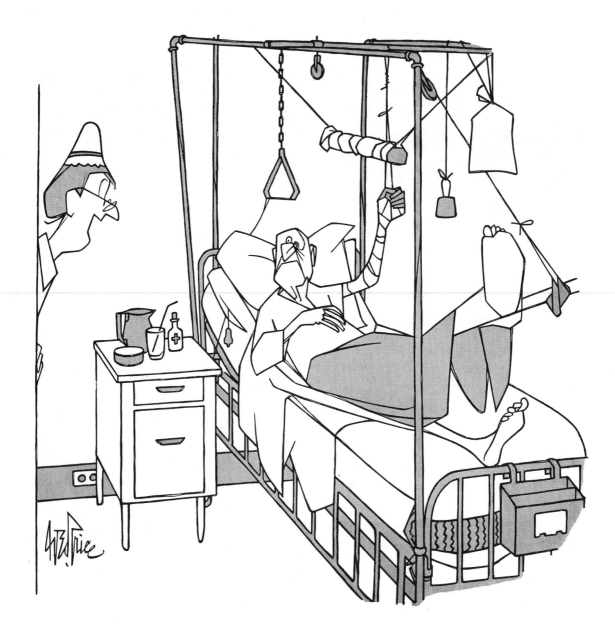

"*Have your pillows been plumped this morning?*"

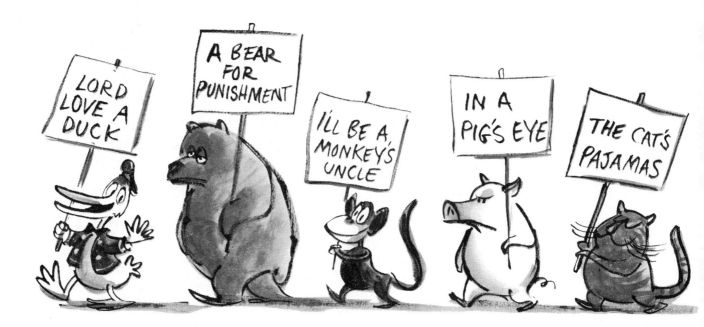

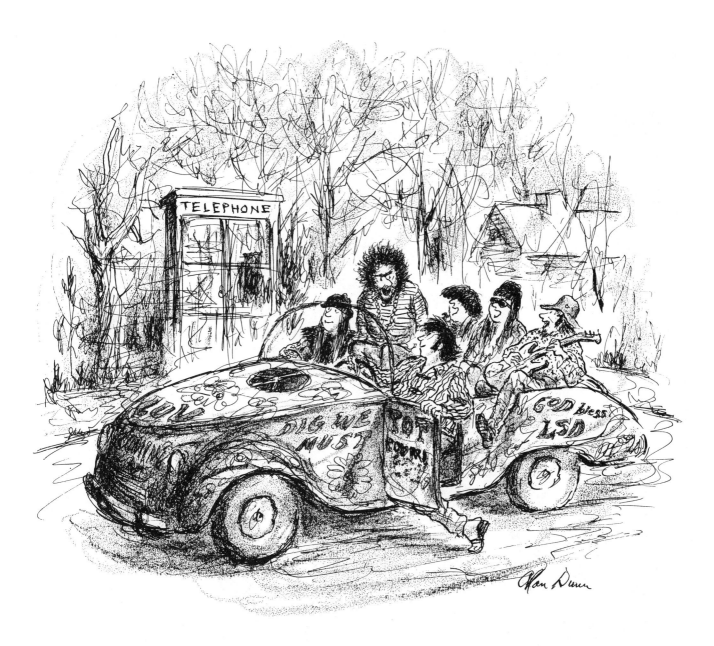

"Why phone ahead? Why don't we just show up?"

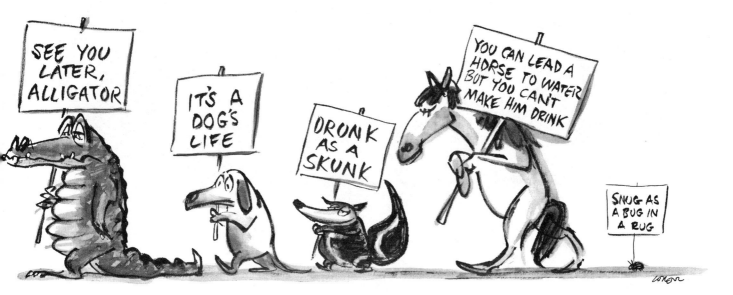

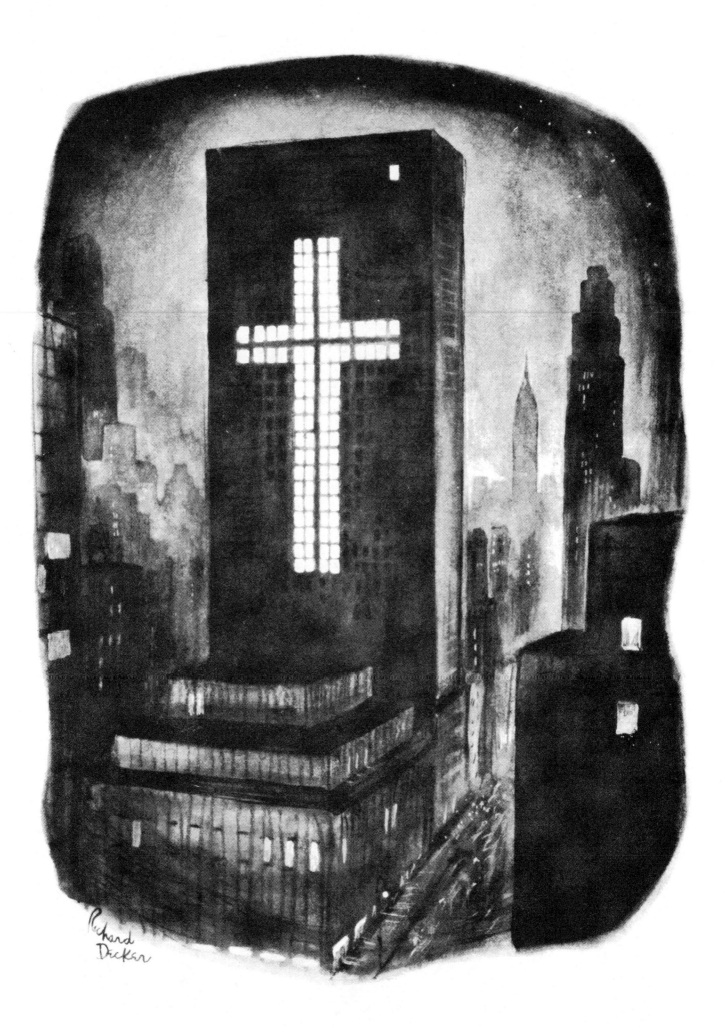

"I can't help that. These invoices have to be in the mail tonight."

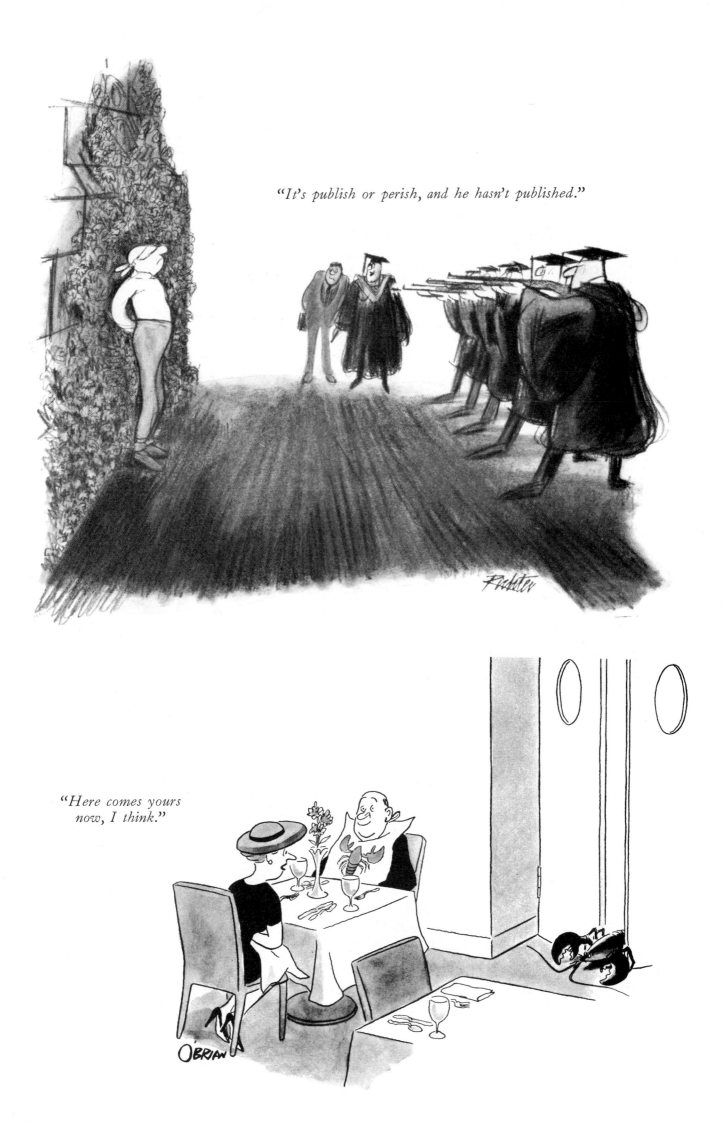

"It's publish or perish, and he hasn't published."

"Here comes yours now, I think."

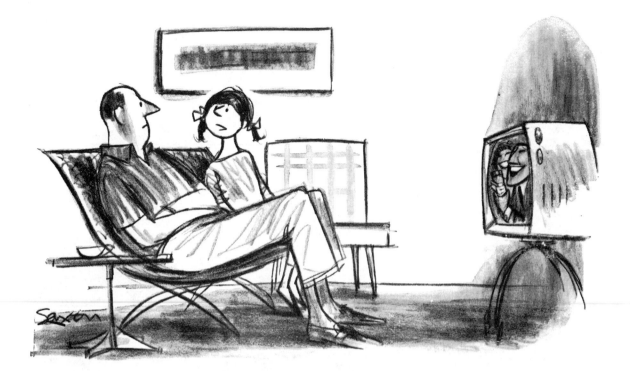

"Why can't they save all the commercials to the end, and then
we could be honor-bound to look at them?"

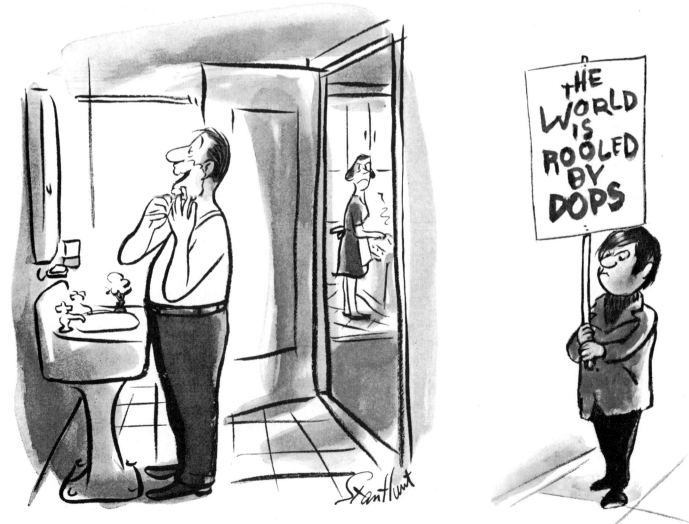

" 'Oh, I've got plenty of nothin'
and nothin's plenty for me.' "

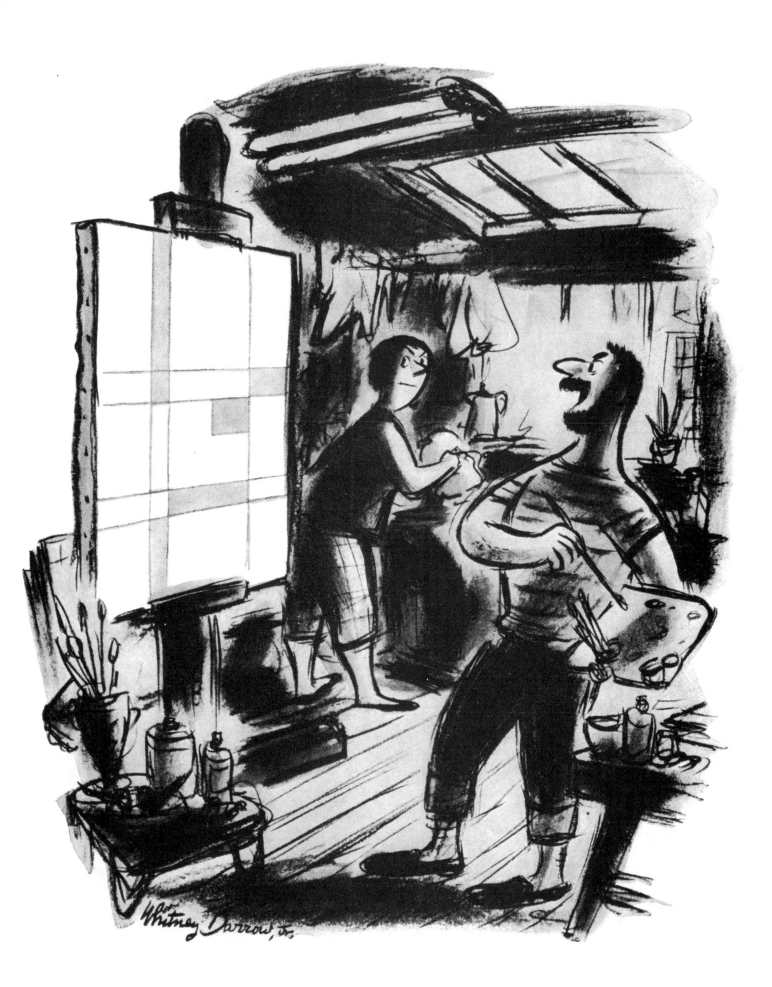

"There! A message of good will for all mankind."

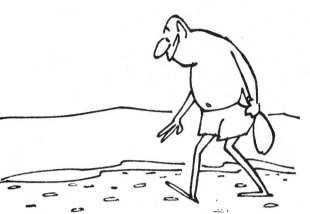

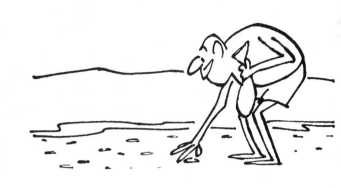

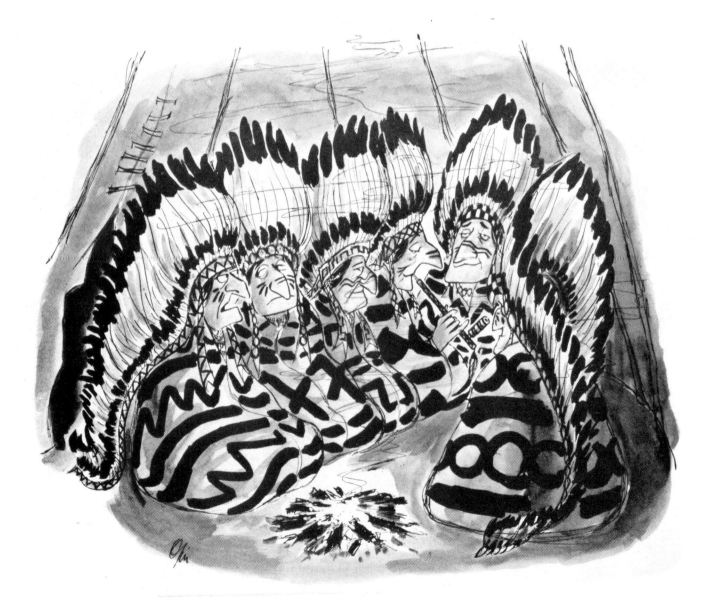

"What kind of powwow is this? I mean like what's in the pipe?"

③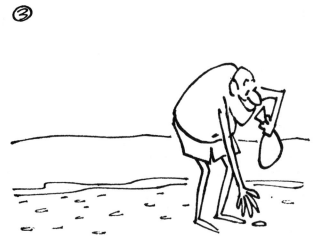

④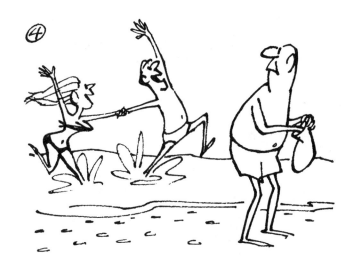

⑤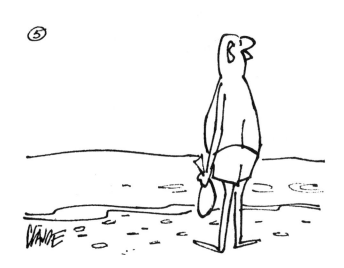

⑥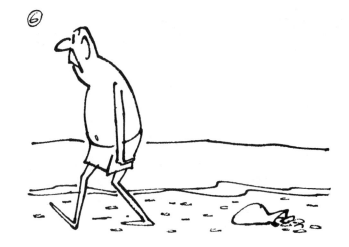

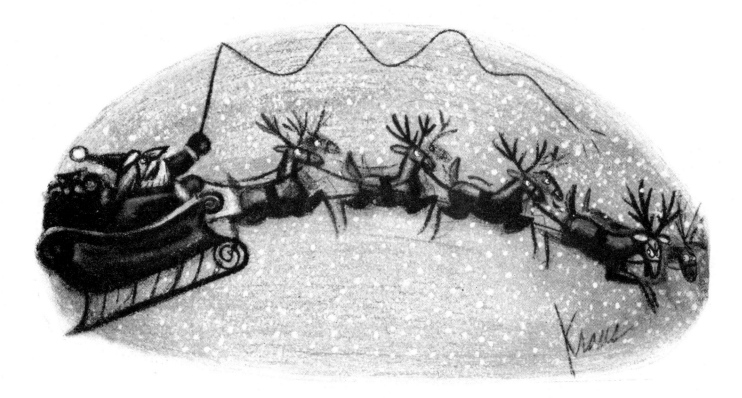

"For a kindly old man, he's mighty quick with the whip."

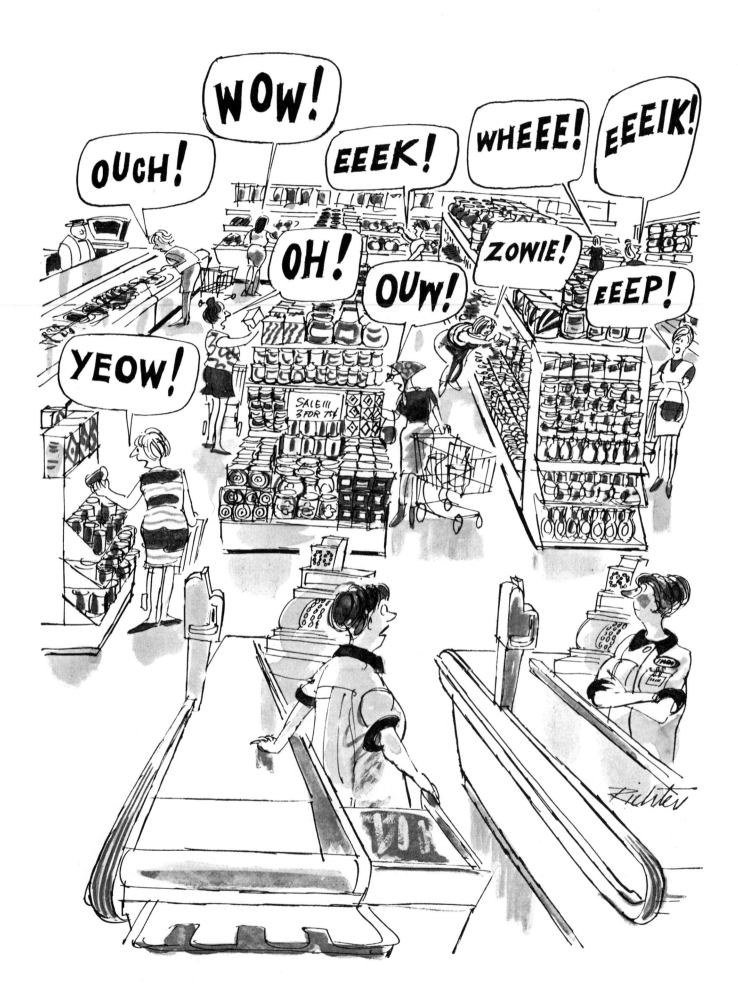

"The cost of living sure keeps going up and up and up!"

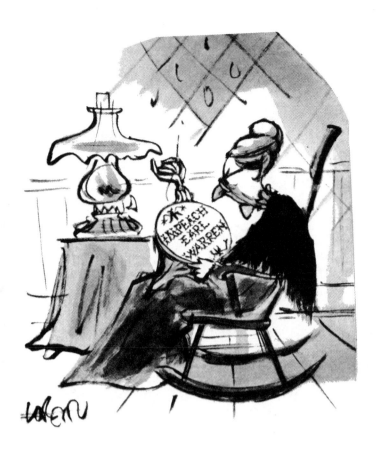

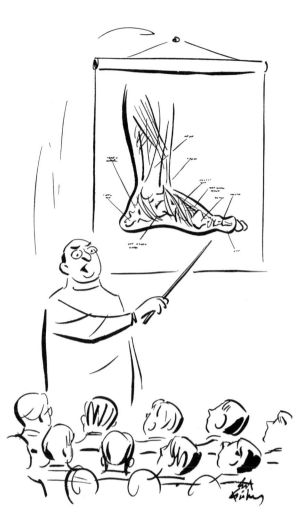

"I realize that those of you who are planning to go into psychiatry may find this dull."

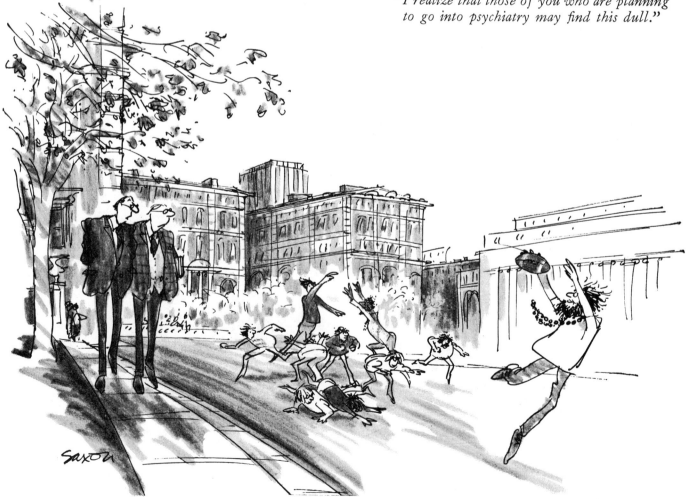

"Perhaps this semester we may see yet another swing of the pendulum."

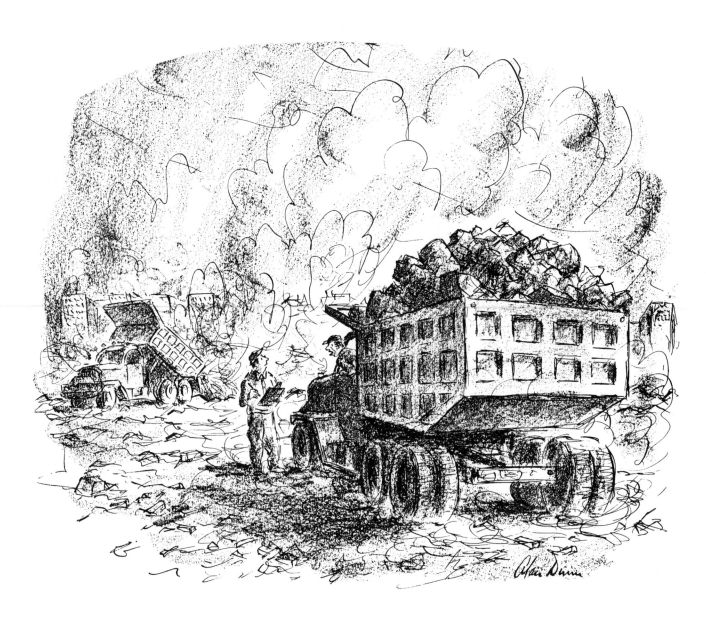

"Where do you want Penn Station?"

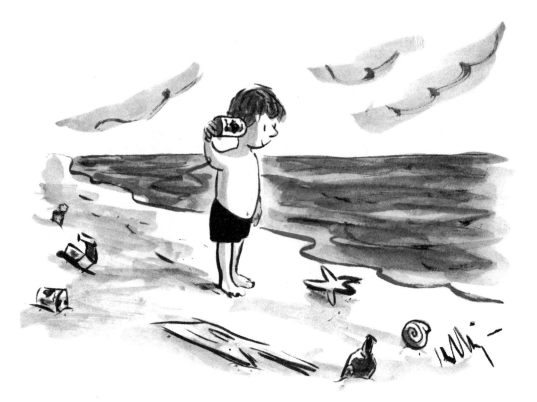

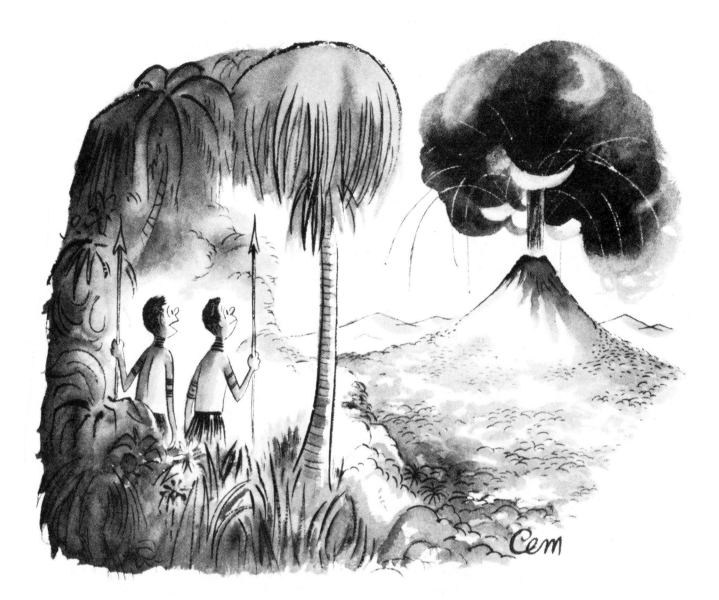

"Now the gods are angry about neo-colonialism."

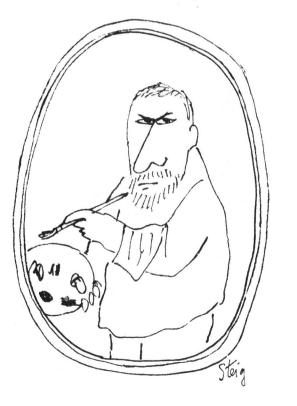

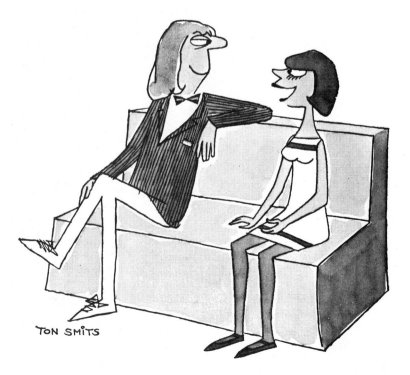

"Your hair looks lovely tonight."

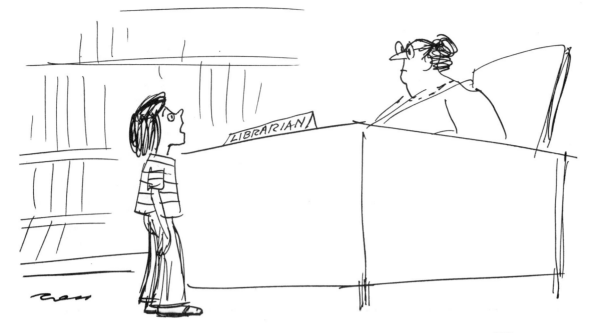

"*I'm very interested in sex education. What would you recommend?*"

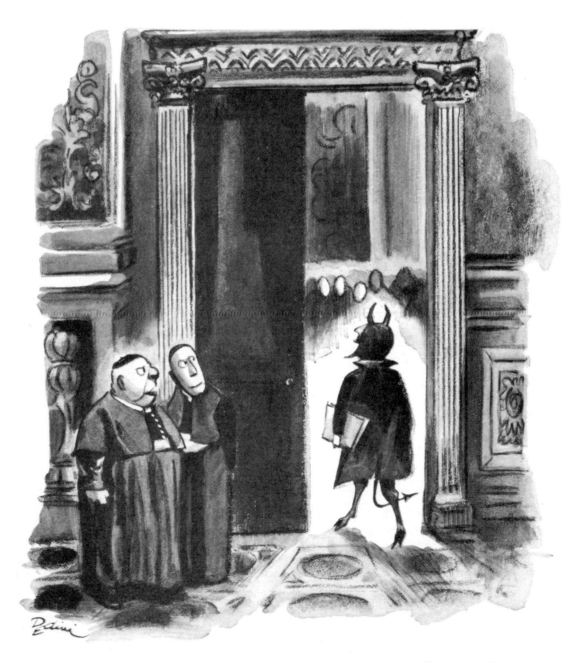

"*Sometimes I wonder if we haven't carried ecumenism a bit too far.*"

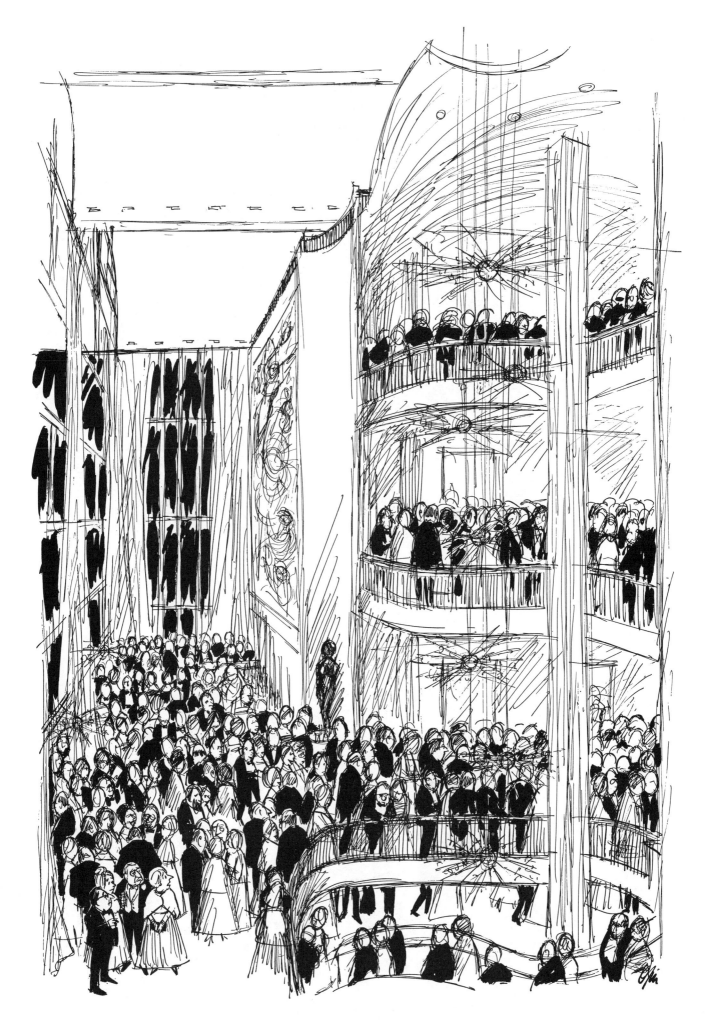

"Oh dear, the bell! We have to go back."

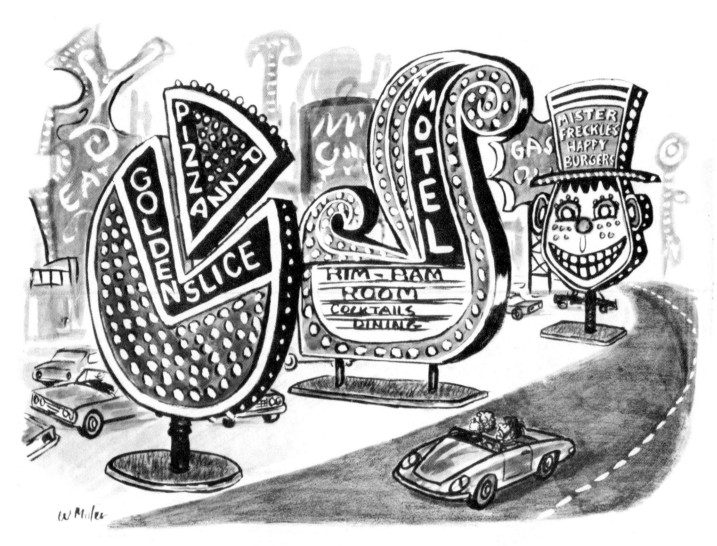

"*Man, it really tears me to think that some squares want to pull down these lovely, beautiful signs!*"

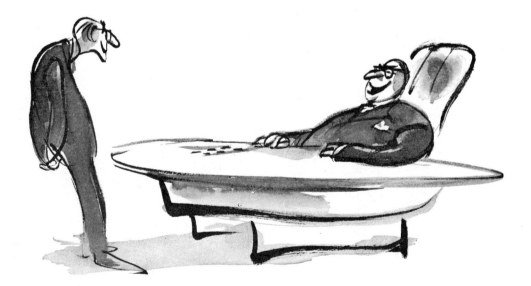

"*As you know, Rogers, when retirement day rolls around here, we don't waste time with a lot of mawkish sentimentality.*"

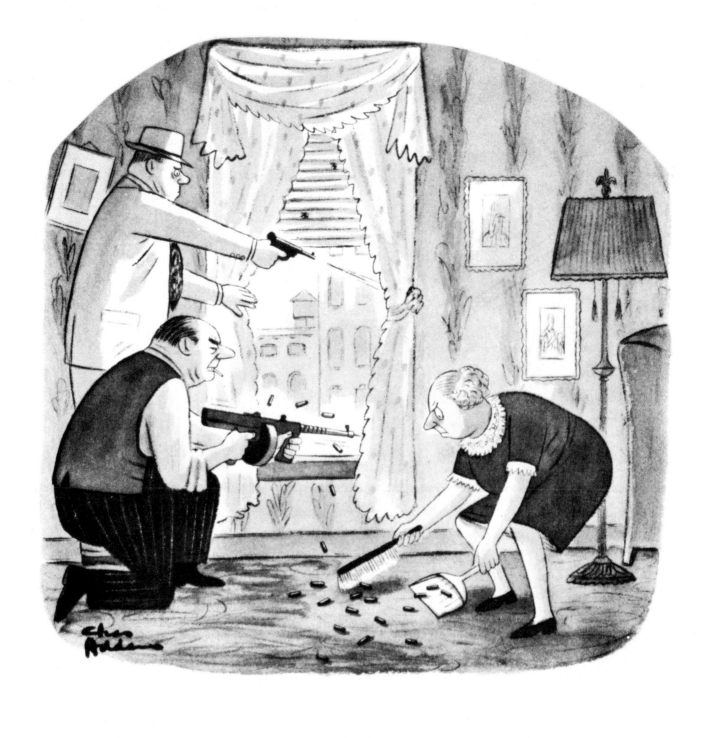

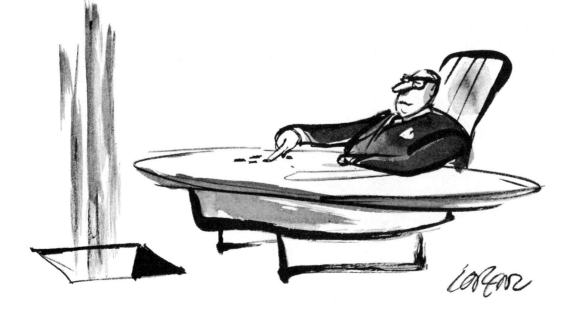

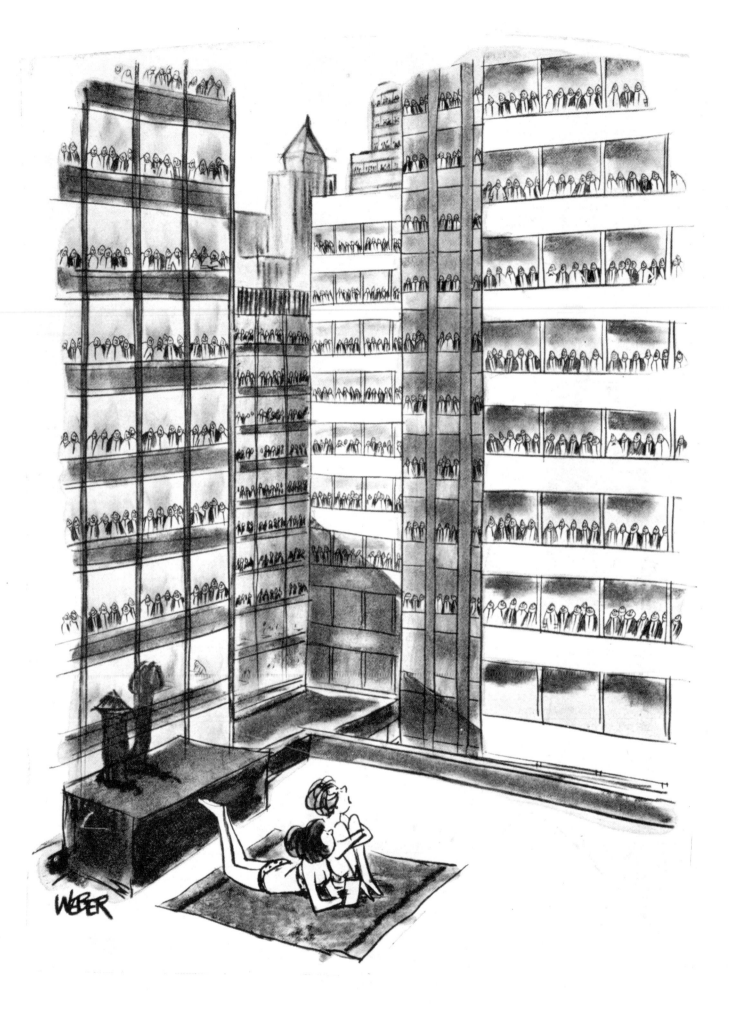

"Men are all alike."

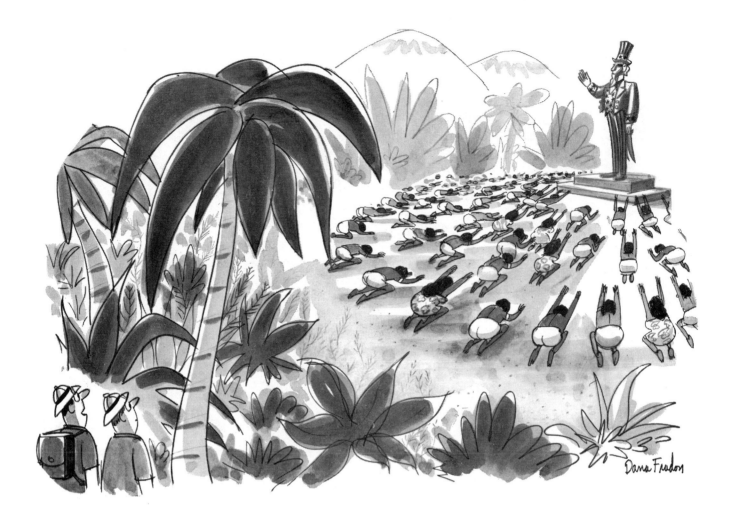

"*It seems the C.I.A. has not been inactive in this area.*"

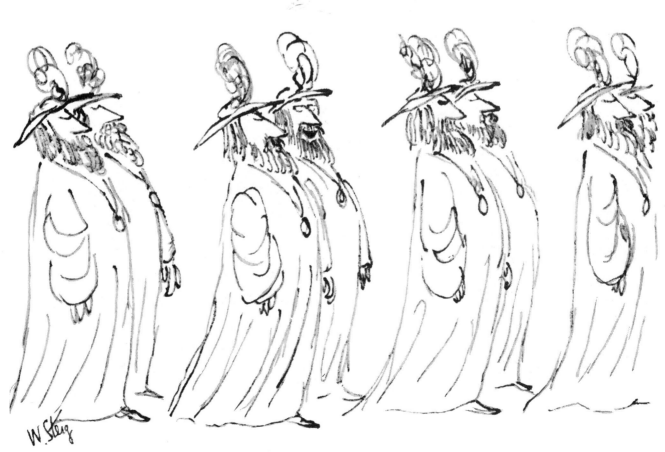

"*I love to walk in solemn procession.*"

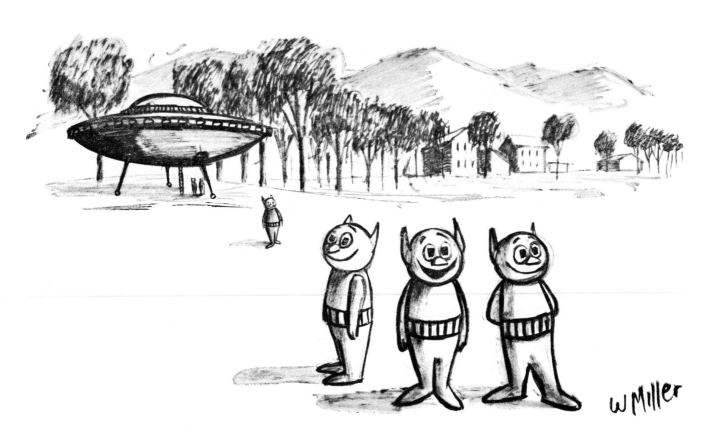

"My goodness, isn't this a pleasant planet!"

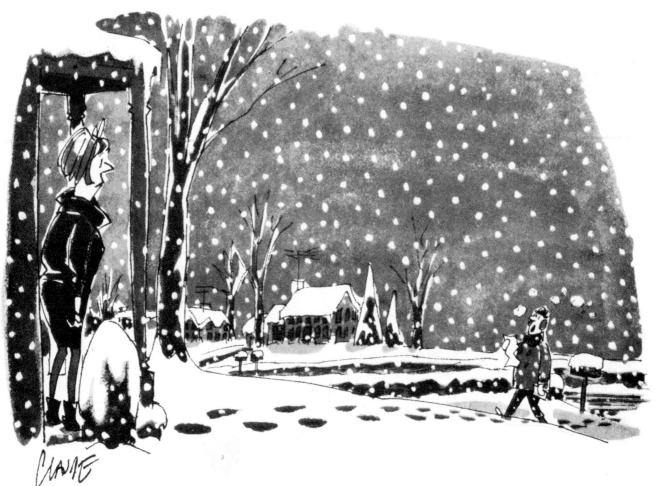

"It's nothing. Just another 'Great Publishing Achievement.'"

STEINBERG

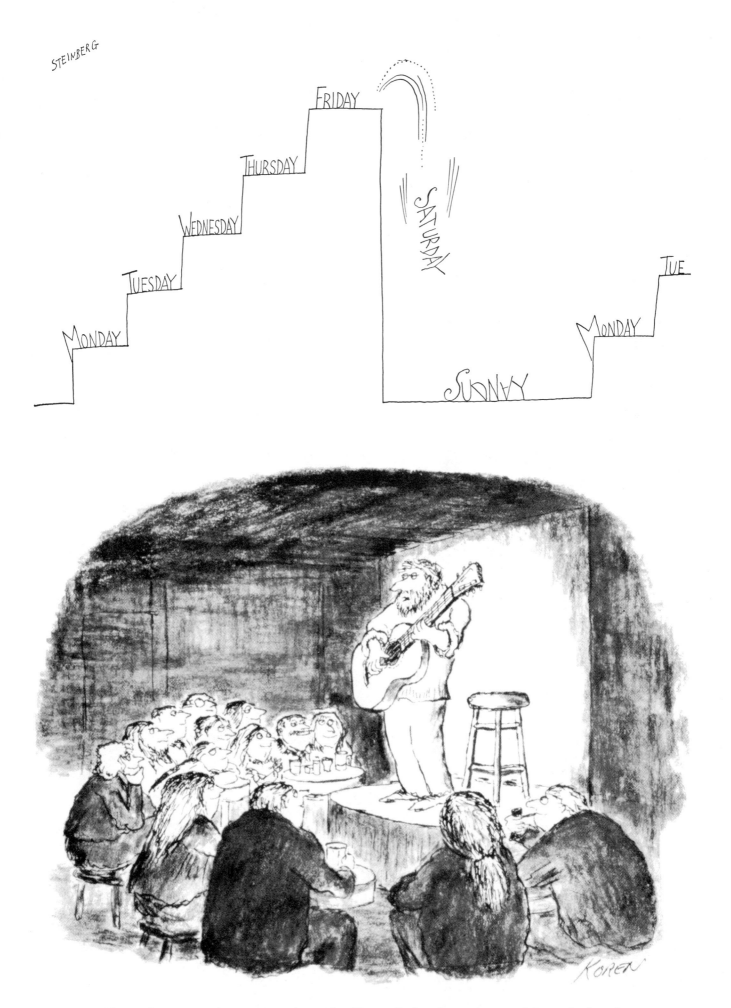

"Next I want to sing a song about the House Rules Committee and how the legislative functions of Congress are tyrannized over by its procedural calendar, dominated in turn by an all-powerful chairman hamstringing the processes of democracy."

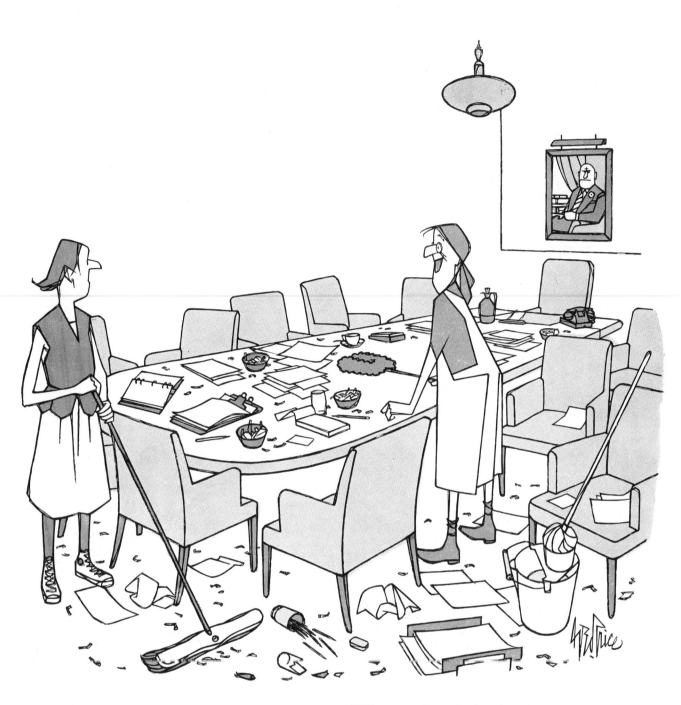

"The tumult and the shouting dies;
The captains and the kings depart."

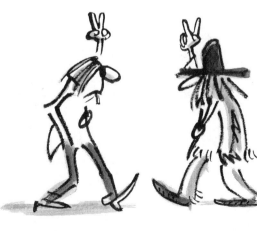

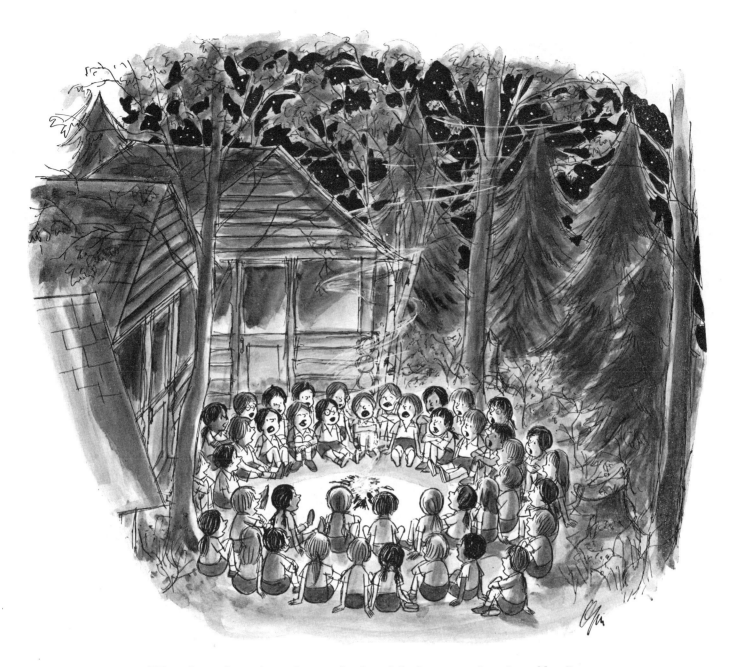

"To thee, first city of our land, with hearts and voices blending,
  We raise a loyal song of praise, with strains of love unending.
We praise thy harbor and thy ships, thy bay renowned for beauty,
  Thy parks with statues bravely decked to tell of faith and duty.
New York, New York, our city loved, to thee in praise we sing.
  Let every loyal heart and voice its loving tribute bring."

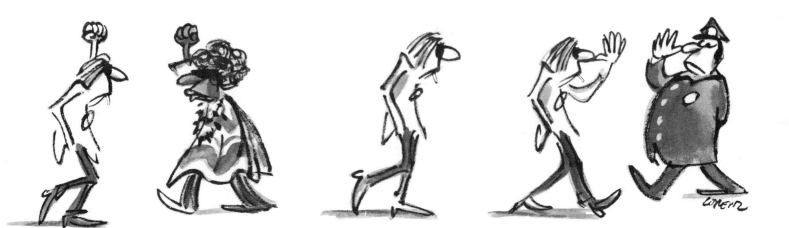

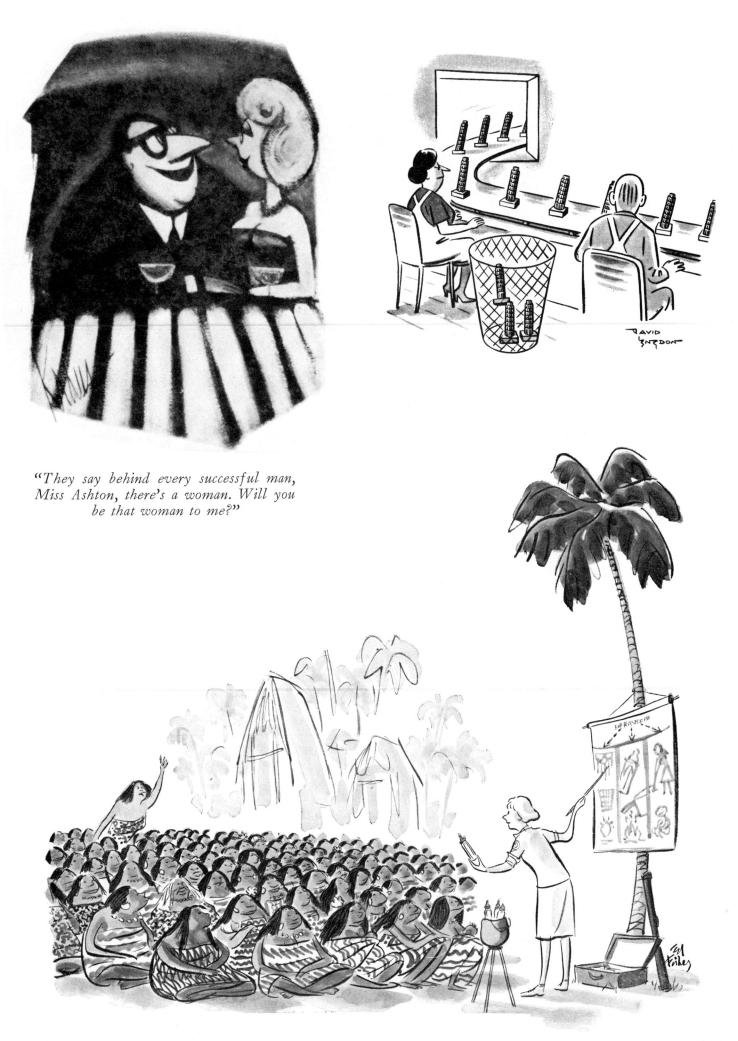

"They say behind every successful man, Miss Ashton, there's a woman. Will you be that woman to me?"

"What about us working mothers?"

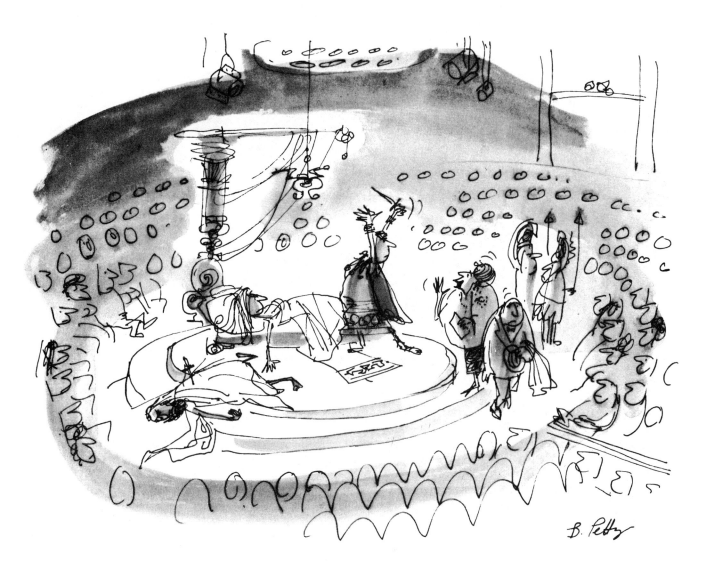

"Love to stay, but we have a sitter."

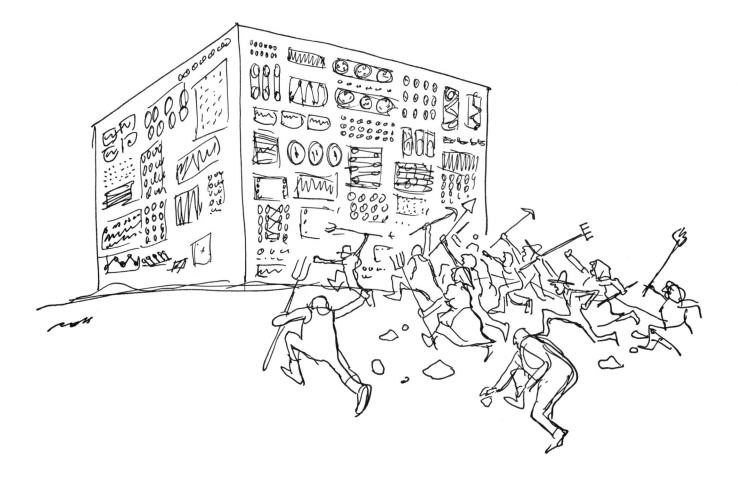

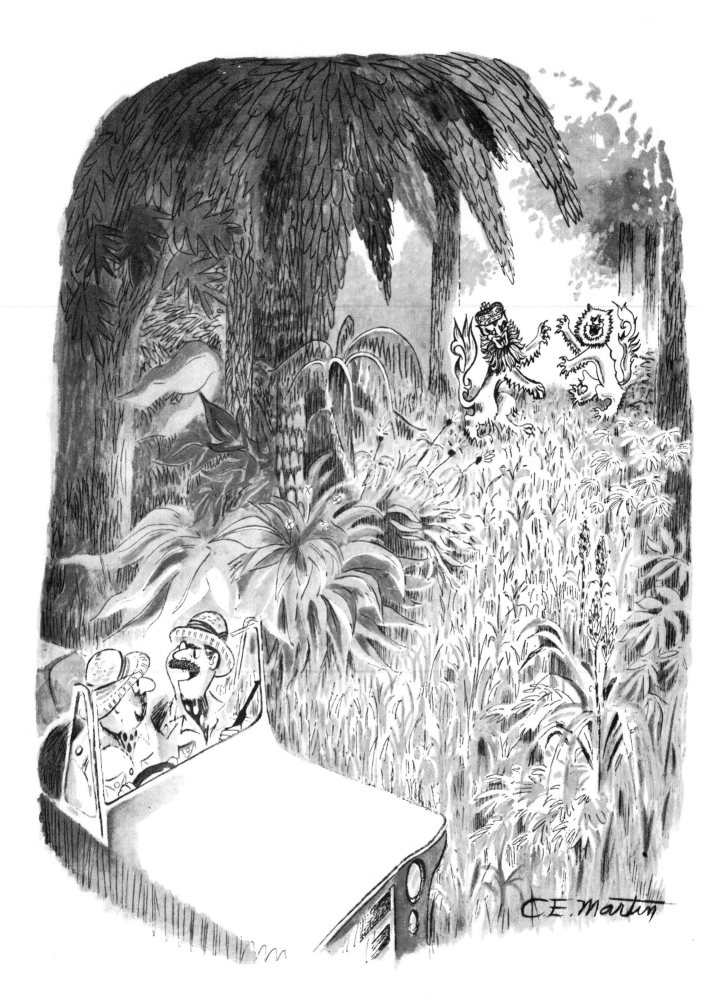

*"It's good to know, Colonel Snively, that there's one small
part of Africa that will be forever England."*

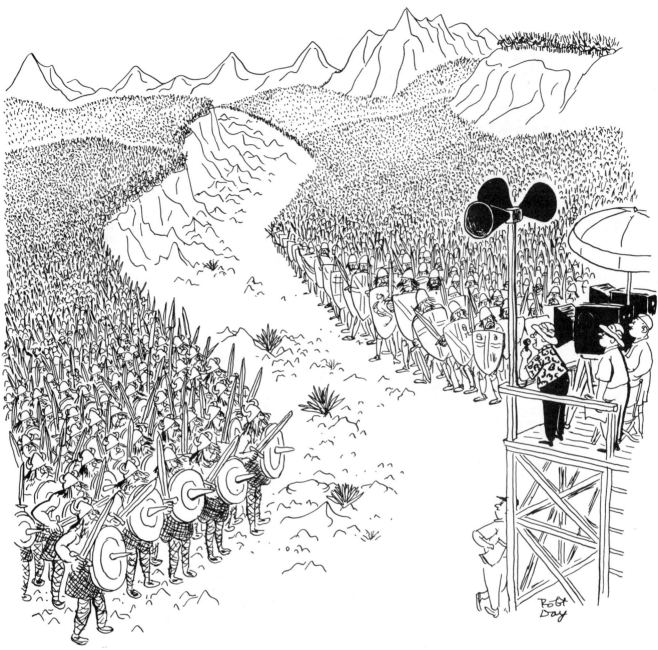

"I've been asked to remind you—please don't bend, fold, or mutilate your I.B.M. cards."

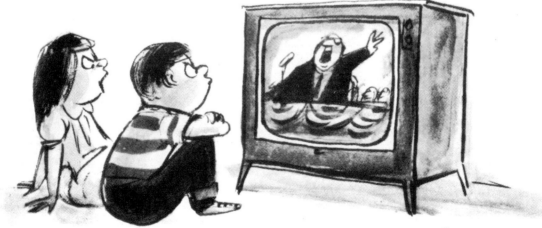

"For this they knocked off 'Wagon Train'?"

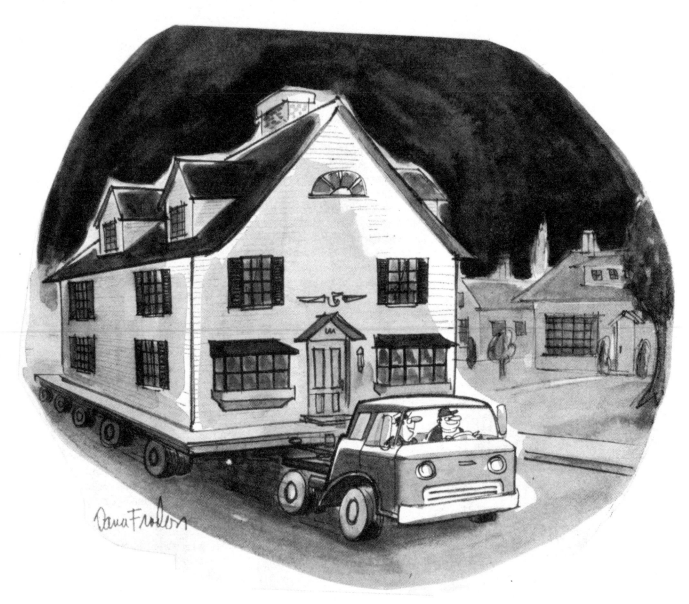

"If we pull this off, we've made burglary history!"

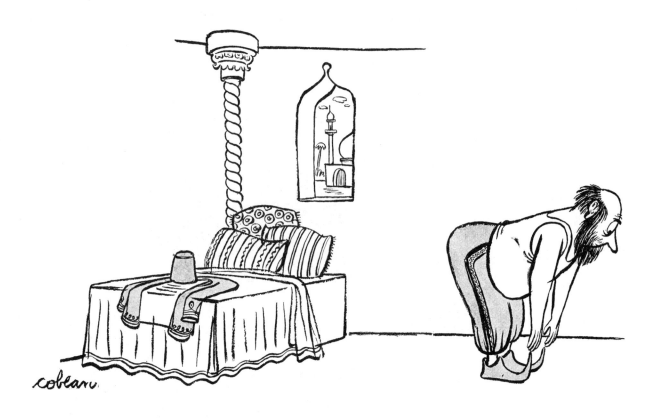

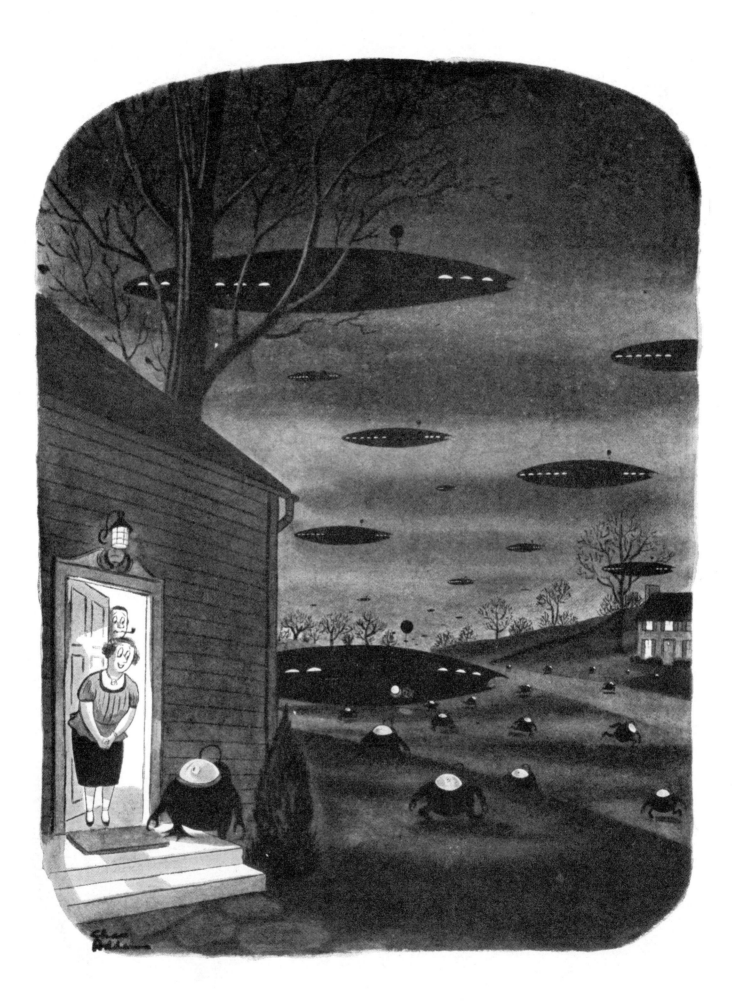

"I'm sorry, sonny. We've run out of candy."

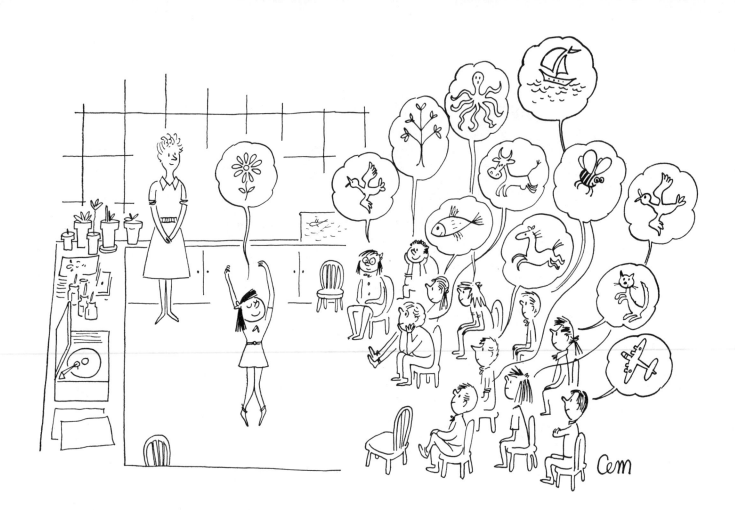

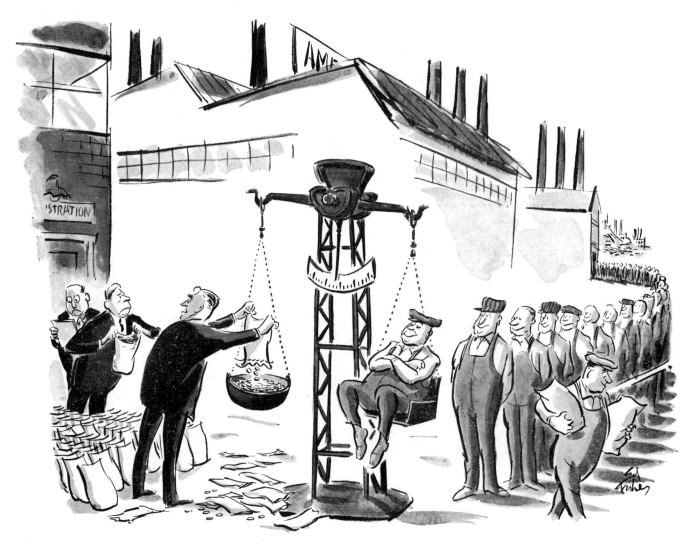

"I'm afraid this is going to play hell with the Presidential guidelines."

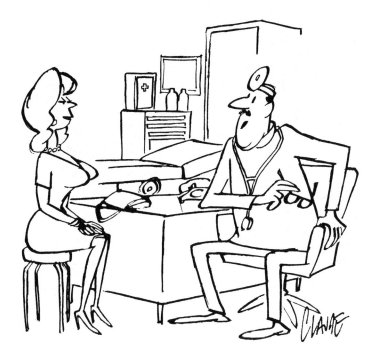

"To begin with, Miss Hughes, the human body is a gorgeous piece of machinery."

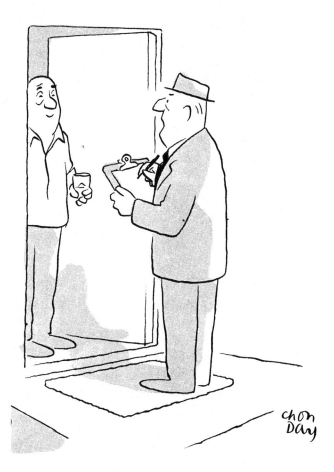

"Old Grand-Dad isn't running."

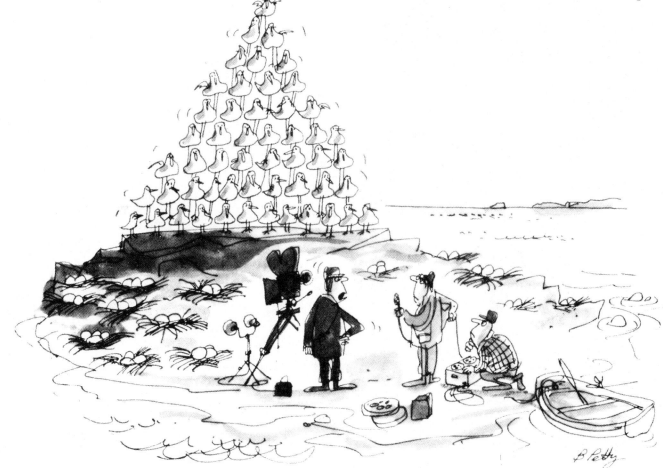

"Are you sure this species has never faced a camera before?"

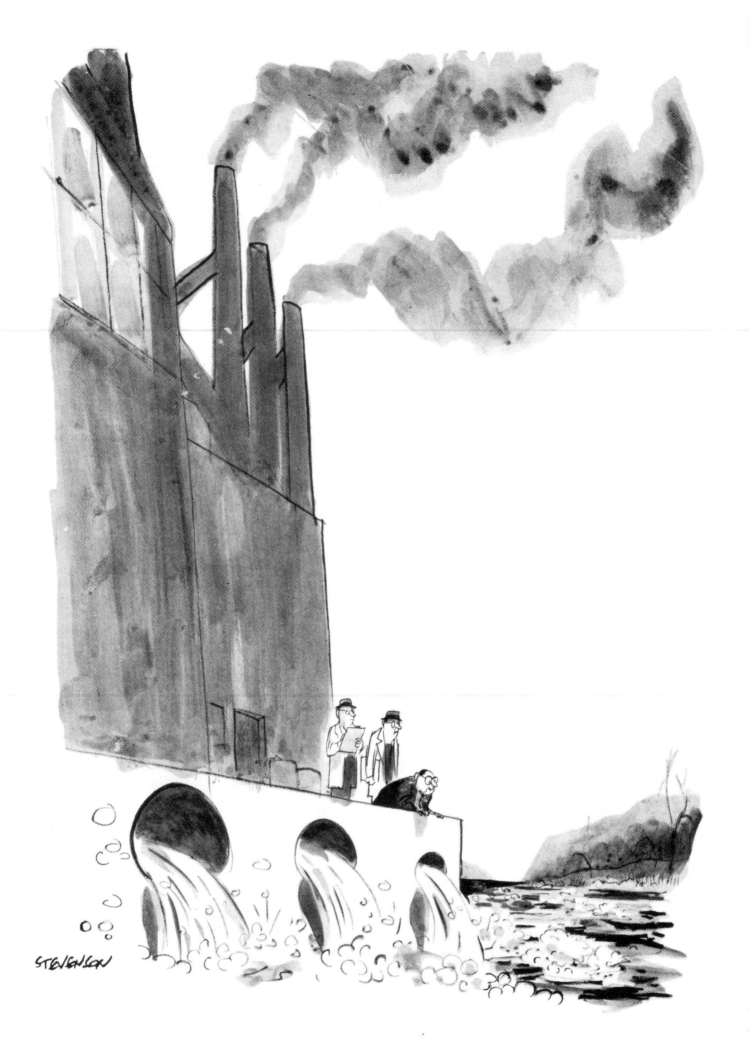

"So *that's* where it goes! Well, I'd like to thank you fellows for bringing this to my attention."

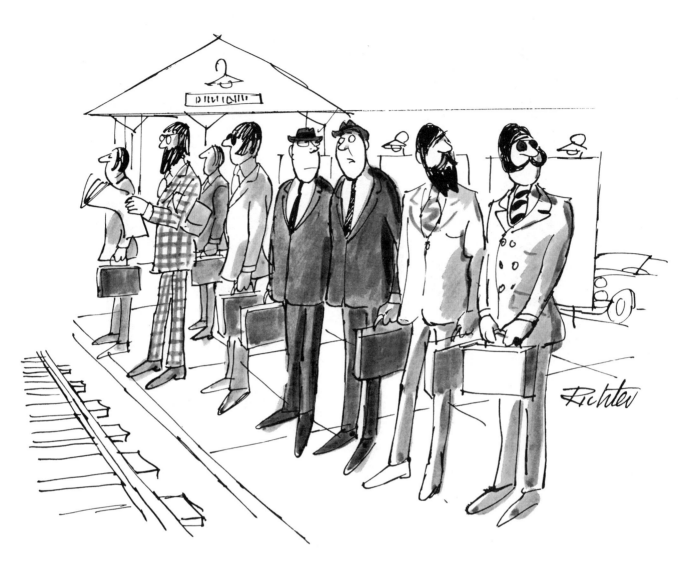

"I feel like a damn fool."

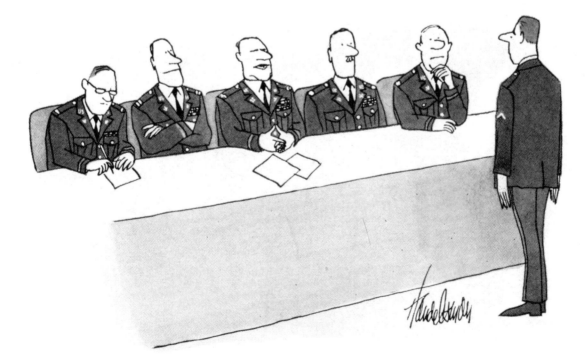

"Aren't you being a little arrogant, son? Here's Lieutenant Colonel Farrington, Major Stark, Captain Truelove, Lieutenant Castle, and myself, all older and more experienced than you, and we think the war is _very_ moral."

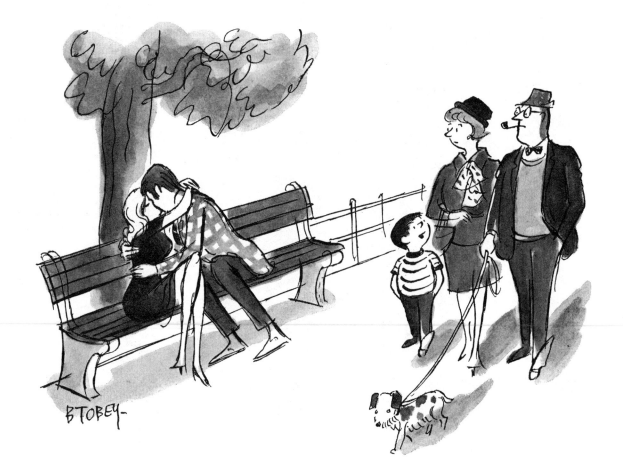

"We had that in school last week."

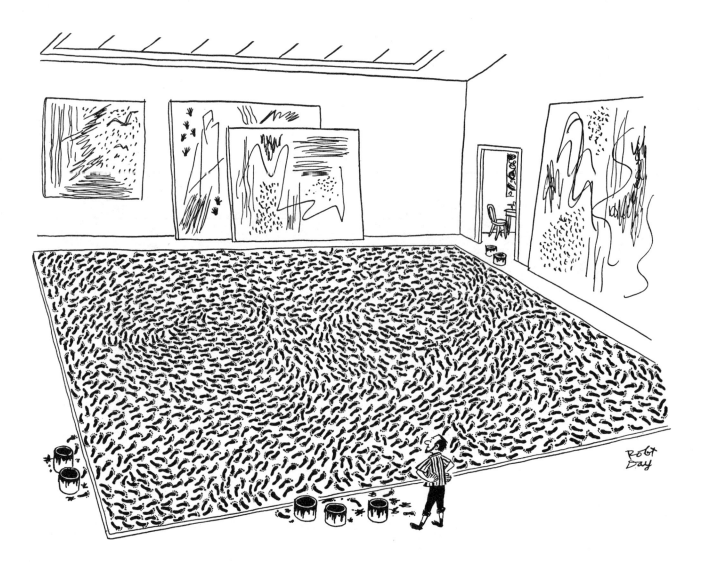

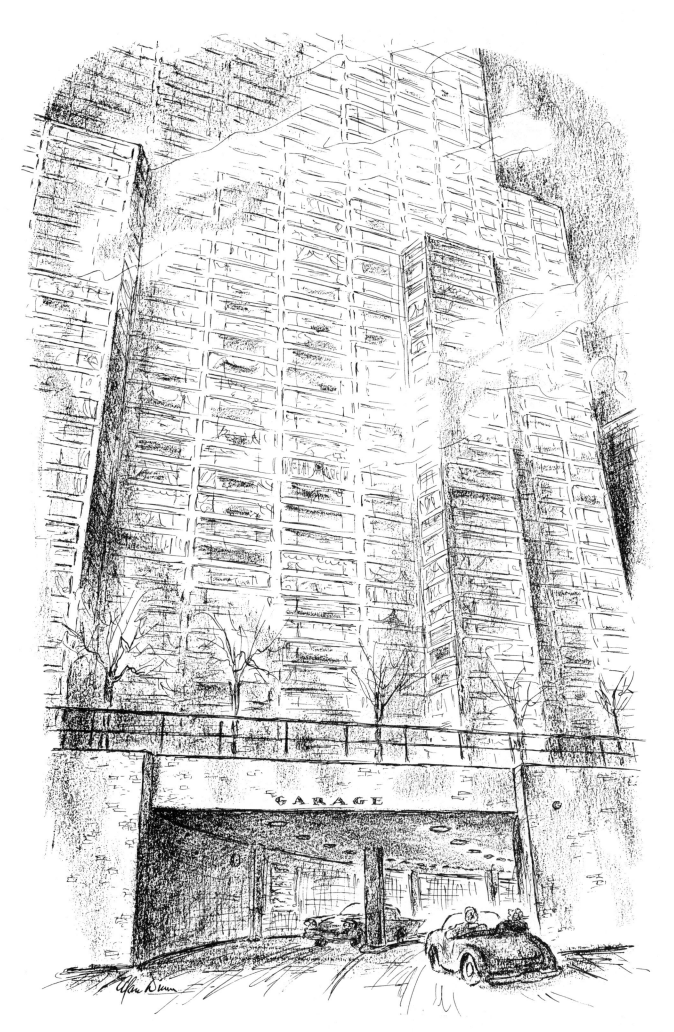

"It's good to get home!"

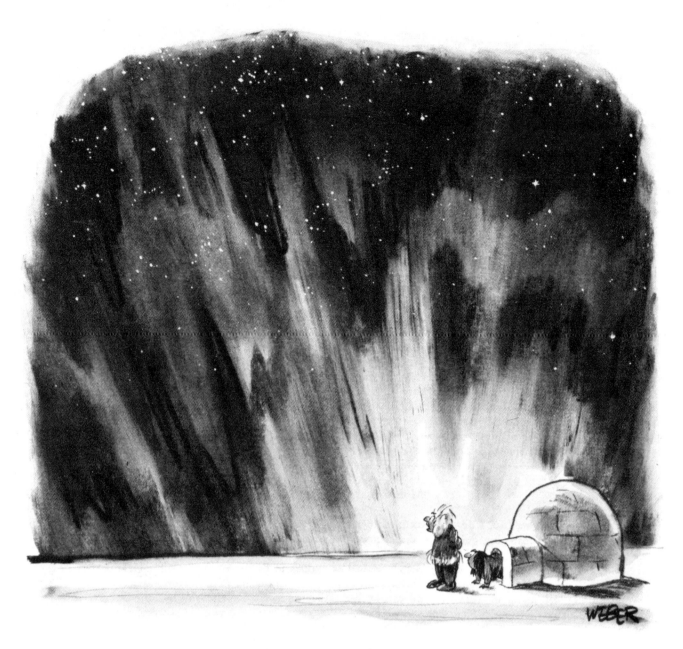

"Same old ice, same old aurora borealis, same old everything!"

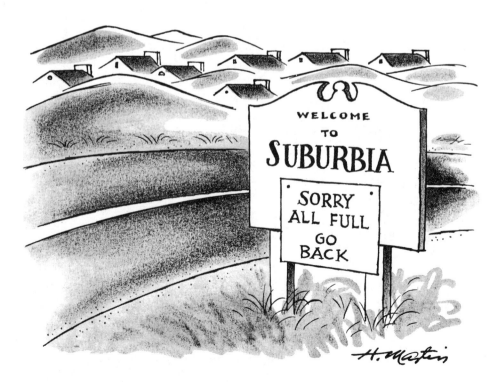

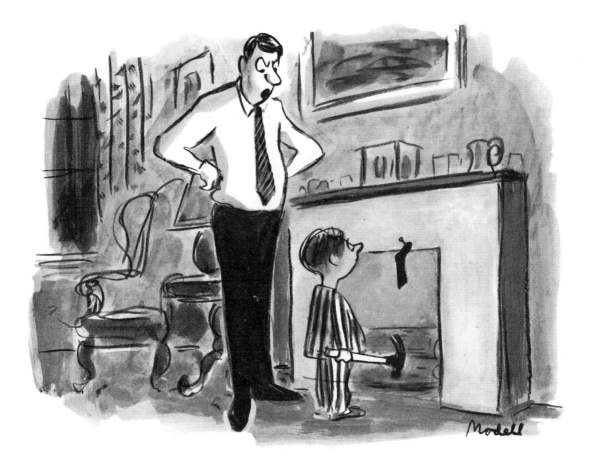

"You call that hung by the chimney with care?"

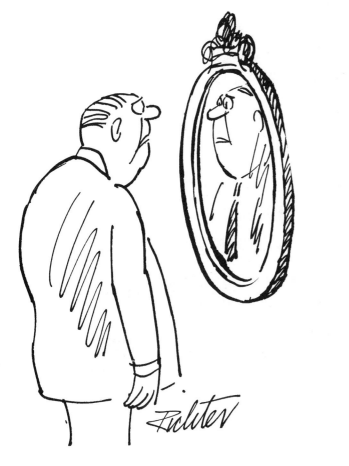

"You're predictable."

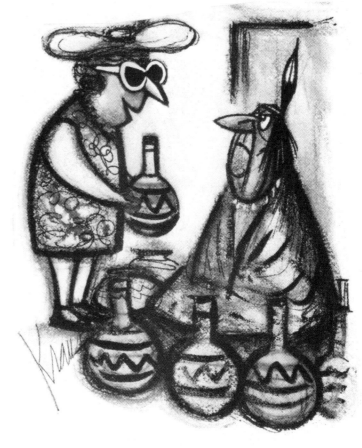

"Absorb the sales tax, and it's a deal."

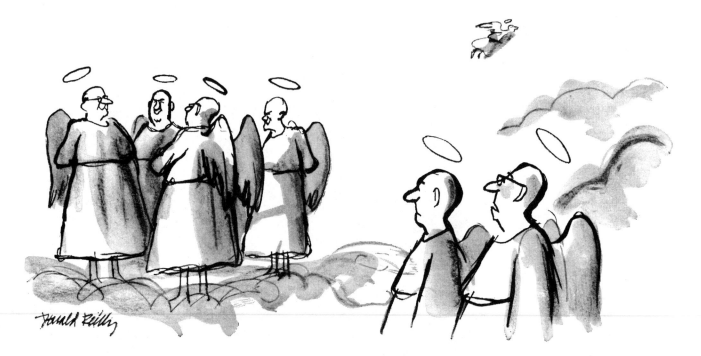

"You just can't talk to that bunch. They all avoided probate."

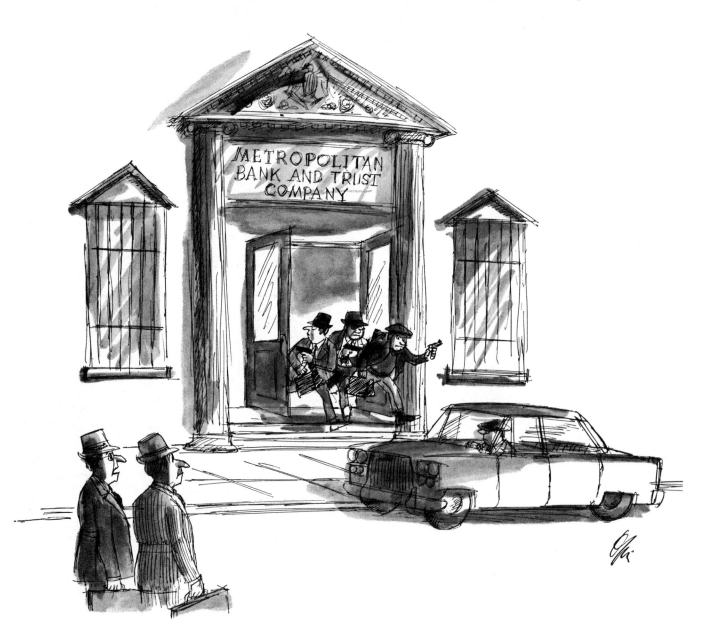

"It's nice to see _some_ people still appreciate the value of a dollar."

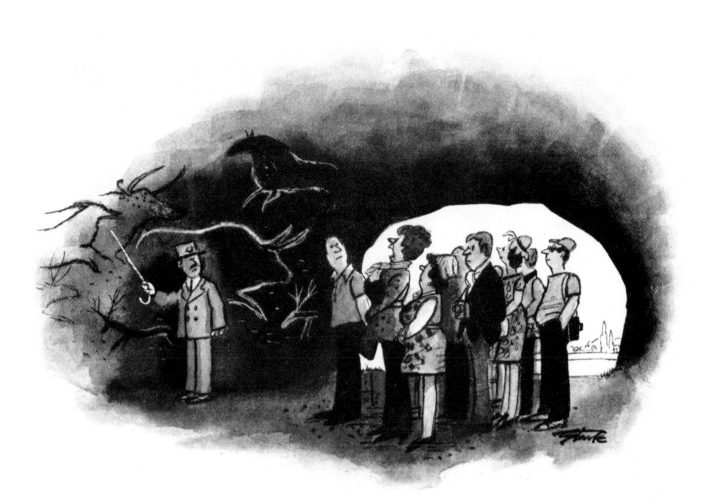

"*It's never occurred to you, I suppose, that they might have been done by a cave-_woman_.*"

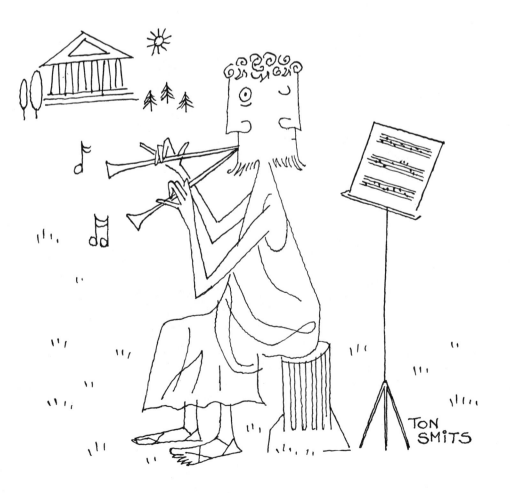

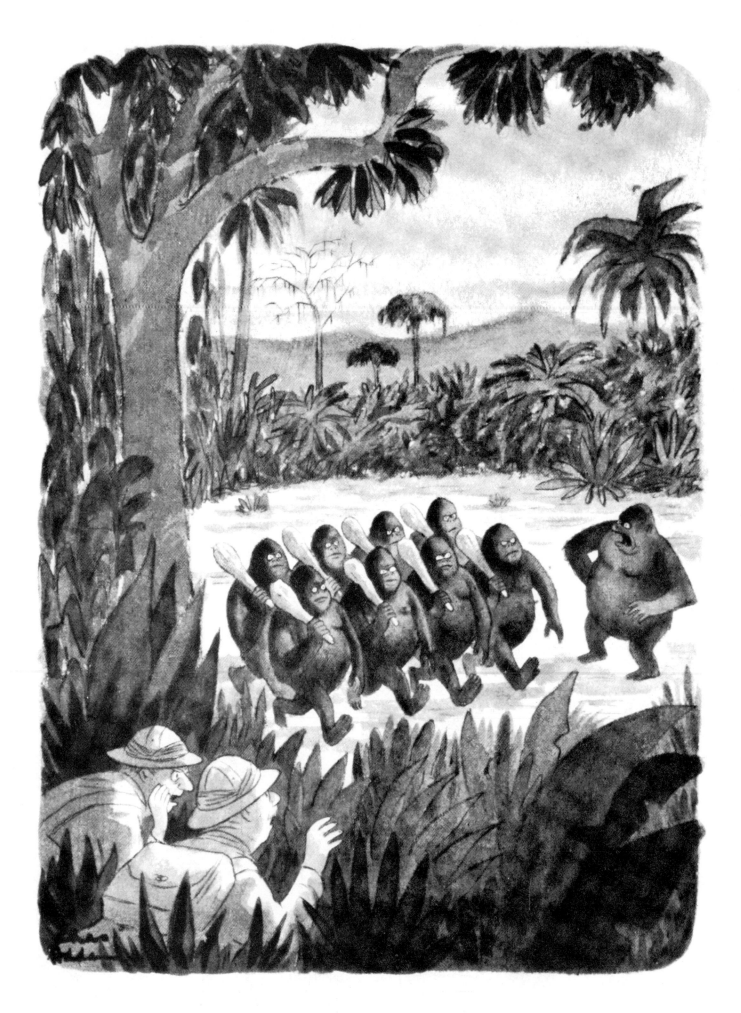

"Well, Kendrick, still think I'm just an alarmist?"

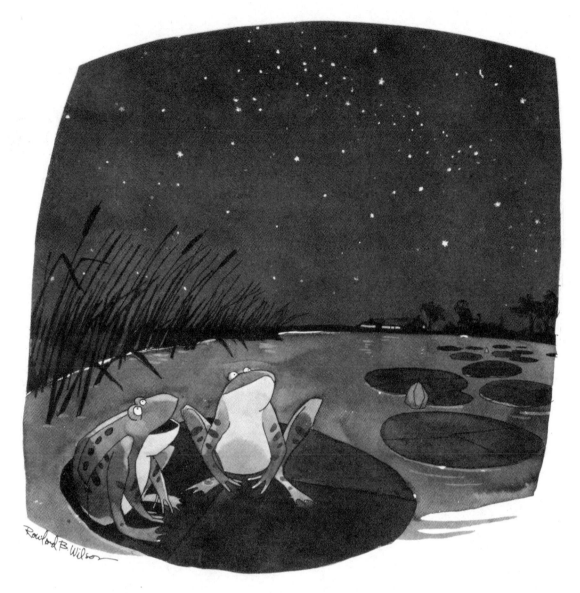

"Do you suppose there's any amphibious life up there?"

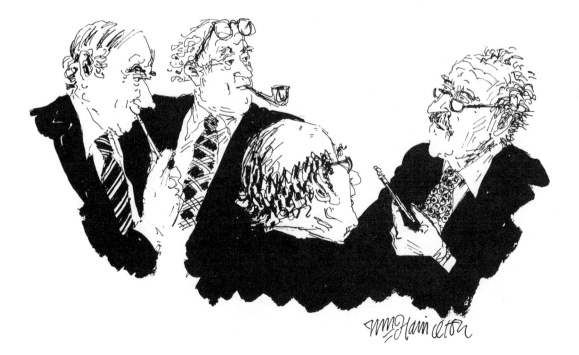

"Even in a think tank, Glebov, nobody likes a smart aleck."

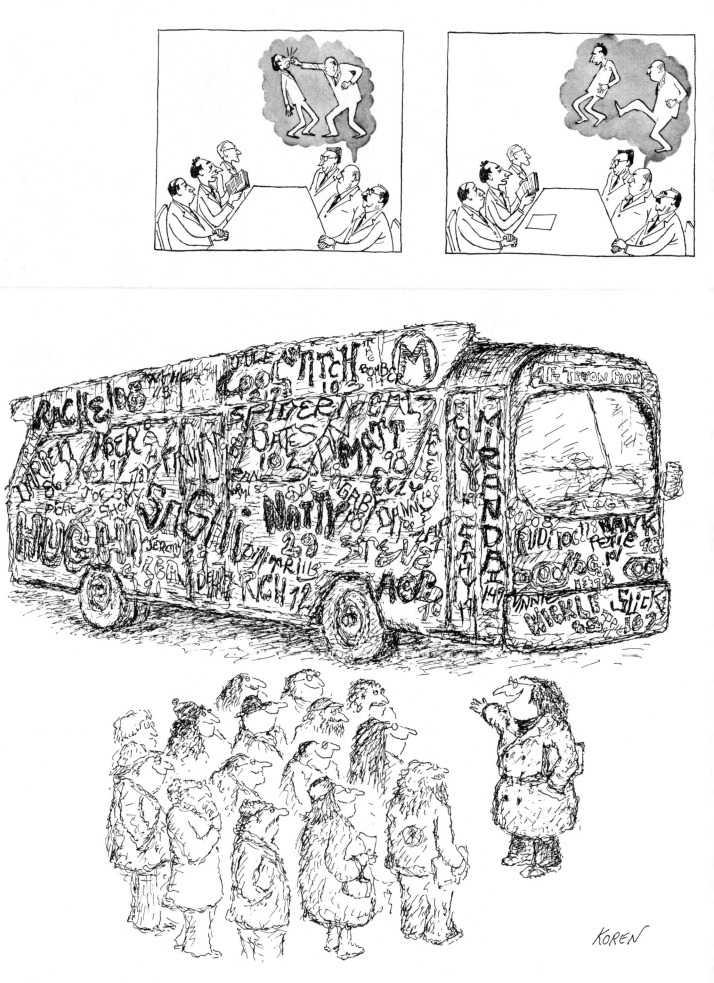

"Note the densely distributed, yet perfectly balanced, relationship between the expressive line and the organic whole—how unity of surface is achieved by overtly lyrical variations of scale, texture, and color, giving three-dimensional form a spontaneous, plastically graphic definition."

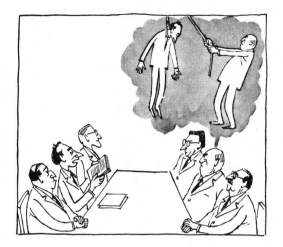

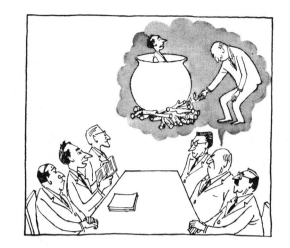

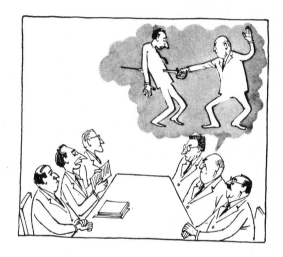

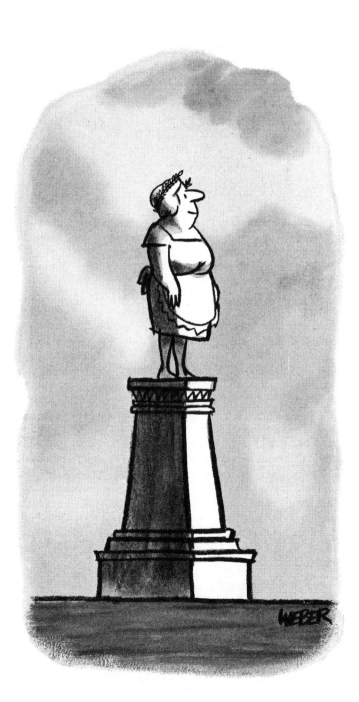

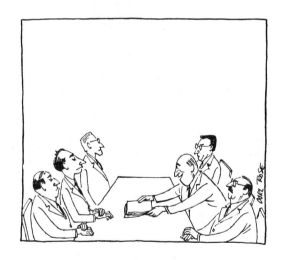

"The Corporation appreciates the clear and cogent outline of your union's demands and promises to give it the most serious consideration. May I suggest that we set a date for our next meeting that will give us enough time to formulate counterproposals?"

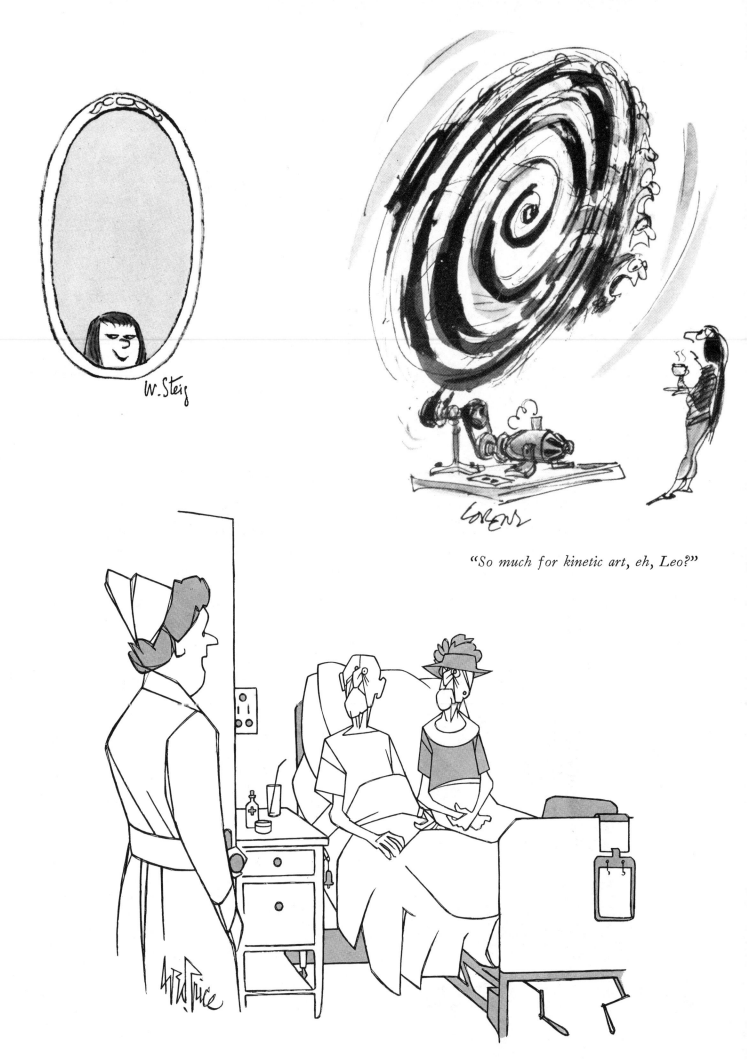

W. Steig

LORENZ

"So much for kinetic art, eh, Leo?"

"Visiting hours are over, Mrs. Glenhorn."

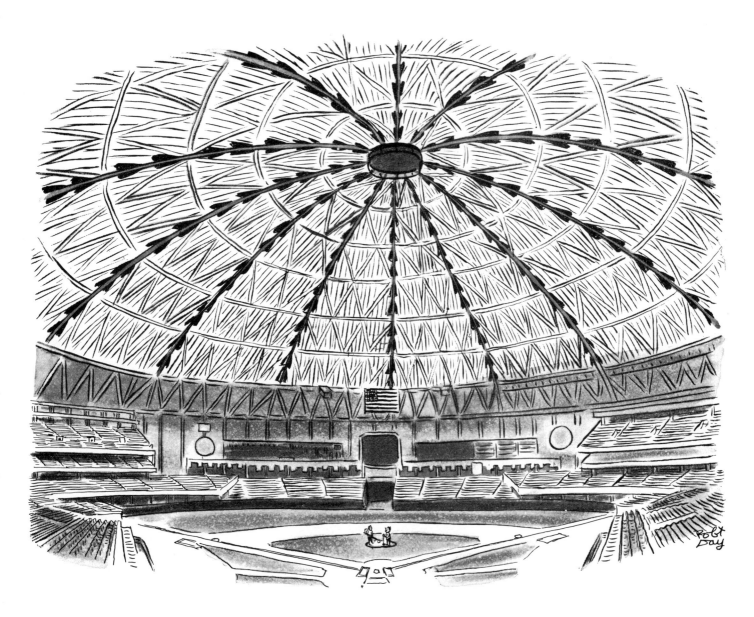

"Do you know what I like? The patter of the rain on the roof."

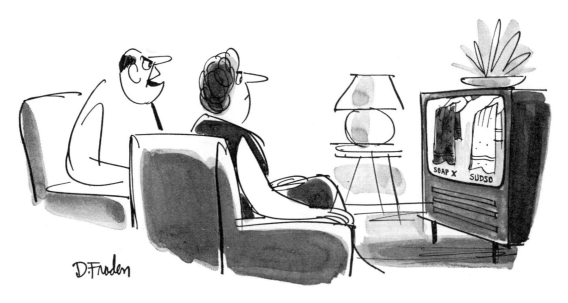

"Have they no shame?"

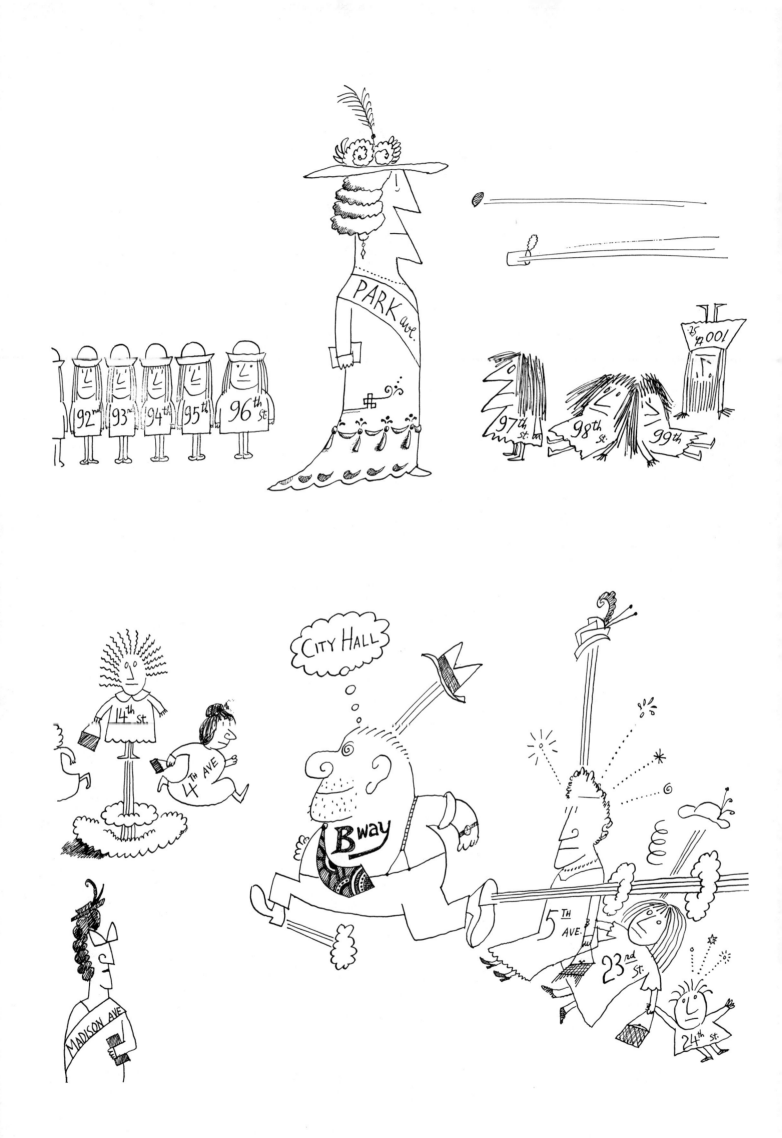

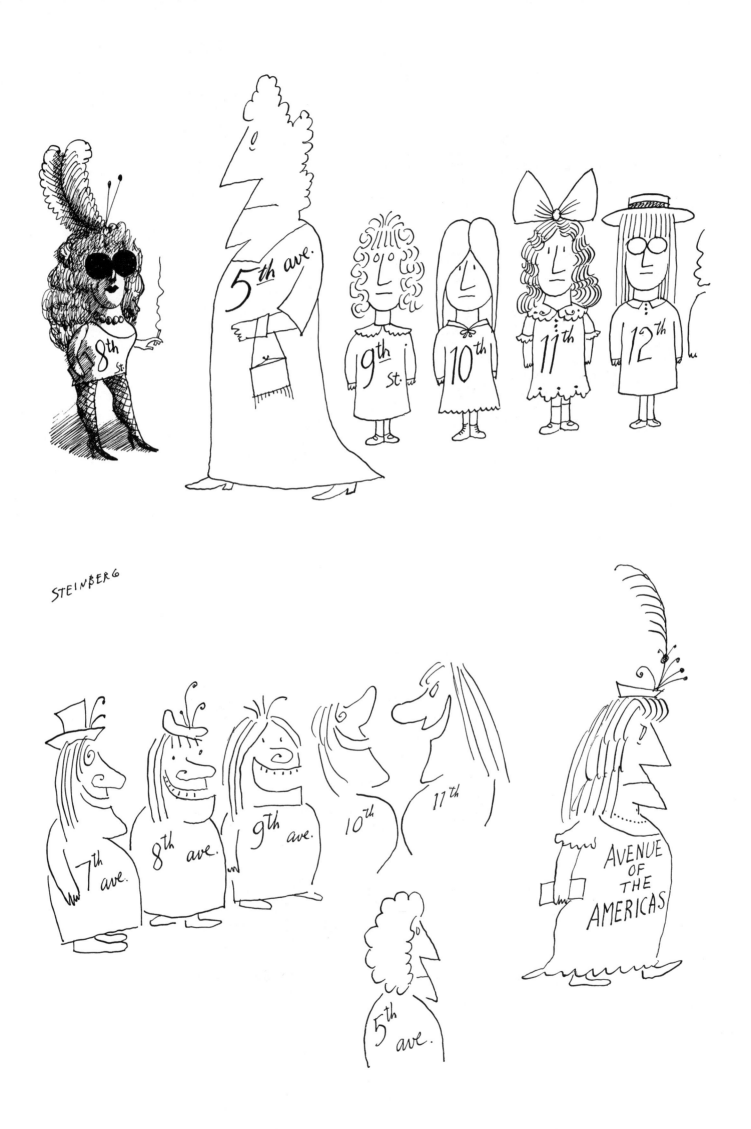

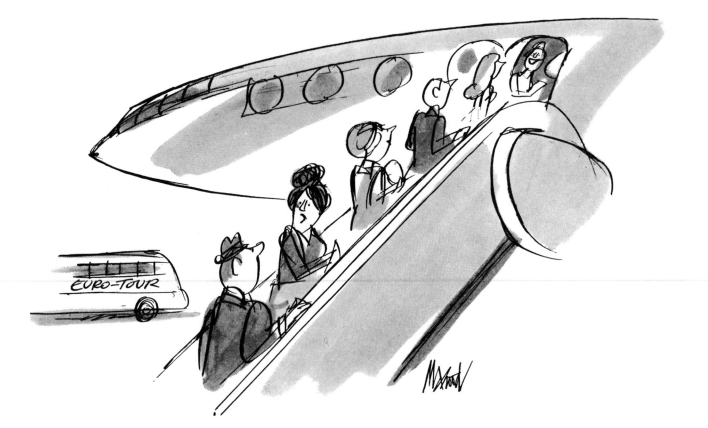

"I hope we get home without a hijack. I don't think I could stand one more country."

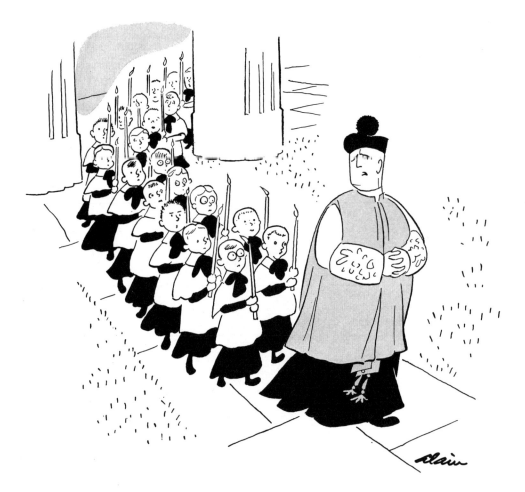

"All right, who has the transistor?"

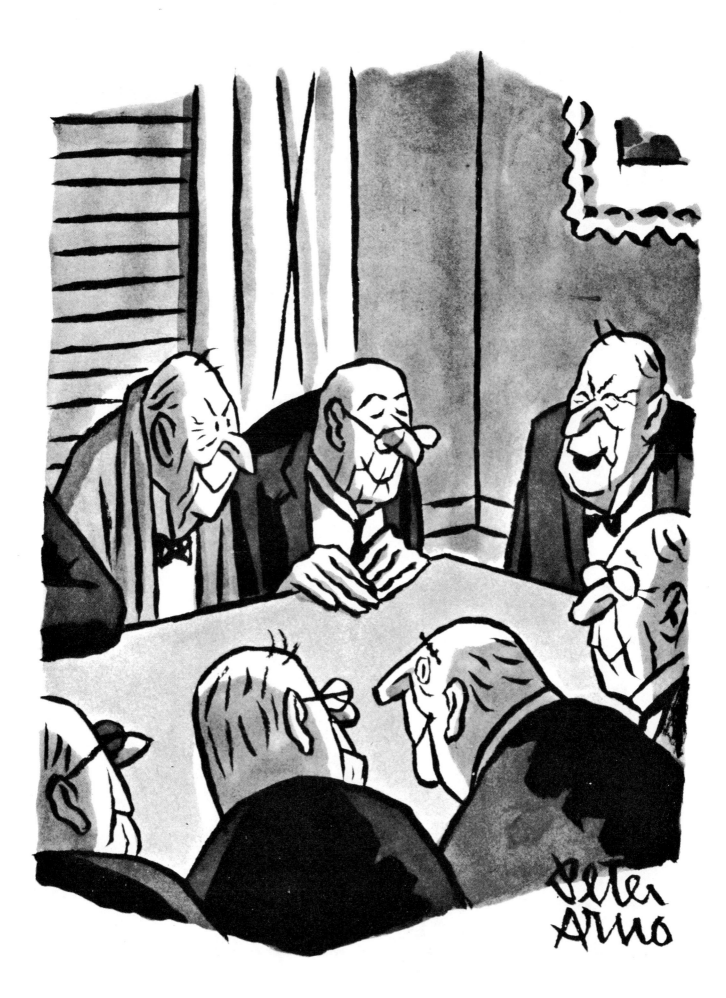

"Then it's moved and seconded that
the compulsory retirement age be advanced to ninety-five."

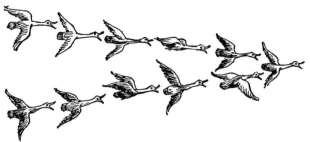

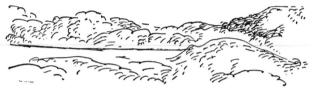

"Honk, honk, honk, honk, honk, honk, honk,

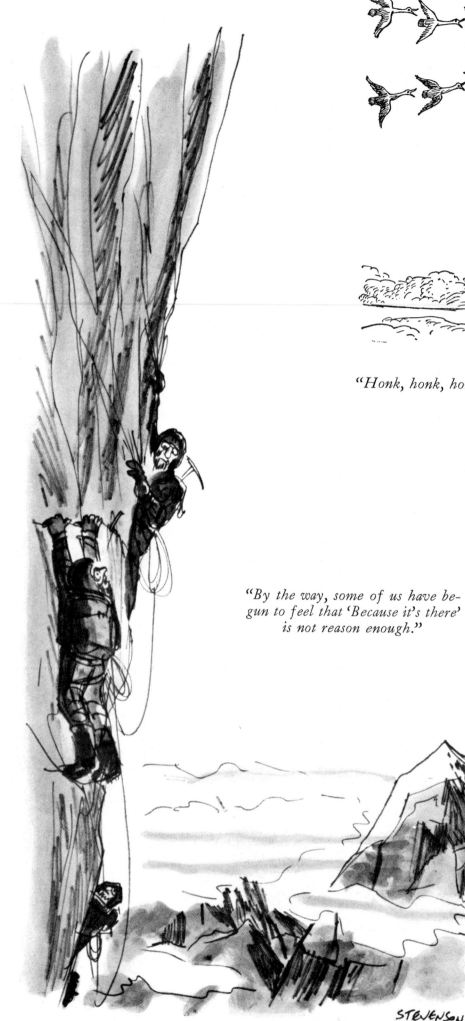

"By the way, some of us have begun to feel that 'Because it's there' is not reason enough."

STEVENSON

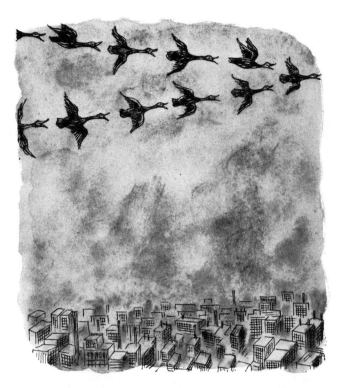

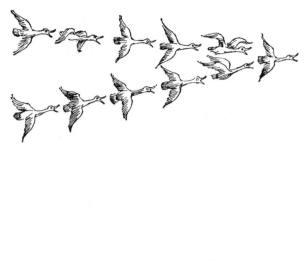

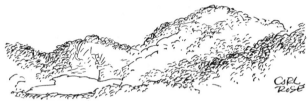

cough, cough, cough, cough, cough, cough, cough,

honk, honk, honk, honk, honk, honk, honk."

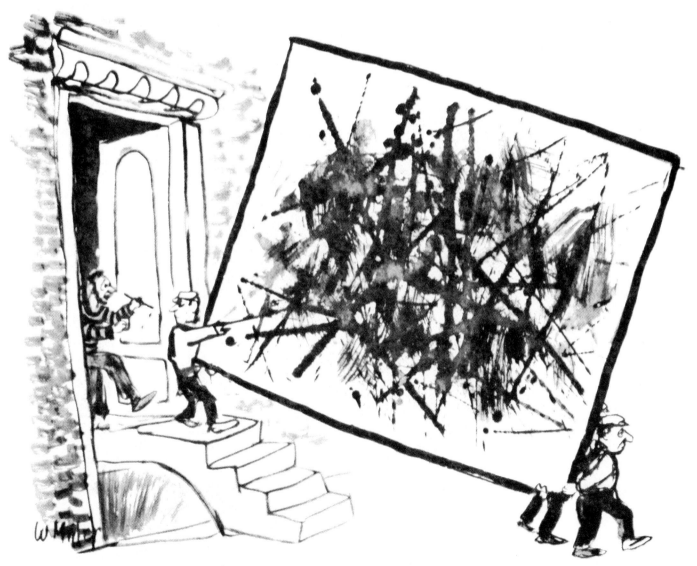

"Wait! I forgot my John Hancock!"

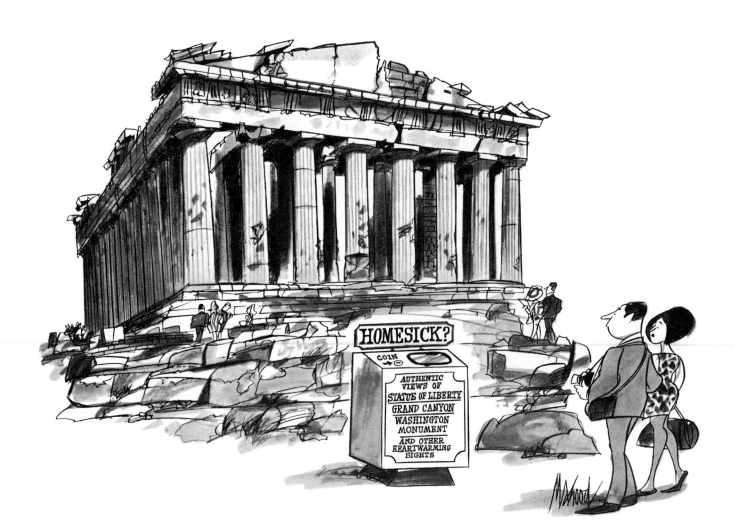

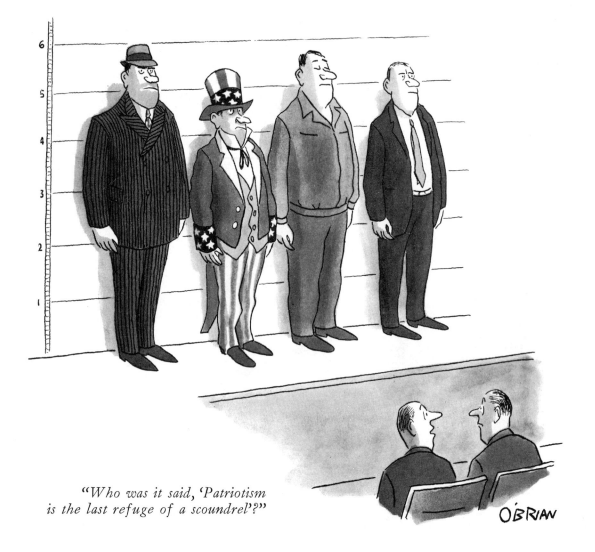

"Who was it said, 'Patriotism is the last refuge of a scoundrel'?"

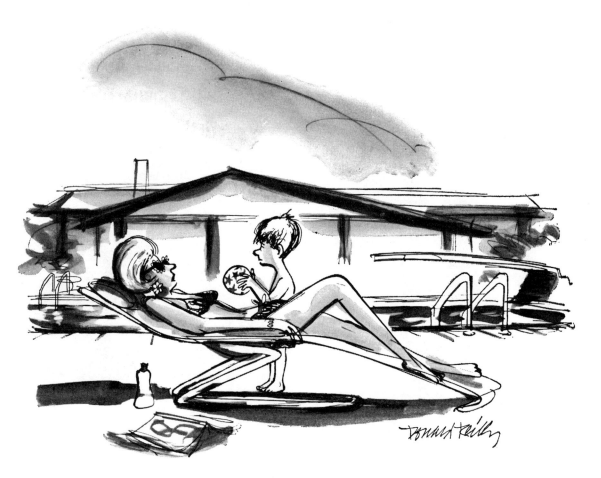

"Children with heated pools are no better than you are."

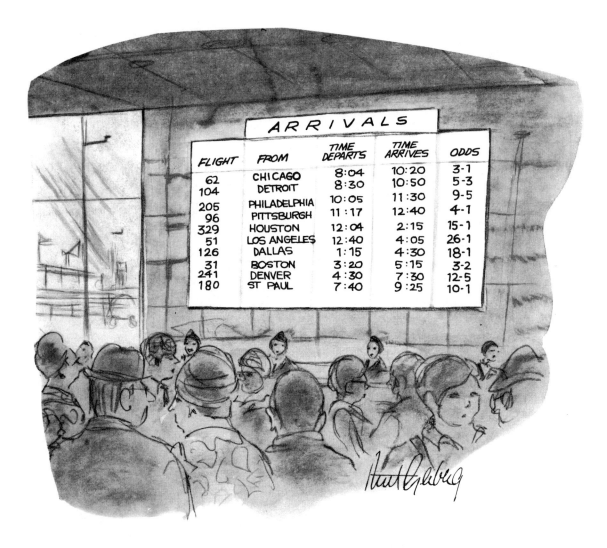

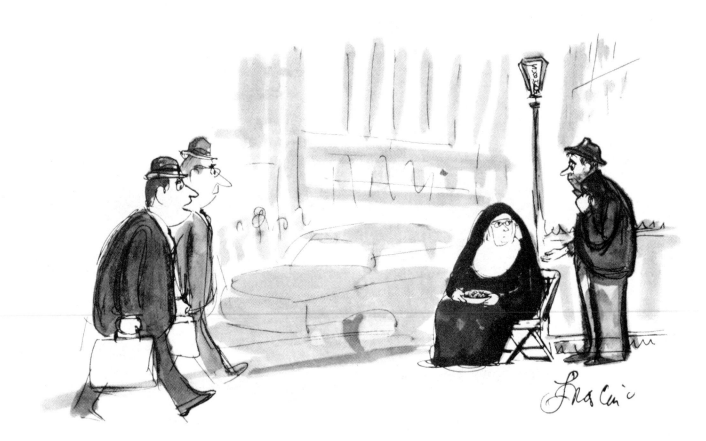

"That's what I call chutzpah."

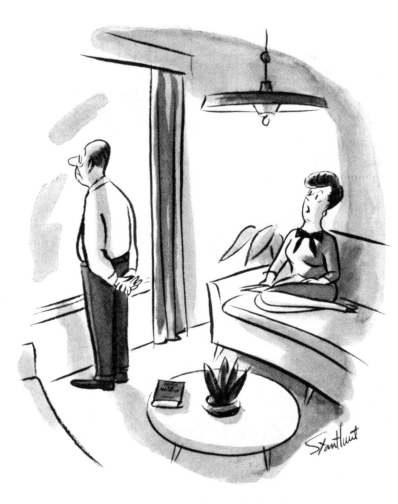

*"What I don't understand is what ever
prompted you to buy a book called 'Being
and Nothingness' in the first place."*

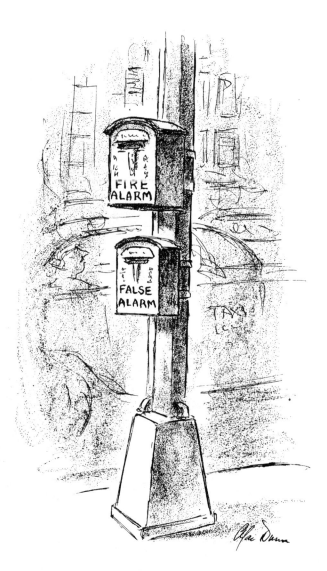

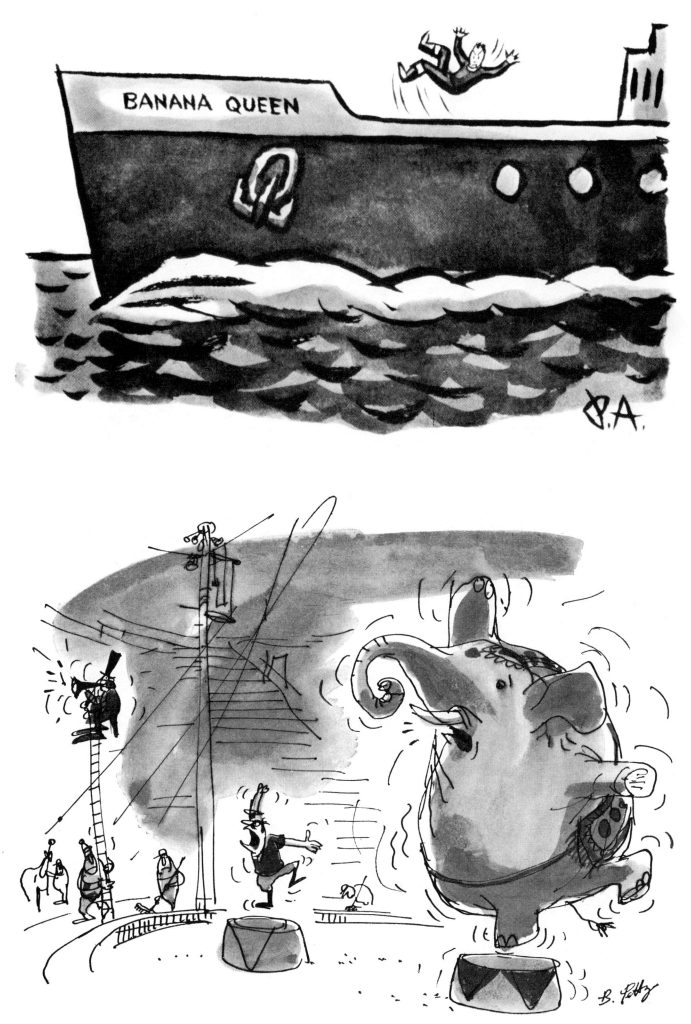

"Can't you see I'm trying to train an elephant?"

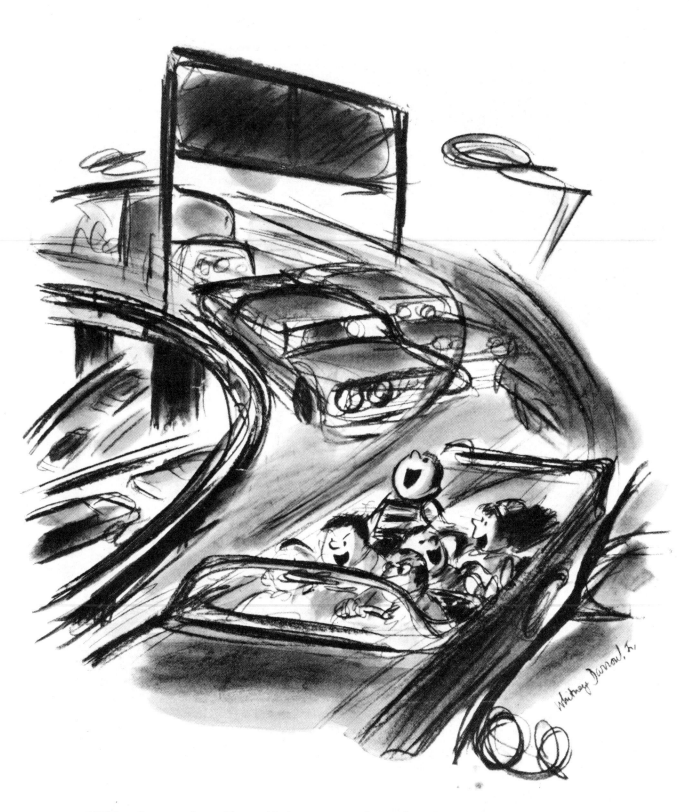

"*The Connecticut Turnpike's connected to the New York Thruway,
The Thruway's connected to the Garden State Parkway,
The Garden State's connected to the New Jersey Turnpike,
The Jersey Turnpike's connected to the Pennsylvania Turnpike . . .*"

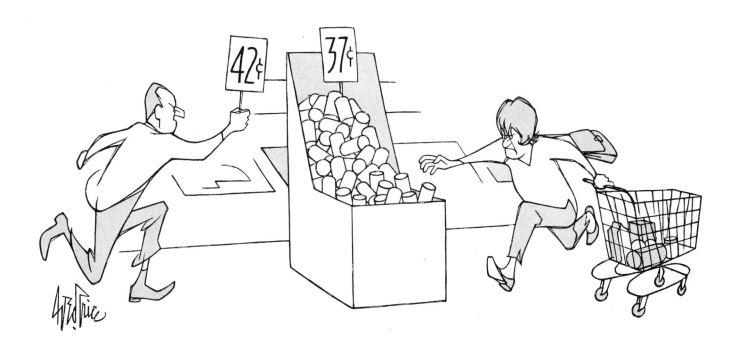

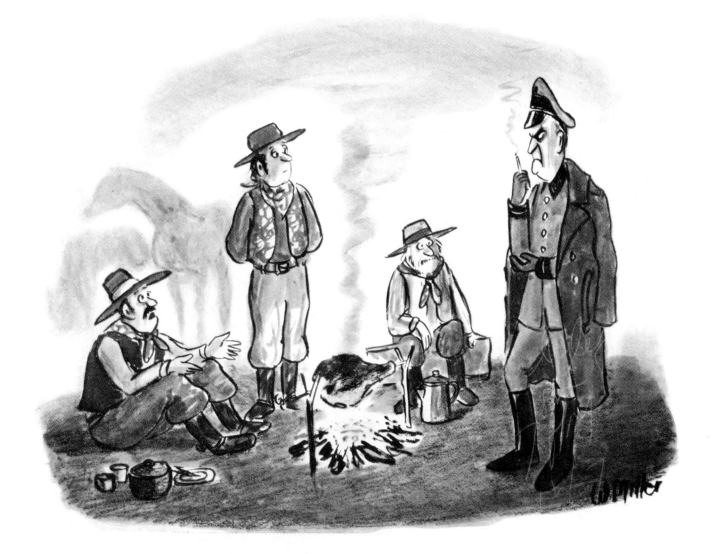

*"No offense intended, José. We were only wondering why you
never dress like the rest of us gauchos."*

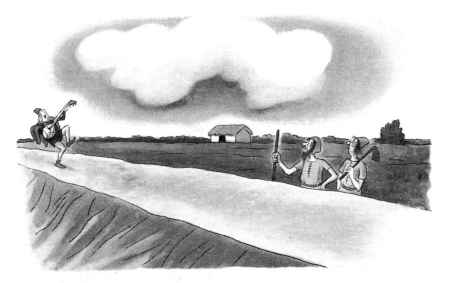

"Sumer is icumen in,
Lhude sing cuccu!
Groweth sed, and bloweth med,
And springeth the wude nu—
          Sing cuccu!"

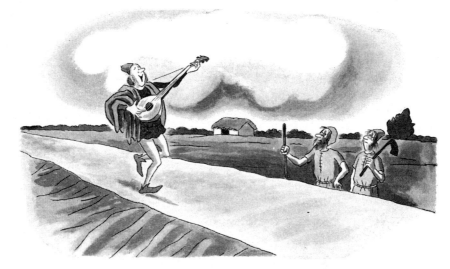

"Cuccu, cuccu, well singes thu, cuccu:
Ne swike thu naver nu;
Sing cuccu, nu, sing cuccu,
Sing cuccu, sing cuccu, nu!"

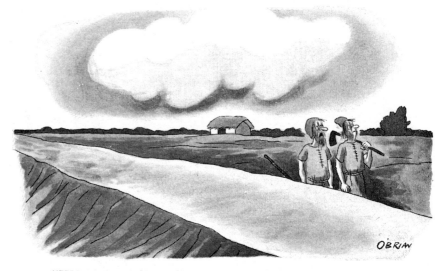

"What the hell do you suppose _that_ was all about?"

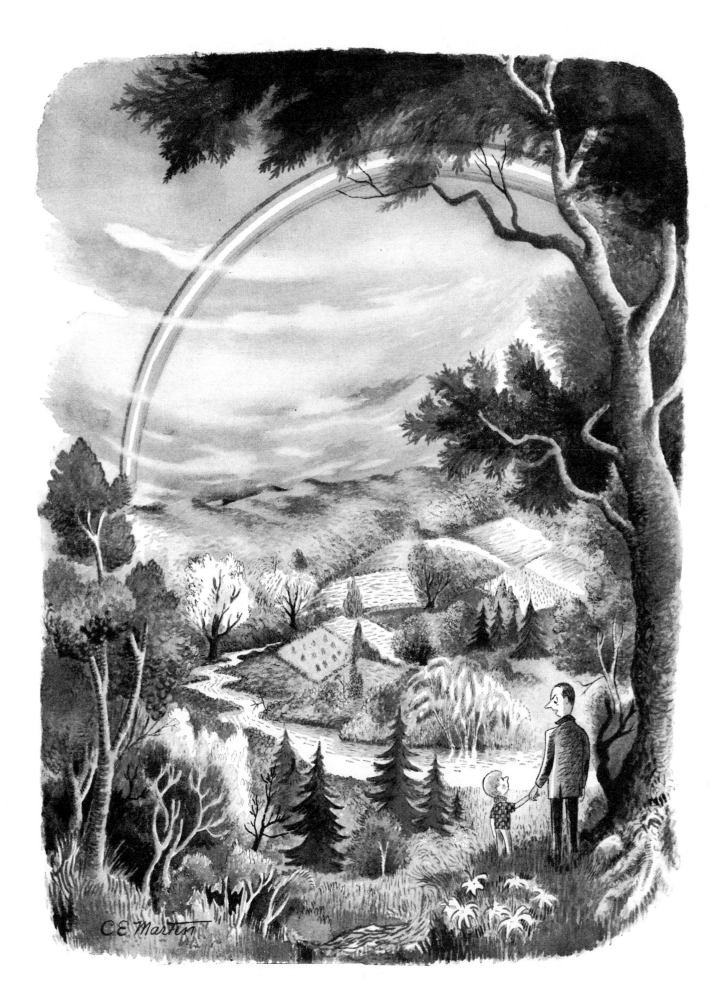

"It's not advertising anything, damn it!"

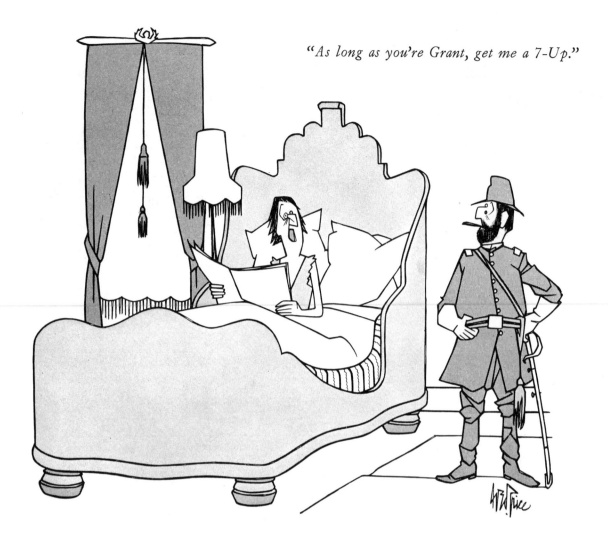

"As long as you're Grant, get me a 7-Up."

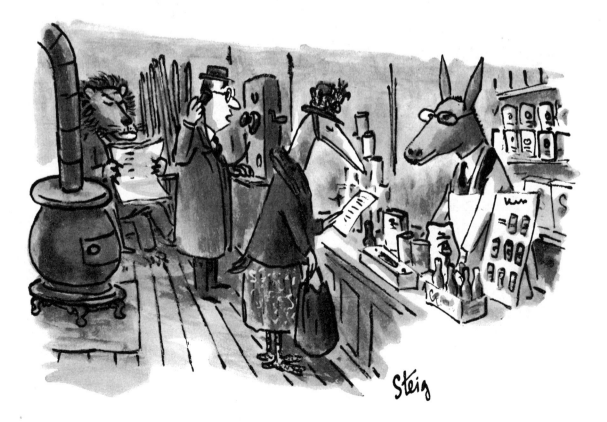

"Nobody here seems to know how I can get back on Route 22."

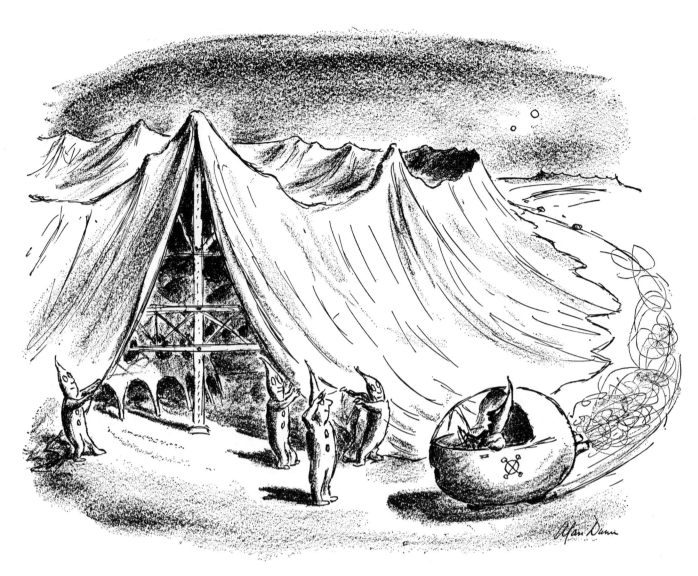

"*All right, men, you can take down those craters now.*"

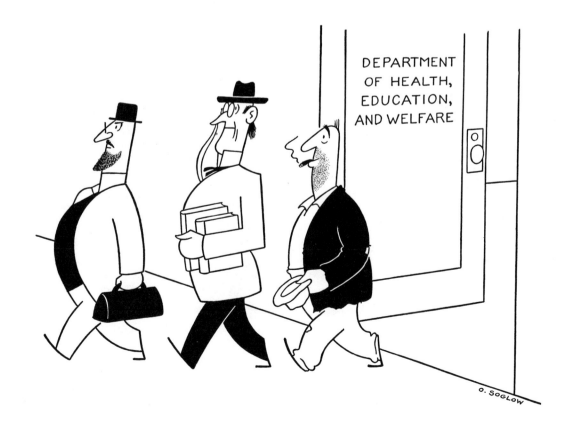

DEPARTMENT
OF HEALTH,
EDUCATION,
AND WELFARE

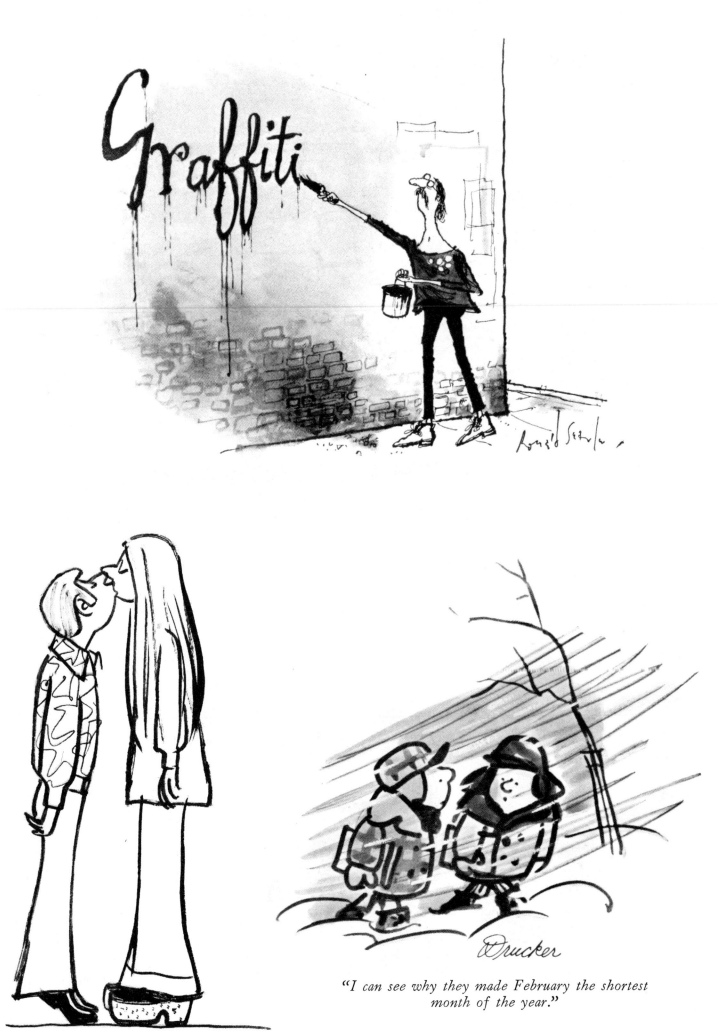

"I can see why they made February the shortest
month of the year."

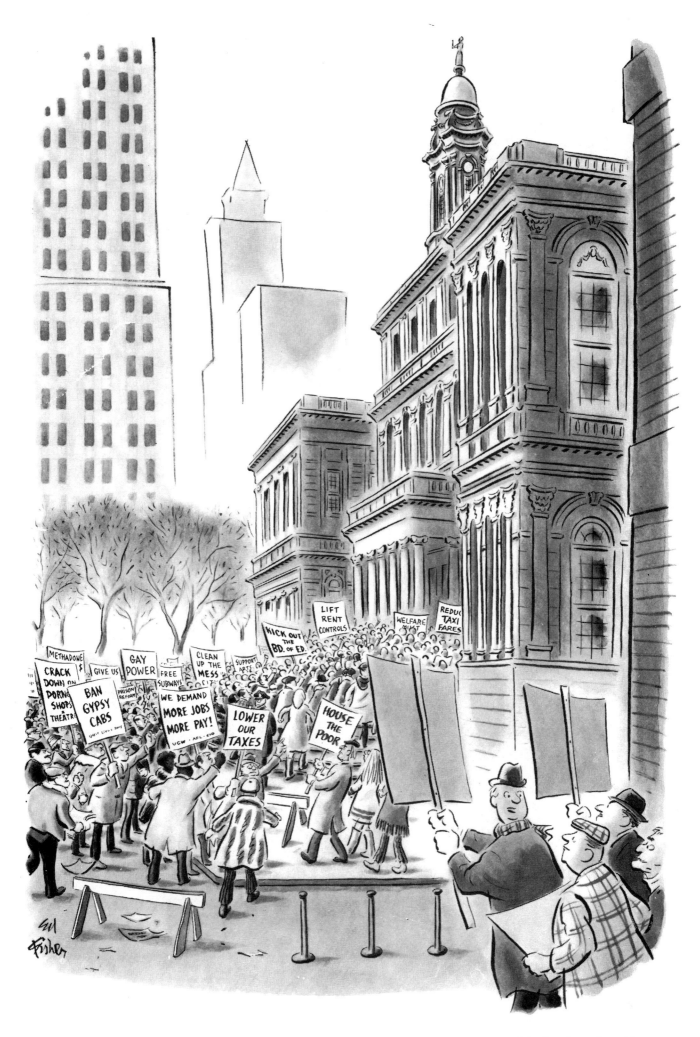

"*Come on, you guys! This is the place.*"

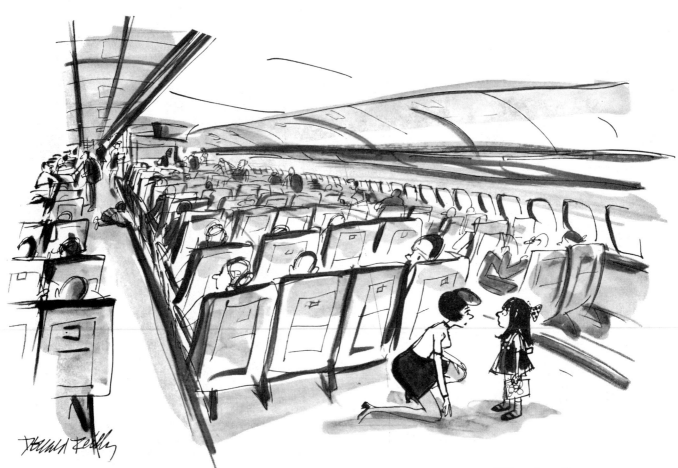

"I'm lost."

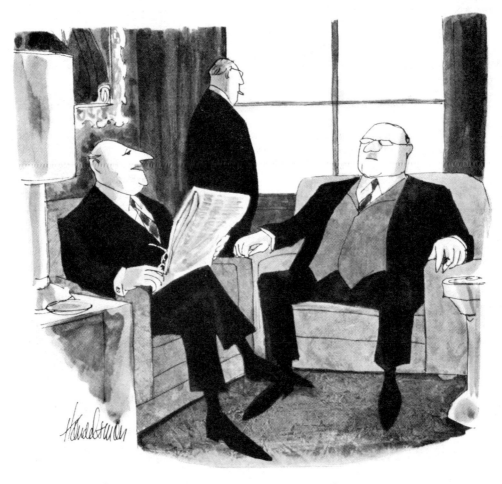

"I feel an intense pride, Robert, that I live in a country rich
enough to have war and peace at the same time."

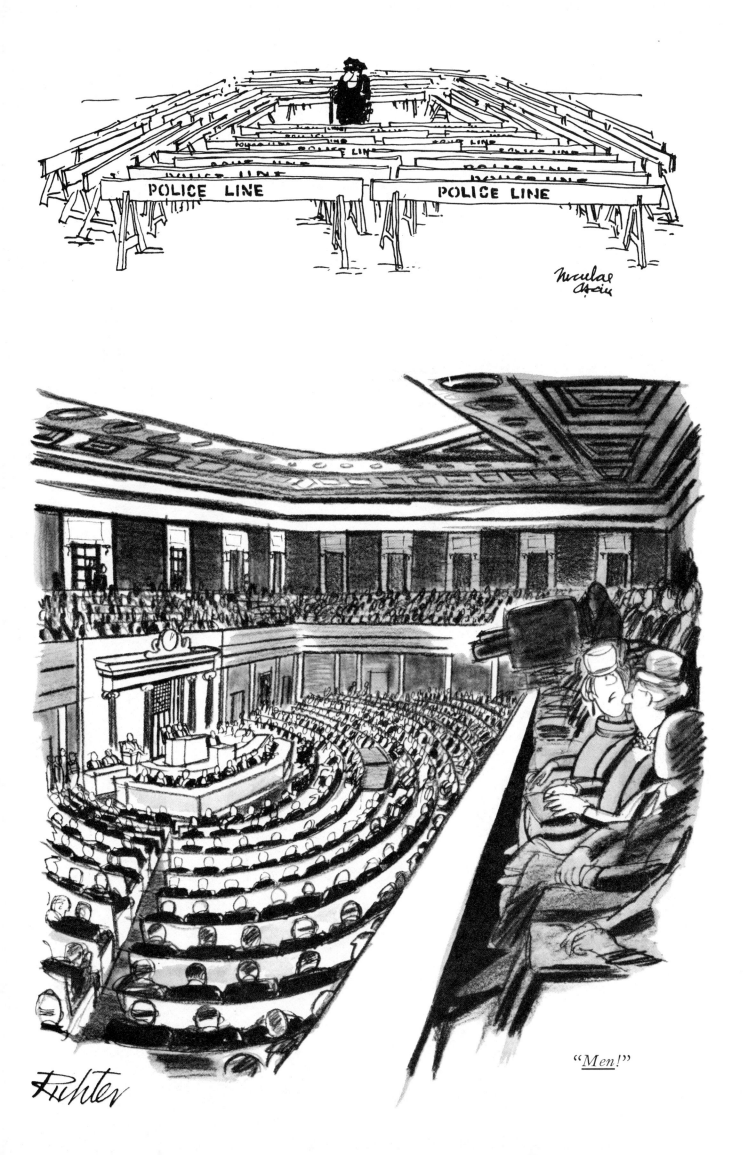

"_Men!_"

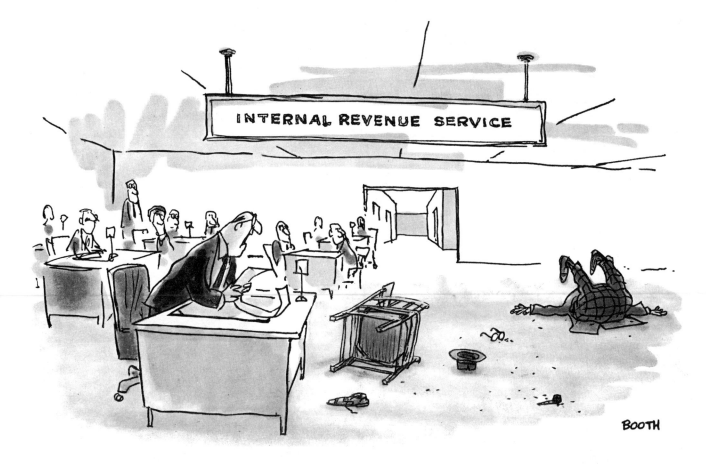

"Other folks have to pay taxes, too, Mr. Herndon, so would you please spare us the dramatics!"

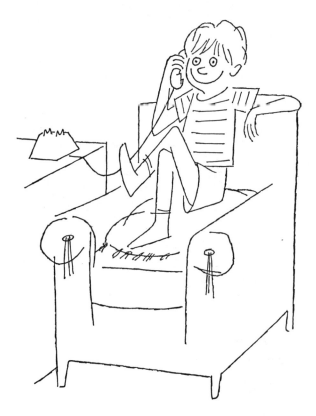

"This is a recording. When you hear 'beep,'
please leave your message. Beep."

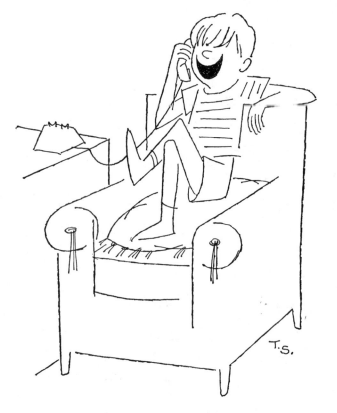

"A grasshopper sitting on a railroad track,
Sing Polly-wolly-doodle all the day;
He sneezed so hard he broke his back,
Sing Polly-wolly-doodle all the day."

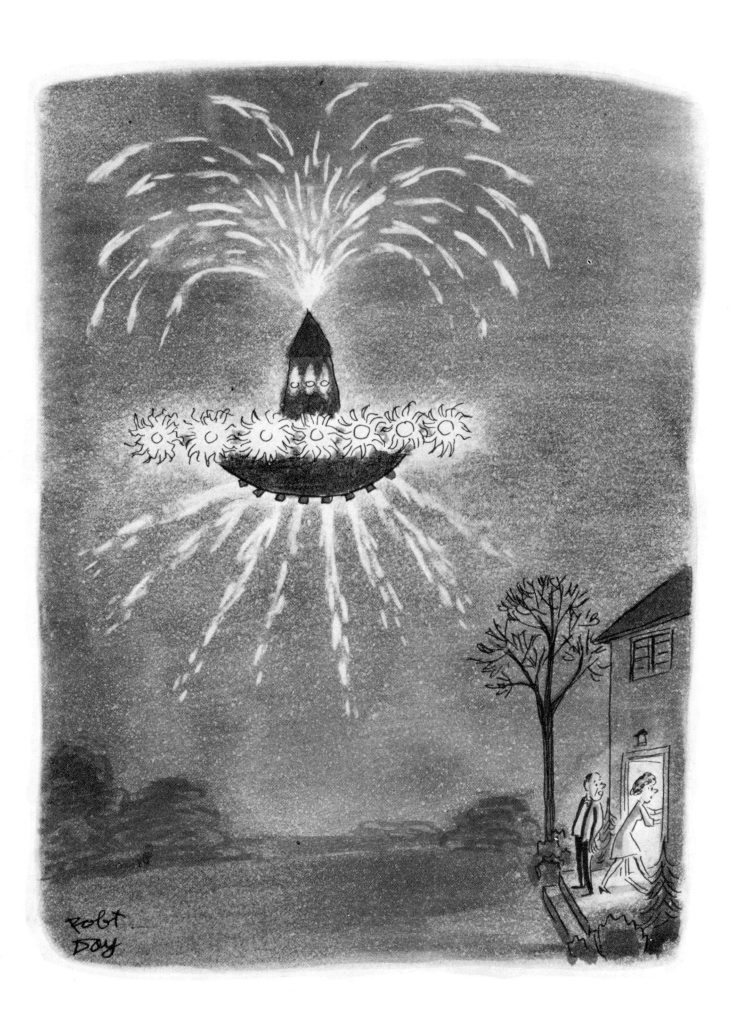

"Why bother to phone? They'll just say it's swamp gas."

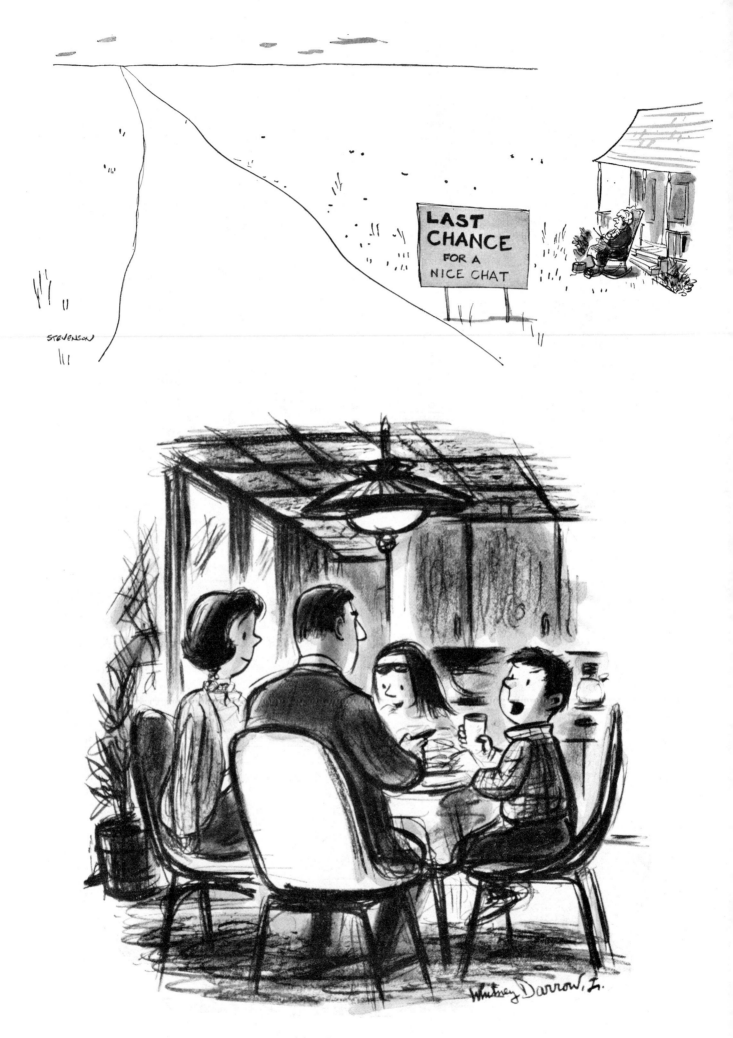

"*Dad, you can't expect to pick up the
basics of the new math in a simple dinner-table conversation.*"

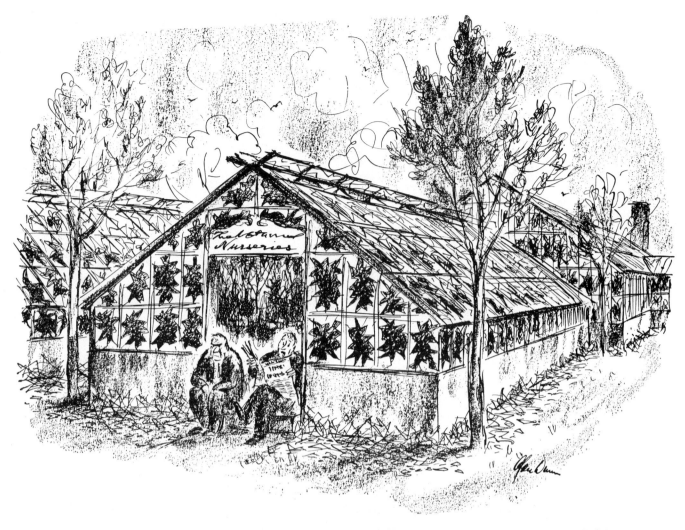

"Would you be interested to know that it broke all records for coast-to-coast flight?"

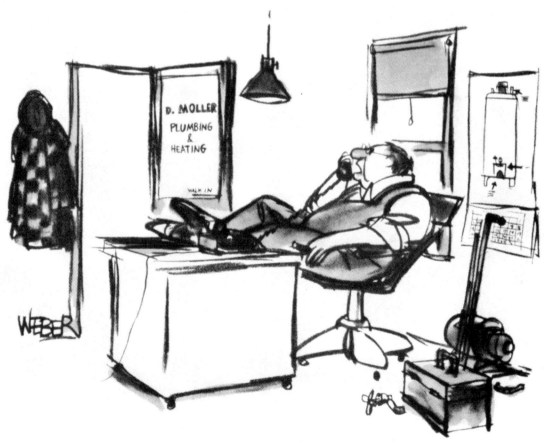

"Say 'please.'"

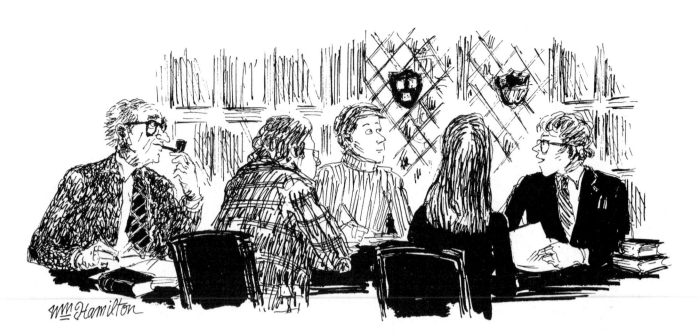

"*The tautology of their symbolism thus begins to achieve mythic proportions in 'A Day at the Races,' 'Duck Soup,' and 'A Night at the Opera.'*"

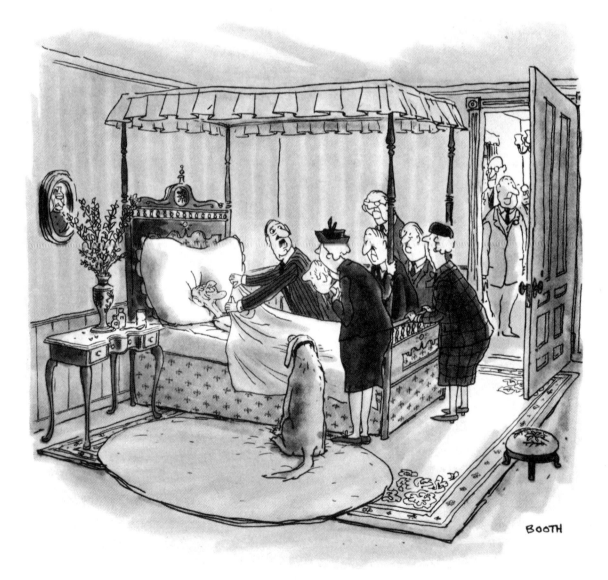

"*He said, 'Tell the Telephone Company to go fly a kite.'*"

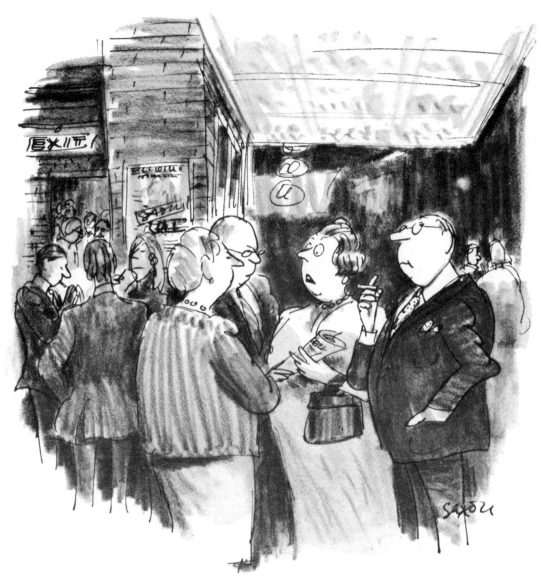

"I'm beginning to think everybody in the whole world is
preoccupied with sex except Henry and me."

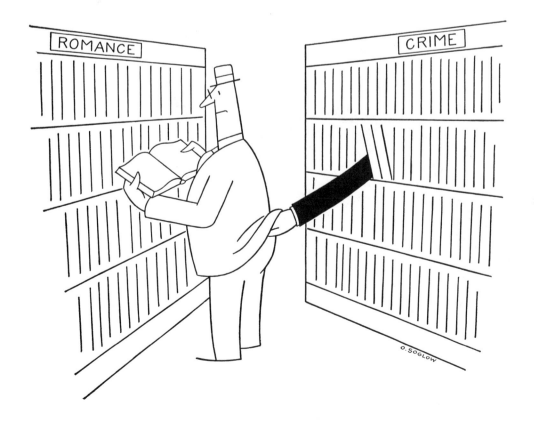

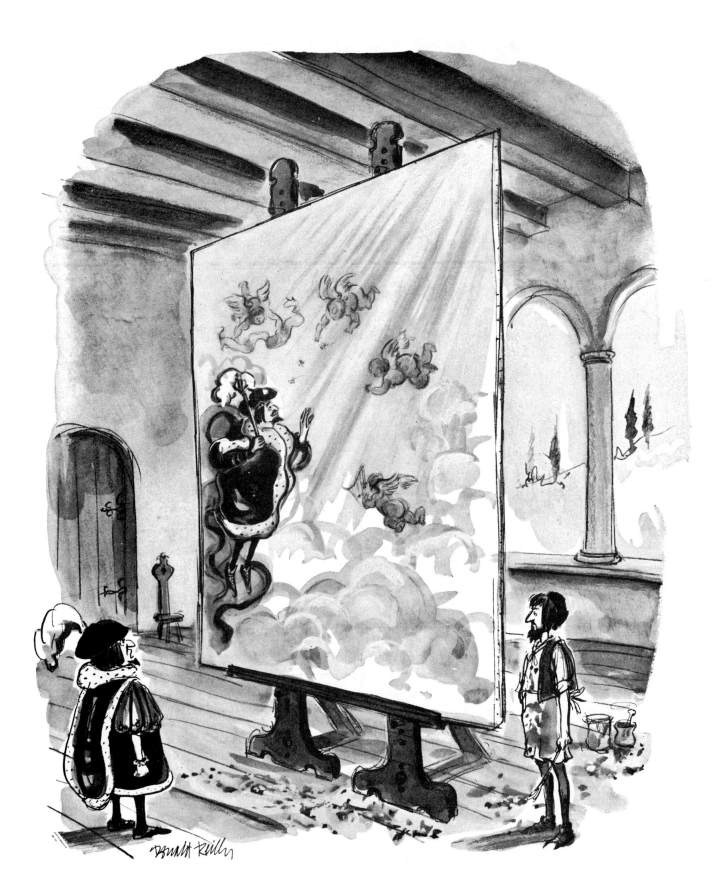

"Give me more angels and make them gladder to see me."

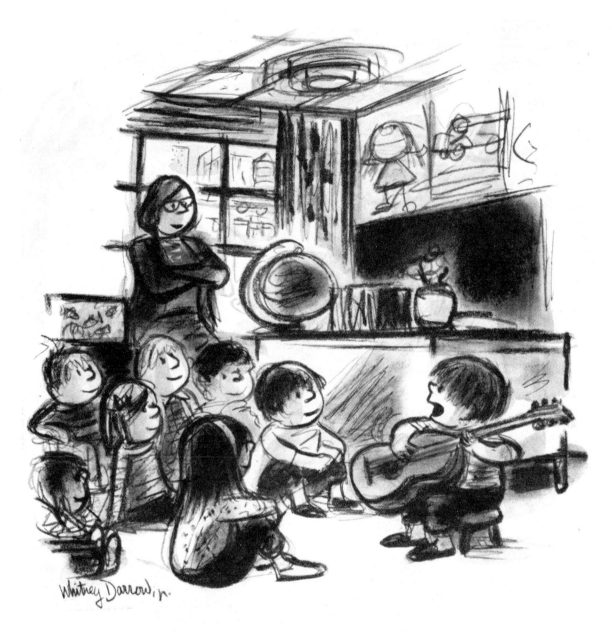

"We can travel the wide world over, but everywhere we roam
We'll find the same hypocrisy we always had at home,
Where parents say we can't read books they've got upon their shelves,
And teach us the value of money by keeping it all themselves."

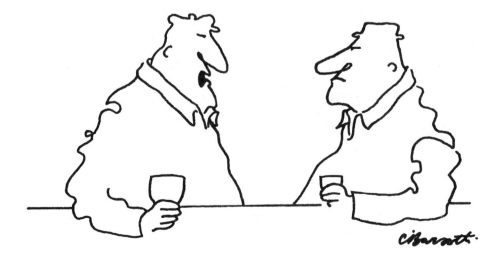

"Look, Nixon's no dope. If the people really _wanted_ moral
leadership, he'd give them moral leadership."

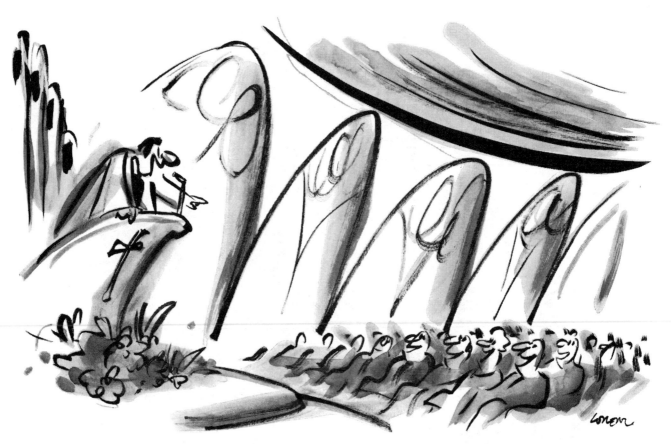

"And so I say unto you, I'm O.K., you're O.K.!"

"Amen, brother! You're O.K. and we're O.K.!"

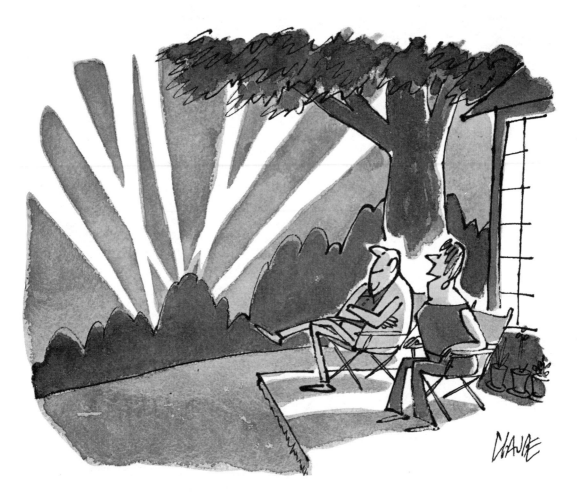

"Well, if it isn't the aurora borealis, I just hope it isn't another of those shopping centers."

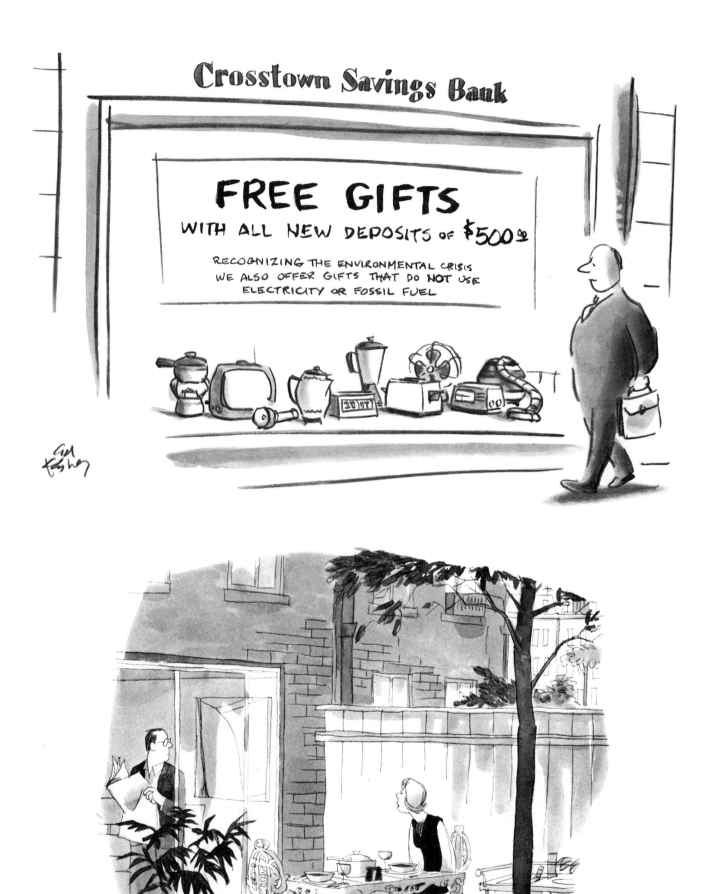

"*Please hurry, Hilary. Your soup's getting dirty.*"

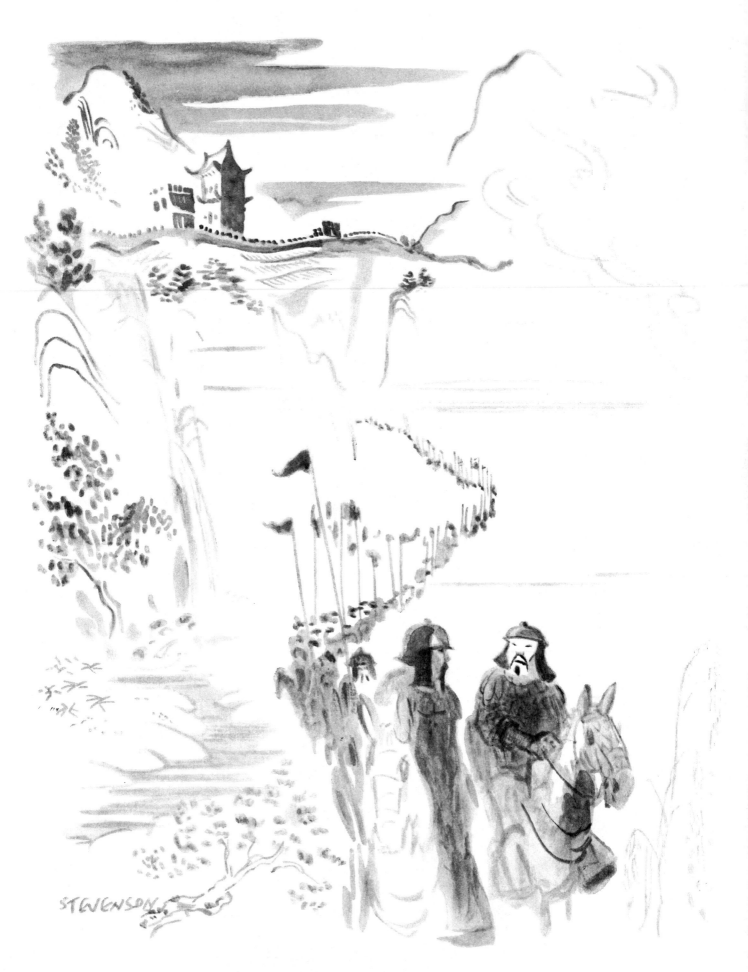

*"That banquet was most delicious, and yet now, somehow,
once again I feel the pang of hunger."*

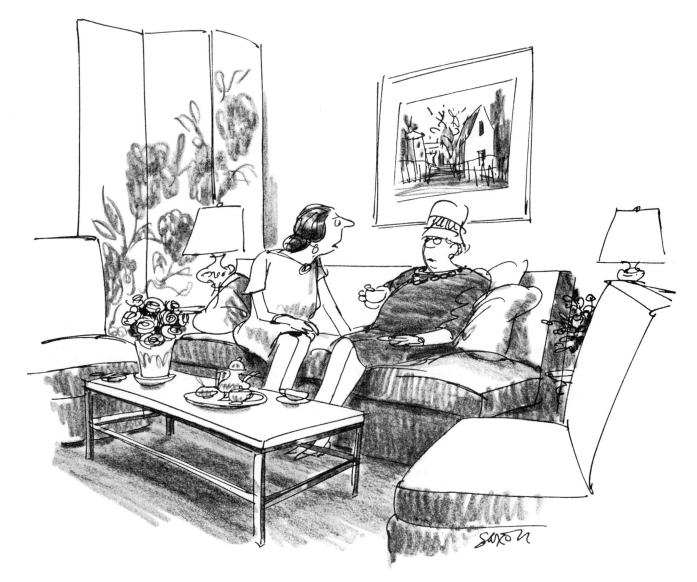

"*I want you to promise me you'll give McGovern one more chance to turn you on.*"

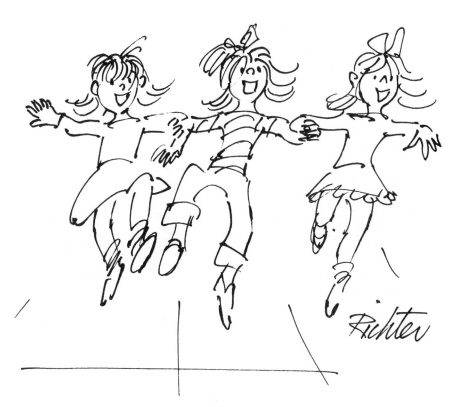

"*Roto-Rooter, that's the name,*
And away go troubles down the drain."

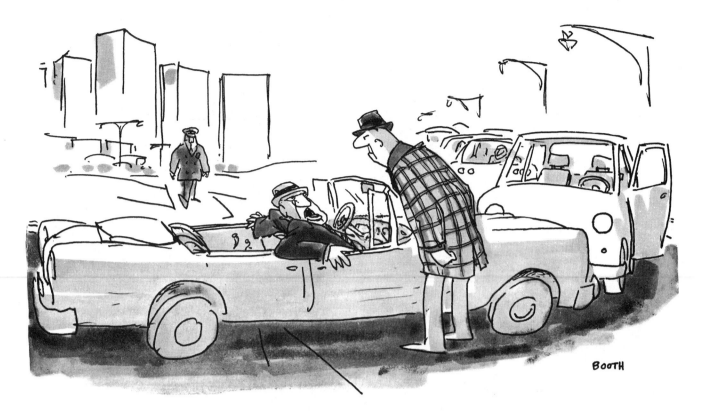

"*The air I breathe is filthy, my food is poisoned, my automobile is a gas-guzzling behemoth, my school taxes have doubled, the Internal Revenue Service plans to take the fillings out of my teeth, my wife is fifty-three and pregnant, my dog bit a lawyer's kid, my son steals, my mother-in-law is a Communist, my daughter ran off with a fink, and now you tell me that if I don't back up and let you have the right-of-way I'll be in trouble.*"

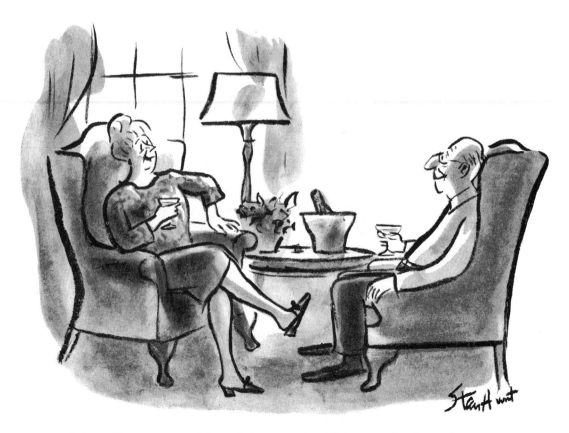

"*According to actuarial statistics, we shouldn't even be here, let alone be sitting here sipping Piper Heidsieck '59.*"

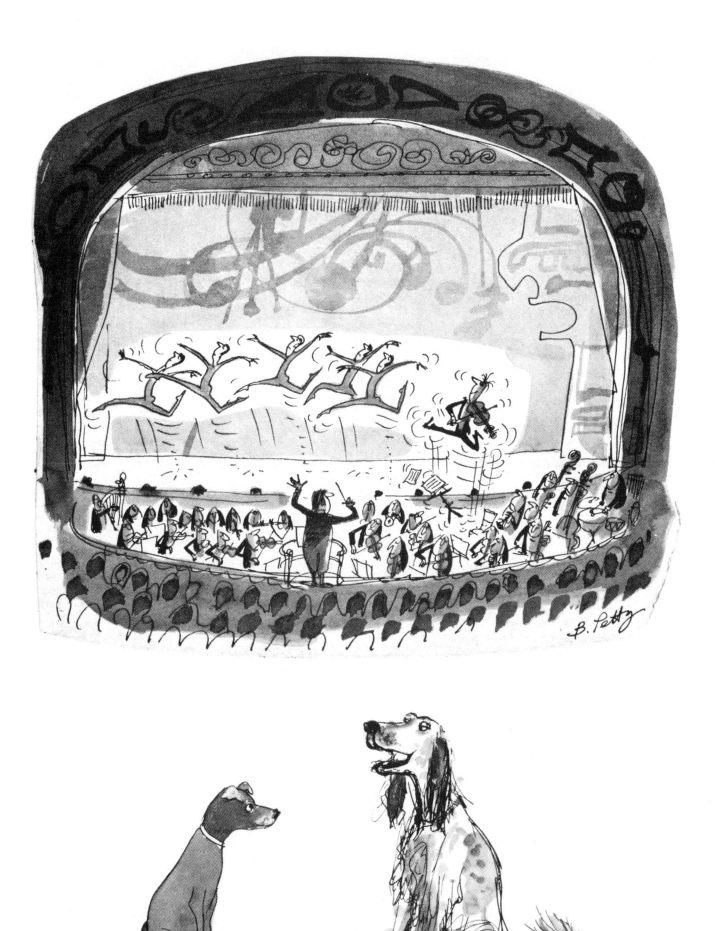

"They never pushed me. If I wanted to retrieve, shake hands, or roll over, it was entirely up to me."

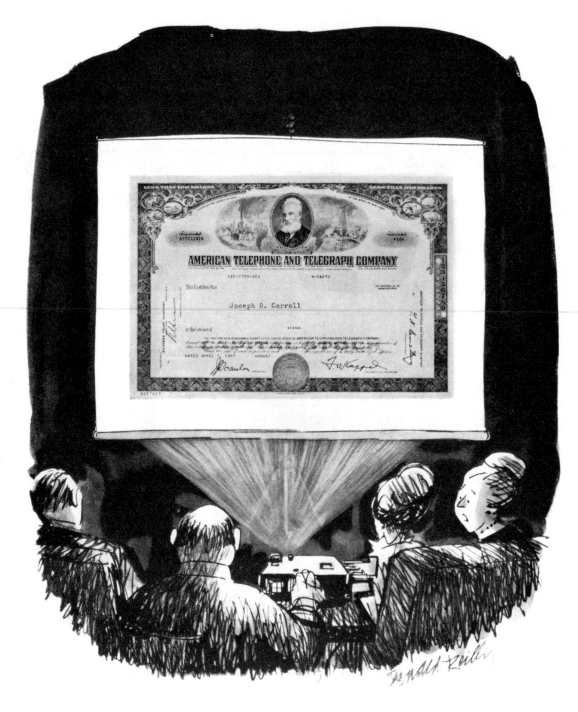

"Oh, Joe, not your portfolio again!"

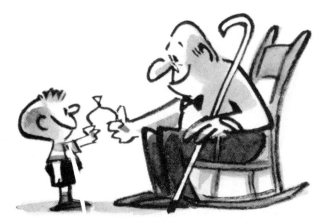
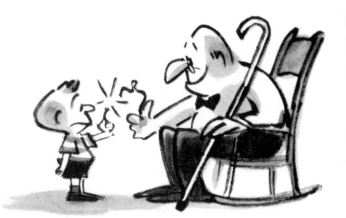

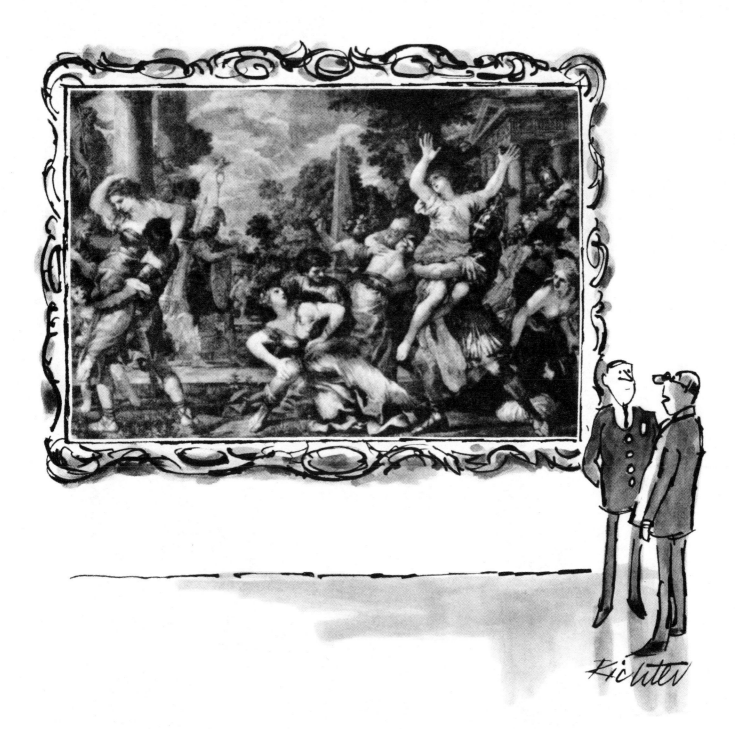

"Getting much flak from Women's Lib?"

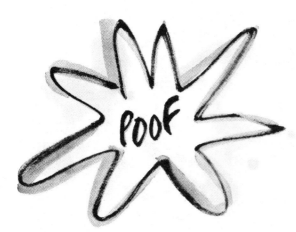
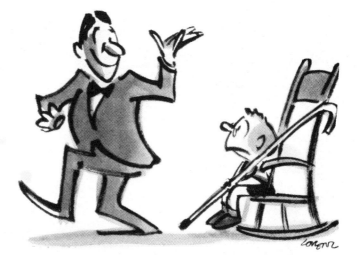

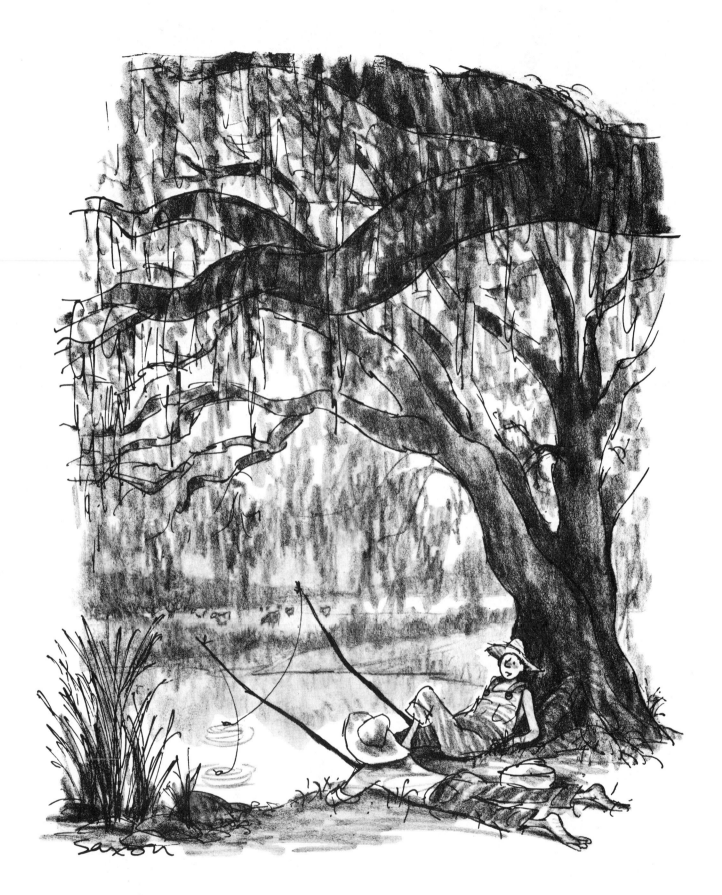

"*What would you do if you had a million dollars—tax-free, I mean?*"

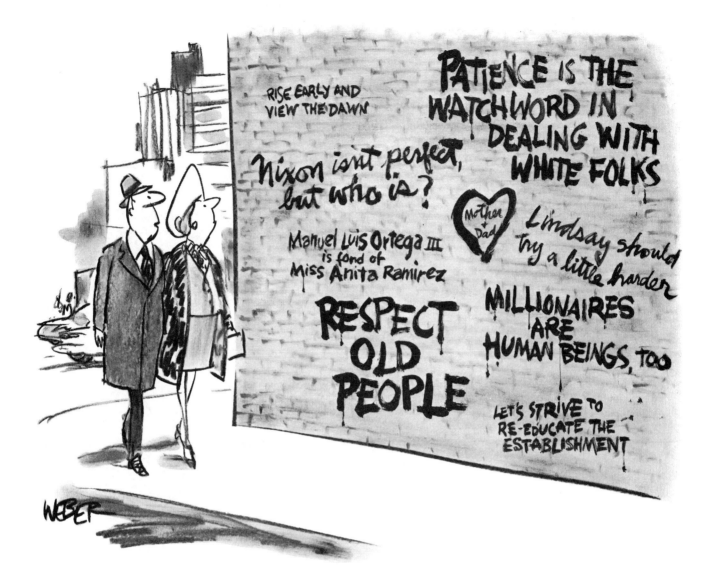

"Well, I must say, this is a heartening change."

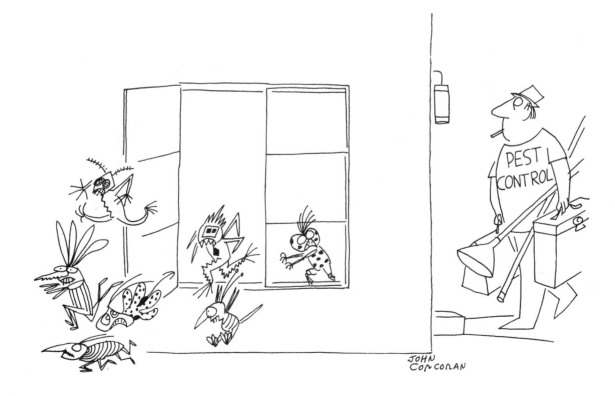

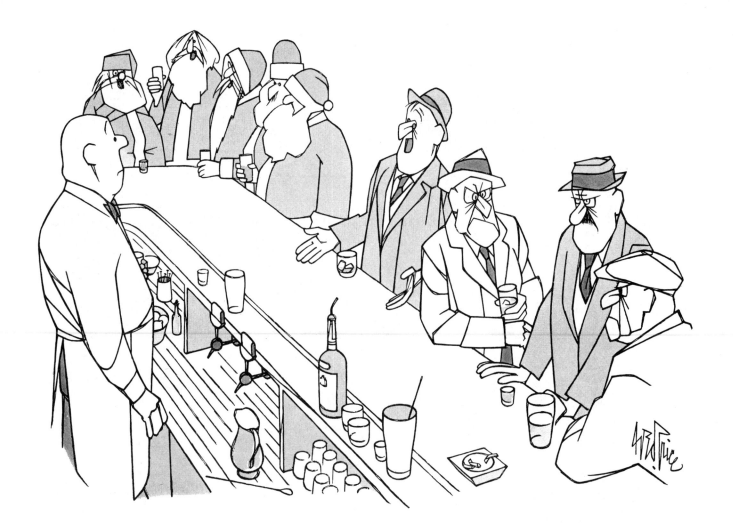

"Between the 'Ho, ho, ho's and the 'Bah, humbug's I've about had it."

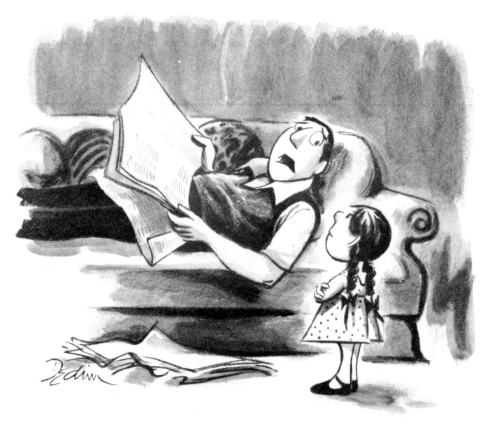

"I _know_ sex is no longer a taboo subject. I just don't
feel like discussing it all the time, that's all."

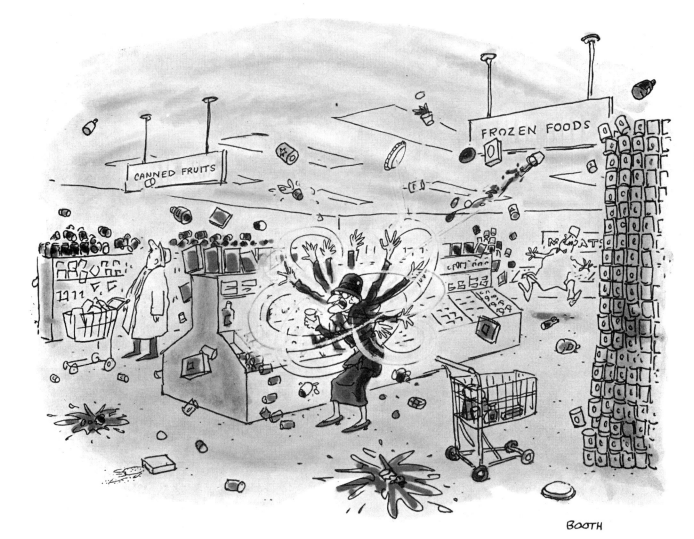

"Artificial coloring, artificial flavoring, artificial glop, artificial slop, artificial this, artificial that . . ."

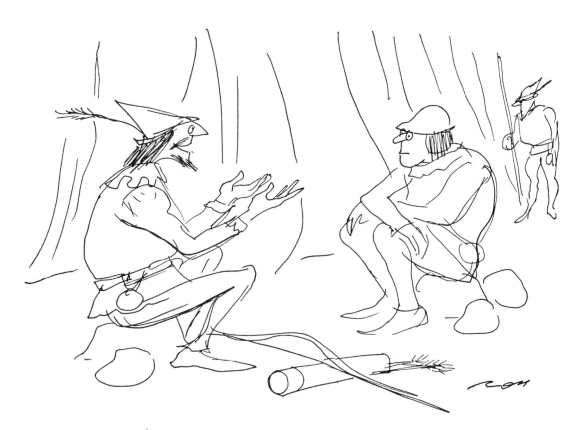

"Here is the way it works: We take from the rich and give to the poor—keeping only enough for salaries, travel, equipment, depreciation, and so on, and so on."

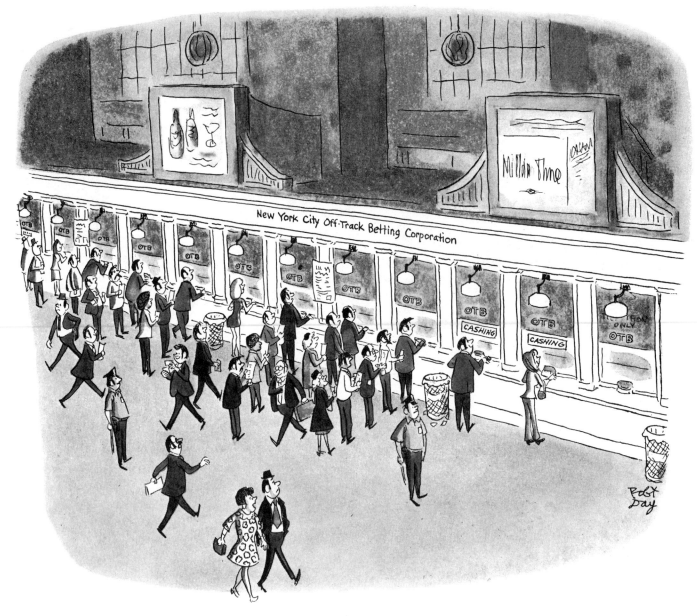

*"All those windows selling tickets and only two windows cashing
them. Doesn't that tell you something?"*

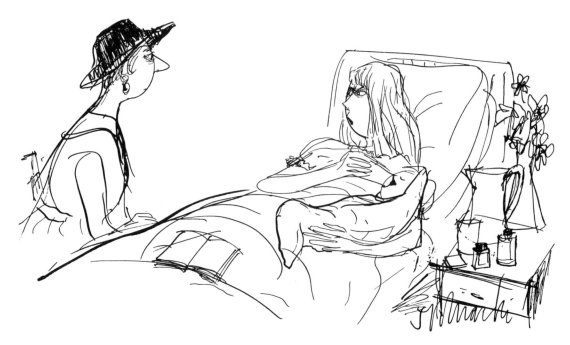

"If you can't trust one of Nader's Raiders, who can you trust?"

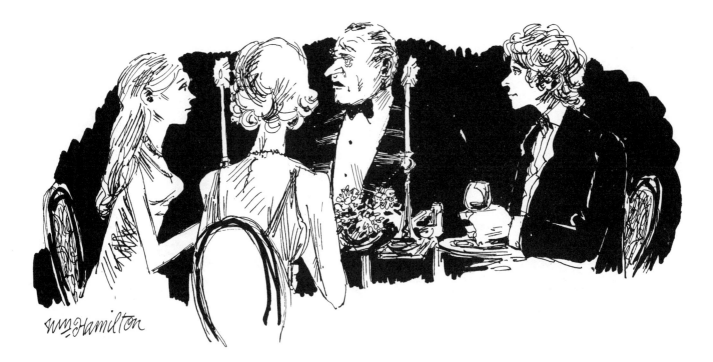

"Tell me, Sara, why does your young man keep calling your mother 'man'?"

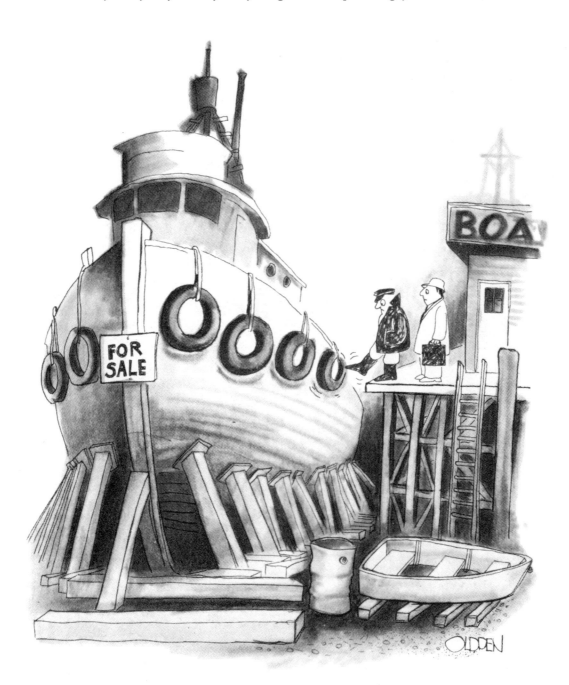

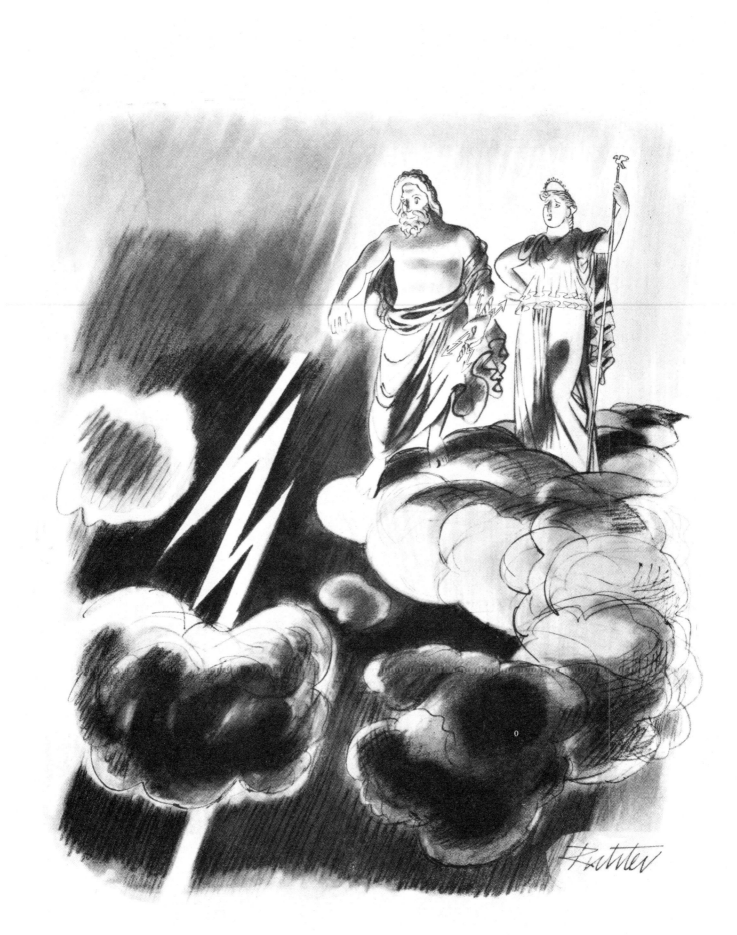

"*If you're so good, why can't you ever strike twice in the same place?*"

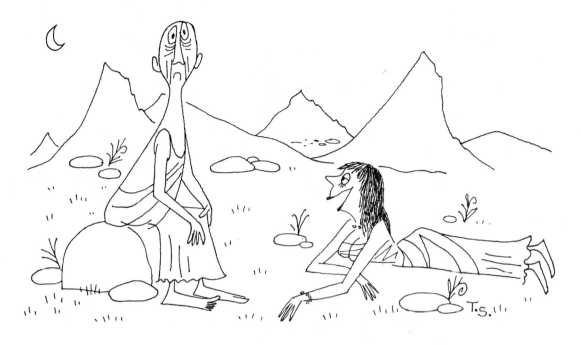

"*Oh, come off it, Methuselah! Seven hundred and eighty-two isn't old!*"

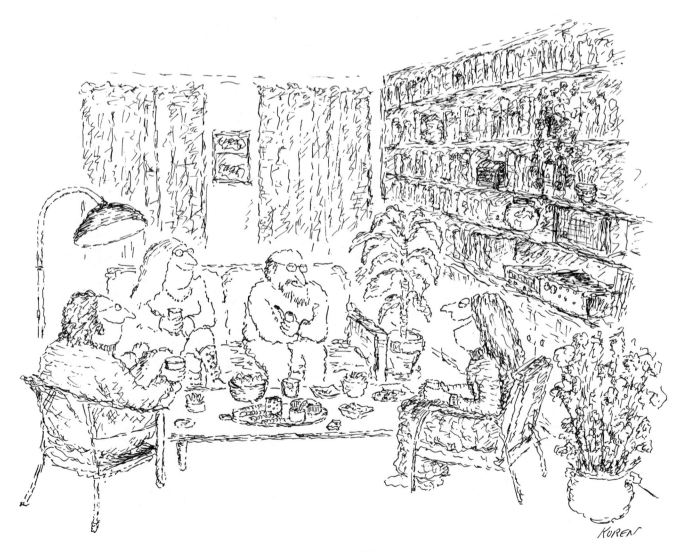

"*Now tell us about your burglary.*"

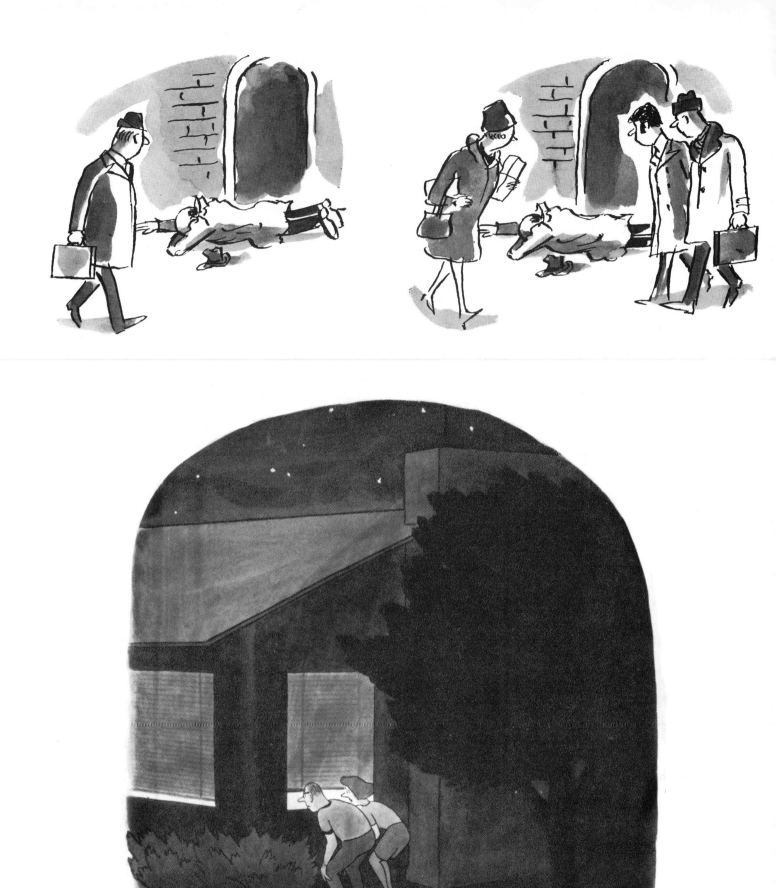

"See, I told you! Their greens and blues are <u>much</u> sharper than ours."

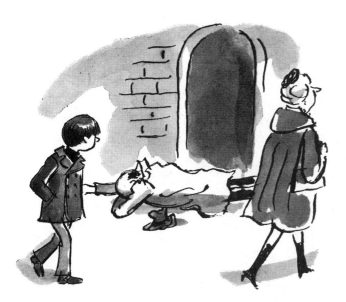

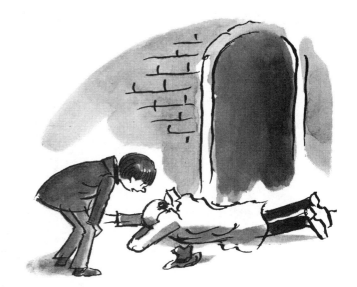

"Are you all right, Mister? Is there anything I can do?"

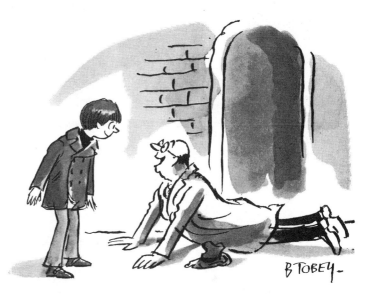

"Young man, you're the only one who bothered to stop! I'm a millionaire and I'm going to give you five thousand dollars!"

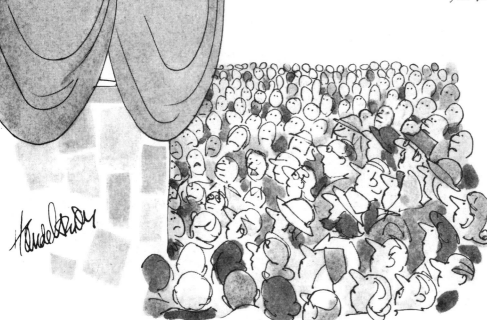

"It is my wish that this be the most educated country in the world, and toward that end I hereby ordain that each and every one of my people be given a diploma."

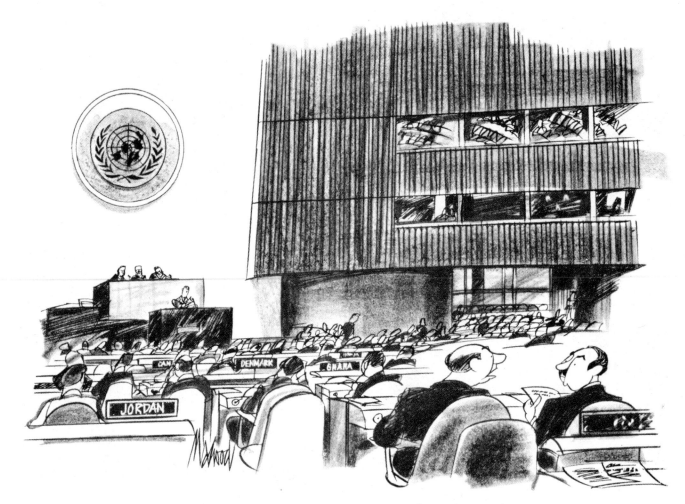

"*What is most depressing is that these platitudes are being simultaneously translated into five languages.*"

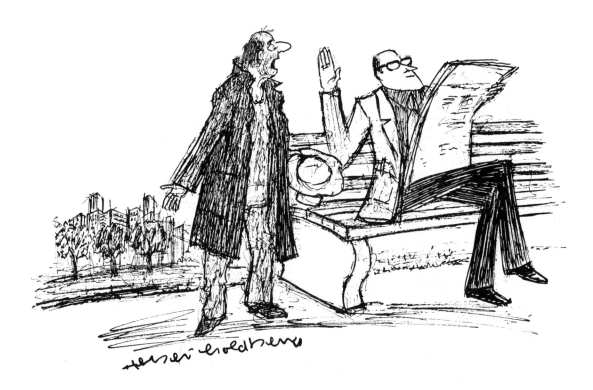

"*This is the compassion of a New York 'Times' reader?*"

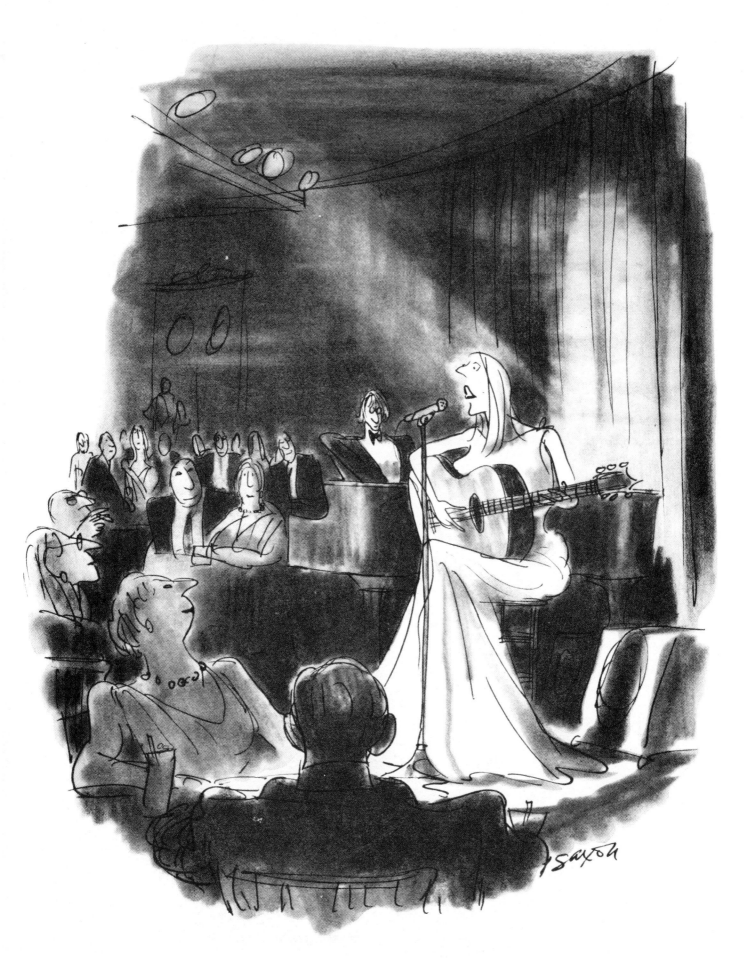

"*Since my songs tonight will not have any special social or political significance, I would like to say now that I am opposed to our military involvement in the Far East, and I'm in favor of legalized pot and of price stability through federal controls, also the boycotting of California table grapes.*"

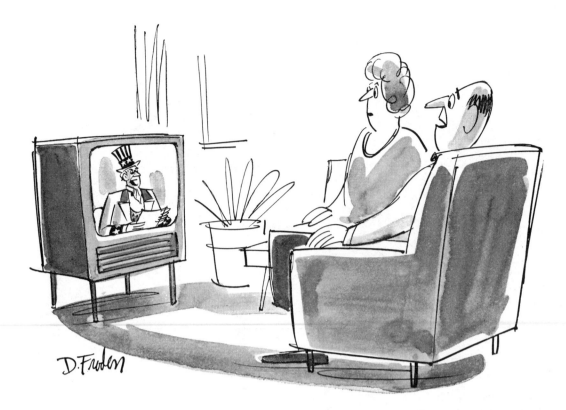

"Don't tell me this news isn't being managed."

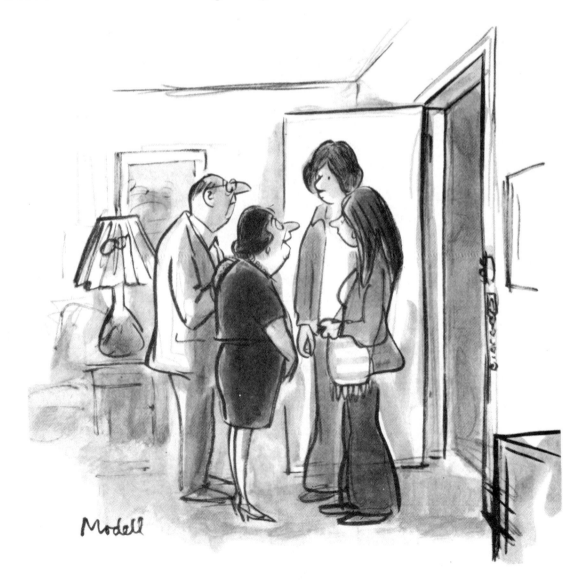

"Your friend is more than welcome, dear, but we just want you to know that your father and I didn't do anything funny till _after_ we were married."

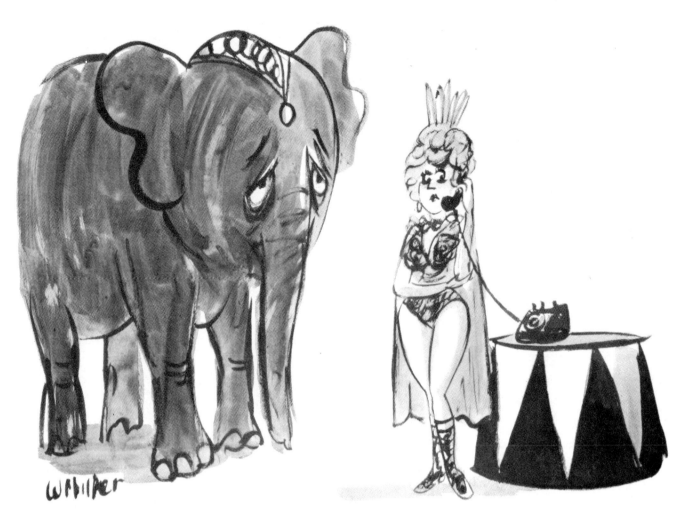

"Give him two bottles of aspirin and call me in the morning."

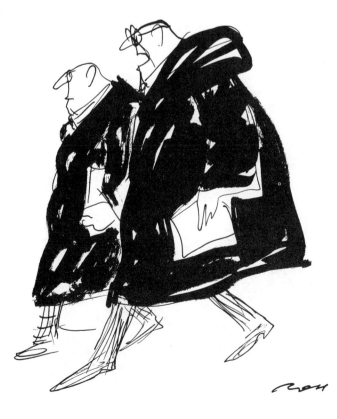

"The way I see it, when you start tempering justice with mercy you've had it!"

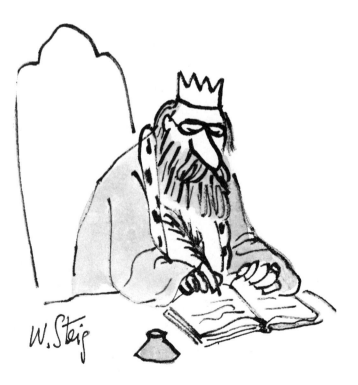

"Do I really want all this power? I think I do."

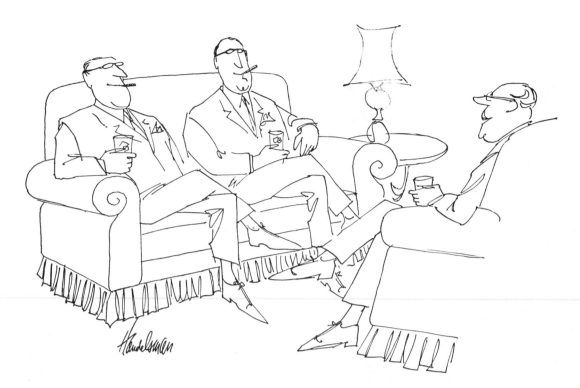

*"What the economy needs is a depression. Just
a small one, and present company excepted, of course."*

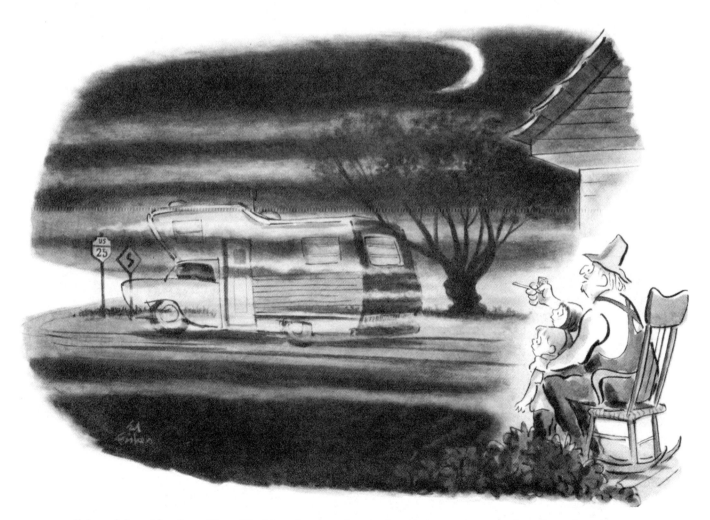

*"Aye, 'tis said when New York's sales tax jumped to seven per cent he slipped across
the line into Connecticut. And when Connecticut passed its tax package he fled to New
Hampshire. And now, the legend goes, he flees from state to state forever."*

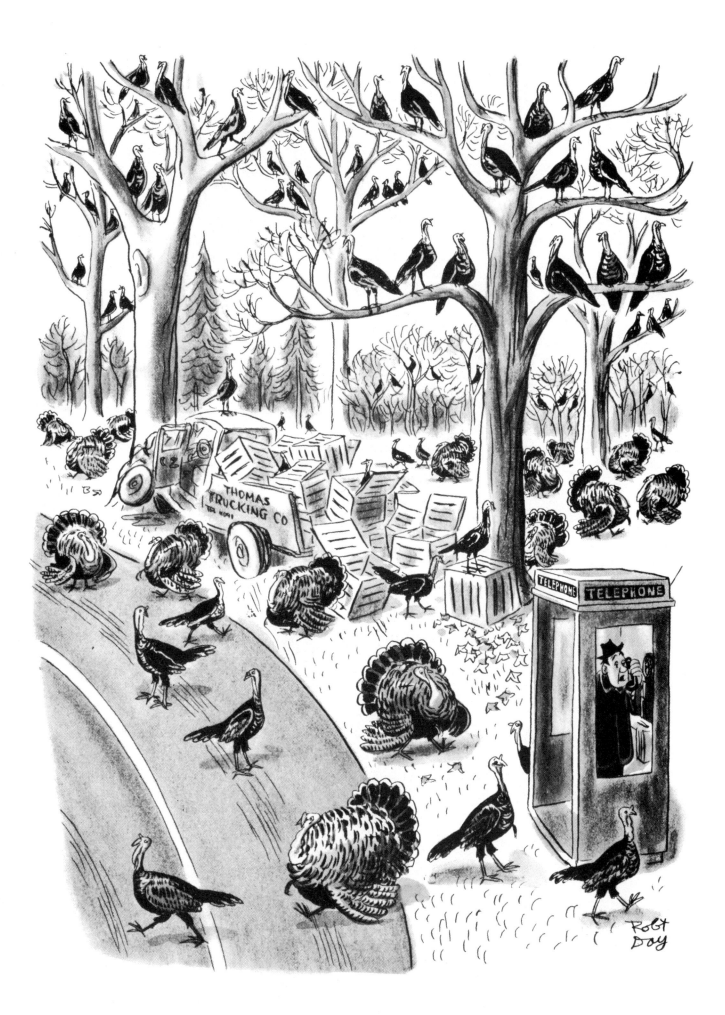

"Boss, I got news for you."

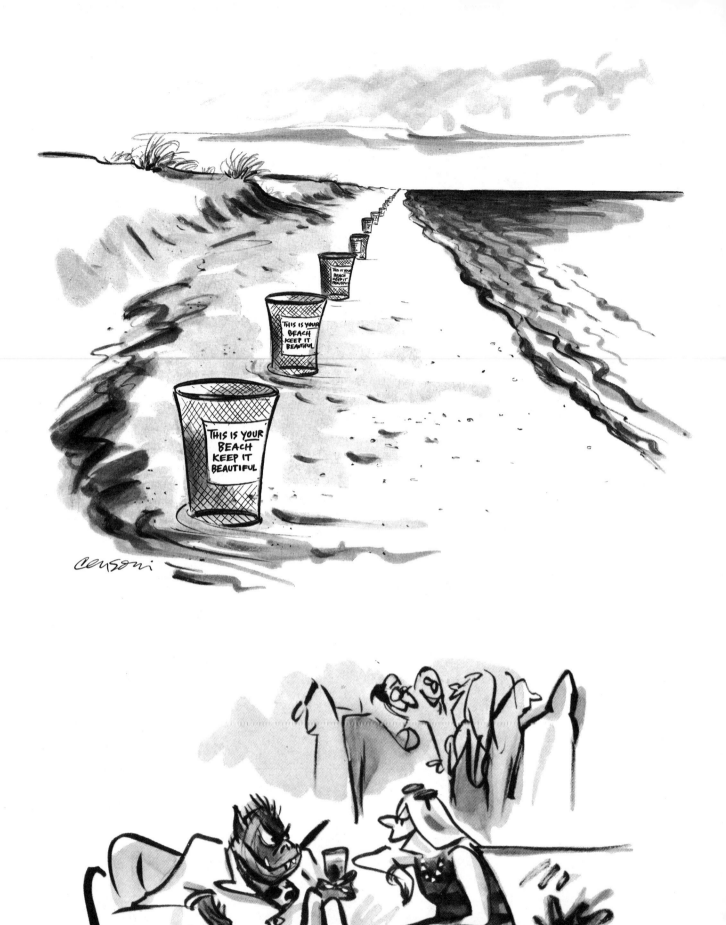

"*All I can say, Mr. Townsend, is thank goodness someone finally had guts enough to bring lycanthropy out of the closet.*"

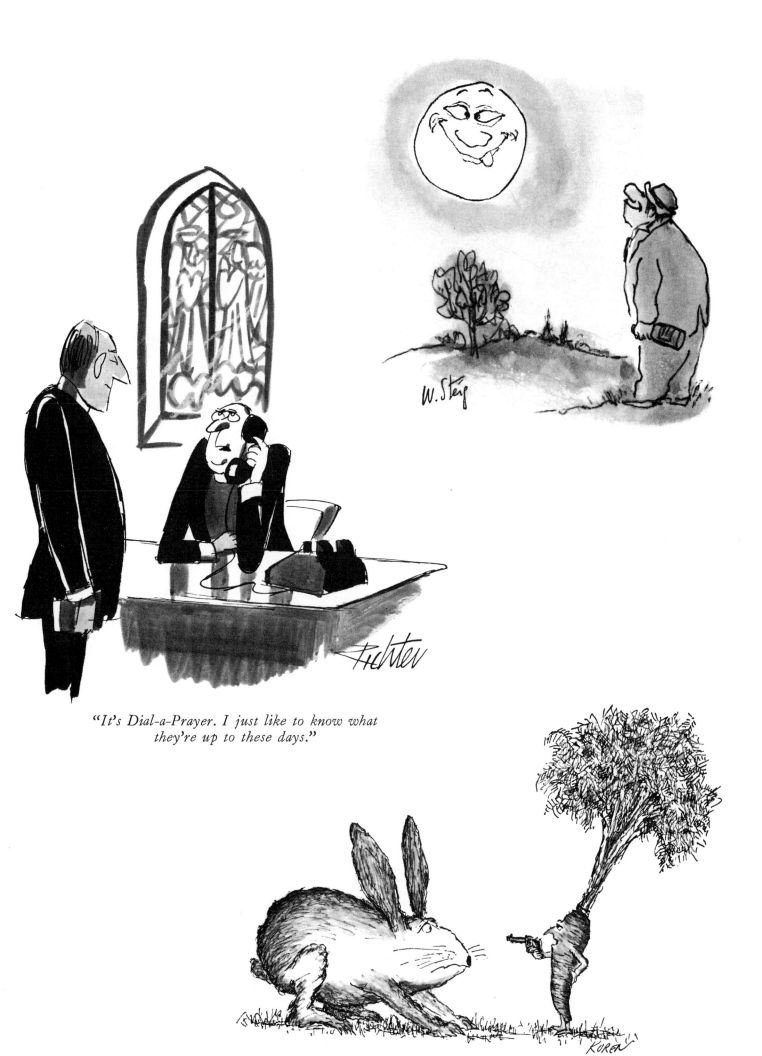

"It's Dial-a-Prayer. I just like to know what
they're up to these days."

"You've just raided your last patch!"

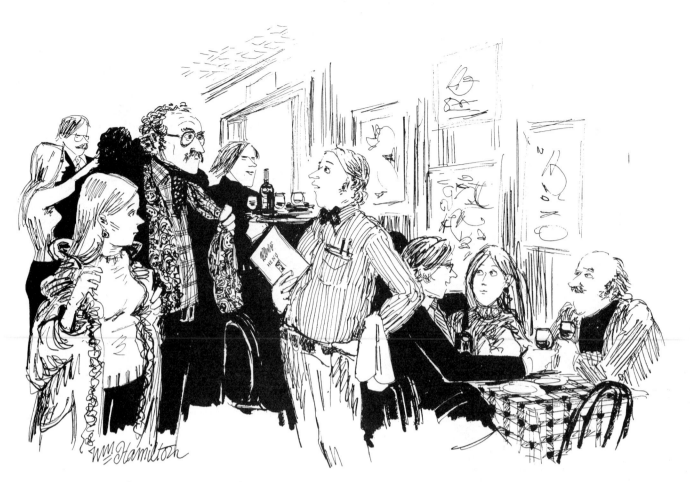

"Sorry, old man. Because of the weak imagery, scanty plot, and pedestrian language in your latest, we've turned your table over to Joyce Carol Oates."

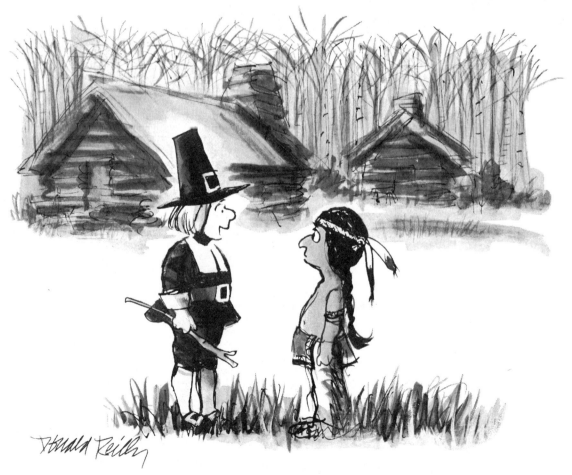

"We're here to escape religious persecution. What are you here for?"

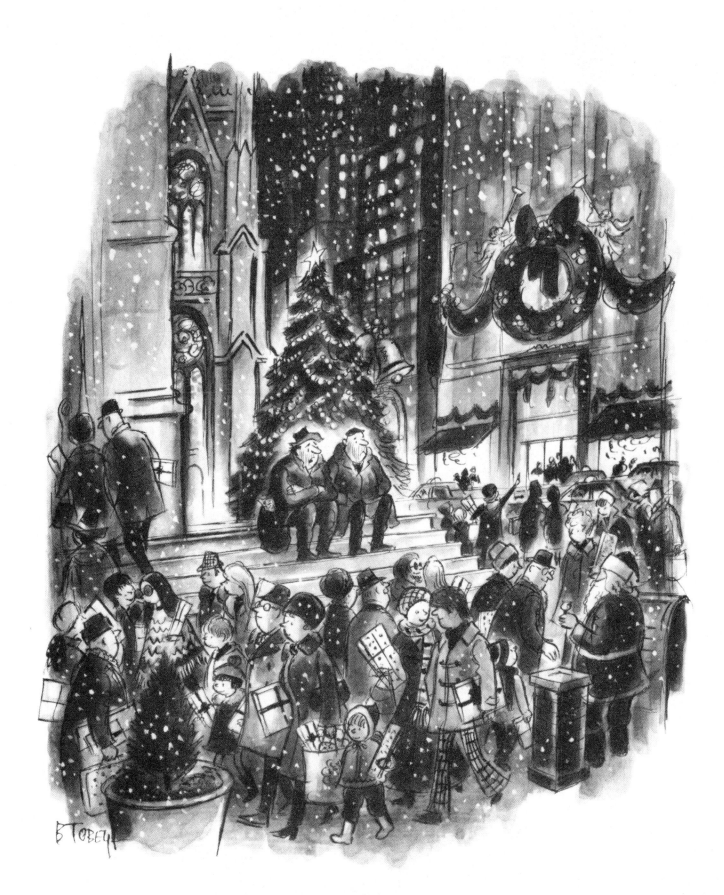

"*This is the time of year I wish I wasn't a bum.*"

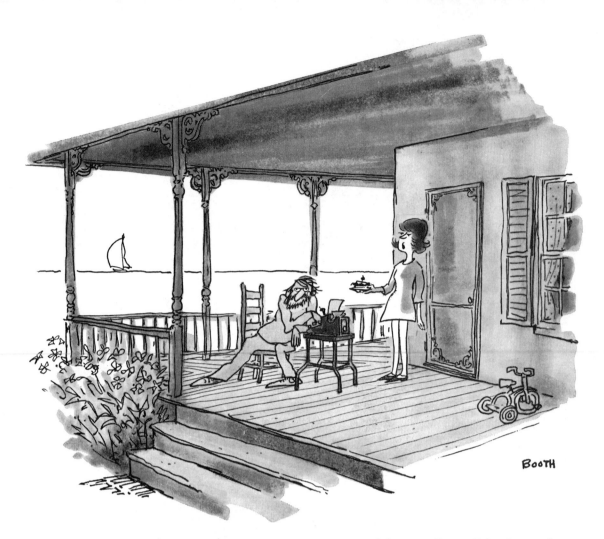

"I've got an idea for a story: Gus and Ethel live on Long Island, on the
North Shore. He works sixteen hours a day writing fiction. Ethel never
goes out, never does anything except fix Gus sandwiches, and in the end
she becomes a nympho-lesbo-killer-whore. Here's your sandwich."

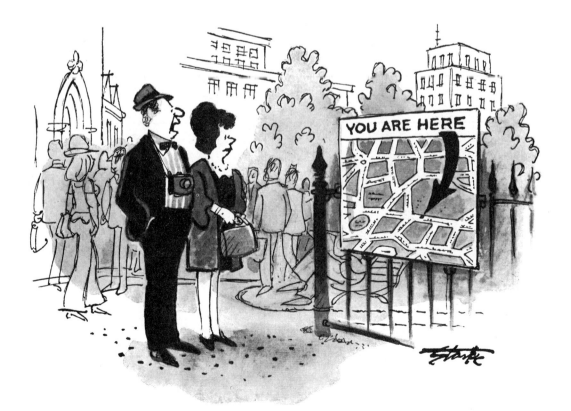

"Bureaucratic busybodies! They keep tabs on you
from the day you're born!"

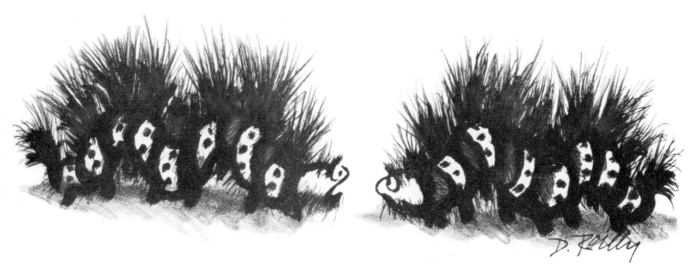

"Well, whatever it is we change into, it can't come soon enough for me."

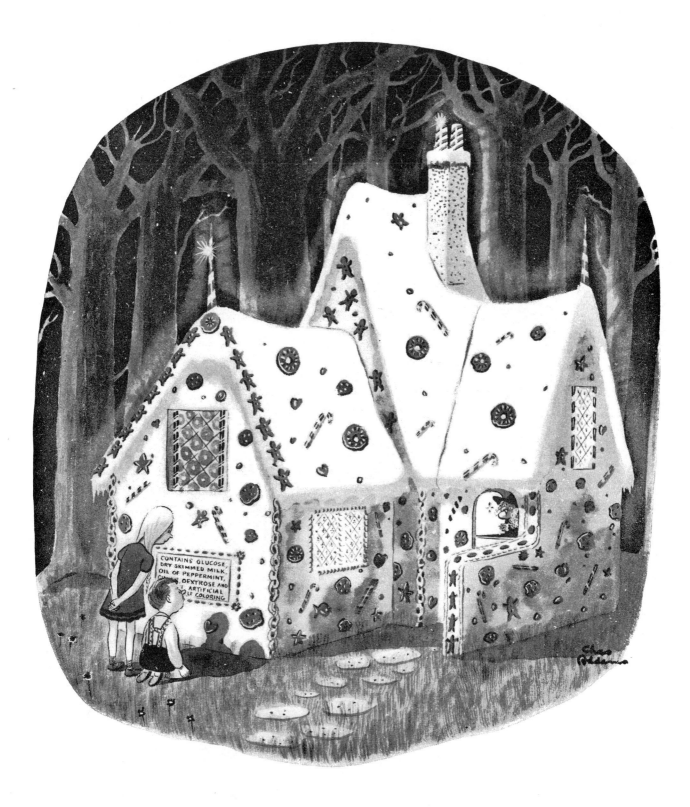

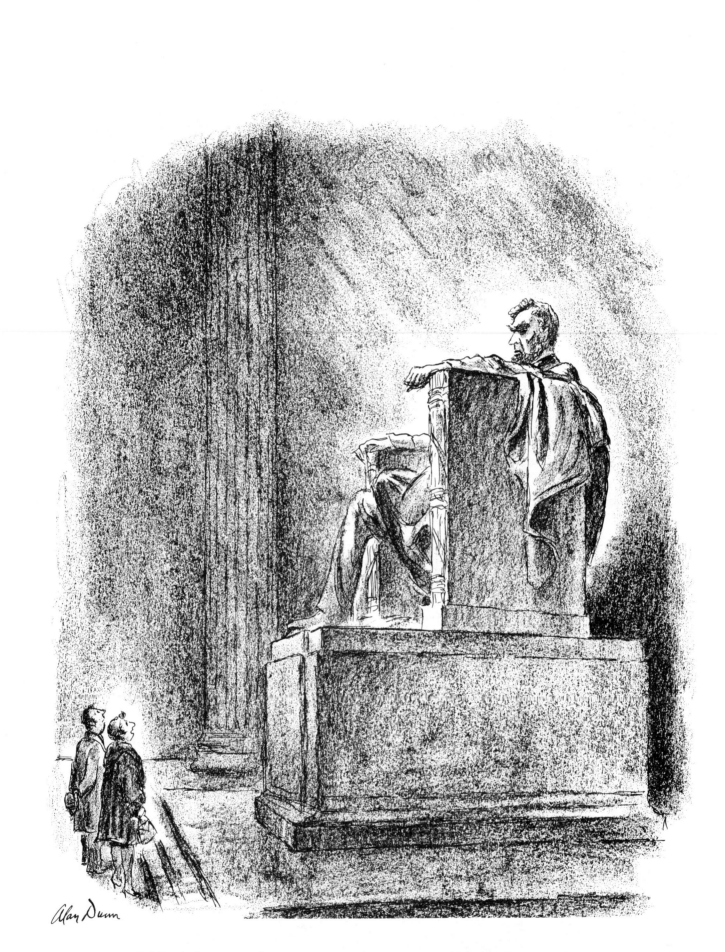

"All right. Muskie's craggy, too, but I bet he never split rails."

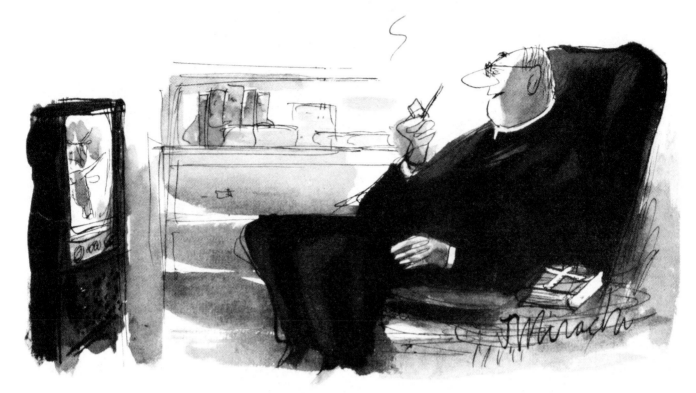

"I'll go you one better, Merrill Lynch,
Pierce, Fenner & Smith. I'm bullish on the whole human race."

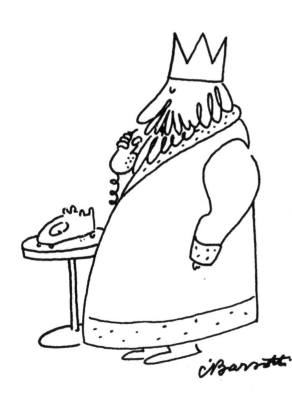

"Operator, I'd like to place a
personage-to-person call, please."

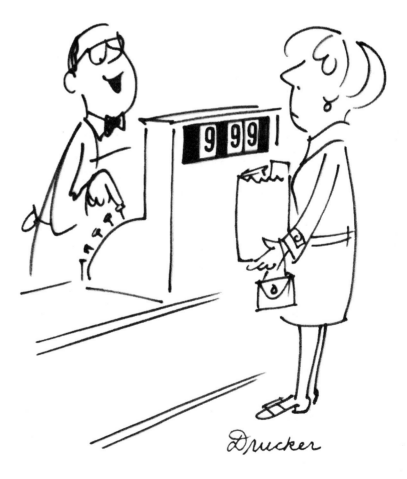

"That sure puts a dent in a ten-dollar bill!"

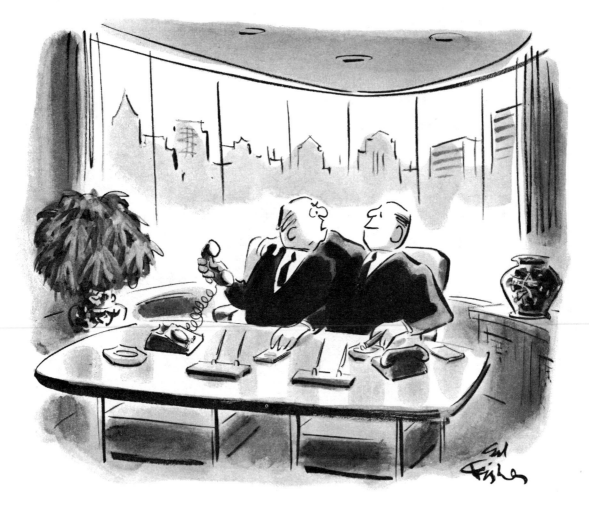

"*When I agreed to the merger, Fairchild, I never contemplated this!*"

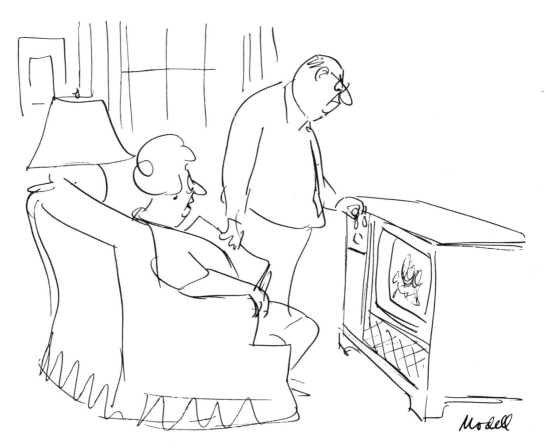

"*Remember when the thing that outraged us most
was the tail fins on the Cadillacs?*"

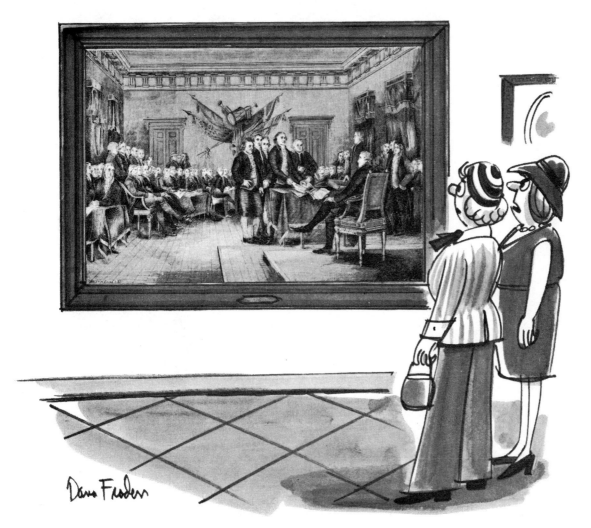

"*Founding Fathers! How come no Founding Mothers?*"

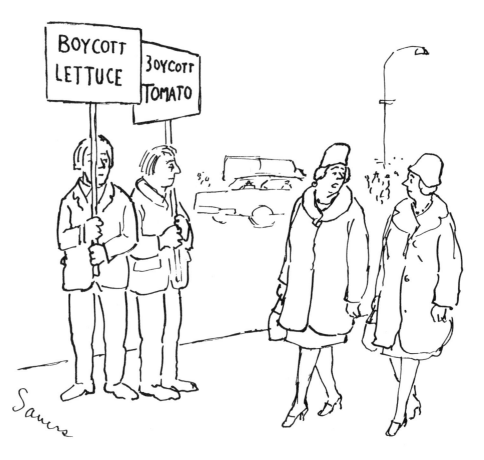

"*Well, there goes lunch.*"

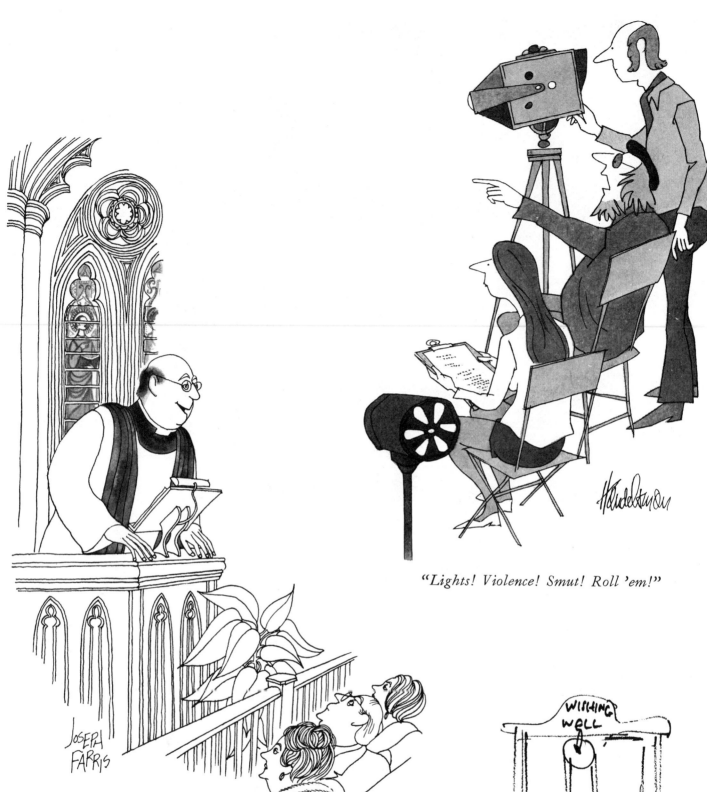

"Lights! Violence! Smut! Roll 'em!"

"Next week is Super Bowl Sunday. It will behoove you all to come here to pray for the team of your choice."

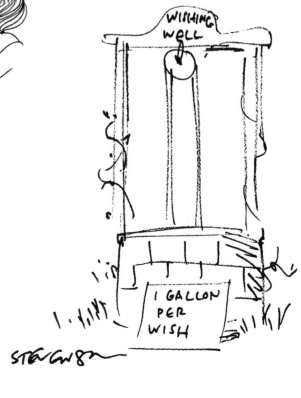

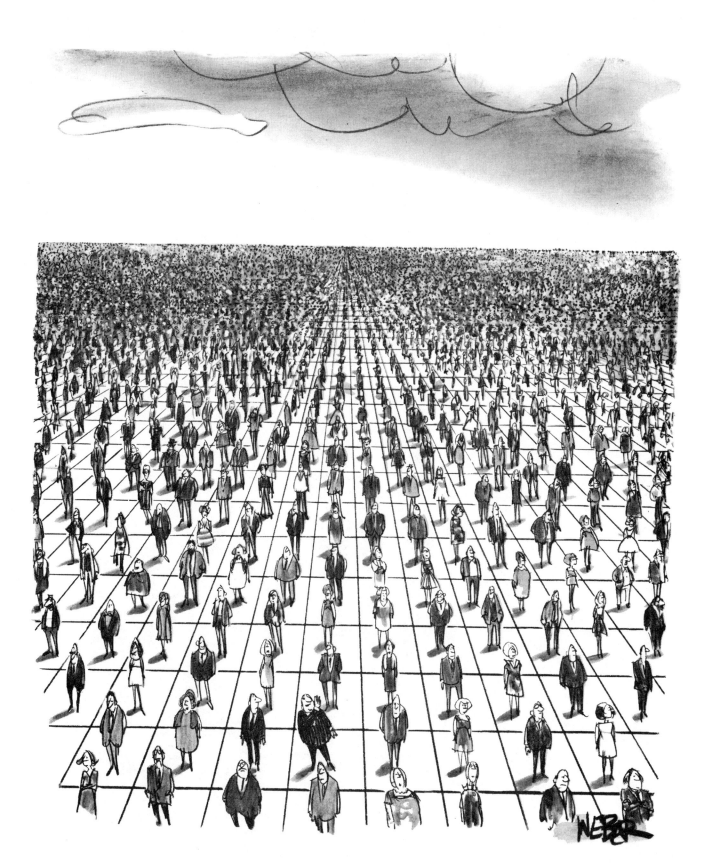

"Excuse me, sir. I am prepared to make you a rather attractive offer for your square."

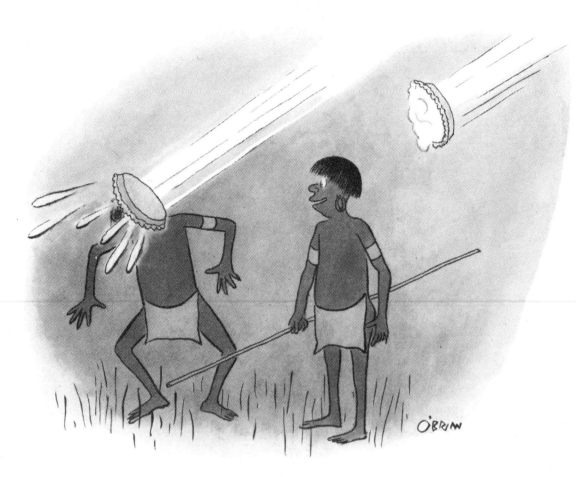

"*The gods are larky tonight.*"

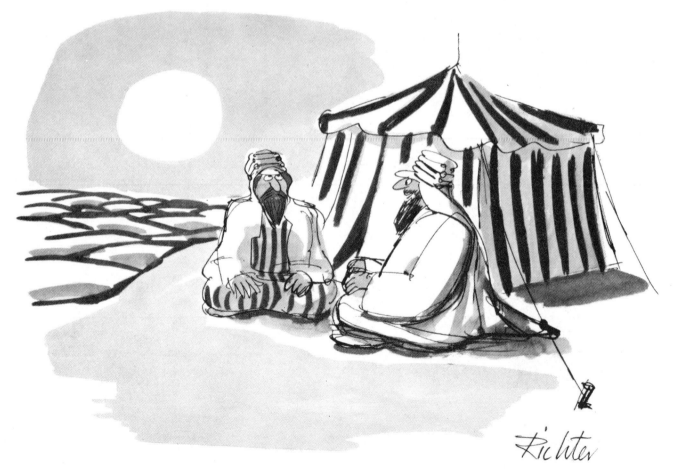

"*Here's another: 'When whippoorwills call and
evening is nigh, I hurry to my' __what__?*"

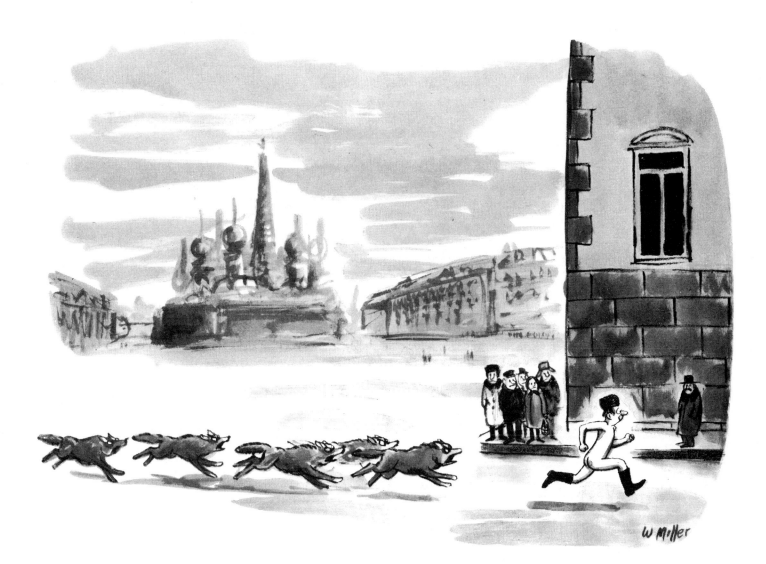

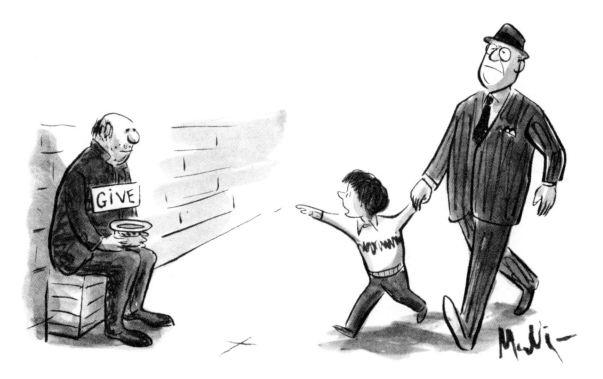

"Look, Granddad, a have-not."

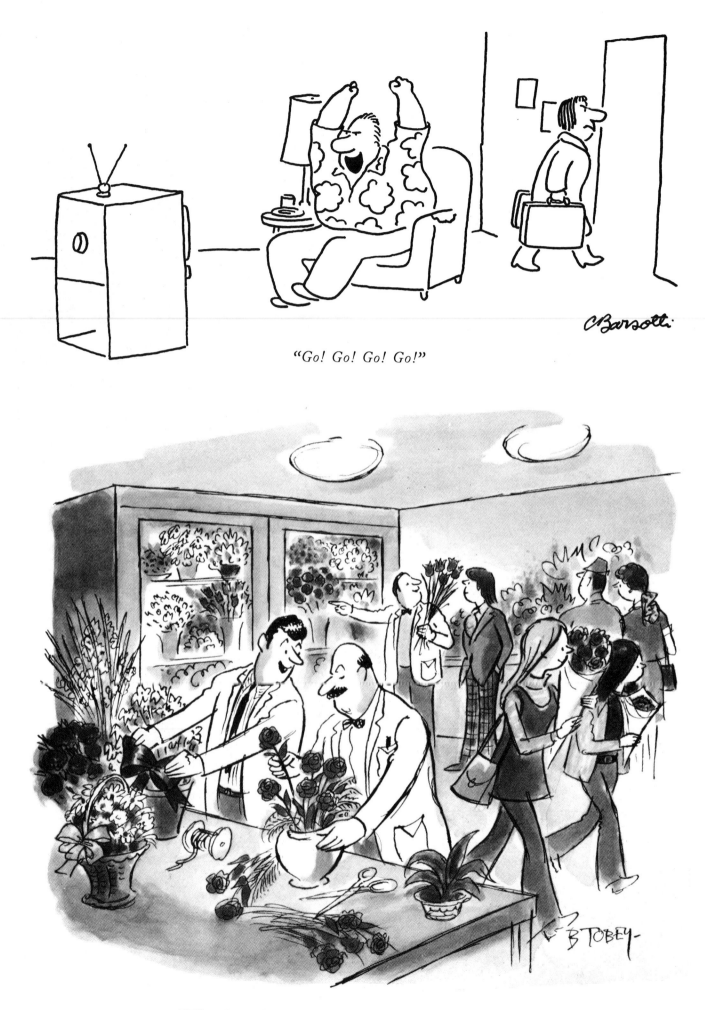

"Go! Go! Go! Go!"

"Thank God Women's Lib hasn't killed Mother's Day!"

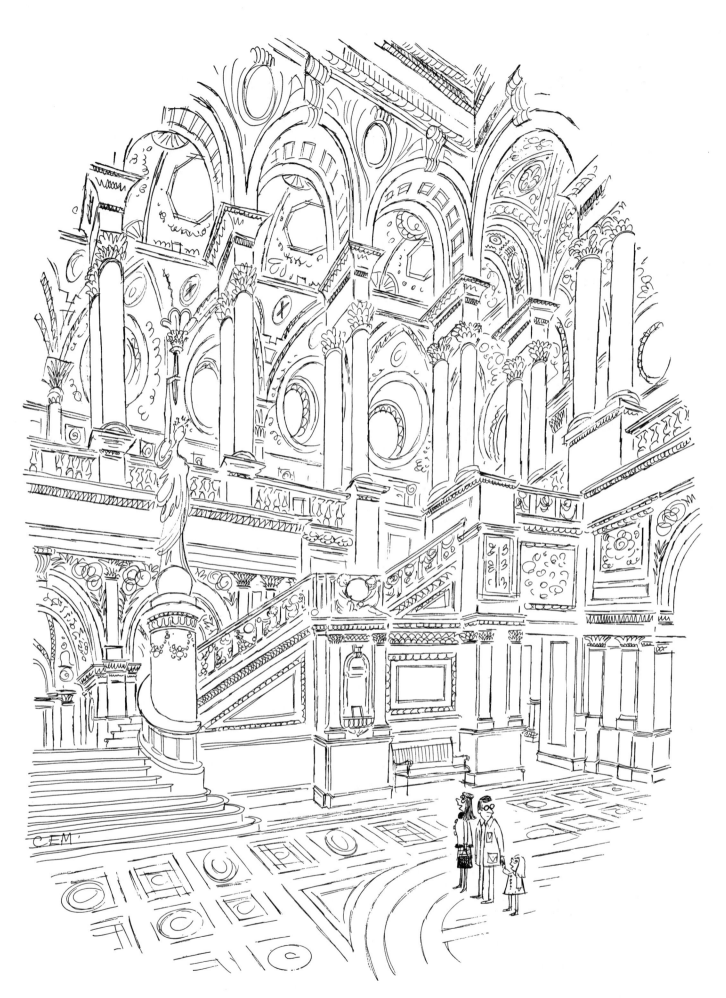

"*Just think! Every book that's ever been published in the United States is right here in the Library of Congress.*"
"*Even 'The Poky Little Puppy'?*"

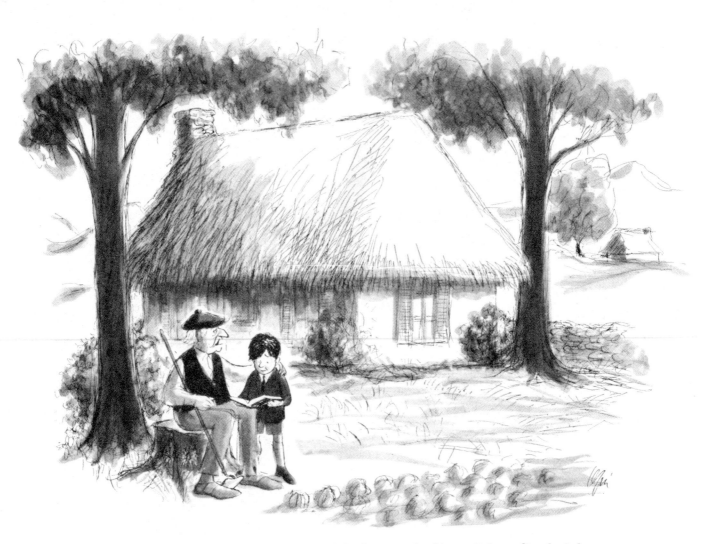

"*My boy, Grand-père is not the one to ask about such things. I have lived eighty-seven peaceful and happy years in Montoire-sur-le-Loir without the past anterior verb form.*"

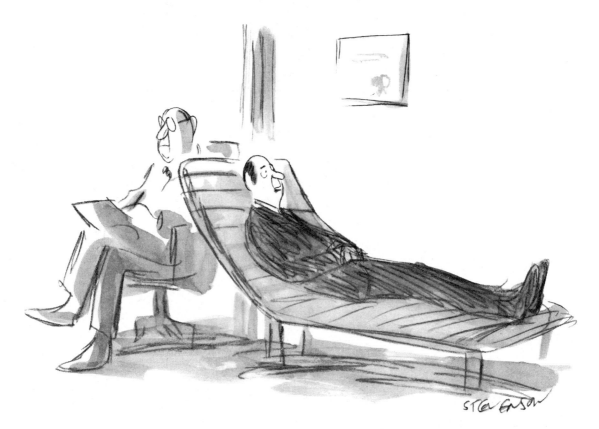

"*All that political paranoia you helped me get rid of, Doctor—what do I do now that it turns out I was right?*"

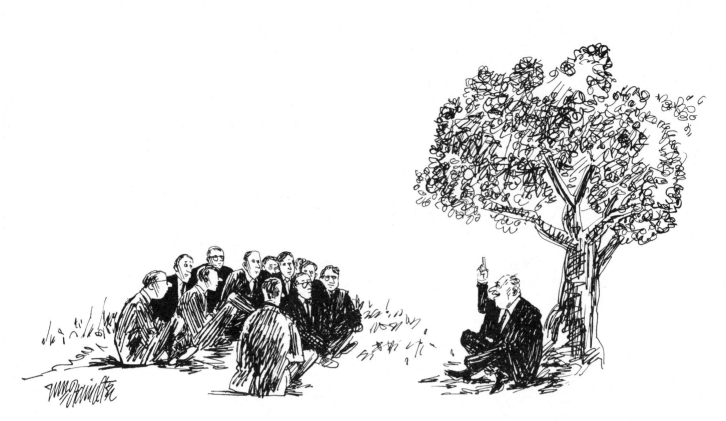

"Buy low, sell high!"

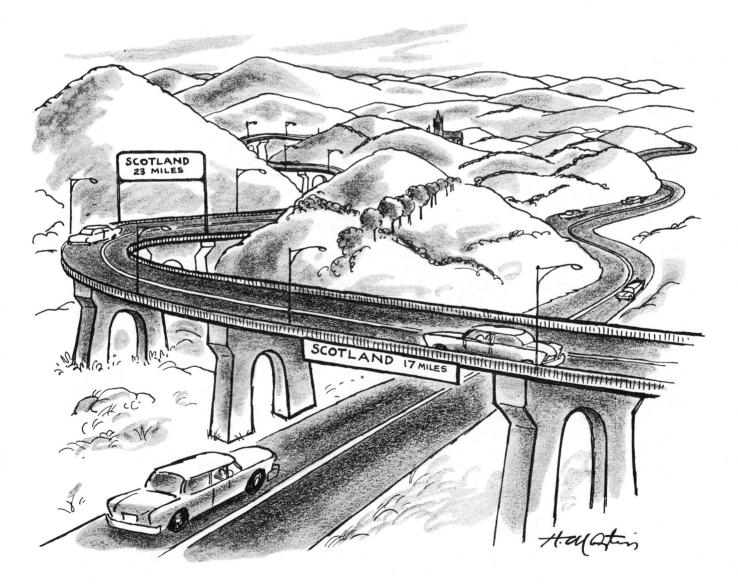

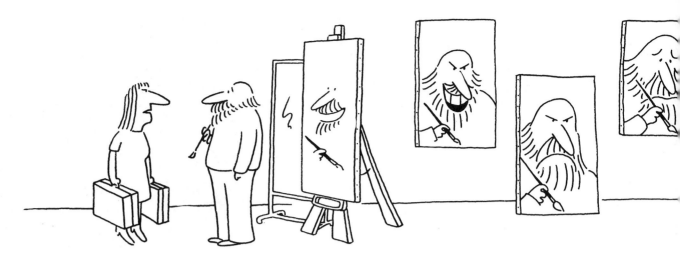

"Charles, I've had it with you and your goddam moods."

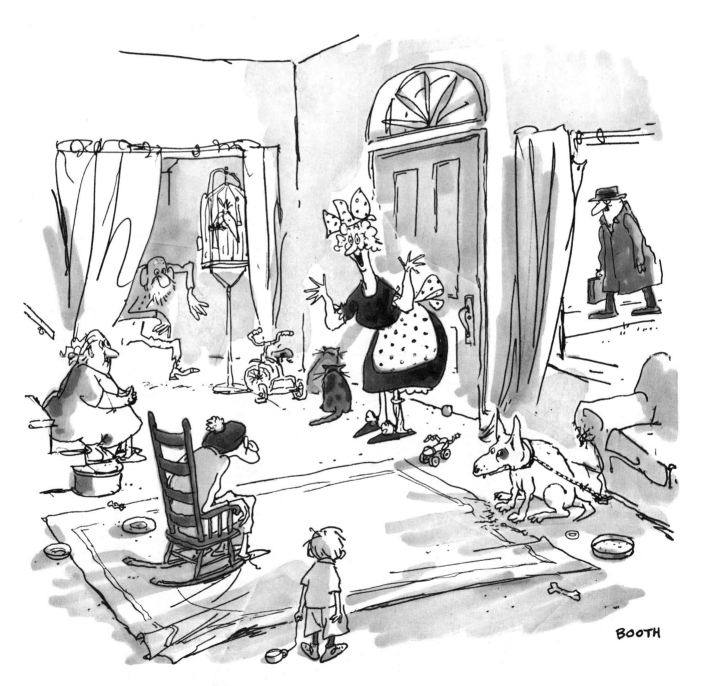

"Attention, everyone! Here comes Poppa, and we're going to drive dull care away! It's quips and cranks and wanton wiles, nods and becks and wreathed smiles."

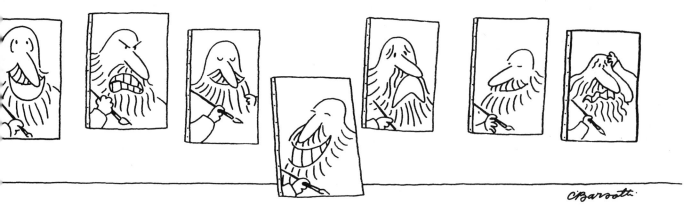

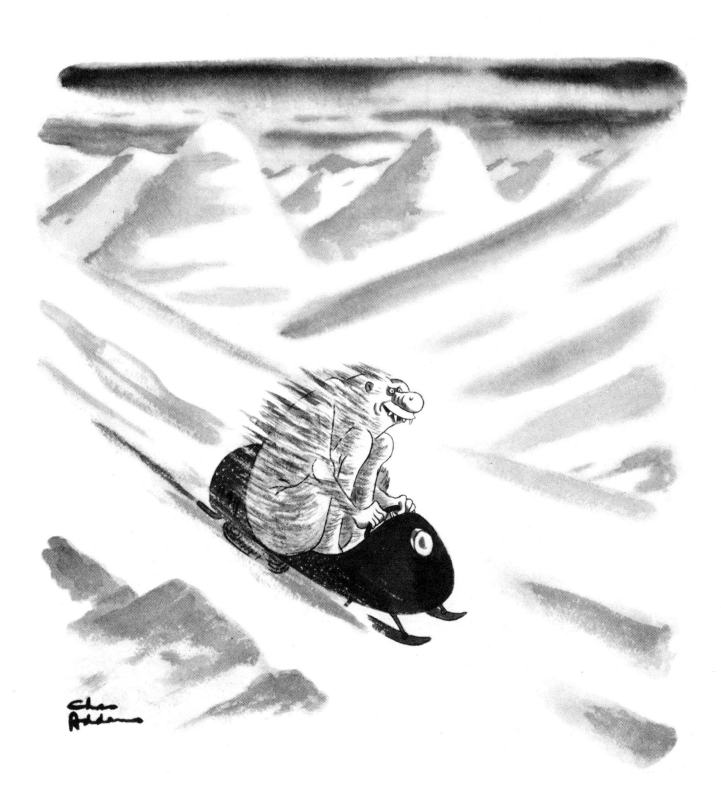

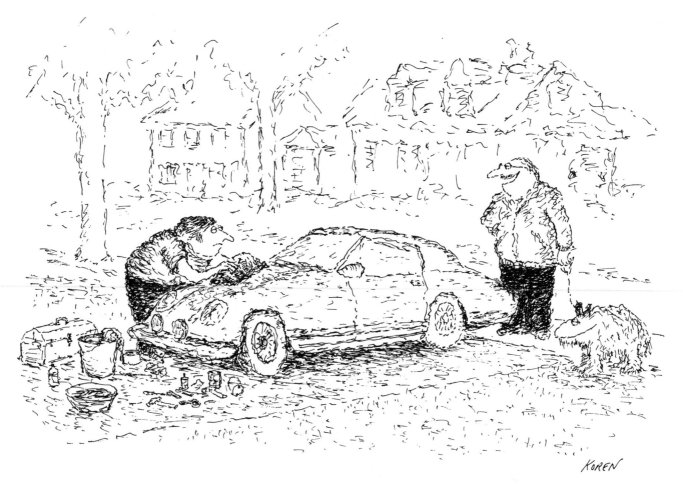

"Have you given any thought to what you'll do with your Saturdays when the world's fossil fuels are used up?"

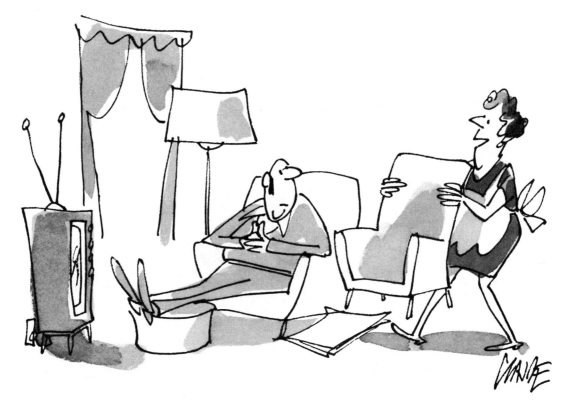

"Well, now that the children have all grown up, I guess *I'll* pull up a chair."

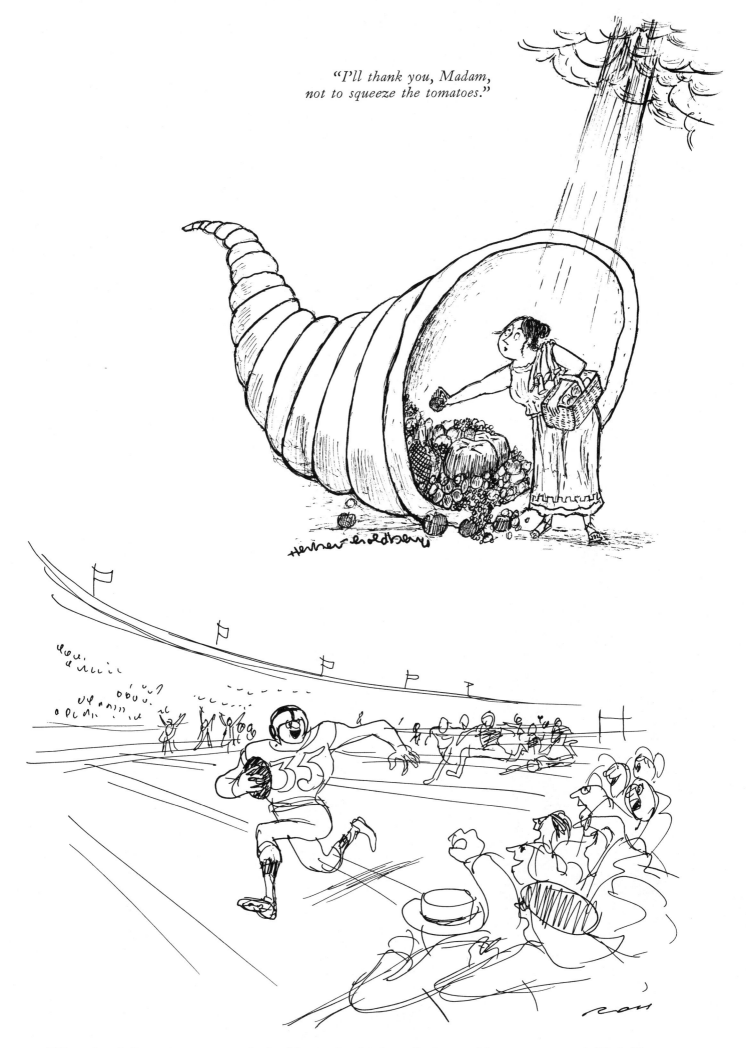

*"I'll thank you, Madam,
not to squeeze the tomatoes."*

"Hey, fans! I've got a separated shoulder and a broken rib, but nothing can stop me! Right?"

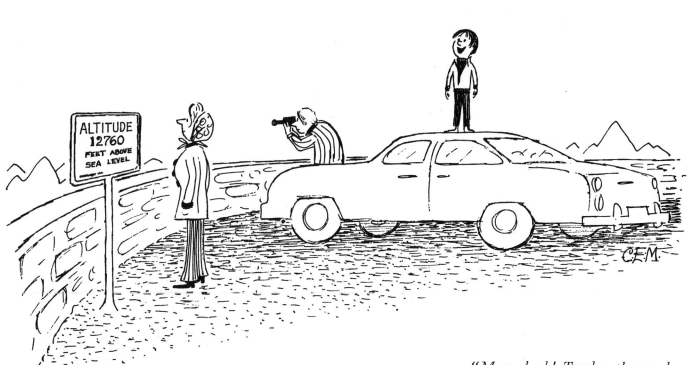

"Mom, look! Twelve thousand
seven hundred and sixty-six feet above sea level!"

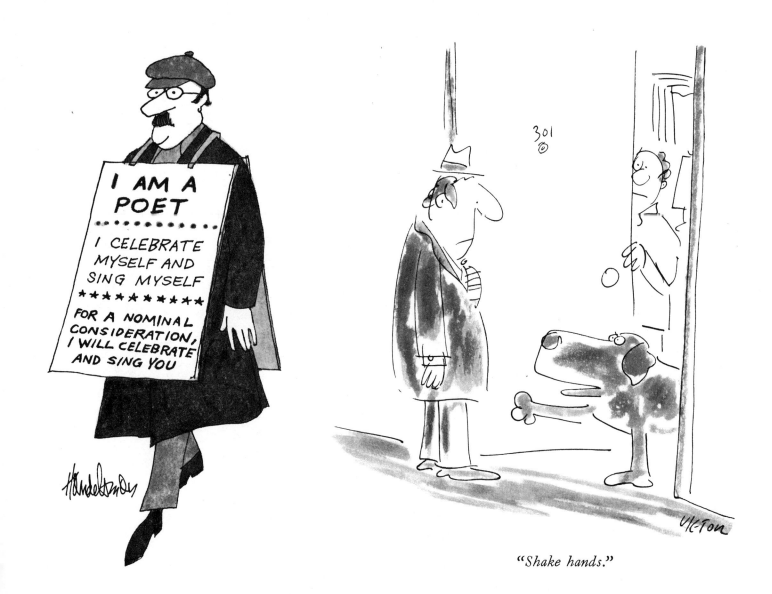

"Shake hands."

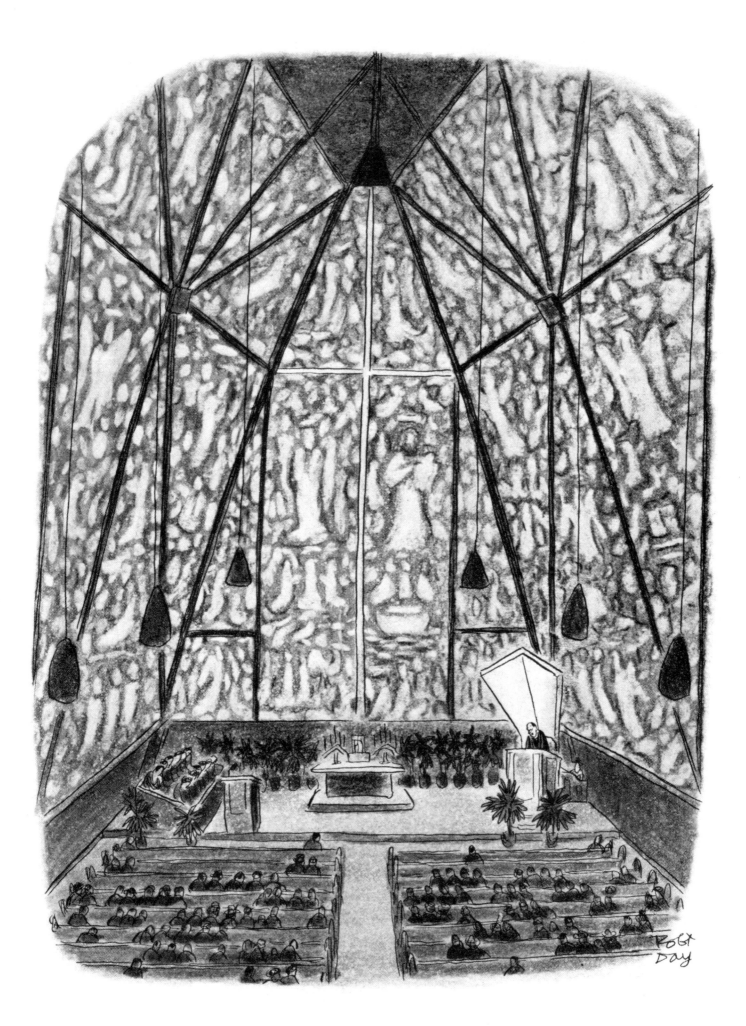

"Give us this day no sonic boom."

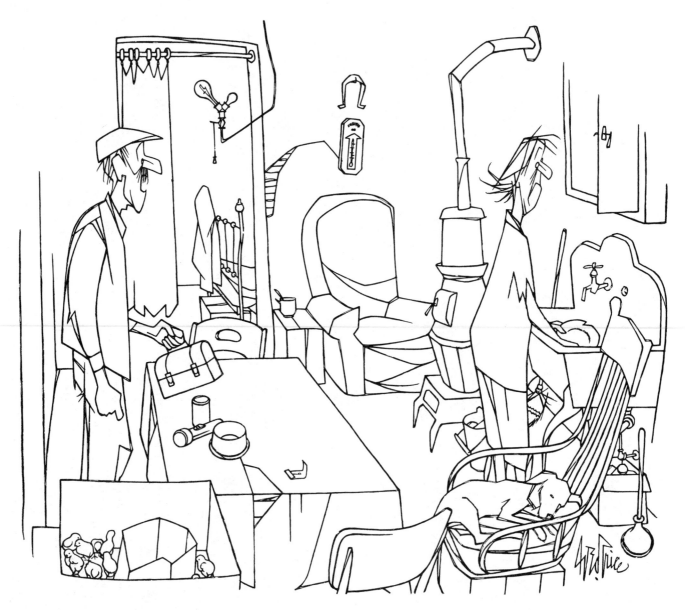

"*I heard a bit of good news today. We shall pass this way but once.*"

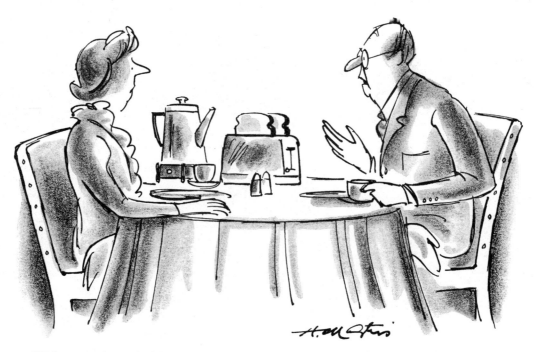

"*The egg timer is pinging. The toaster is popping. The coffeepot is
perking. Is this it, Alice? Is this the great American dream?*"

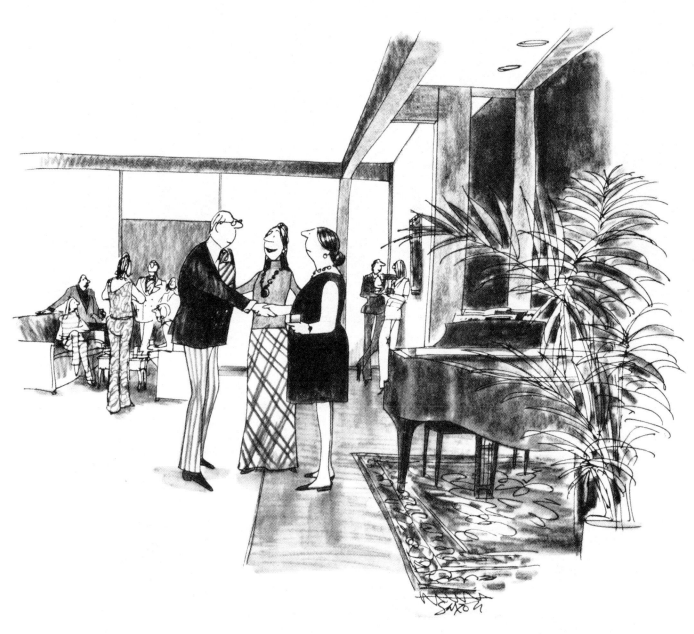

"Dear, you remember Mrs. Leeming. We met way back during Civil Rights."

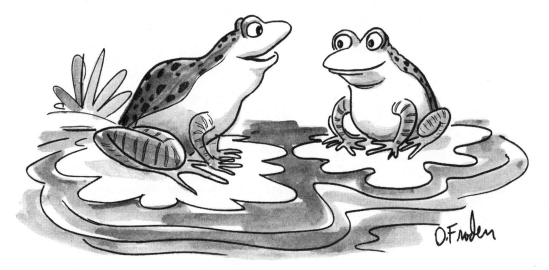

"Jeepers creepers, where'd you get those peepers?"

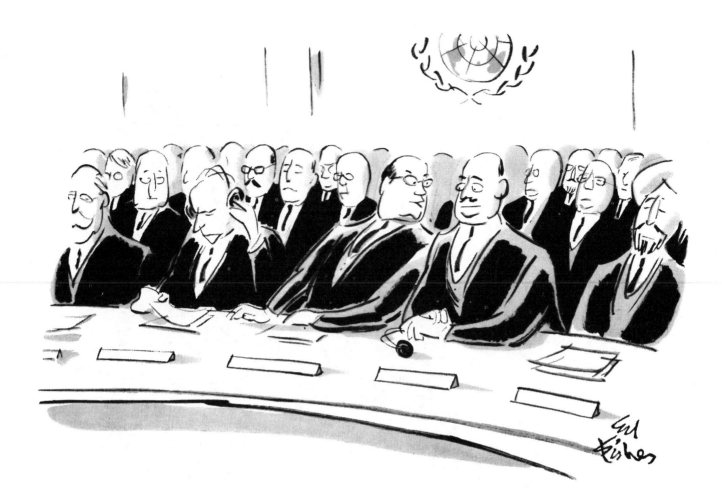

"Tell you what I'll do. You back me on the Trusteeship issue and my wife will lend your wife our Mrs. Twickins for two afternoons a week."

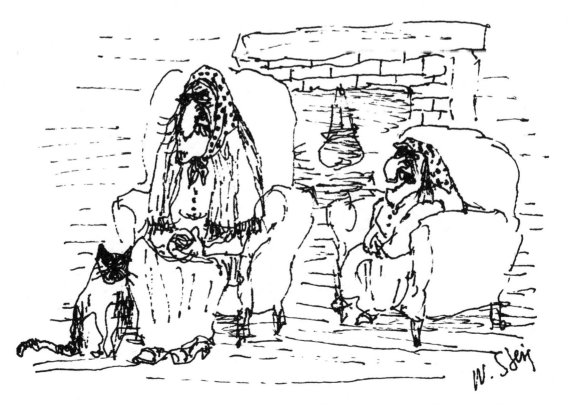

"We haven't done anything really crummy for a long time."

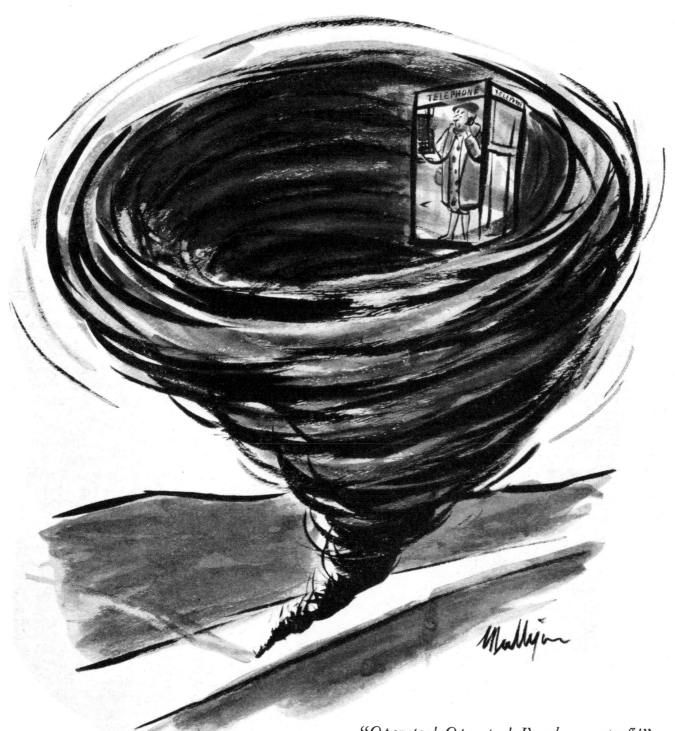

"Operator! Operator! I've been cut off!"

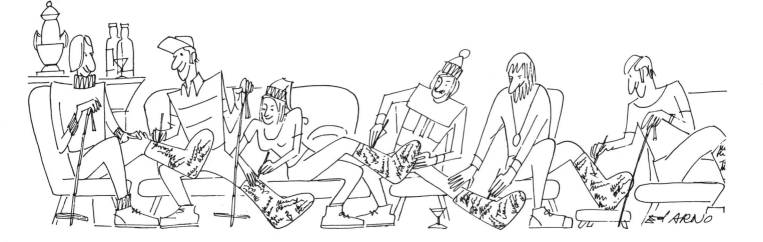

ARRIVALS & DEPARTURES

NAME	ARRIVE	DEPART
YELLOW-BILLED CUCKOO	EARLY MAY	LATE SEPT.
RUBY-THROATED HUMMINGBIRD	MID-MAY	MID-SEPT.
RED-HEADED WOODPECKER	EARLY MAY	LATE SEPT.
YELLOW-SHAFTED FLICKER	MID-MARCH	LATE OCT.
EASTERN KINGBIRD	EARLY MAY	EARLY SEPT.
EASTERN PHOEBE	MID-MARCH	MID-OCT.
PURPLE MARTIN	MID-APRIL	LATE AUG.
BROWN CREEPER	LATE SEPT.	EARLY MAY
HOUSE WREN	LATE APRIL	EARLY OCT.
CATBIRD	EARLY MAY	EARLY OCT.
BROWN THRASHER	LATE APRIL	LATE SEPT.
ROBIN	EARLY MARCH	MID-NOV.
THRUSH		MID-
HERMIT THRUSH	EARLY APRIL	
EASTERN BLUEBIRD	MID-MARCH	

NAME	ARRIVE	D
CEDAR WAXWING	MID-MAY	M
SHRIKE	EARLY AUG.	
YELLOW WARBLER	EARLY MAY	
BLACK & WHITE WARBLER	LATE A	
WARBLER		
YELLOWT		
OVENBIRD	EARLY MAY	
WATERTHRUSH		
M		M
WARBLER		
RED-EYED VIREO		
BOBOLINK		
MEADOWLARK		

STEVENSON

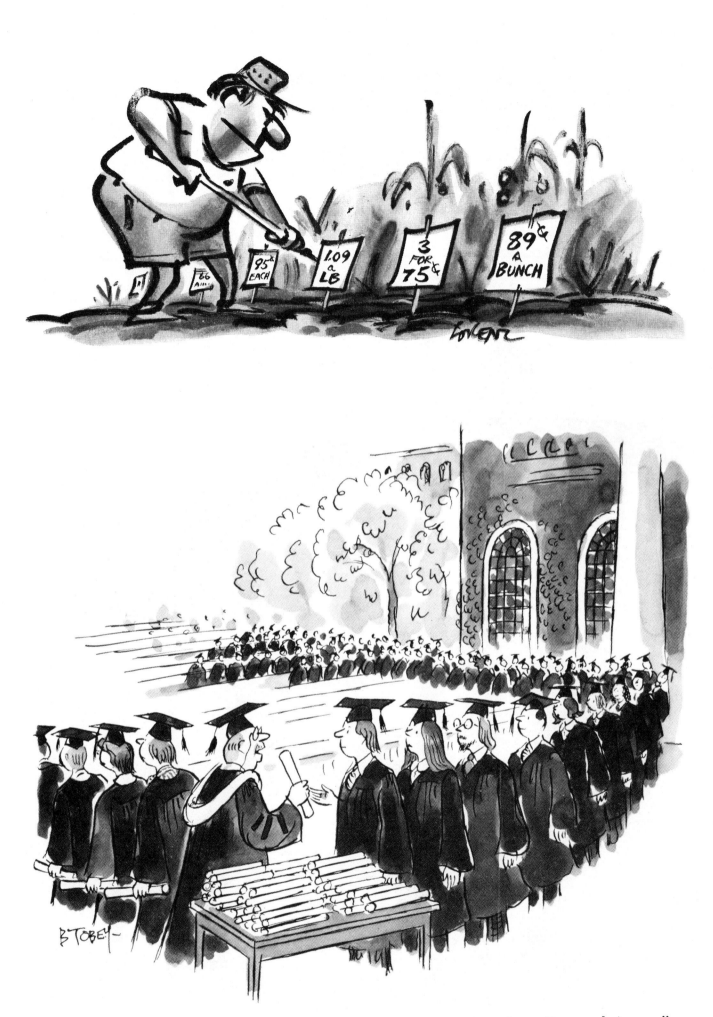

"Congratulations, keep moving, please. Congratulations, keep moving, please. Congratulations . . ."

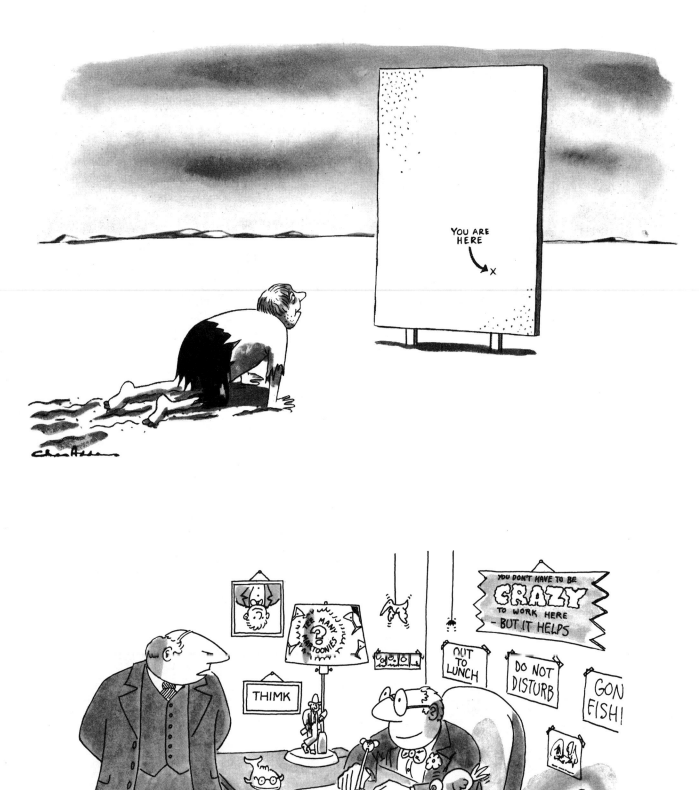

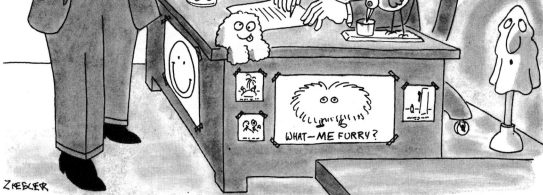

"When you can spare a minute, Benton, I'd like a word with you."

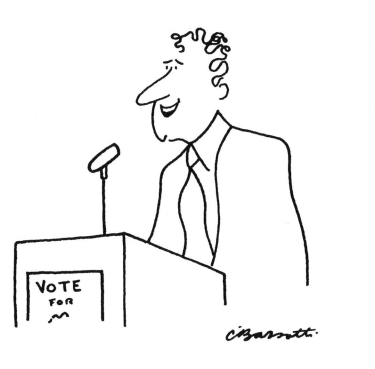

"And if elected I promise to remain as charming as I am today."

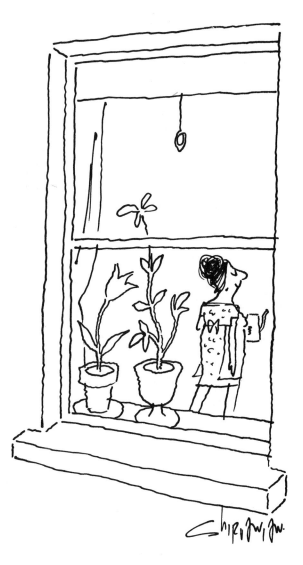

"I thought she'd *never* shut up."

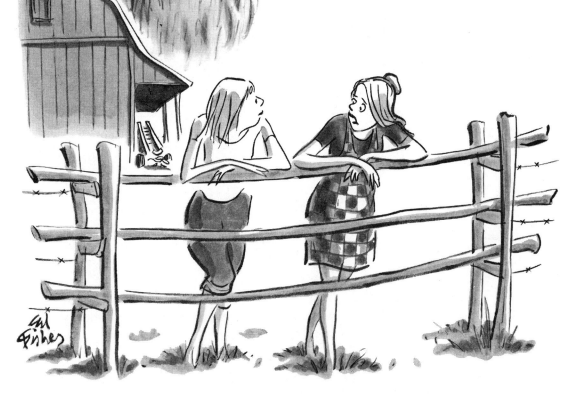

"Well, he didn't come right out and *ask* me to marry him, but he sure talked a lot about preserving America's one-family-farm system."

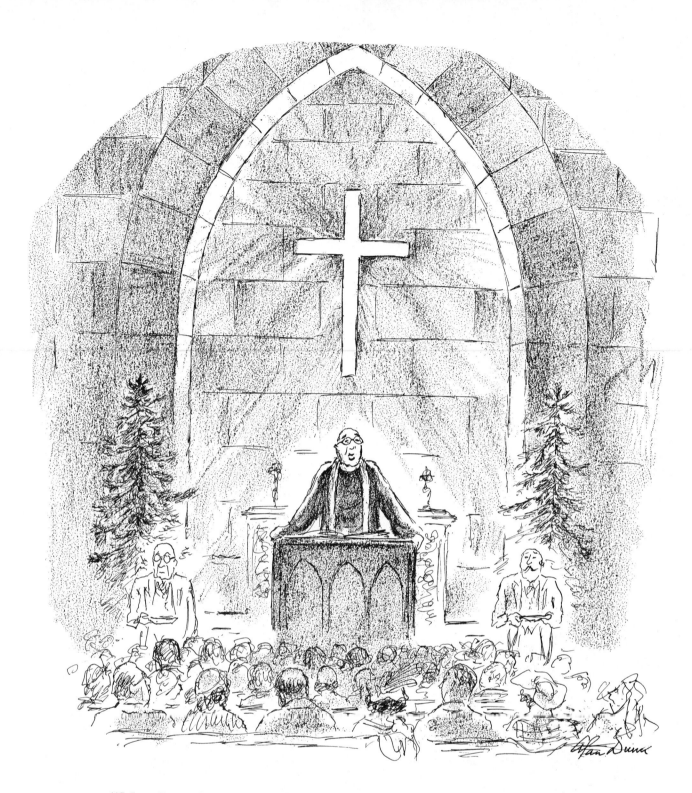

"May I remind you that Phase Two does not apply to the Offertory."

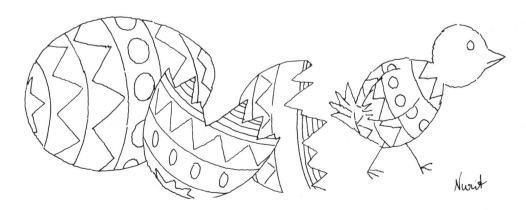

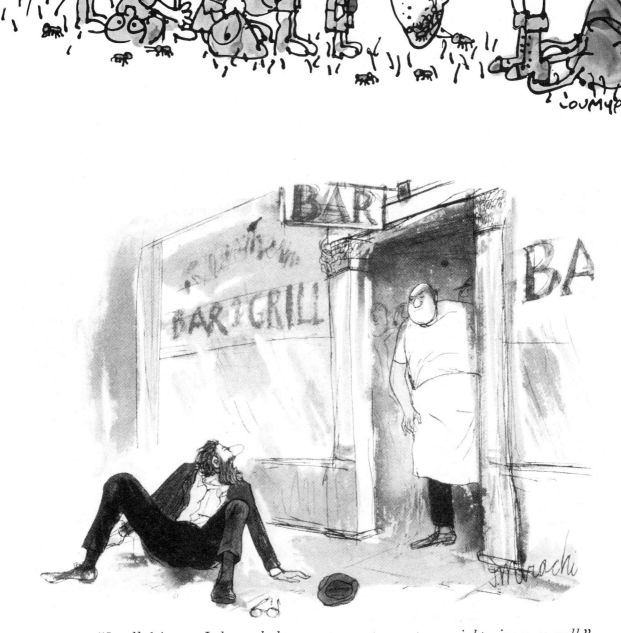

"Survival out here is many things. It is thin layers of birch bark, shredded to make tinder. Likewise dry moss, grass, lichen, fuzz from pussy willows, milkweed, and the heads of goldenrod. Insects are good eating, and far more fortifying than meat or fish. Among them are dragonflies, moths, and mayflies."

"In all fairness, I demand that you toss out an extreme right-winger as well."

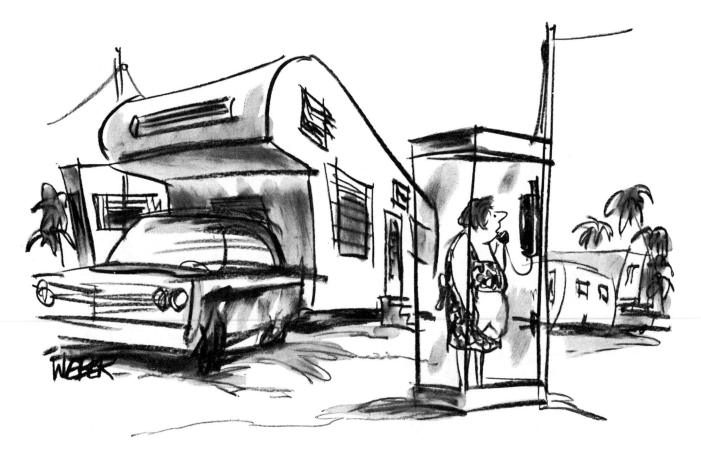

"Well, would you make a house call if we brought the house over?"

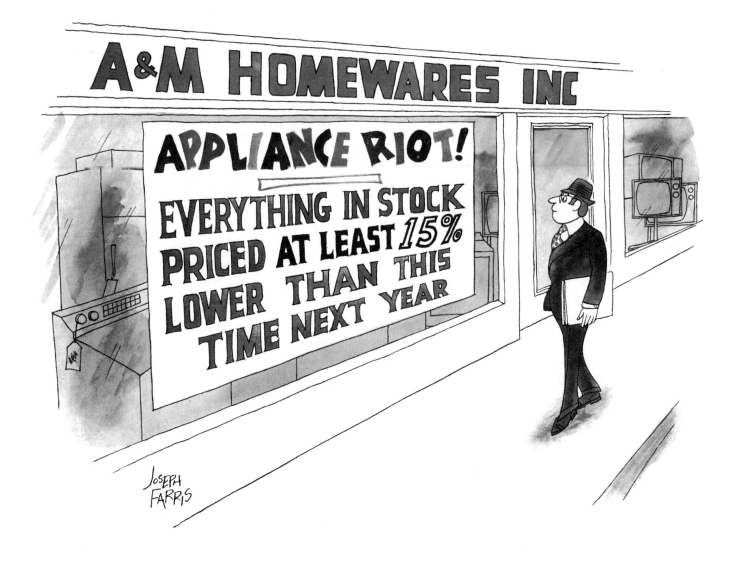

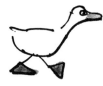 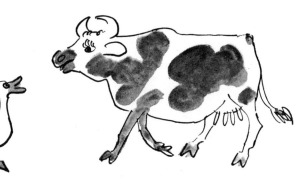

"Quack."   "Moo."

 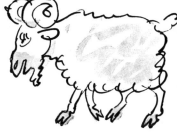

"Quack."   "Baa."

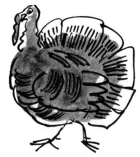 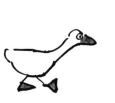 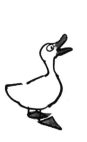 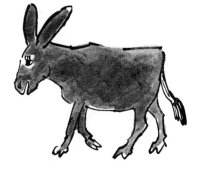

"Quack."   "Gobble-gobble."   "Quack."   "Hee-haw."

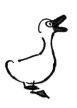   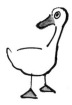

"Quack."   "Oink."   "Quack."   "Quack."

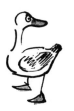 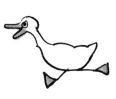 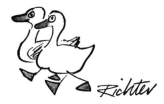

"Quack!"

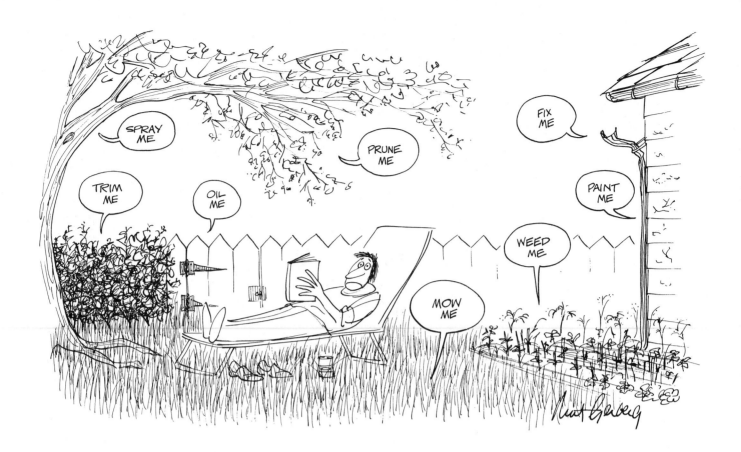

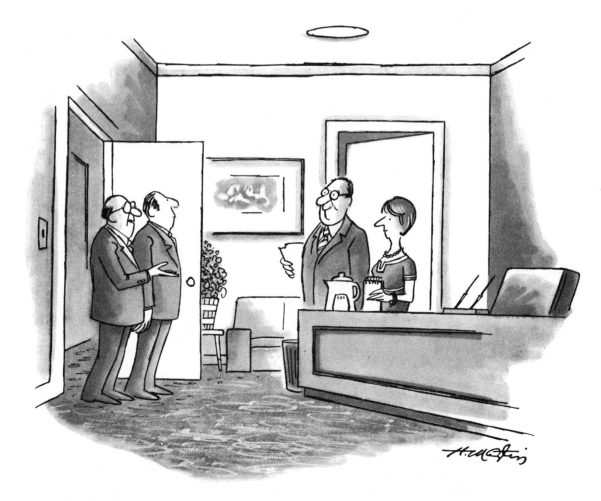

"This is my executive suite and this is my executive vice-president, Ralph Anderson, and my executive secretary, Adele Eades, and my executive desk and my executive carpet and my executive wastebasket and my executive ashtray and my executive pen set and my . . ."

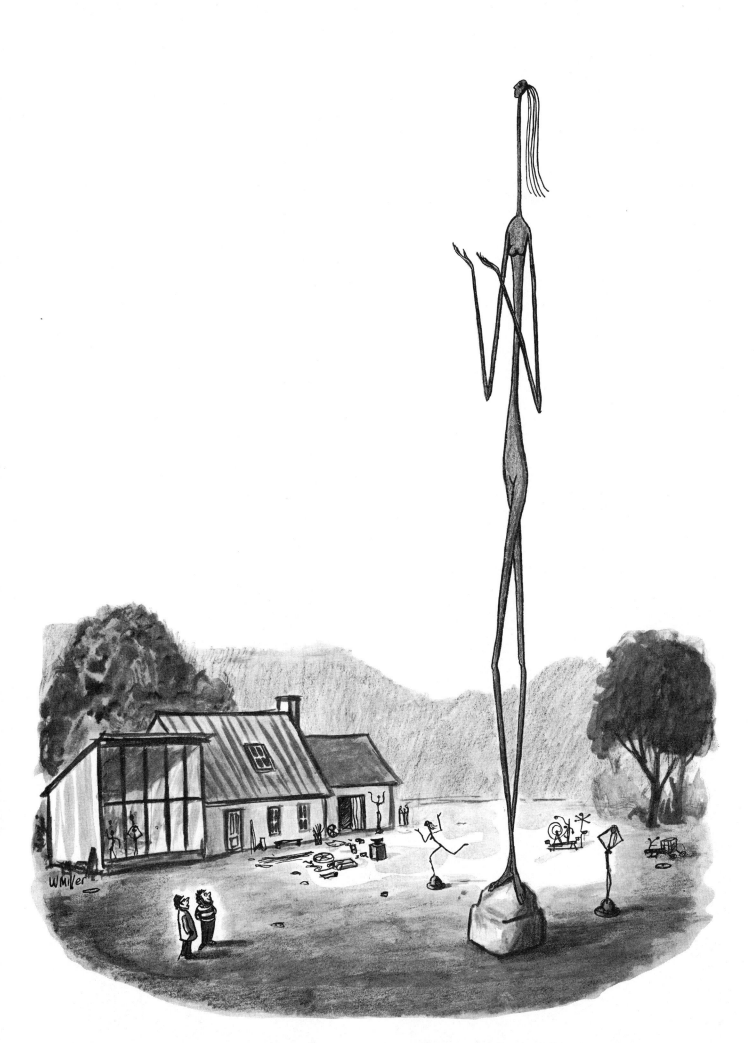

"Sam, it's the most sensitive thing you've ever done!"

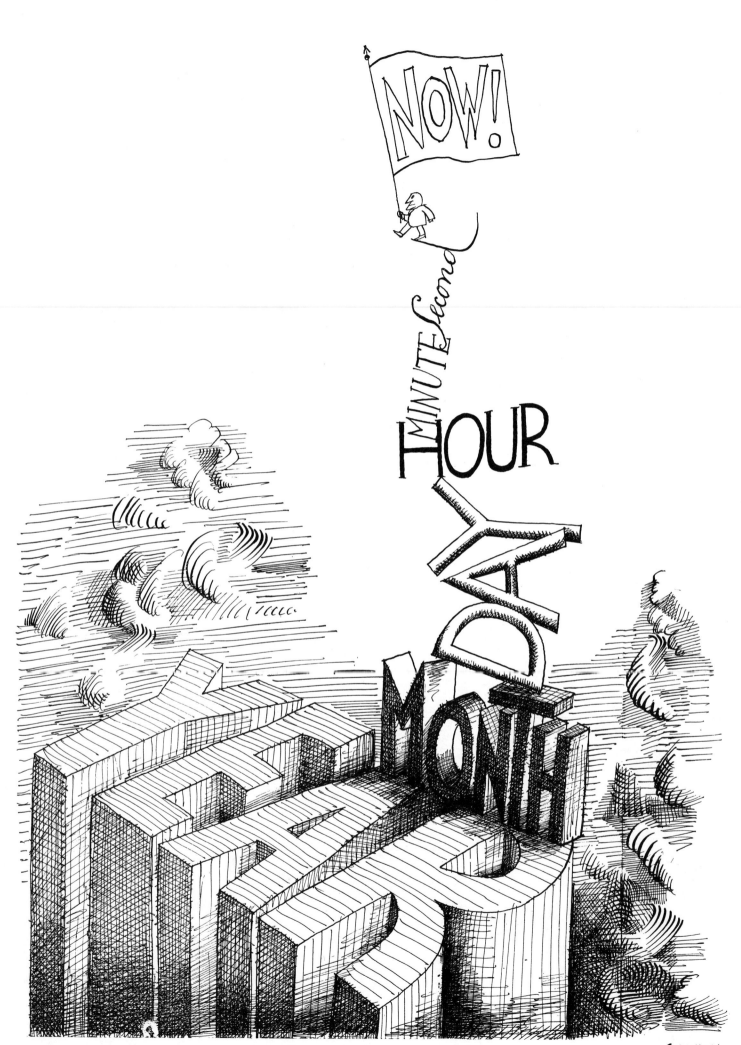

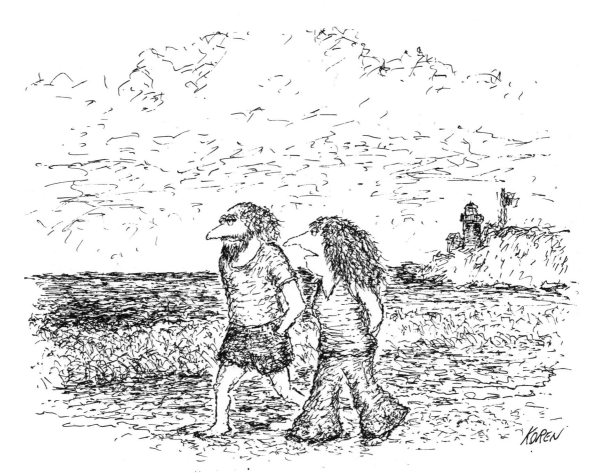

*"I do think your problems are serious, Richard.
They're just not very interesting."*

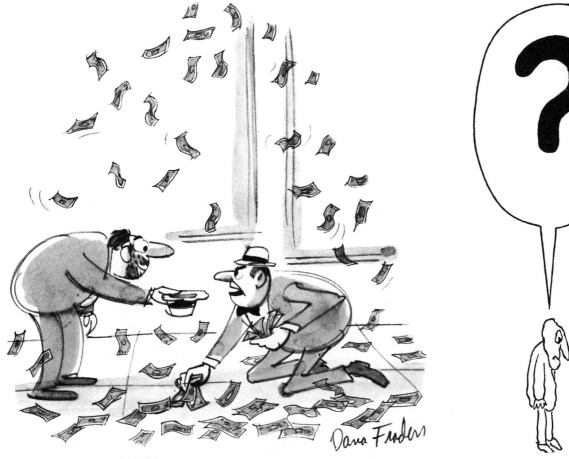

"For God's sake! Pick up your own damn money!"

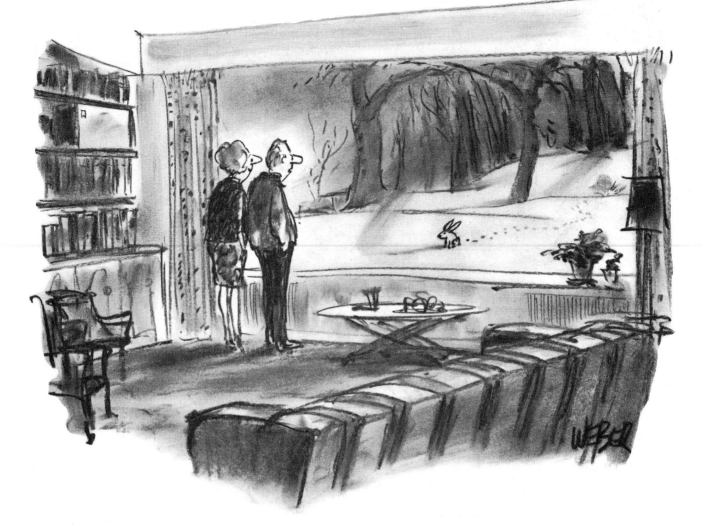

"If this is the high point of our day, then I say something is radically wrong."

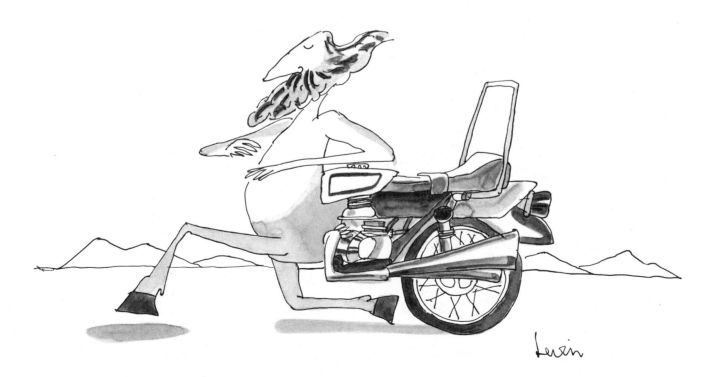

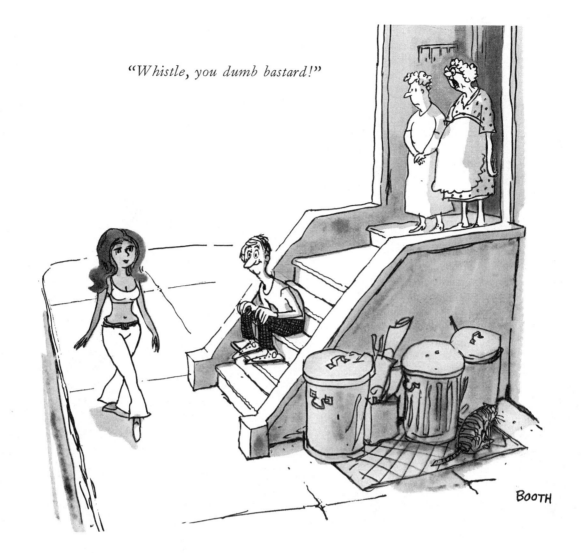

"Whistle, you dumb bastard!"

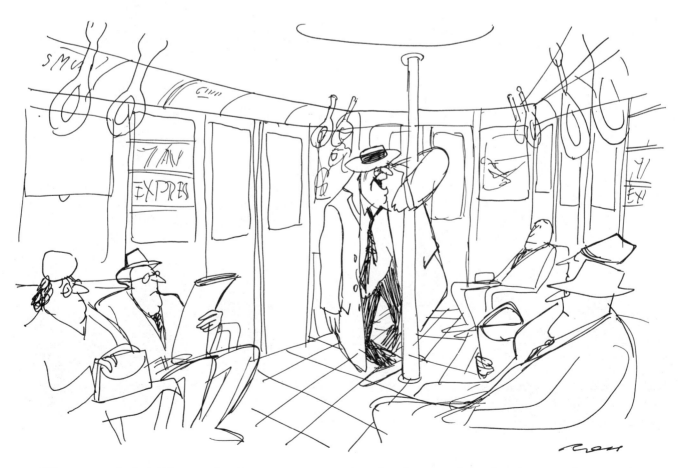

"Hey, everybody! It's exactly three years ago today that I stopped smoking! How about that?"

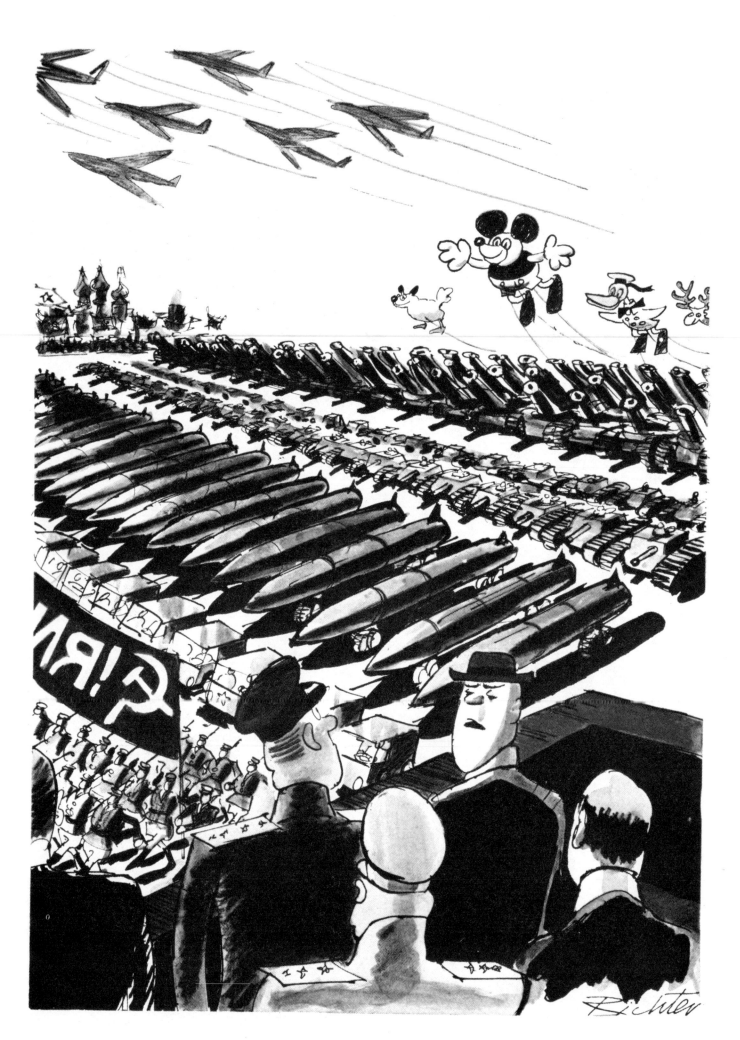

"Détente."

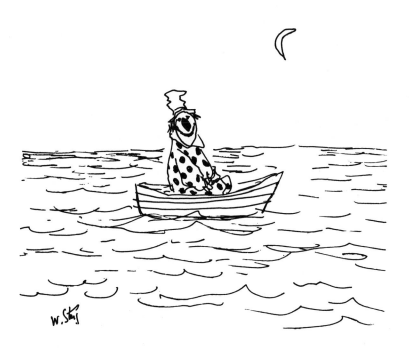